Indigenous Poetics in Canada

Indigenous Studies Series

The Indigenous Studies Series builds on the successes of the past and is inspired by recent critical conversations about Indigenous epistemological frameworks. Recognizing the need to encourage burgeoning scholarship, the series welcomes manuscripts drawing upon Indigenous intellectual traditions and philosophies, particularly in discussions situated within the Humanities.

Series Editor

Dr. Deanna Reder (Métis), Assistant Professor, First Nations Studies and English, Simon Fraser University

Advisory Board

Dr. Jo-ann Archibald (Sto:lo), Associate Dean, Indigenous Education, University of British Columbia

Dr. Kristina Bidwell (Labrador-Métis), Associate Professor, English, University of Saskatchewan

Dr. Daniel Heath Justice (Cherokee), Associate Professor, English, Canada Research Chair in Indigenous Literature and Expressive Culture, University of British Columbia

Dr. Eldon Yellowhorn (Piikani), Associate Professor, Archaeology, Director of First Nations Studies, Simon Fraser University

For more information, please contact:

Lisa Quinn
Acquisitions Editor
Wilfrid Laurier University Press
75 University Avenue West
Waterloo, ON   N2L 3C5
Canada
Phone: 519-884-0710 ext. 2843
Fax: 519-725-1399
Email: quinn@press.wlu.ca

Indigenous Poetics in Canada

EDITOR Neal McLeod

WILFRID LAURIER
UNIVERSITY PRESS

Inspiring Lives.

This book has been published with the help of a grant from the Canadian Federation for the Humanities and Social Sciences, through the Awards to Scholarly Publications Program, using funds provided by the Social Sciences and Humanities Research Council of Canada. Wilfrid Laurier University Press acknowledges the support of the Canada Council for the Arts for our publishing program. We acknowledge the financial support of the Government of Canada through the Canada Book Fund for our publishing activities.

Canada Council for the Arts   Conseil des arts du Canada

ONTARIO ARTS COUNCIL
CONSEIL DES ARTS DE L'ONTARIO
an Ontario government agency
un organisme du gouvernement de l'Ontario

Library and Archives Canada Cataloguing in Publication

Indigenous poetics in Canada / Neal McLeod, editor.

(Indigenous studies)
Includes bibliographical references and index.
Issued in print and electronic formats.
ISBN 978-1-55458-982-1 (pbk.).—ISBN 978-1-77112-009-8 (pdf).—
ISBN 978-1-77112-008-1 (epub)

    1. Indian poetry—Canada—History and criticism. 2. Canadian poetry—Native authors—History and criticism. I. McLeod, Neal, editor of compilation II. Series: Indigenous studies series

PS8147.I6I53 2014   C811.009'897   C2014-901705-7
                                                                   C2014-901706-5

Cover image: *mistahi-maskwa (Big Bear)* by Neal McLeod, 2012 (acrylic and oil on birch panels, 8 feet × 6 feet), University of Saskatchewan Art Collection. Photo by Blair Barbeau. Cover design by Martyn Schmoll. Text design by Daiva Villa, Chris Rowat Design.

RECYCLED
Paper made from recycled material
FSC
www.fsc.org   FSC® C103567

"Small Birds / Song Out of Silence," copyright © 2014 by Joanne Arnott
"Getting (Back) to Poetry: A Memoir," copyright © 2014 by Daniel David Moses
"Interview with Armand Garnet Ruffo," copyright © 2014 by Armand Garnet Ruffo
This book is printed on FSC® certified recycled paper and is certified Ecologo. It is made from 100% post-consumer fibre, processed chlorine free, and manufactured using biogas energy.

Printed in Canada

Contents

Poetics of Performance

Poetics of Medicine

Preface

Neal McLeod

This book emerged during the Ogamas Aboriginal Festival in Brandon in the fall of 2009. One panel, which included Randy Lundy, Louise Halfe, and Duncan Mercredi, discussed the creative process within Indigenous poetry. Randy Lundy talked about the nature of poetic language, Louise Halfe talked about the power of yôtin (wind) and breath, and Duncan Mercredi spoke of the sound of the rapids. A lively and rich discussion ensued. Marilyn Dumont suggested writing a book on creativity in the context of Indigenous poetry. At the break, I asked Randy Lundy if he would help me edit a book on Indigenous poetry and poetics to which he agreed. I could sense that there was momentum in writing such a book and using it for teaching and research. During the festival, I asked many of the poets if they would contribute. They agreed and were supportive of the project.

The next stage of the book involved applying for a SSHRC workshop grant. There were only ten days until the deadline, and Randy and I worked very hard to complete the grant application. In the spring, I was notified that we were successful in obtaining the grant. Randy, unfortunately, was unable to complete the project. However, without his help, this book would not have been possible. I would also like to acknowledge the support of my fiancée, Natasha Beeds.

At the workshop in early November 2010, writers and academics gathered to discuss Indigenous poetics. Daniel David Moses remarked that this was perhaps the first gathering devoted to Indigenous poetics in Canada. To the best of my knowledge, this is the case, and indeed it was an honour to facilitate this process.

The book is divided into four sections. The first section, "The Poetics of Memory," examines the dynamic way in which classical poetic narratives intersect with the living Indigenous present. The second section, "Poetics of Place," examines the embodiment of Indigenous consciousness, and the way in which Indigenous oralities are animated through performance. Third, "The Poetics of Performance" examines one of the central elements of Indigeneity: namely, the consciousness of specific places that emerges as people dwell in specific places over long periods of time. Fourth, "The Poetics of Medicine" has the power to heal collective trauma, and to imagine and dream new possibilities.

I have deliberately not written a conclusion because I think that readers should arrive at their own understandings, and to imagine the possibilities of Indigenous poetics for themselves. My father, Jermiah McLeod, who passed way during the writing of this book, always taught me that I had to find the meaning of stories and words ultimately for myself.

It is hoped that this book will contribute not only to the discussion of Indigenous poetry but also to expand how we think of Indigenous consciousness in the larger context of Indigenous poetics.

All author royalties for this book will go towards a scholarship in the name of Marvin Francis.

Neal McLeod
Peterborough, 2014

Acknowledgements

This book would not have been possible without the assistance of many people. First and foremost, I would like to thank all the contributors to the volume. Without their work this volume would not have been possible.

I would like to give special thanks to Randy Lundy, whose early support of this project was very important. Although he was unable to see this project to completion, I am grateful for his early and invaluable support.

I am especially grateful to my mânahcikan, Tasha Beeds, not only for her paper but also for editing mine. She also helped in preparing the SSHRC workshop grant application, and played a central role in the fundraising for the gathering and author readings.

I would like to acknowledge the SSHRC workshop fund, which allowed many of the contributors to gather and share their ideas. I am also thankful to Louise Halfe, who was able to attend the gathering and help inspire us all.

I would like to thank various units and people of Trent University for their support: Department of Indigenous Studies, Graduate Students' Association, Office of the President, Frost Centre, Department of English, Carol Williams, Gzowski College, Canadian Studies, and the Department for International Development. I would also like to thank the Symons Trust Fund for the support to help pay for the indexing of this book. I would also like to thank Rob Kohlmeier, of Wilfrid Laurier University Press, for his assistance in helping the book take its final form.

I would also like to thank several Peterborough businesses for their support as well: the UPS Store, Natas Café, Catalinas, Sam's Place, Dreams of Beans, East City Bakery, Blackhoney, Hi-Ho Silver, Maggie's Eatery, and La Hacienda Restaurante Mexicano.

I would like to thank all of my students from INDG 2480 and INDG 4480 who contributed in various ways, including moderating the panels.

I would also like to thank several of my graduate students who played a key role in assisting. I would like to thank Mara Heiber, who helped with overall logistics. I am deeply indebted to both Christine Sy and Danielle Jeancart, who assisted with formatting the essays and fixing the endnotes.

Finally, I would like to thank Deanna Reder, the editor of the series of which this book is a part. Also, I am very thankful to Lisa Quinn of Wilfrid Laurier University Press, who believed in the book and who was very supportive throughout the process.

Introduction

Neal McLeod

wâpamon (the mirror)

I.

There is an old Cree-Anishinaabe story about when Cree and Anishinaabe people first acquired the mirror (wâpamon). The story goes something like this.[1]

Once there was a Cree man who went to a fur-trading post, which was cluttered with all sorts of items. There were shiny metal goods that bore fragments of luminosity, catching only the rough shadows of things but not their fully articulated forms. There were stacks of blankets and other trading goods. The place was not very well lit and was quite dark in places. As the man looked across the store, he saw a person a few aisles away. At first, when they gazed directly at each other, that person seemed to be just as startled as the Cree man. He could tell the man was an Indian, but because of the light, he could not make out the full details of his appearance.

He looked again and tried to stare him down, thinking to himself, "Who was this Indian to come into the store and try to get solid? The other Indian[2] just stared right back at him. "There is no way I am going to lose this staring contest," the Cree man thought with great bravado.

The staring match went back and forth, with the other Indian matching every crazy face that he could make. The Cree was not accustomed to losing a staring match. He even went so far as to throw something on the floor, trying to make a loud sound to intimidate the other man. And, sure enough, the other person did the same, seemingly just as quickly. After the Cree man had made another grimacing expression, the Hudson's Bay factor, who had been standing there watching him for some time, finally said to him in bewilderment, "What are you doing, my good friend?"

1

In reply, the Cree said, "Who is the man over there? He keeps looking at me in an angry fashion. I don't really like that." The store factor laughed, his belly moving as it pushed the limits of the fabric of his shirt. The Cree man added with great seriousness, "You should really kick him out."

The factor paused, looked at the Cree right in the eye, and said, "Why would I want to do that? He is my best customer."

The Cree guy looked down, disappointed, "You mean even better than me?"

The factor laughed again. "He is you."

The Cree looked at him, confused, "Cha. What do you mean?"

"You are looking at yourself in what is called a mirror. It reflects back what is in front of it."

"Oh," said the Cree man. "It is like water that thing. It just reflects back."

"Yes, but only sharper," the factor replied. He paused and dug around in a little box for a bit. "Here, take this. It is a little mirror. You can have it as a gift. You have been such a good customer over the years."

The Cree man smiled widely and put the mirror in his bag.

II.

As soon as he came back from the HBC post, the Cree man left again. He always seemed busy, and his young wife began to wonder what he was up to. Finally, one night while the man was asleep, she went through his bag to find clues to tell her where he had been. She saw something shiny at the bottom of the bag.

She pulled out this shiny thing, looked at it, and then said, "wahwâ, mitoni ê-nipahi-miyosit![3] For this is the reason why my husband goes out all the time!"

The next morning, she woke her mother. Her mother had been concerned about her daughter and knew she had been unhappy for the last little while. While the family was slowly starting the day, the daughter showed her mother the object from her husband's bag. Indignantly, she said, "wâpam. Look at her. This is who your son-in-law has repeatedly gone out to see." The mother pulled the mirror close to her and said, "nitanis. Don't worry. You really have no reason to worry. It will be okay. This woman is not very pretty and she's way too old!"

The woman's father had been puttering around that morning and had lit his little smoking pipe. Sitting down, he said, "mahti ôma."[4] He held the mirror close to his face, exclaiming, "wahwâ! She does resemble my late father and as such she is quite homely for a woman!"

The story is important for a variety of reasons. It gives us narrative insight into some Cree people's first experience with the mirror. There is a whole genre of stories that deal with Cree encounters with European technology. Here, the technology is the mirror, but in this genre I would also include stories about television. My late father told me the story of how people clustered around the first television on our reserve, and some would even stand outside the window, puffing warm air onto the window, fogging it up, and obscuring the view for others. Crees, like other Indigenous peoples, have always taken various elements of technology and woven them into their lives. The story of the mirror is one example of this process, but causes us to think about the nature of our perceptions and the way in which we construct meaning.

For instance, the story of the mirror links generation after generation of Cree and Anishinaabe people through the act of storytelling, but also through the action of weaving the old stories with new contemporary realities. Undoubtedly, the story had currency in the time of the fur trade as it was a narrative way of incorporating new realities into the Cree mindset and life. Often this process involves humour as we can see from the mirror story.

The story of the mirror presents certain Indigenous—in this case Cree and Anishinaabe—conceptions of the world. Narratives also provide a basis for theoretical reflection grounded in the culture it is "mirroring." Our interpretation of the world is often mediated by our own experiences and our way of seeing the world. Each person who looked at the mirror brought certain interpretations in terms of what and how he or she saw and understood of the reflection in the mirror. It is my contention that a great deal of what we might call Indigenous poetics is not only embedded in contemporary forms of poetry or poetic narrative, but also in the classical narratives of various nations. Part of the poetic process, in an Indigenous context, is bringing the narrative power of our old stories into the present. By examining various narratives, we can begin to articulate Indigenous theories of narrative understanding. Indigenous poetics is, fundamentally, a theoretical activity grounded in narratives and language.

Indigenous Poetics Articulated

I have discussed the nature of Indigenous poetics, but want to articulate what it means. I want to avoid a reductionist definition, and instead put forward an organic and contextualized understanding of Indigenous poetics. First, I would like to acknowledge Lee Maracle's[5] suggestion of framing this book with the concept of "poetics" rather than simply the conventional term of "poetry." By framing this book as poetics, it allows one to understand the connections to classical Indigenous narratives, and to move beyond the conceptions of what poetry is from the Anglo-môniyâw[6] interpretative matrix. By shifting the nomenclature slightly, one is able to engage the topic from an Indigenous theoretical and cultural conceptual basis. There has been a past tendency in the Anglo-môniyâw[7] publishing world to not consider Indigenous poetry as "poetry" or to see Indigenous literatures as not meeting their expectations of what poetry is supposed to be. For instance, a review of Louise Halfe[8] held that the line between poetry and prose took away from regarding *Blue Marrow* as poetry per se. From a Cree perspective, rather than being a weakness, the narrative elements in Louise Halfe's work strengthen the text because they link it to older classical Cree narratives that are foundational to Cree culture—namely, the âtayôhkêwin[9] Rolling Head.

Indigenous peoples had poetics long before môniyawâk[10] and English departments existed in our territories. I believe strongly that we have to return to our own conceptions and frameworks, and rage against simple conventions of mimicry. As Gail MacKay writes in her chapter, "Indigenous poetics reach beyond western literary theoretical orientations to bring Indigeneity to the forefront of all factors being considered."[11] Duncan Mercredi, one of the senior Indigenous poets and storytellers active on the circuit today, further articulates Mackay's point. He states that:

> Let's not lose our voices, ones that have been evolving for generations, to please those that believe that to gain acceptance we must lose something of ourselves. Because once that happens, we are no longer seeing the universe from our perspective and our stories become indistinguishable from all of the other stories out there.[12]

Not only does Duncan bring the Cree language into his work, but also the paradigm of classical Cree storytelling as Cree poetics. He talks of traditional storytellers as poets.[13] I have always thought the same.

I remember some of the editorial advice I received when I was writing my first book of poetry. Much of it was quite sound. However, my editor also noted that I concentrated too much on my family and that I should move beyond them. I think that Anglo-môniyâw editors sometimes miss the point of Indigenous poetry—for example, its rhythms and movement through our respective languages, the meaning and significance of Indigenous words, our poetic humour, and the societal context from which our words are derived.

Indigenous poetics is the embodiment of Indigenous consciousness. The "Poetics of Performance" section in this book examines this aspect. Academic books such as this are important in articulating Indigenous poetics, and also the lived embodied work of Indigenous poetics. The late Marvin Francis, who was a pivotal poetic force on the Prairies, notes in the interviews some of the playful elements of his performance. Indeed, Indigenous poetics were vibrantly manifested in the 1990s to the present through such collectives as the Winnipeg Aboriginal Writers' Collective, and also the Crow Hope Café, of which I was one of the founders. There was a need recognized some time ago to publish Indigenous voices by Indigenous peoples. Kateri Akiwenzie-Damm's development of Kegedonce Press is a prime example of this consciousness. Much of this writing was, at times, outside of the paradigmatic norms of Anglo-môni-yâw poetic practice and conventions. Dub poetry in Canada has undergone something similar. At a dub poetry event in Peterborough, Lillian Allen spoke about the time when the League of Poets debated whether or not dub poetry was poetry (from an Anglo-môniyâw perspective).[14] Both point to a need to find other vehicles for the dissemination of these poetic voices outside of those of the mainstream.

Indigenous poetics, as well as pushing the boundaries of English, also involves the celebration of the elasticity within Indigenous languages. My late father spoke of an old man named côhcam[15] whom he remembered. My father said he would close his eyes when côhcam spoke and richly visualize the storyscape that he was creating with his words. Poetics also involves metaphorical play within these storyscapes.

The Cree language is full of rich metaphors and groups of sounds that point to other things in the world. Often in Cree, things are kiskino, pointed to, but never completely articulated. This space allows the listener or reader to arrive at his or her own understanding. This contextual narrative poetic play is created through the dense and compacted language of poetry.[16] The words and sounds created represent a variety of possibilities. Through the ambiguous process of kiskino, pointing, the possibilities of these words or signs are expanded in our interpretation. Furthermore, this rich meaning is added when "sometimes two ordinary words are placed unexpectedly side by side"[17] and "can energize each other."[18] Indigenous peoples have often valued the multiple possibilities of understanding a story and, indeed, words, particularly through images. Once when I was visiting the late Clifford Sanderson, he pointed to four trees outside his house. Like the mirror story, he saw his life reflected in the imagery of those trees. Those trees were compacted symbols and the expansion of those meanings into our lives is an example of Indigenous poetics.

Indigenous Poetics as Theory
Indigenous poetics can move toward the richness of knowledge stored in the manifold plurality of Indigenous consciousness. Within these poetic condensed cores of Indigenous consciousness, we can find the tools to not only articulate the beauty of our tradition, but also deal with our collective trauma as experienced in residential schools and the spatial diasporas from

our own homelands. Indigenous poetics, while an articulation of classical poetic knowledge at the cores of narrative centres, is also a critical impulse. Christopher Teuton, in *Deep Waters*, describes the "critical impulse" as "the life force of cultural production."[19] The late Marvin Francis, whose interview with Rosanna Deerchild and Shayla Elizabeth is included in this volume, was a powerful poetic force whose writing reflected this life force. This is an example of Indigenous poetic consciousness manifesting within an urban landscape.

Inspired by Francis's poem "Edgewalker," Warren Cariou discusses the importance of the embodied poetic consciousness, stating: "For me one of the most important functions of poetry in an Indigenous context is to help decolonize the imagination by bridging the ideological boundaries that often separate the beneficiaries of colonialism from those who are objectified and impoverished by it."[20] This is a movement toward the edges and imagining other possibilities. Cariou adds, "Though he doesn't explicitly say this in the poem, I think that Marvin would agree that the poet is the ultimate edgewalker."[21] Janet Rogers, an important spoken-word artist based in Victoria, articulates this visionary process of Indigenous poetics: "We, as poets, are here to witness, ruminate and creatively express our stories, in verse to all that has gone, all that is now and visions of the future."[22] This element of Indigenous poetics allows us to imagine other possibilities and gives us a poetic map to reshape the world.

A key function of Indigenous poetics is to puncture holes in the expectations and understandings of contemporary life. For instance, in Lesley Belleau's chapter in this volume, she discusses the way in which the old story of cihcipiscikwân can be used to understand contemporary times through the poetry of Louise Halfe. As noted before, Indigenous poetics can point to other pathways and other possibilities. Indigenous poetics can puncture holes in how we see the world, and is also a way of retrieving the feminine, to follow Lesley Belleau's analysis. Thus, not only is Indigenous life contemporary, it can also question the way traditions are articulated and understood.

Classical Indigenous Poetics

To me, a pictograph is a novel.[23]

—Marie Annehart Baker

The statement by Marie Annhart Baker is quite profound, and radically re-shifts the way we think of the relationship between orality and the written text. It puts the old pictographs on par with the classics of Europe. The

Mississauga Anishinaabe are the caretakers of the petroglyphs in their traditional territories. When you look at the petroglyphs, you can see layers of drawings. The image is always changing, depending on the angle, direction, and flow of light. There are literally hundreds of archived iconic memories housed at this spot, along with endless interpretations throughout the generations. Interestingly, Bon Echo Provincial Park, where there are many ancient rock paintings along the waters' edge, is called mazinaw in Algonquian, which is etymologically related to the Cree and Anishinaabemowin word for "book," masinahikan (mazinahikan). These ancient pictographs are records of historical Indigenous consciousness whose meaning stretches back through countless generations, and they do function as "texts." They are a fundamental core of many Indigenous nations that are constantly being reanimated by new experiences and new nuances.

The engagement with classical poetics is part of the critical-theoretical poetical standpoint. Sam McKegney, in his chapter, "Writer–Reader Reciprocity and the Pursuit of Alliance through Indigenous Poetry," speaks of the narrative of Aionwahta by Tom Porter, noting that it "provides such a space for mobilizing the living oral tradition in contemporary contexts to awaken alternative political and aesthetic critical possibilities."[24] The engagement with this classical poetic narrative of the Haudenosaunee demonstrates Aionwahta's "poetic intellectualism of a sense of duty to the individuals he condoles, to their communities, and to creation more broadly and out of profound respect for the integrity of poetic voice."[25] From this classical narrative, we see Aionwahta as a poet who offers us maps to help us understand the contemporary world and to negotiate our place in it.

Another example of the way in which classical poetics are still a function of contemporary times is the various Apache narratives that Keith Basso worked with. Throughout his chapter, David Newhouse talks about how Basso's narratives are "texts" that can be read in the landscape. Newhouse describes the "textuality" of these narratives as "the construction of meaning from symbols, the symbols in this case being features and places in the landscape."[26] The land is a compressed poetic icon whose meaning is expanded and animated through storytelling and performance.

Duncan Mercredi discusses the importance of the visceral nature of oral poetics and the importance of kinship in the context of transmission: "These words, spoken in the old way, simple yet spoke volumes and the words flowed like water over the rapids in a singsong chant long into the night, and a child cradled in his Kookum's arms would drift off to sleep."[27] Traditionally, counselling narratives (kakêskihkêmowina) allowed this transfer of collective wisdom to others, often close relatives. One of the most important contributions of Gail MacKay's chapter, "Learning to Listen to a

Quiet Way of Telling," is to demonstrate that the classical genre of kakêskih-kêmowina can be applied in the context of contemporary literature, namely *Half-Breed*. The classical poetic narratives of Indigenous peoples have the power to help us make sense of the contemporary world and also to centre us in the field of Indigenous memory.

Poetic Narrative Icons and aniskwâcimopicikêwin

One way of describing the relationship of narratives to one another without privileging the written text in Cree would be aniskwâcimopicikêwin.[28] As noted before, many of the authors in this volume expand the notion of "text" as a poetic icon. These are narrative poetic strands that stay relatively stable over a period of time. In turn, they are reanimated through performance and through the weaving of the narrative elements with the context of the present. I prefer to use the term "narrative poetic icons" in lieu of "texts" for two main reasons: first, the term "text" has a Western literary bias and certain connotations. Second, my term "poetic narrative icons" tacitly acknowledges the constant interplay between orality and written forms, and goes against the notion of a progressive understanding of the orality-written continuum as put forward by thinkers such as Walter Ong. In addition, I use the term "aniskwâcimopicikêwin" to build upon this. It literally means "the process of connecting stories together." I propose this term to replace the term "inter-textuality," which often presupposes an "oral-written" binary.

There is a constant play between orality (performative elements) and narrative poetic icons, which could include a vast array of things, including the land itself, dreams, petroglyphs, classical narratives, hide paintings, and so on. I think of many cases where this play happens with contemporary Cree, but then goes from spoken to mediation with written dictionaries and back again to orality. In fact, when I created the Cree Word a Day project,[29] people would write various words that they had heard, bundle them in written form, and then "unbundle them," to use Greg Scofield's term metaphorically.[30]

To build upon the points made previously about the critical impulse, the process of aniskwâcimopicikêwin connects various poetic narrative cores together. The dissonance between these spaces of being allows us to see each poetic element in new ways. The critical impulse allows our awareness to grow and then in turn to add to the "collective sound bundle."

Indigenous poetics involves this connection of narrative poetic icons and is indeed a process of interpretation. There are many examples of this primary poetic act of interpretation, including the poetics of Black Elk, Seth Newhouse, Basil Johnston, narratives collected by Freda Ahenakew, and the work of Kim Anderson and Edward Ahenakew. The "narratives holes" allow for fluidity in terms of interpretation. By this I mean there is a narrative dissonance created between two points of understanding. Theory, then, is a conversation between these poetics-narrative cores, these points of understanding, and is embodied in our lives, our bodies, and our understandings. By examining the work of Scott Momoday, Christopher Teuton explores this theoretical process: "Rather than reifying western literature or Native oral tradition, *Rainy Mountain* aims at placing these traditions in conversation by invigorating the critical impulse."[31] All of the old people knew this, and that is why storytelling is so close to their beings. And, I think, that is why they valued independent thinking so much. My late father gifted me with an understanding of our Cree history and language. In the process of imparting this gift, he taught me that I had to come to my own understandings. I would call this the essence of the critical impulse and the essence of Indigenous poetic theory.

The Poetics of Space and Embodiment

Indigenous poetics involves embodiment, not only in the land around us, including urban landscapes, but also in our understanding. Janet Rogers writes of this embodiment: "Our words are like stars that helped navigate our ancestors."[32] These stars are like a map and are manifestations of iconic memory. Lindsay "Eekwol" Knight describes the dynamic process of embodiment within Indigenous poetics: "As a performer I also succumb to the ways in which the energy within each word or phrase embodies my actions and movements."[33] The performative act is essentially one of letting the body sound poetic knowing. Within the work of both Janet Rogers and Lindsay "Eekwol" Knight we see this sounding of the body; through their performances and their recordings are poetics icons. There is a stability of these recordings as we can return to them over and over again. Furthermore, their poetic meaning is enriched over time as new possibilities of understanding emerge.

Not only do contemporary writers exemplify this layering process, but it is also represented by an engagement with classics poetics. As Leanne Simpson writes, "Our bodies collectively echo the sounds of our ancestors, the sounds of the land, and (o)depwewin,[34] the sound of our hearts."[35] She adds that the land itself anchors this echo: "for the land retains a spatial memory of ancestral languages."[36] Her chapter, "'Bubbling Like a Beating Heart': Reflections on Nishnaabeg Poetics and Narrative Consciousness," and Niigaanwewidam James Sinclair's chapter, "The Power of Dirty Waters: Indigenous Poetics," describe the importance of places and their stories. Their work on Indigenous poetics helps to populate the landscape with Indigenous consciousness, and helps us retrace the wisdom and knowing of the ancestors through poetic meditation on place names. These place names are poetic narrative markers and condense the richness of our classical narrative traditions as well as the contemporary elements. Alyce Johnson, in her chapter, adds, "The land holds many layers of stories, not only in time, but also with peoples that occupy that time and place in a past, present, and future context."[37] The land can also help us to imagine all kinds of possibilities. Indigenous poetics maps the past by retracing previous collective experiences and imagines future possibilities in the world, allowing us, as Indigenous peoples, to move beyond a sense of the limitations that we sometimes feel.

One of the challenges of contemporary Indigenous poetics is to move from a state of wandering and uprootedness toward a poetics of being home. The poetics of being lost is perhaps most eloquently found in the ghost within the Daniel David Moses's play *Almighty Voice and His Wife*. The ghost wanders the Earth alienated from his sense of home and his identity as manitowêw (Almighty Voice). It is the interlocutor, who, through dialogue and the articulation of narrative dissonance, helps the ghost regain his identity as Almighty Voice. Lee Maracle, in her collection of poems, *Bent Box*, notes this process of moving between the space of displacement and the movement toward home and belonging: "Beware, settler, for the language of suffering humanity is breathing, liberation to the winds of freedom."[38] The poetics of retrieval helps us to find our place in the world and balance in our lives. Leanne Simpson discusses the importance of word maps and narrative maps in the context of the Indigenous territory around Trent University:

> When I heard or read the word "Otonabee," I think "Odenabe," and I am immediately connected to both a physical place within my territory and a space where my culture communicates a multi-layered and nuanced space meaning that is largely unseen and unrecognized by non-Indigenous peoples. I am pulled into an Nishnaabe presence, a decolonized and decolonizing space where my culture understanding flourish.[39]

In Christine Sy's work, "Through Iskigamizigan (The Sugarbush): A Poetics of Decolonization," she uses the Anishinaabe term "biskaabiiyang," which she translates as "returning to ourselves."[40] It is interesting to conceive of a poetics of place as a return to ourselves, indicating that our home is already within us.

In this way, this process is of "returning to ourselves" involves Susan Gingell's notion of sound identity.[41] "Sound identity" involves moving beyond the linguistic registers of the mainstream society and moves toward a process of "returning to ourselves." As Gingell states:

> Sound identity as I am using the term here, then has three dimensions: the constitution of dynamic identity by oral practices both musical and linguis-

tic, the sounding of the depths of self and community in order to know those depths more fully, and the sounding out of expressive dimensions of self in community, their restoring psychic and spiritual health.[42]

Lillian Allen further articulates the social importance of poetic practice with both a dub and Indigenous context:

> Indigenous poets, like dub poets, have seized poetry as a necessary means to not just counter the meta-narratives and the absence of Indigenous and black communities, and communities seeking, empowerment from the official version, but also a way to vindicate our experiences, enrich our cultural voice, and to be fully in our humanity of art, ritual, and communication that the art of writing, reading, performing is.[43]

Lillian Allen adds that "much of Indigenous poetics like dub poetry is about freedom."[44] Indigenous poetry and dub poetry use alternative englishes. Derived from other sources, they puncture and put holes in the surface and skin of the English language.

Part of the process of dwelling at home in English involves the process of trying to poetically resolve the trauma that Indigenous peoples have experienced. Lesley Belleau describes the process of working through embodied trauma as found in the work of Louise Halfe:

> Louise Halfe in her book documents in many ways the "lived experience" of Indigenous peoples, and in particular the trauma that many Indigenous peoples have experienced. I can easily see how this narrative could resonate with someone at the time of residential schools. I can only imagine how mothers and fathers must have felt when the children were taken from them and how the narrative of Rolling Head in some ways would have mirrored that reality. The children would have been cut off from the nurturing aspects of their mothers—and this way their love and the capacity for embracing a loving relationship.[45]

Halfe's work, *The Crooked Good*, describes how the narrative of cihcipiscikwân's journey maps out the land. Her body marks the land the same way that wîsahkêcâhk did in all of his wandering. While I am not a singer, I am grateful for having heard a song of wîsahkêcâhk's wandering sung by the late Beatrice Lavallee.[46] It is the singing of these old songs and the performance of these old poems that will help to make us whole again.

Conclusion
Throughout the histories of Indigenous peoples, there has been a grounding of Indigenous poetical memory in spatial landscapes and within pools of collective memory. Alyce Johnson's chapter, ""Kwânday Kwańdur—Our

Shagóon,"[47]demonstrates a consciousness deeply and profoundly grounded in place. She stresses the importance of place names, and how they are like bodies, where old sound gathers. We are a part of these bodies as we speak and sing those names again and again into new generations. Various kêhtê-ayak,[48] authors, writers, poets, and storytellers have all, in their own ways, contributed to this song and voicing that is Indigenous poetics. The articulation of Indigenous poetics is multi-layered and cannot be exhausted by one person, including one editor—in this case myself. It is the hope that other writers and other editors, and indeed other storytellers, will build upon this work and add, in their own ways, to the conversation of Indigenous poetics.

Indigenous poetics is inherently political because it is the attempt to hold on to an alternative centre of consciousness, holding its own position, despite the crushing weight of English and French. The Cree language has many ways of playfully describing this alternative conception of reality, and the experience of the dislocations caused by colonialism, for example, iskonîhkan (the leftover), sarcastically referring to reserve land. I remember once my late father said the word "okimâhkan"—a fake leader, a fake chief, often used to refer to "Indian Act chiefs"—while we were driving by the place where the deer with great horns was said to exist. I remember another time kayâs[49] when my father and his friend, who had run for chief, and other supporters were gathered after the election had been lost. One person laughed and said "m'nânitâw. okimâhkan piko."[50] Then, of course, there was the sardonic term sôniyâw-okimaw, which means "money boss" or "one who has authority over money." It was a term used for "Indian agents," and perhaps one could apply this today to third-party managers.

Of course the great Cree leader mistahi-maskwa also used the Cree language and Cree metaphors. For instance, he said "môy ê-nôhtê-sâkawêpinakawyân." That could be translated as "I do not want to be dragged around like a horse." This was mistahi maskwa's way of saying that he did not want to be colonized—that he didn't want someone to tell him how to live. Through his use of Cree metaphor, he pointed out the narrative dissonance between his lived experience, and indeed his anticipation of future lived experience, and illustrated the richness of his poetic home.

One thing that the Idle No More movement demonstrated, particularly in the winter of 2012–13, is the persistence and power of Indigenous consciousness. This consciousness was manifested poetically in round-dance singing, other genres of singing, poetic oratory, and literature. All these events demonstrated the power of Indigenous poetry, in all its forms, to inspire, and the power of Indigenous poetry to transform political spaces.

It is hoped that this volume will contribute to creating a space to speak of Indigenous poetics. There is a virtual renaissance of Indigenous writing occurring right now in Canada. There is an increasing number of Indigenous literary readings and an explosion in the published works of Indigenous authors. Also, there is an increase in the number of Indigenous peoples who are using Indigenous languages, and also an increase in the number of online resources (such as creedictionary.com) to support the learning of Indigenous languages. More work needs to be done to explore not only the classical forms of Indigenous poetics as found in the old stories, but also the forms of Indigenous poetry as found in contemporary Indigenous poetry.

Notes

1 My understanding of this is based on versions I heard from Guy Albert, Basil Johnson, and other sources.
2 This is the term my father and many older Crees always used where I grew up.
3 Translation: "She is truly very beautiful!"
4 Translation: "Hand it over" or "Let me see."
5 Personal communication, 2010.
6 Translation: "English-white."
7 môniyâw in Plains Cree means "European."
8 Theresa Shea, "Review of Blue Marrow," http://www.quillandquire.com/reviews/review.cfm?review_id=3886.
9 Sacred story
10 Europeans
11 See Chapter 28 (MacKay) in this volume.
12 See Chapter 1 (Mercredi) in this volume.
13 Ibid.
14 Lillian Allen, panel discussion, "What Do Dub and Indigenous Oralities Have in Common?", Trent University, Peterborough, February 26, 2010.
15 It is Cree convention not to capitalize Cree words.
16 In the interview with Armand Ruffo (Chapter 2 in this volume), he refers to the "compact" nature of poetic language.
17 Ibid.
18 Ibid.
19 Christopher B. Teuton, Deep Waters: The Textual Continuum in American Indian Literature (Lincoln: University of Nebraska Press, 2010), 36.
20 See Chapter 3 (Cariou) in this volume.
21 Ibid.
22 Janet Rogers, transcript of Indigenous Poetics workshop, Trent University, Peterborough, November 4 and 5, 2010, 404.
23 Quoted by Renate Eigonbrod, "Studies in America's Indian Literatures" 22, no. 1 (Spring 2010): 1–19, cited in Annharte Baker, "Borrowing Enemy Language: A First Nations Woman's Use of English," West Coast Line (1993): 59–66.
24 See Chapter 5 (McKegney) in this volume.
25 Ibid.

26 See Chapter 7 (Newhouse) in this volume.
27 See Chapter 1 (Mercredi) in this volume.
28 The act of interconnecting stories together; is similar to intertextuality, but avoids a basis of only conceiving of this as written "text."
29 This was a Facebook project that I initiated in the winter of 2011. The goal was to post at least ten words a day on different themes for a total of one hundred days. In addition to posting words, people would contribute their words and note dialectical variations. Arok Wolvengrey edited the Cree in the project. A book based on the project will be published under the title *Cree Word a Day* by the University of Regina Press in 2015.
30 Greg Scofield uses this term throughout Chapter 25 in this volume.
31 Teuton, *Deep Waters*, 54.
32 Rogers, transcript of Indigenous Poetics workshop, 404.
33 See Chapter 20 (Knight) in this volume.
34 The word means "truth" in Anishinaabemowin.
35 See Chapter 10 (Simpson) in this volume.
36 Ibid.
37 See Chapter 12 (Johnson) in this volume.
38 Lee Maracle, *Bent Box* (Penticton: Theytus Press, 2000), 94.
39 See Chapter 10 (Simpson) in this volume.
40 See Chapter 14 (Sy) in this volume.
41 See Chapter 22 (Gingell) in this volume.
42 Ibid.
43 Ibid.
44 See Chapter 23 (Allen) in this volume.
45 See Chapter 27 (Belleau) in this volume.
46 She played a tape of this song for me in 2000 at the Saskatchewan Indian Federated College.
47 See Chapter 12 (Johnson) in this volume.
48 Translation: "Old Ones."
49 Long ago
50 Translation: "It is okay. The person [who won] is just a fake chief."

Bibliography

Baker, Annharte. "Borrowing Enemy Language: A First Nation Woman's Use of Language." *West Coast Line* 10, no. 27/1 (Spring 1993): 59–60.

Dumont, Marilyn. *that tongued belonging.* Owen Sound, ON: Kegedonce, 2007.

Eigenbrod, Renate. "A Necessary Inclusion: Native Literature in Native Studies." *Studies in American Indian Literature* 22, no. 1 (Spring 2010): 1–19.

Maracle, Lee. *Bent Box.* Penticton: Theytus Press, 2000.

Shea, Theresa. "Review of *Blue Marrow.*" http://www.quillandquire.com/reviews/review.cfm?review_id=3886.

Teuton, Christopher B. *Deep Waters: The Textual Continuum in American Indian Literature.* Lincoln: University of Nebraska Press, 2010.

Poetics of Memory

1

Achimo

Duncan Mercredi

Kayask ooma
[It was a long time ago]
Nata agamick
[Over there, across the river]
Egota ka kewegit ana ka ke machwit napaw
[It was where he lived and hunted]
Aha, mona ki kokayaw ana napaw
[Yes, one didn't visit this man]
Moch atigay
[No, no way]
Tapa wan na e pataw ana napaw awapamisk at ta kosinyan
[Yes, if that man saw you coming]
Mona kiskanitamuk ininowak kagone whoma ka kitootuk awa napaw
[No one knew, the people, what this man had done]
Mona a weyak we achimoo
[No one would tell his story]

These words, spoken in the old way, were simple yet they spoke volumes and the words flowed like water over the rapids in a singsong chant long into the night, and a child cradled in his Kookum's arms would drift off to sleep.

I would dream of this man, who allowed no one onto his property. I would dream I am walking into his yard and he would run out of his house, brandishing an axe, ready to strike me dead. I stand frozen seeing his rage and I can only ask him in my dream before he struck me, "I only want to know your story."

I can't speak for all those who are contributing to this anthology on the topic of the poetics of poetry because my teachings didn't come from the halls of academia, where one's words, placed upon the pages of a book or a letter to a loved one, are dissected to find the underlying meanings.

My teachings came from the mouths of people whose ability to read was basic at best, but many were unable to read yet they were unequalled in their ability to relate a story, a story that flowed like water in a stream, soothing, calming, then at times angry, raging like rapids released from the icy grip of winter. I was held spellbound by these storytellers, who travelled far distances to tell their stories, stopping at each village to share their gift, and in return would be given a gift to take with them as they continued their journey up the river. I would sit enthralled for hours listening to that song they sang with their words, sometimes barely a whisper, other times bellowing with rage, and at other times soothing, tempting the unwary, trapping those who ventured too close with a caress of a word or a phrase blowing gently into their ears.

My Kookum was a storyteller and all the stories she told were told in Cree. Now we had people who would come from down along the Saskatchewan River, which was also known as Misipawistik (Grand Rapids) or (the term I've grown to love) the Singing Waters. They would travel from Cumberland House, Saskatchewan, to Opaskwiyak (The Pas), Moose Lake, and Chemawawin. These storytellers would come down the river in the wintertime. They would tell stories at each village at the local storyteller's house. They would gather family stories, which they would share at each village they visited, gather stories from each of these villages, and carry these to their next stop. This is how we kept in touch with family along the river from Cumberland House, Saskatchewan, to Grand Rapids, Manitoba. We would then tell our stories and the storytellers would carry these stories back to repeat on their journey home. It was important that these stories be told exactly as they heard them. It was very, very important that they did not digress whatsoever from the way they were told. It had to be very, very clear and precise because once you changed, even slightly, the order of the story, it could affect the whole family and would continue to affect them for years. Once rumours or little mistakes are made, they have a way of growing and once they are repeated, it is almost impossible to correct. It was up to us to listen to these stories very carefully and with utmost attention.

My Kookum had chosen me to be the storyteller or, if you prefer, the keeper of the fire, and I still struggle with that task or gift she bestowed upon me.

When the storytellers reached our village, they would come to my Kookum's house. My Kookum would wake me up (more often than not, the storytellers would arrive at night) and I would be expected to sit and listen as they related the stories they had gathered on their journey. I am not certain when this training began, but it probably started quite early in my life—my best guess would be when I was around four years old. I was not allowed to go to sleep while the stories were being told. The next day, the storytellers would repeat their stories and this time it would be to the rest of our family. This process would be repeated on the third day, except it would be to the community. Interested families would drop in and sit while the storytellers related the messages they had been given from our visitors' families. Our visitors would then pass along their stories to the storytellers to take back with them. On the fourth day, our family would gather again and we would relate our family stories, knowing they were in the good hands, minds, and hearts of the storytellers. They would leave right after we were done, hoping to make it to Chemawawin later that night.

Life would return to normal after this visit, and there would be much talk about what was happening in our distant relatives' lives and villages, speculations on the genders of expected newborns, not knowing for sure until the next visit or maybe a surprise visit from our cousins come the next summer.

Usually three or four weeks later, my Kookum would have me come sit next to her and she would ask me to tell her a story that I had heard when the storytellers had visited. I had learned early on that Kookum didn't want to hear the first or the last story I had heard that week but maybe the fourth or the sixth story. She would sit and listen as I talked. Every once in a while she'd count, piyuk, one; then I'd continue again, niso, two; continue, nisto, three; don't stop, neyo, four; now you stop noosim. You've made four mistakes, so tomorrow you do four chores. Now as I was a young boy who resisted doing chores at any time, being told by my Kookum that I had to do chores because of mistakes I made in telling a story, I would argue it wasn't my job to do chores. I'd argue because the chores I had to do consisted of carrying water from the river for washing, cooking, drinking, etc., cutting firewood and filling the woodboxes, emptying the slop pail, and—the worst task of all—emptying the chamber pot. Now in a house that consisted of eight or more people, the chamber pot was without a doubt the most vile, smelly piece of household equipment ever to be used in a northern cabin, and sometimes accidents would happen when carrying this concoction of human waste. I leave the rest to your imagination.

As soon as I finished complaining, my Kookom would say, in that quiet way of hers, without raising her voice or looking at me, "Maybe next time you will listen better. Now go to bed. You have a lot to do tomorrow." As I would trudge up the stairs, shoulders and head down, she would quietly say, "How you remember the story and how you tell it has consequences that could last a lifetime—remember that."

I would sit and watch wide-eyed as the storytellers slip into each character, becoming that persona, that creature with ease, watching that transformation and not knowing if it was the shadows that played tricks or if they really did have the ability to shape-shift, depending on the story.

They were poets, these storytellers, whether they were aware of it or not. Each story they told had its own rhythm, rising and falling, melodic when required, monotonic if it made the story interesting.

But what made these storytellers? What drove them to relate stories they had acquired over their travels? Did they feel the need to share or did they know that these stories were given to them to share so that we as a people would not forget who we were, that the mistakes we had made in the past were instilled in our memories so we would not repeat those mistakes? Did they believe, as I do, that in order to know where we are going, we have to know where we have been?

Personally, I believe that storytellers are chosen by other storytellers. Now, as to how they are chosen, that is to be discussed in another forum. Let's just say that once chosen, the storyteller's path in life is set. Now, whether the storyteller takes that path early in life or in his later years, how that is determined, I believe, is left entirely to the storyteller.

Where was I going with this train of thought?

> Omsi itayew ana kisano,
> [This is what the old man said]
> Agota whoma kayapit
> [Over there where he sat]
> Achimot
> [Telling stories]
> Iskew, itayew, at ta koosik
> [A woman, he said, came in]
> Whochawasimisa a wechayogut
> [Her child came with her]
> Piyuk who ta wasi michuk a ahkoosich
> [One of her children was sick]
> We che in, atayew, ahkoso awasis
> [Help me, she said, my child is sick]

And so the story would begin, the old man gesturing with his hands for emphasis, but also to keep a child's attention, tenable at the best of times. It was important for the child to pay attention for the smallest detail of every story was important as it could affect the reputation of the person telling the story as well as that of the person the story was about.

Now, in this day and age, is this as important as it once was or do we merely skim the edges of truth to hold the attention of a generation who have grown up in the age of instant news and sound bites? Do we do justice to our teachers or do we want to capture the attention of those who have a passing interest in who we were, but really have no interest in who we have become? Another question we should ask ourselves is: Who dictates what is to be considered serious writings?

Is it those among academia who decide what we should be writing, dissecting our words, and then deeming them worthy for the masses to read? Or do we let those who do have an actual interest in what we are saying and actually purchase our books because they find our voices unique? Many times I have read and heard, even from "our peers," that only those who are considered "learned" should have their works considered for publication, lest the lesser "learned" embarrass those who have achieved some success in both the literary and publishing world.

But does the fact that one has studied in institutions of higher learning make that person more qualified to judge the writings of others, or have they also become elitist?

There is that danger, the desire to become accepted instead of celebrating our ethnicity with its uniqueness in its view of the world. We tend to lean toward those in the mainstream and their idea of what they consider acceptable. When that happens, we have lost touch with who we are and once that happens, it is difficult to go back.

We are in essence discarding our past to embrace a new way of expressing our stories so that we can join the mainstream.

Recently the Truth and Reconciliation Commission began their task of gathering stories from the survivors of the residential school experiment of indoctrination. Their stories were told in a manner consistent with the way stories were related when I was a child. These were emotional, gut-wrenching stories, told from the memories and hearts of the storytellers so that they would have the most impact but, more importantly, they were told in such a way that they would remain embedded in the memories of those hearing them for the first time. They were poetic, with a rhythm that would rise and fall, depending on the emotion in which the story was told.

Will that same emotion, that same rhythm, be captured on the written page? I'm not sure unless you happened to be there to hear the story first-hand. To have the same impact, these stories should remain as close to the way they were told by the storyteller, the survivor, without too much interference from those who will be editing the stories to somehow make them more professional in form and substance. When we do that, we are taking away the heart of the story—the rhythm and cadence are lost in translation.

Much the same way happens when we translate from our Indigenous languages a poem we have written. Once we see it in translation, we tell ourselves, that's not what we meant.

Let's not lose our voices, ones that have been evolving for generations, to please those who believe that to gain acceptance, we must lose something of ourselves. Because once that happens, we are no longer seeing the universe from our perspective and our stories become indistinguishable from all the other stories out there.

Ekosi ma, asa mistayi ayamin, kayask ka ki pimatisyan, ekosi, kayask ka ki ski no machik.
[That's all. I have talked too much, I have lived a long time now, that's all. It was a long time ago I was taught by my nookimak ago nimisomuk, mona nataw ka kintan, ekosi whoma ka ke tachik, how, Grandmother and Grandfather, I don't know it all. That's what they would say, how.]
Kasipatan, mona ma wanaw katotan.
[I leave now, but I won't go too far.]

2

Interview with Armand Garnet Ruffo

Conducted by Neal McLeod

NEAL MCLEOD (NM): Your first book of poetry, *Opening in the Sky*, seems to be more political than the next two books. What was going on in your thinking when you wrote?

ARMAND GARNET RUFFO (AGR): *Opening in the Sky* consists of poems that I wrote specifically for the collection and others that had been kicking around for a while which I thought would be suitable. And, yes, as you point out, much of the poetry is political and, I might add, even angry because, to use a cliché, you cannot be Native in this country without being political and angry unless, of course, you are in major denial. Maturity and healing help temper this, but if you know anything about the history of this country, I don't think it ever totally abates. From a literary perspective, you just find ways of dealing with it. For example, there are different literary strategies one can use. In *Opening in the Sky*, though, much of the writing is straightforward and "in your face," meaning that it isn't couched in humour, satire, or whatever to make it more palatable. In hindsight, I think it was a process that I had to go through. Growing up in the sixties in a town that had a residential school, I don't think I knew any Native people who had not suffered the repercussions of it in one way or another. Of course all I had to do was look and see what had happened or was happening to my own relations, so I guess *Opening in the Sky* is a much more immediate book than the others. I was looking around me, and I had a lot to say before I could take a breath and explore other forms of writing.

NM: How did various readings and performances of your poems from this book help shape them and help you edit them?

AGR: I actually didn't read much from the manuscript prior to publication. I read some of the earlier poems at a couple of coffee houses in Ottawa as part of a small group of Native poets who had hung out together in the early nineties. Because of the lack of opportunity for Native writers, we even self-published a small anthology of our work called *Voices from Home: The W.I.N.O. Anthology.* I have to say that I was not part of the mainstream literary scene and consequently received very few invitations to organized readings. In fact, nearly all of the work that I sent out to literary journals in the 1980s was rejected. The usual comment was that it was too polemical, too political. I guess that's one of the reasons it took me a long time to think that I could actually publish a collection. *Opening in the Sky* was eventually published by Theytus Books, and I worked with Greg Young-Ing and Jeannette Armstrong to finalize the manuscript. When it came out, Theytus arranged a reading for me at the Vancouver Writers' Festival, and I ended up on stage with Al Purdy not too long before he passed away. He gave me a nod of approval after I did my reading, which I will never forget because I felt it was confirmation that I was on the right track.

NM: Who were some of your early poetic influences?

AGR: This is an interesting question because, as you know, there were very few Native poets publishing actively in the 1970s and 1980s in Canada when I took an interest in writing. As a matter of fact, coming from northern Ontario, I can say that my exposure to contemporary poetry was, to say the least, limited. My grandmother wrote poetry and her influence was Pauline Johnson, but I found the form archaic, so as a teenager I really had little interest it. It was only later when I realized what Johnson was actually saying that I revisited her work. However, as a teenager, I was actively listening to the music of singer-songwriters such as Gordon Lightfoot, Bob Dylan, and Johnny Cash, and two things happened to me quite by happenstance when I was in grade eleven. First, one of the girls in class loaned me a Bob Dylan album, which had Dylan reciting a poem on it. I found it amazing. Second, my older sister, who had been living in Toronto, moved back to town and had a copy of Leonard Cohen's first album, the one with "Suzanne" on it, which I ended up playing over and over. That year our English teacher, who happened to be rather innovative, asked us to do a presentation on a Canadian musician, and I chose Leonard Cohen. This led me to his poetry. I even had the school bring in the early NFB film about him. There was something about his use of language that captivated me. In the mid-1970s I moved to Toronto myself to go to York University, and I enrolled in a Canadian literature course with the Jewish Canadian poet and critic Eli Mandel, and I was suddenly introduced to the whole Toronto scene—Irving Layton, bp nichol, Michael Ondaatje, Gwendolyn MacEwen; I saw them all read. A few years later, I moved to Ottawa to work for *The Native Perspective* magazine, and I was introduced to the work of writers like Duke Redbird, Rita Joe, George Kenny, and Wayne Keon. As Jeannette Armstrong has eloquently written, it was these writers who really spoke to her, and they spoke to me. That said, I guess there have been a lot of influences along the way.

NM: When did you write your first poem?

AGR: The first kind of writing that I did was actually songwriting. As a teen I was learning to play the guitar and managed to string three chords together. As for poetry per se, I wrote my first poem in high school, but I kept it to myself. I mean I come from a hockey town! It wasn't something you mentioned. I kept the songs and poems I was writing in a notebook, which eventually disappeared. The writing was obviously forgettable because I barely remember doing it. At York University I continued to write, but I was struggling to find my voice. The poems I was writing had little to do with my own reality and more to do with the contemporary non-Native writers I was reading at the time. Then one day I was visiting my grandmother and she read one of her poems to me and something just clicked. I guess she got me to start thinking about where I come from and all the implications of that. I went back to school and wrote a poem that I would later publish in *The Native Perspective* magazine.

NM: How has Indigenous poetry in Canada changed since you published your first book?

AGR: It's like night and day. When I began writing, there were very few Native writers in Canada and, therefore, I had precious few writers for role models. Certainly there was quite a growing scene in the USA, but I didn't know about it, nor did I have access to it. Today, a young person can go to nearly any library or bookstore and find something by a Native writer or poet. There's also so much on the Internet.

NM: In what ways does poetic form allow you to tell a story in a way that prose sometimes cannot?

AGR: What I like about the poetic form is that the language is compacted and charged in a way that prose is generally not. By this I don't mean that the language has to be out of the ordinary; on the contrary, sometimes two ordinary words placed unexpectedly side by side can energize each other, much like two colours placed side by side can vibrate. I liken poetry to language that is about to surge and explode off the page, at least for me it should, and by its nature it allows you to provide a lot of information in a short space. And, of course, there is a musical, oral quality to it in the way you can employ rhythm, sound value, repetition, etc. And because the bedrock of poetry is ellipsis, the form is able to capture our thought processes, and it therefore lets the reader make his or her own connections. Everything doesn't have to be spelled out. Prose, on the other hand, generally meanders along at a slower pace; it twists and turns and needs room to be expressed fully. Simply put, the two forms have different qualities. And, of course, these observations are not absolute; these days there's a lot of blurring of the genres, and I guess I'm as guilty as anyone of doing that.

NM: As you started to gather poems, when did you realize that you had enough for a book?

AGR: Each book is different. Sometimes you just get to a mass of work that tells you to stop; other times you are never sure if you have enough material or, better yet, the right material. I think it's somewhat easier if a collection has a theme, or maybe even a plot, some kind of glue holding it together, and it comes to a natural conclusion. I think the problem these days is there seems to be a rush to put out one collection after another when the poet has little new to offer. Because I teach at a university, I am constantly being sent books from publishers and despite the laudatory commentaries on the back covers, I generally end up feeling sorry for the trees that went into making the book. Am I calling for fewer poets? No. Just more conservationists.

NM: In your poem "For Duncan Campbell Scott," you talk about how Duncan Campbell Scott sees his poetry. He "says it will make us who are doomed / live forever" (Opening in the Sky, p. 25). How do you see your poetry as contributing to challenging this assumption of Duncan Campbell Scott?

AGR: Ah, good question. We are still here, aren't we? Yes, some of us may be paler than our mothers (or fathers), but we still see ourselves as Native, and I don't think Duncan Campbell Scott's work speaks to that reality. In fact, I wouldn't hesitate to say that he thought quite the opposite. He believed that with "a little push," we would all assimilate and that would be the end of the "Indian problem." My poem presents him and everything he stood for from a Native perspective, and the very fact that it exists as a document in spite of what he did to try and get rid of us is testimony that we are not going away.

NM: What were some of the challenges in telling the life story of Archie Belaney in poetic form?

AGR: When I set out to write Archie Belaney's story, I intended to write it in third-person prose. For various reasons it didn't work. Then I decided to write it from Belaney's perspective, but I found it too limiting. I wanted to give the reader information about Belaney that he himself might not necessarily be aware of. I also found that the voices that came to me were too disparate and they were all vying for space. It all seemed too chaotic. For a while I stopped writing, but kept thinking about it, and then one day I knew it was time to sit down and start writing again. Like magic, one of the voices just jumped on the page and started to tell his or her story about Belaney, then another, and another, and before I knew it, the book was writing itself. I basically started to record what these various characters were telling me. Whether a particular "story" was going to be in a more prose-like or poetic form simply depended on what came to me. So to answer your question, once I found the right form to tell Belaney's story, or rather my subconscious did, the book kind of wrote itself.

NM: In *Grey Owl: The Mystery of Archie Belaney*, you talk about how Belaney will "learn their language, the stones / he will later use to remake himself" (p. 18). In what way did the poetic/narrative exploration of Archie Belaney help you remake yourself?

AGR: Someone else once asked me this same question, and I think that the only real influence that writing the book had on me was that it made me more confident as a writer. By the time I wrote *Grey Owl* I was secure in my skin so to speak and had already gone through my own identity crisis years before. And I have to say that for me it was never really pronounced because I have strong family roots in the Biscotasing region of northern Ontario, where we have a long, long history and have always taken pride in our identity. That my great uncle was Grey Owl's Ojibway canoe partner only further confirmed this to me.

NM: In the prose poem "John Tootoosis, 1936" you write: "We know Wa-Sha-Quon-Asin is not born of us, and we say nothing. For us, it is of no importance. We do not waste our words but save them, because we know in this struggle of generations / they are our strongest medicine // The man flies for us true and sharp, and we are thankful he has chosen our side." I have heard this story of when the late John Tootoosis met Grey Owl in Ottawa, and was struck by the poetic empathy that John had for him. What do you think people like John B. Tootoosis saw in him?

AGR: One of the things that I have always believed is that our ancestors went through things we can only imagine, and by this I mean it is often too easy to pass judgment on events from a contemporary perspective. John Tootoosis's generation endured residential school, pass laws, segregation, disenfranchisement, you name it, and when he met Grey Owl, he saw someone who in his own way was trying to do something positive on behalf of Native people. Remember, Native people couldn't vote, couldn't hire a lawyer, the cards were stacked against us, and here was Grey Owl getting a private audience with the king of England, not to mention the prime minister. I'm sure John recognized that Belaney had his own demons to contend with. By the time they met, Belaney was an alcoholic, but Tootoosis also saw someone who wanted to help, and it didn't really matter where he actually came from. Furthermore, as you know, historically, we have always adopted people into our tribes, and so having Belaney on side was both useful and not necessarily out of the ordinary.

NM: How do see your own narrative family history as being interwoven with the history of Archie Belaney/Grey Owl?

AGR: Well, that's the reason I took on the project in the first place. If it hadn't been for the stories that I had heard about Belaney from my grandmother and great uncle, then I probably wouldn't have been drawn to his story. In fact, when it first occurred to me to write something, I envisioned a handful of poems at best. Of course, the more I learned, the more material I had to draw upon, and probably the central thing that I learned is that it was my family, the Espaniel family, among other Native peoples, who actually helped create Grey Owl. They taught him the language, taught him how to see the world from a Native perspective; as a young girl, my grandmother even dyed his hair black! He certainly couldn't have pulled it off by himself, and for this reason, my family, along with other Native people, are central to his story. I mean there's a reason that when he was unmasked by the *North Bay Nugget*, most Native people at the time just shrugged it off while the general public was in shock, many feeling betrayed.

NM: In a poem called "fallout" (p. 14) in *At Geronimo's Grave*, you wrote that: "As through the heirs of Columbus had a special claim to affection for those like us / caught in between" (p. 12). How do you see your poetry and prose as a way of negotiating this space "in between"?

AGR: Hmmmm. There are a lot of mixed-blood writers out there, and I think it was Laguna Pueblo writer Leslie Marmon Silko who pointed out that this may be because we are constantly negotiating the "in between space." Maybe it's because people in the middle, so to speak, often get to experience two sides of everything. The poem you are referring to is about the fallout of residential school where Native kids returned to their communities without ever having experienced real affection. They, in turn, had children and didn't necessarily know how to express their love to them. They had never been taught. This terrible experience, of course, didn't happen to the "heirs of Columbus," the Europeans who came to Canada, and they could express themselves in any way they wanted. As a child I experienced these two worlds first-hand, and it left an indelible impression on me.

NM: How do you see your new work on Norval Morrisseau as extending your previous work?

AGR: For the record, the manuscript is finished and will hopefully be published next year. I had to stop working on it in order to finish my film *A Windigo Tale*, but I finally got back to it last year, and it's done. My original plan was to include a number of ekphrastic poems based on Morrisseau's art to accompany the prose text, but as it stands I think I have too many poems. Ostensibly I may end up with two books. We'll see. What I can say about it in the context of my previous work is that while *Opening in the Sky* is primarily about my own coming to voice in a political way, and *Grey Owl: The Mystery of Archie Belaney* is primarily about identity and what it means to be "Indian," and *At Geronimo's Grave* is about history and resistance, *Norval Morrisseau: Man Changing into Thunderbird* is really about art and spirituality. Of course it is about many other things as well, but I would say these things are the essence of the book. What I can also say is that writing this book allowed me to explore territory that was new to me, gave me insight into a whole art movement, and so I hope it will be new and exciting to potential readers.

Note
Interview was conducted by Neal McLeod through e-mail.

Bibliography
Ruffo, Armand Garnet. *At Geronimo's Grave*. Regina: Coteau Books, 2001.
———. *Grey Owl: The Mystery of Archie Belaney*. Regina: Coteau Books, 1997.
———. *Norval Morrisseau: Man Changing into Thunderbird*. Edited by Greg Hill. Ottawa: National Gallery of Canada, 2006.
———. *Opening in the Sky*. Penticton, BC: Theytus Books, 1994.
———. *A Windago Tale*. Written and directed by Armand Ruffo. Ottawa: Six Nations Reserve, 2010.
———. *Voices from Home: The W.I.N.O. Anthology*. Ottawa: Agawa Press, 1994.

3

Edgework: Indigenous Poetics as Re-placement

Warren Cariou

Poetics, a Greek Word

Contemporary poetry is an arena of edges and boundaries. There are competing schools and styles, pitched battles for supremacy in the pages of review journals. Manifestoes proliferate. Cliques and cadres and coteries. Young poets are encouraged or required to choose between language and lyric, concrete and spoken word, New Formalism and old free verse. Poems these days are being inscribed into the DNA of bacteria; they are being written by algorithms.

Where does "Indigenous poetry" fit in this tumultuous field? Is it a style, or a school, or a way of relating language to the world? Does it have to jostle for space against all these other contemporary aesthetic categories that trumpet their principles so fiercely—or does it exist in a fluid relationship to them, flowing through and around their borders? Does it point toward their obsession with boundaries? I like to think that it infiltrates the colonial aesthetic categories and shows them that there is more to art than drawing distinctions.

Aristotle, too, was a drawer of boundaries. Sometimes that makes me wish Indigenous artists had a different word for the thing he defined as poetics. But on the other hand, that might be inviting further marginalization of Indigenous literary art. Literature as rez. The colonial boundaries drawn on the land have caused troubles for generations and, as many Aboriginal writers will tell you, the bookstore categories are bad enough. The more I think about it, the more I have come to believe that Aristotle's dusty old Greek word is as good as any for what this particular kind of Indigenous expression tries to do. *Poesis: to make, to create.* To be all verb. To move beyond the old restrictions, making way for something new. That verbal quality is what is most appropriate to Indigenous ways of thinking, in which the entire world is always *doing* or relating rather than simply being. "Cree-ing loud into my night," Louise Halfe writes in a line that gestures toward her inspiration for writing *Blue Marrow* as well as her practice of creating it.[1] Cree-ing is the pronunciation of identity, an assertion that the speaker is connected to her people, to a way of life that is larger than herself. I think each Indigenous nation expresses its identity and its uniqueness in a similarly active and verbal way. Poetry as a cry, a *cri*, that echoes through communities and through the land itself, moving across the lines of class and race and epistemology toward something more elemental in us all, something that we feel in our bodies like the sound of a drum.

Edgewalkers

For me, one of the important functions of poetry in an Indigenous context is to help decolonize the imagination by bridging the ideological boundaries that often separate the beneficiaries of colonialism from those who are objectified and impoverished by it. Marvin Francis's poem "Edgewalker" is an important work for me in this regard because it focuses on the lines that divide different communities in North America, showing how people in a sense become invisible to each other on the basis of nearly unconscious judgments about race and class. "Society edges the other from others,"[2] he writes, suggesting that the process of "othering" is essentially a drawing of boundaries around people and places that society would rather not acknowledge. These boundaries can quickly become so hardened that people can't see past them; they become "edges that cut off our mind / from the crack baby"[3] and from other terrible injustices that we would otherwise have to confront and acknowledge. This process of "edging" is in a sense what creates slums and Indian reserves, and also what enables the relatively wealthy and privileged to enjoy their place in the nation without being bothered by the horrific inequities that typify colonial reality on this continent.

On the other hand, an "Edgewalker," in Francis's conception, is someone who travels along those boundaries, making them visible again and providing a necessary window across them. Though he doesn't explicitly say this in the poem, I think Marvin Francis would agree that the poet is the ultimate edgewalker. Certainly Francis exemplified this in his own life as a poet of Winnipeg's grittiest streets. I learned a lot from Marvin in the time I knew him, though I was supposed to be his teacher at the University of Manitoba, where he had begun to work on a Ph.D. a couple of years before he died. Whenever I talked to him, it always seemed like he was the one who was doing the teaching. After his untimely death, I was given the honour of editing his posthumous second poetry collection, *Bush*

Camp, which taught me a great deal more about Marvin's sly awareness of the societal boundaries that so often disrupt relationships between individuals and between communities.[4] In my own poetic practice now, I am constantly thinking about how poetry can be used to expose those edges that Marvin was so interested in because we need to open our eyes and see what is really right in front of us if we are to have any kind of authentic understanding of where we live and what extraordinary difficulties we have inherited from our colonial history.

While poetry is undoubtedly a marginalized genre in mainstream Western society today, I believe it retains the capacity to shake up the divisive mindset that is endemic in our class-inflected and still-colonized world. It can destabilize those edges that keep Aboriginal peoples marginalized in contemporary North American culture, and it can do this by holding different realities side by side: by juxtaposing the received mainstream perception of colonial reality with a perception that is rooted in Aboriginal experience. In my poem "Louis Speaks to Gabriel Through the Ground,"[5] I have tried to juxtapose the meaning of the Canadian Museum for Human Rights in the non-Native community with the meaning that it has for many Aboriginal peoples, who wonder whether the museum's goal is in fact to deflect attention away from Canada's treatment of Aboriginal peoples throughout the nation's history. In the poem, Louis Riel describes Canada's contemporary rhetoric of human rights as "a bland directionless goodwill / that crushes the bones of our dead." The poem is a reminder that the site of the Museum for Human Rights remains Indigenous space even though the builders would prefer to think otherwise. (As many Aboriginal peoples in Winnipeg have pointed out, the builders neglected to do a complete archaeological survey of the museum grounds before construction began, and thus no one knows whether sacred items or even the remains of Aboriginal ancestors have been covered up by the construction.) To me, this purposely obtuse approach to the museum's construction is an act of "edging" in Marvin Francis's sense: an attempt to push aside an uncomfortable reality in favour of a more sanitized and gentrified imagining. It involves a wilful forgetting, a choice to not look at something that might destabilize Canada's wholesome idea of itself.

Because poetry so often deals with the realm of the unspoken—with suggestion and metaphor and the half-forgotten realms of the unconscious—I think it is an ideal medium for edgewalking. Even at the level of linguistic play, Indigenous poetics can work to shake up prevailing colonial mindsets by taking colonial icons, phrases, and stereotypes and setting them in a new and revealing context. Marvin Francis does this throughout his collection *City Treaty* by taking text from actual treaty documents and then subjecting this text to playfully poetic rewriting and recontextualiza-tion.[6] I have tried something similar with my poem "Ipperwash Litany,"[7] which is an extended meditation on former Premier Mike Harris's alleged comment during the 1995 Ipperwash crisis: "I want the fucking Indians out of the park." Harris later insisted that he hadn't made this statement and that this was "not the kind of language" he would use in a meeting. In the poem I tried to imagine what Harris might have actually said in the meeting that was allegedly misheard by Attorney General Charles Harnick. The result is a playful series of homophones that echo the alleged comment but gesture toward other possibilities in the situation, rather like a series of Freudian slips: "I taunt the lucky / Indians / just for a lark." By placing these plausible though outrageous lines alongside Harris's official denial, I try to raise readers' awareness of the alternate story that lurks outside of official colonial discourse, beyond where our political leaders want us to look.

Written in Stone/Written in Breath
Of course it's not only the poetry of irony and critique that can assert Indig-enous values. The poetry that grows out of particular Indigenous traditions provides perhaps a better way of accomplishing this. Most of the time I feel that I lack the traditional knowledge to do this myself, but I am in awe of the poets who can draw upon the philosophy and the storytell-ing traditions of their people in order to create new works of imagination. One great example of this is Jeannette Armstrong's extraordinary work in her collection *Breath Tracks*, which powerfully proclaims that traditional Indigenous ways of understanding this place are still very much alive today.[8] Armstrong's poems in the sequence entitled "From the Landscape of Grand-mother" consist of grid-like collections of image-words that seem almost to be written on the landscape itself, thus gesturing toward a traditional mode of writing that has been practised in Armstrong's Okanagan homeland for countless generations: rock painting.[9] By presenting us with these words "From the Landscape of Grandmother," she helps to make the Earth visible to us again in a way that is new to the colonized mind, but also very old to those who are acquainted with Okanagan traditions. Similarly, poetry based on Indigenous oral traditions, such as much of Gregory Scofield's and Louise Halfe's work, which draws from their knowledge of the Cree language, points out to readers that Indigenous modes of expression are in fact very contemporary: they exist all around us, often in forms that non-Native listeners don't know how to listen for. In other words, poetry of this kind asserts the contemporary strength and vitality of Indigenous cultures. It clears a place for Indigenous peoples to be acknowledged and respected in their humanity, their complexity, and their strength of tradition. And

it also provides a kind of ground, a medium through which Indigenous peoples can recognize themselves and one another. I can think of nothing more valuable than this in the ongoing struggle for decolonization.

The New *Terra Nullius*

Indigenous spaces such as reserves and certain urban neighbourhoods like Winnipeg's north end have essentially become blank spaces in the colonial imagination. While imperial nations at the onset of colonialism considered north America a *terra nullius* or empty land, open for their own claims, I believe that non-Native North Americans now once again see Indigenous spaces as blank, but in a different sense: they don't imagine these spaces as tantalizingly empty zones of potential wealth and possibility; instead, they don't see them at all. Indigenous space has become terra nullius in terms of being seen as wasteland, as something that doesn't even register in the colonial mindset at all. To me, one of the things that Indigenous poetry and other arts can do is to help shake up this kind of compartmentalized thinking by placing different realities side by side, thereby showing readers what they sometimes prefer not to notice.

Very often, a face can be an empty territory, one that we have no desire to claim. We walk on past someone without even registering his or her existence. This is especially true when that person fits into any number of stereotypical images we already carry in our minds, thick skins that we grow over our eyes. I think of Sherene Razack's book *Looking White People in the Eye*. She talks about the need for people of colour to lift their eyes upward, to present themselves boldly as faces for those around them who would prefer not to see them at all.[10] Implicit in all this is the unwritten corollary to her book, the decolonizing how-to text that has yet to be written: *looking brown people in the eye*. How do non-Native people register the Indigenous presence in their lives, in their spaces?

I think poetry by Indigenous writers can help to make that presence recognized, can re-map the terra nullius once again, so that Indigenous faces and voices can no longer be ignored. Indigenous poetry can accomplish this by opening our senses to what is already there, by giving us the tools to see past the boundaries that colonization has put in place. It can do this by reinvigorating the English language with Indigenous concepts, rhythms, accents, and forms. It can do this by engaging in *poesis*, the kind of making that might also be known as Cree-ing, or Anishinaabe-ing, or Dene-ing: a making that is a cultural and artistic assertion of something good, something that will endure.

These poems can accomplish such important things partly because they are often based upon the old stories, the oral traditions that contain so much of the knowledge of Indigenous peoples. But at the same time, the poems are not exactly the same as oral stories because they do something different with language. At their best, each line of such poems has a kind of flexibility or athleticism that moves readers subtly out of their accustomed realities. These poems trip the reader up just a bit with their words, not so that the readers fall down and lose their way in the poem, but so that they lose their balance a little. Louise Halfe is so extraordinarily good at this. Her language is a bolo lobbed artfully among our feet, forcing us to dance. Her lines, snares. For years now I have been halted, brought up short, whenever I think about a particular couplet from *Blue Marrow:* "Columbus wrote: / *"my wound has opened again."*[11] Writing as a wound, but a wound for whom, by whom? The ambiguity is endlessly compelling; it brings me to a place where the usual interpretive categories disintegrate. This is what Indigenous poetry can do: teach us new ways to question. It can take an old story, an old history, and make it again mysterious, make it present to us in ways we could never have predicted.

Not Just a Platform
I went back to the blueberry-picking place where we've gone all my whole life, and found a sweat lodge there. Yes, it's true. A light willow frame, wrapped in kinikinihk, open to the Sun and my amazed eyes. Washed boulders nestled like eggs in the centre. Toward the lake, the huge poplar trees were wrapped in sacred colours, and there was a path that led down to the water. I stood there at the edge and looked out at the wide bay, the sandy shallows, the shadows of trees extending out into the clear water, quivering along the bottom.

I had been here before, and yet not. You see, it had once been the Catholic Church summer camp. The ruins of the old cookhouse, which was also a makeshift chapel, were still there on the shore, a stark parallelogram of concrete punctuated by the stumps of burned wooden pilings that jutted up like rotting teeth. In my childhood, when we used to come to this place, there was often a church function going on: a barbecue or a softball game or a singalong. Sometimes we joined in, but most of the time we focused on the berries. Then about fifteen years ago, the church abandoned its claim on the site—the insurance had become too expensive, apparently—and the place became quieter, more tranquil. We saw evidence that people had continued coming here: fire rings, wooden benches carved with chainsaws. I assumed these people were coming for the blueberries, too, or maybe for the fishing.

But when I saw the sweat lodge there, I understood. I had always felt that this was a special place, but I had never thought much about why, or for how long. Seeing the sweat lodge was a shock in a way, and yet it was also utterly *in place* where we saw it, as if it had been there for generations. Suddenly I realized: it *had* been there for generations. Yes. It was not that the sweat lodge had ever been out of place, but that the place itself had for a while been shifted, defined in a different way. And now it had shifted back. The boundaries of belonging and exile had fallen away. This frail-looking structure of twigs and branches, and the coloured cloth wrapped around the trees, and the footpaths worn into the sandy soil, were freshly visible manifestations of something that had been there all along—a kind of writing on the Earth. Traces of ceremony. Transitory-seeming, perhaps, but I know somehow that it will always be there.

In My Dream

I was teaching Emma LaRocque's "My Hometown Northern Canada South Africa" the first time I asked my Canadian literature class how many of them had been to an Aboriginal community.[12] Two hands went up at the back, behind a forest of blank faces. Two out of fifty.

"No more than that?" I said. "Are you sure?"

It's amazing how they look away when they don't want to be asked. A force field of inattention, like my face was an eclipse of the Sun.

"Think about it," I said. But I'm not sure they did. It was putting-away-the-books time, smoke-break time, texting-the-homies time, and they were already on their way.

So I asked them again at the next class, and again every few days, all term. "How many of you have been to an Aboriginal community?"

Same answer, same eyes.

They're starting to dislike me. But I'm going to keep asking that question until it becomes something of a poem, a line recited again and again until it echoes in the right way, pushes at the edges, jostles an opening.

That day, in my dream, the hands will all go up at once and their voices will announce: "We live in one!"

Notes

1 Louise Bernice Halfe, *Blue Marrow* (Toronto: McClelland and Stewart, 1998), 14.
2 Marvin Francis, "Edgewalker," in *City Treaty: A Long Poem* (Winnipeg: Turnstone, 2002), 1, 18.
3 Ibid., 11: 10–11.
4 Marvin Francis, *Bushcamp* (Winnipeg: Turnstone, 2008).
5 This poem is part of a manuscript in process entitled *Emergent*, which traces the history of the Western concept of emergency from its beginnings in seventeenth-century England to its deployment in North American Aboriginal communities up to the present day. Many of the poems focus on taking apart the colonial rhetoric of crisis that surrounds acts of Indigenous resistance.

6   Marvin Francis, *City Treaty: A Long Poem* (Winnipeg: Turnstone, 2002), 16–18.
7   This poem is also from the collection in progress entitled *Emergent.*
8   Jeannette Armstrong, *Breath Tracks* (Stratford: Williams-Wallace/Theytus Books, 1991).
9   Ibid.
10 Sherene Razack, *Looking White People in the Eye: Gender, Race, and Culture in Courtooms and Classrooms* (Toronto: University of Toronto Press, 1998).
11 Halfe, *Blue Marrow*, 13.
12 Emma Laroque, "My Hometown Northern Canada South Africa," in *Making Space for Indigenous Feminism*, ed. Joyce Green (Halifax: Fernwood, 2007), 216–20.

Bibliography

Armstrong, Jeannette. *Breath Tracks.* Stratford: Williams-Wallace/Theytus Books, 1991.

Francis, Marvin. *Bush Camp.* Winnipeg: Turnstone, 2008.

———. "Edgewalker." In *City Treaty: A Long Poem.* Winnipeg: Turnstone, 2002.

Halfe, Louise Bernice. *Blue Marrow.* Toronto: McClelland and Stewart, 1998.

LaRocque, Emma. "My Hometown Northern Canada South Africa." In *Making Space for Indigenous Feminism*, edited by Joyce Green, 216–20. Halifax: Fernwood, 2007.

Razack, Sherene. *Looking White People in the Eye: Gender, Race, and Culture in Courtooms and Classrooms.* Toronto: University of Toronto Press, 1998.

4

Pauline Passed Here

Janet Marie Rogers

I know I am spoiled because even with all the biographical material written about her, the numerous museum objects owned by her, the many stories and poems penned by her, and the seemingly small file of photographic likenesses of her, I still want one thing. I want her voice in my ear. I want to hear Pauline Johnson's voice, husky as it has been described, reciting her verses. I want to hear the theatrical inflections, the dramatic pauses and hushed phrases as I can only imagine it to be.

One of my favourite places to visit is the Library of Congress in Washington, D.C. In the summer, the library's air conditioning is cranked to the max while us humanoids start to shiver and shake over our rare literary finds. I hold out for as long as I can. The library is a magical place where researchers and readers alike are given access to a vast collection. Pauline holds a very secured place there. She'd be pleased. However, no audio files, no wax cylinder of Miss Pauline is filed there. Perhaps "technology" was not her thing. Perhaps her fundraising efforts (family wampum belts sold to the Smithsonian) could afford her only tours and not something as advanced as voice recording.

I am a Pauline enthusiast. I devour volumes of her biographies and excitedly exchange information about her with other fans. She was a Mohawk poet from the Six Nations reserve. I, too, am a Mohawk poet from the Six Nations reserve. The parallels between E. Pauline Johnson and myself have not gone unnoticed, not by me or other readers of our works. I would never make the claim to be Pauline reincarnate. It delights me to note that I was born in the city of Vancouver, the same city Pauline adopted as her own upon retiring from extensive touring. Vancouver, British Columbia, is also the city where Pauline left this earth, three days shy of her fifty-second birthday in 1913. I grew up in southern Ontario just outside of my father's reserve, Six Nations, in Stoney Creek and Hamilton. I presently live on

Coast Salish territory, the capital of British Columbia known as Victoria, and have been here since April 1994. Geography is not all we have in common. Pauline developed her poetry into theatrical recitals, complete with costume changes. She recited her poems in this manner and for fifteen years made both a career and a living by doing so—something we call spoken word today. I present my poems as spoken word and also engage in performance poetry, recorded poetry with music and video poetry.

There are also aspects of our personal lives that mirror one another; I am chronically single and chose not to reproduce. After a botched engagement, Pauline, too, never married or bore children. Rumours circulate about her collection of lovers. I've even heard that she kept samples of pubic hairs from her various conquests, although that would very difficult to prove. Plus it's just plain bizarre. But I believe it was her love of adventure that kept her on the road, crossing the country nineteen times, reaching out to remote communities as well as the prestigious halls in more populated cities. She was dedicated to poetry and she loved the road. Having travelled the width and length of my beloved British Columbia, I am dedicated to her and it would take nothing short of great love or a great salary to budge me from here. The road and roads less travelled informed Pauline's poems as they do mine. I love a good road movie and a long road trip. As I travel, especially through the interior of this colonized province, I can't help but think "Pauline passed here too."

When business brings me back to Vancouver, I have been known to stop by her stone monument in Stanley Park, erected by the Women's Canadian Club. There, I place gifts of flint (wooden matches) and speak words of gratitude to her. I make prayers to Pauline—that if, in anyway , she sees what I do as a continuation of her work, may I be guided to do it with honour by carrying on to the best of my ability and represent her and our people of Six Nations in a good way.

In 2000, during a residency at the Gibraltar Point Centre on Toronto Island, I had the notion to pen a play starring our Pauline and co-starring Emily Carr. You can't live in Victoria, British Columbia, without bits of Emily's history attaching itself to you, so I put these two artists together, only ten years apart in age and of two different disciplines (although Emily wrote too). Through fictional theatre writing I had Pauline and Emily meet through their mutual love of canoeing. The turn of the century (1900s) may not have been so accepting of these freedom-loving, adventurous, artistic chicks. Through the story they become allies, then form a deep friendship and an unanswered question of a lesbian relationship arises. The last scene in which Emily pays a reluctant visit to Pauline in the hospital before she succumbs to breast cancer never leaves a dry eye. Now—before this begins to sound too much like one-sided testimony—truth to tell, as Pauline would say, I am not so much a fan of either of these women's work. Pauline's rhymes are far too naive for my liking and, quite frankly, I find the couplings annoying. As for Emily, her paintings make me feel like I'm fighting my way through fog. Her colours are muddy and there's that underlying question of cultural appropriation with her. I enjoy her writings more.

I remember that during a stage reading of the play simply titled *Pauline and Emily, Two Women*, renowned Cree artist Joanne Cardinal-Shubert was in attendance. She asked me, "Did Pauline Johnson really die of breast cancer?" "Yes," I told her, knowing that she, at the time, had beaten the disease. Many years later Joanne lost that battle and joined Pauline in (her words) the Happy Hunting Grounds. These pioneering women of the arts have left in their wake great inspiration. In my mind, leaving a void where these women stood can never be an option, so I write and read and teach others coming up to fill her space, my space, with greatness.

5

Writer–Reader Reciprocity and the Pursuit of Alliance Through Indigenous Poetry

Sam McKegney

At the *Sounding Out: Indigenous Poetics Workshop*, Métis poet Joanne Arnott responded to an audience question regarding the significance of clothing in her work with the declaration, "I love to wash the clothes of those I love." Arnott's assertion is instructive not only in its delineation of a form of allied relationship between washer and wearer (bound in this instance by "love") but also in the potent metaphor it provides for audience engagements with poetic creation. The clothes we've worn tell stories; they offer cryptic maps to where we've been and what we've been doing; they attest to our triumphs and failures; and they carry traces of our experiences—indeed of our physical selves—to be decoded by those with the skill and awareness to turn those traces into meaning. Yet none of this occurs in a determinate fashion. Clothing is not an unambiguous synecdoche for its wearer's identity; rather it offers semiotic, tactile, and olfactory signals that, under careful analysis, can be coaxed into a series of interpretative possibilities. The first point here is that the washer, like poetry's audience, is crucial to the process of meaning creation. The second is that the clothes in the laundry hamper, like lines of poetry on a printed page, are encountered at a remove from their wearer—from their creative source.

In an evolving cadence that concludes each of the chapters of *The Truth about Stories*, Thomas King invites his audience to "[t]ake [this] story.... It's yours. Do with it what you will. Tell it to friends. Turn it into a television movie. Forget it. But don't say in the years to come that you would have lived your life differently if only you had heard this story. / You've heard it now."[1] By entreating his listeners to do what they will with the story he has gifted them, King affirms the lives taken on by stories and poems beyond the creative control of their tellers. Although traceable to the vision of the author, poetic images are converted into meanings and affective responses within the minds and bodies of readers. Even in oral settings—in which poets and storytellers have the opportunity to contextualize their work through introductory and concluding commentary, to guide interpretations through bodily gestures, tone, and performance, and to respond to audience questions—the meanings of words and lines and stories inevitably multiply as they collide with the thoughts, memories, and spirits of audience members, who perform acts of creative translation through engaged listening.

Arnott frames the act of washing clothes as a gesture of love on the part of the washer toward the beneficiaries of her or his labour, which strikes me as a form of allied commitment to the well-being of those who soiled the clothing in the first place—who, by means of the analogy I'm trying to make, are poets. But the focus of the task at hand is the restoration of cleanliness (or symbolic health) to the clothes themselves so that the loved ones can again be warmed, nurtured, and protected as they prepare to circulate in a world all too often hostile. So while the primary commitment of the loving launderer must be to those who don the clothing being washed, the expression of that commitment becomes attentiveness to the needs of the clothing itself: gentle cycle for some items, handwashing for delicates, like colours, lay flat to dry. It is the same with poetry. While the act of reading, listening to, and interpreting Indigenous poetry needs to commence from a foundation of respect for the poet's voice, the expression of that respect ought, in many cases, to include critical engagement with the poetry itself—engagement that asks not what the poet intended to mean, but what the form and content of the poetry engenders.

In her seminal essay "Native Literature: Seeking a Critical Center," Chippewa scholar Kimberly Blaeser argues for the value of "critical methods and voices that seem to arise out of the literature itself."[2] What I wish to argue in this piece is that attentiveness to the cues to criticism emanating from poetry honours the participatory and reciprocal creative relationship between poet and audience in a manner that aspires toward generative alliance.[3] Through the willingness to be inspired, guided, even seduced by the poetry without abdicating the critical responsibility to question and challenge, critical readers of Indigenous poetry can, I suggest, do more to foster the balanced cloak of words envisioned in Arnott's discussion of clothing than they can through passive allegiance to author intentionality—provided such engagement is undertaken from a position of commitment to the well-being of the author and the communities out of and for which she or he writes.

Antagonistic Communities? The "Tribe" of Indigenous Poets and the History of Academic "Poaching"

Elsewhere in this volume, Cree poet Rosanna Deerchild posits two crucial maxims about poetic creation: "The story must be kept, and the story must be given away."[4] Crafting poetry requires exercises of memory and insight refracted through intellect, inspiration, and imagination: the alchemical reaction between experience and artistry metamorphosing into an offering. The story is "kept" because by committing it to words (spoken or written), the poet creates an archive, a reinforcement of memory, which, through its peculiar and precise expression, renders the tale ever more the artist's own. Yet, when the poem is spoken aloud to an audience or committed to paper for publication, the tether to its creative source is loosened; its meaning is no longer nourished solely by its creator but comes to rely on outside engagement to achieve impact and effect. The story is "given away" because its meaning becomes contingent on interaction with other minds and bodies, which it influences, moves, and sways, but which bring to bear upon it distant experiences, understandings, and ideas.

Giving the story away undoubtedly induces anxiety. To share one's intimate imaginative creations—which so often work through both positive and negative personal, familial, and cultural experiences—involves vulnerability, a factor exacerbated among those who have been subject to dispossession, marginalization, and stigmatization. Sto:lo author Lee Maracle writes in *I Am Woman* that "[t]he result of being colonized is the internalization of the need to remain invisible. The colonizers erase you, not easily, but with shame and brutality. Eventually you want to stay that way. Being a writer is getting up there and writing yourself onto everyone's blackboard."[5] To write oneself onto everyone's blackboard is to subject not only one's words but one's sense of selfhood and often one's family, community, and culture to public scrutiny. And given the authority often claimed erroneously over textual meaning by those with peculiar forms of cultural capital (like professors of literature like me, or publishers and literary reviewers), the danger of misrepresentation or further acts of erasure is very real—as illustrated by the impermanence of the blackboard medium in Maracle's analogy.

Métis poet Gregory Scofield dramatizes this danger in his recent poem "The Dissertation," wherein the speaker describes an academic figure "over[taking] his poetry like a landlord, / rent[ing] him a room in his life."[6] At first this attention is "flattering" to Scofield's poet-speaker, "But then arrived the microscope / and she set to work, the academic, / prodding and jotting, / jotting and prodding."[7] The divestiture of control here is acted out through the relative positionality of academic "landlord" to poet-tenant, with the former setting the terms of engagement while constraining the poet's artistry through physical confinement in a life over which he can no longer claim full autonomy. The arrival of the microscope again places not only the poetry but indeed the poet under invasive surveillance as he becomes immobilized like T. S. Eliot's "patient etherised upon a table,"[8] then dissected and absorbed within the academic's critical narrative. Here the poet is indeed "annexed" as the hegemonic voice of academic authority sterilizes the dynamism of the creative process, reducing poetics into discrete bits of information in an anatomy textbook.

Given the history of unscrupulous research in Indigenous communities by scholars, the fear connected to "giving the story away" in Scofield's poem—or, more accurately, having it taken away—is understandable. Scholars are but one audience of Indigenous poetry and very seldom are they the primary audience. Yet scholars remain disproportionately influential because of their capacity to affect dissemination and reception. Many readers first encounter Indigenous poetry in a classroom setting, and what they encounter generally depends on decisions by publishers, editors, and pedagogues; the pieces anthologized,[9] the texts available from publishers, and the works studied within particular courses can all be influenced by the decision-making of scholars—decision-making that engenders political and economic consequences. This is, of course, somewhat unnerving given that the academic study of Indigenous literatures has historically involved the appropriation and misrepresentation of Indigenous cultural materials, knowledges, and stories; the documentation of images of the "vanishing Indian" according to touristic impulses that appease settler guilt by invoking tropes of tragedy; and the replication of stories of Indigenous social dysfunction with neither recognition of strength and continuance nor accountability to Indigenous communities struggling with the legacies of colonialism. Cherokee scholar Jace Weaver refers to such scholarship as academic poaching: stealing cultural materials in a manner akin to stealing land and profiteering from adverse conditions in Indigenous communities while failing to respond in tangible ways to the articulated needs and goals of Indigenous nations.[10]

That being said, the roots of the study of Indigenous literatures on the northern half of Turtle Island have been tended predominantly by Indigenous intellectuals, many of whom identify first and foremost as writers and poets.[11] Writers like Kateri Akiwenzie-Damm, Jeannette Armstrong, Maria Campbell, Thomas King, Emma LaRocque, Lee Maracle, Daniel David Moses, and Armand Garnet Ruffo produced the foundational critical insights that have provided tools for analytical engagement with Indigenous literatures for generations of academics to follow, often publishing in Indigenous-run presses like Theytus, Kegedonce, and Pemmican. Their work continues to be engaged with, adapted, developed, supplemented, and questioned in valuable ways by Indigenous critics like Janice Acoose, Natasha Beeds, Warren Cariou, Jo-Ann Episkenew, Kristina Fagan, Neal McLeod, Deanna Reder, Leanne Simpson, and Niigaanwewidam Sinclair. And while the voices of settler scholars continue to contribute valuable insights to the field—scholars like J. Edward Chamberlin, Renate Eigenbrod, Margery Fee, Susan Gingell, Keavy Martin, and Pauline Wakeham—it would be a mistake to consider the field of Indigenous literary studies in Canada dominated by non-Indigenous voices.

This does not, of course, mean that threats of unscrupulous research and oppressive poetic analysis are anachronistic. As a settler scholar who exists outside the community of poets that Gregory Scofield referred to with great affection at the Sounding Out conference as "my Tribe,"[12] I am aware of the economic and status-related incentives for me as a recently tenured faculty member at a Canadian university to produce as much critical commentary as possible on Indigenous literary production, which can mean subduing my attentiveness to critical methods arising "out of the literature itself" and subjecting Indigenous poetry to pre-formulated methodologies indebted to Eurocentric philosophical traditions that are perhaps anathema to particularized Indigenous world views, thereby replicating acts of imposition. I could simply bring out the microscope and prod and jot, jot and prod. However, such decontextualized analysis for the purposes of academic poaching would contravene the reciprocal responsibilities I want to suggest ideally obtain between writers and readers—a relationship that can be understood as aspiring toward ethical alliance. In this formulation, the critic or reader's primary means of fulfilling her or his commitment to the poet and the communities out of and for which she or he writes involves engaging rigorously with the poetry itself—much like Arnott's launderer whose "love" for others manifests in care taken toward their clothing. In the next section of this paper, I will examine the traditional Haudenosaunee tale of Aionwahta as a teaching that might guide critical readers toward relationships of reciprocal responsibility with the potential to enliven their work by making it more meaningful for—and accountable to—Indigenous writers and Indigenous communities.

Aionwahta and Poetic Possibilities for Healing and Change

In *Red on Red: Native American Literary Separatism*, Creek scholar Craig S. Womack argues that the Indigenous peoples of Turtle Island "have our own canon, a large body of written and oral work authored and spoken by Indian people, both primary literatures and commentaries on those literatures in written and oral forms, which have existed for centuries and must surely provide models for interpretation and principles of literary aesthetics."[13] Thus, Womack contends not only that the oral tradition has "always contained within it [a] level of political critique,"[14] but also that it has always contained aesthetic and methodological directives of value to the study of poetics. Cree poet Neal McLeod notes that "[t]hinking poetically involves the movement away from the epistemological straitjacket and the colonial box that the social sciences have often placed on Indigenous narratives. Thinking poetically gives us a space to recreate, although imperfectly, the narrative thinking of the greatest of our kêhtê-ayak, Old Ones, and our storytellers."[15] The Haudenosaunee sacred story of Aionwahta, as told by Bear Clan Mohawk Elder Tom Porter (Sakokweniónkwas) in his book And Grandma Said... Iroquois Teachings as Passed Down Through the Oral Tradition, provides such a space by mobilizing the living oral tradition in contemporary contexts to awaken alternative political and aesthetic/critical possibilities.

The tale of Aionwahta offers political teachings that seek to characterize just and equitable governance structures at the same time that it offers critical teachings about the contours of ethical engagements with Indigenous literary art—and it does so in language immediately recognizable as poetic.[16] Meanwhile, it provides a template for ceremonies of condolence by delineating the responsibility of those within the Haudenosaunee web of kinship to bring those who have been thrown out of balance by grief, trauma, and oppression back to what Taiaiake Alfred refers to as "the power of reason."[17] In these ways, the Aionwahta story addresses alliance: commitment to the well-being of others with whom one is in relationships of reciprocal responsibility. It speaks volumes about the role of poetics and narrative in the attainment of community health while, I will suggest, providing a prototype for forms of ethical critical engagement with Indigenous literatures.

Aionwahta was a man living in Onondaga at the time of the Peacemaker's journey to unite the clans and nations of the Iroquois Confederacy under Kaianere'kó:wa, the Great Law of Peace. A man of witchcraft desired Aionwahta's wife, but she rejected his advances, so "the witchcraft man" produced medicine that made her grow sicker and sicker until she died. "'Because if I can't have her, nobody's gonna have her.' That's what he thought."[18] This man then sought the love of Aionwahta's seven daughters one by one, each of whom rejected his advances and each of whom he killed, leaving Aionwahta utterly broken and disconsolate. In despair, Aionwahta began to walk "aimlessly, in no particular direction. He just walked." He even walked into a small lake "covered from shore to shore with a blanket of geese and ducks," not caring if he should drown. When the birds flew up out of his way, however, they carried in their feathers so much of the water that they drained the lake—"that's how many were in there." As he walked upon the lake's muddy bottom, Aionwahta spied quahog shells, which he picked up and began to thread upon strings of sinew so that they "formed different variations of white and purple." And as he finished each of his strings, Aionwahta declared:

> "With this string I made from this wampum that I found, if there is somebody in the world that is as sad and tearful, as full of grief as I am, with nothing to live for...I would go see them. And I would take from the very beautiful blue sky a pure eagle feather. And I would wipe the dust of death from the sad one's ears, so that he could hear the children talk and sing and laugh again. So that he could hear his children and nephews when they speak to him. That's what I would do with this wampum if I knew somebody who was as sad as I am. I would console them by taking the death from their ears."
>
> And then he picked some more up and he strung them. And he said, "If there was somebody as sad as I am, walking this earth, I would take, from the very beautiful clear blue sky, a soft little deer skin that's like white cotton. And I would wipe the tears from his eyes. I would use that cloth to wipe the tears, the pain of lonesomeness away from him. So he can see again the beauty of our Mother Earth and the beauty of his children and nephews and nieces. So he can see life again. That's what I would do, if there was somebody as sad as I am, to lose their whole family that they love."
>
> Then as he continued to walk, he found some more of those same beads on the ground. And he strung them up. "With this wampum," he said, "if there was somebody in this world who was as sad as I am, with heaviness upon them, what I would do is I would take from the very beautiful blue sky, a medicine water and I would offer it to him. So when he drank it, it would dislodge the grief and the sadness, about the loved ones who died in his family. That way he could eat again and the food would taste good. And that way he could speak without a stutter to his loved ones, the ones that remain on earth.... And that's what I would do, if there was somebody who was in as much grief as I am."[19]

Porter's version of the Aionwahta tale is generically and thematically complex. In terms of genre, the tale acts as sacred story *and* political treatise, as oral tale (spoken by Porter) *and* written document (transcribed by Lesley Forrester), as traditional teaching reaching back centuries *and* contemporary telling attuned to the present concerns of the People, and— perhaps most significantly for this chapter—as poetic creation *and* critical gloss. In terms of theme, the Aionwahta tale is concerned with love and commitment, with violence and abuses of power, with loss, grief, and despair, and with ceremony as a vehicle for the restoration of balance to individuals, clans, and nations. The tale is also about writing. As Aionwahta strings together the quahog shells of various sizes and hues in a specific order, he mobilizes a symbolic system of non-alphabetic writing that can be translated into meaning by knowledgeable readers. The strings of wampum he places in his pouch—like pages in a book, like poems in a collection—act as an archive of his experience, detailing Aionwahta's despair at the loss of his family. This creative act, however, does more than document the past; it transforms past experiences into a creative offering capable of inspiring change in the present and future. Aionwahta is here not simply historian or biographer but poet. His creative distillation of experience arises from a place of profound personal suffering to become a public artistic gesture that seeks a horizon of possible effects through the catalyzing force of an envisioned audience. Porter depicts Aionwahta not as an autonomous creative talent in the European Romantic tradition, but rather as a communal actor with duties and responsibilities, wedding him to the fate of family, community, and nation.

Porter's depiction of Aionwahta thus resonates with Uruguayan writer Eduardo Galeano's contention from "In Defense of the Word" that "[a]t times, [writing] answers—years in advance—the questions and needs of the collectivity, if the writer has known how to experience them first through inner doubts and agonies. Writing springs from the wounded consciousness of the writer and is projected onto the world; the act of creation is an act of solidarity."[20] Aionwahta demonstrates solidarity with others by describing his intention to restore perspective to the aggrieved, and that solidarity is reciprocated when Aionwahta eventually meets the Peacemaker and is condoled in precisely the manner that he had envisioned for others. With his "rationality"—to borrow Alfred's term—restored, Aionwahta is then able to accompany the Peacemaker on his journey to bring the Great Law of Peace to the nations of the Iroquois Confederacy.[21]

In Porter's rendition of this story, Aionwahta's words and actions delineate a teleological purpose: to cleanse the aggrieved individual of impediments to her or his perspective and to restore her or his place within the web of tribal kinship. Poetic utterances become elevated to rituals of condolence in which Aionwahta symbolically "wipe[s] the dust of death from the sad one's ears, so that he [can] hear the children talk and sing and laugh again"; "wipe[s] the tears [from the sad one's eyes] ... [s]o he can see again the beauty of our Mother Earth"; and "dislodge[s] the grief and the sadness [from the sad one's throat, so that he can] speak [again] without a stutter to his loved ones." As the repetition of "so" between the clauses above suggests, Aionwahta's statements pursue a causal relationship:

speaking the ritual instigates a model of action through which particular goals might be realized. Yet the ritual itself, sculpted in Porter's evocative language, remains essentially open-ended. Aionwahta seeks not to impose a particular perspective upon the aggrieved individual but rather to open that individual up to perspectives ever more her or his own. The recipient/reader's eyes are opened so that she or he can see the world more clearly. Her or his ears are cleansed so that the words of others are less likely to be misinterpreted and so that the relationships solidified through community interaction can be reaffirmed and celebrated. And her or his throat is unclogged, not so that she or he can parrot the views of Aionwahta the poet, but so that she or he can reclaim her or his own voice. The re-establishment of the aggrieved individual's voice in this process is every bit as important as is the voice of the poet-condoler in the first place.[22] Aionwahta seeks neither to persuade nor to instruct; rather, he uses words and actions to create conditions in which the voice of the aggrieved might be raised in a self-determining and healthy way.

Critical Alliance Rather Than Interpretive Allegiance: Tentative Conclusions

All of this, it seems to me, bears practical implications for the study of Indigenous poetry and poetics. The Aionwahta story speaks not only to what Indigenous poetry does; it speaks as well to what honouring Indigenous poetry might mean as a critical ethos emerging from Indigenous intellectual and poetic traditions. In his commitment to the well-being of aggrieved individuals and to the health of the communities in which they circulate, Aionwahta harnesses emotions that erupt from his own traumatic experiences and sculpts them into words and rituals capable of responding to what he has understood through careful analysis to be the needs of others. Aionwahta might therefore be interpreted not only as a poet but also as a form of critical reader; he reads and intuits the needs of others and responds through carefully crafted language. To paraphrase Blaeser, Aionwahta (as imagined critic) invokes analytical methodologies arising out of the self-expressions of those to whom he is committed: the aggrieved individuals reveal themselves to be veiled by the "dust of death," which leads Aionwahta to turn to critical tools like the "pure eagle feather," the "soft little deer skin," and the "medicine water." These Aionwahta employs to reawaken the power of the aggrieved individuals' voices. Aionwahta is neither dictatorial nor dogmatic, but rather struggles in the service of greater understanding, employing his critical knowledge and experience out of a sense of duty to the individuals he condoles, to their communities, and to creation more broadly.[23] And he does so with profound respect for the integrity of poetic voice.

Aionwahta's posture as imagined critic, therefore, aspires toward a form of open-ended alliance. Alliance requires attentiveness to a dynamic and evolving relationship in which multiple parties maintain forms of reciprocal agency. Allegiance, on the other hand, involves unidirectional and static obedience to a particular point of view. Both the Aionwahta story and Arnott's discussion of washing her loved ones' clothing champion active roles for readers in which they respond to poetic creation in creative ways. These responses demonstrate respect for the voices of artists, but do not obligatorily endorse everything those voices might say. Aionwahta strings together the wampum in order to create conditions in which the voices of those he honours—the poets—can resonate more clearly and unhindered, yet he does so in recognition that the perspectives of those he honours might very well be flawed; that is why, in Alfred's terms, they might need to be "brought back to the power of reason" through the condoling capacity of Aionwahta's work. Arnott's launderer lovingly tends to the needs of soiled clothing in order to restore them to a condition in which they will serve its wearers—the poets—in their interactions with the world; her respect is demonstrated metaphorically by her engagement with the words themselves (if clothing = poetry and loved ones = poets) rather than through strict allegiance to the wearers' desires. Both Aionwahta and Arnott's launderer prove committed to the creative beings with whom they interact, but not in a passive manner.[24] Their interpersonal alliances are not expressed through inevitable endorsement of others' perspectives but rather through their own creative and critical labour—intriguingly configured in both cases as acts of cleansing.

To draw this back to a discussion of critical strategies for engaging with Indigenous poetic art, Porter's and Arnott's teachings seem to imply that the audiences of Indigenous poetry ought not seek to intuit what authors *intend* or purport to be the *true meanings* of their creations; rather we should seek to honour the words of Indigenous poets by responding to cues to criticism within the poetry itself, using those cues to form rigorous albeit non-definitive understandings, and striving to extend the poetry's capacity to engender positive change. We should allow ourselves to be shaken by the movement of the words and to honour that shared energy by drawing together our minds, hearts, and bodies in a ritual of catalytic engagement—a ritual that requires something of us as active participants rather than passive recipients. Gregory Scofield explained to me in a recent interview that "when [a poet is] reading aloud and they're shaking the rattle, the spirit is being flung, the spirit is being directed, it is being moved around the room, so you have no choice but to move. It's like a wave. You have no choice but to move with that spirit and to be taken by it. And the spirit will resonate with you, even after the poet stops speaking."[25] The key is to honour that resonating spirit by carrying the energy that's been shared to new and distant places while, in acts of reciprocity, reflecting gratitude and engagement back to the poet herself or himself. Creative energy is not a finite resource that dilutes and disappears when shared; it grows and crescendos and is nurtured from spark to flame. As a critical reader of Indigenous poetry—and by critical reader, I mean one who is inspired and moved by, yet analyzes and interprets Indigenous poetry—I might demonstrate my gratitude for the way the poetry has symbolically cleansed my eyes, ears, and throat by mobilizing the strength of my newly awakened voice to engage with issues emergent from the poems themselves, but not in a programmatic way predetermined by author intentionality. Osage scholar Robert Warrior reminds readers of "the importance of dissent—especially dissent from the ideas of those who share a critic's political commitments."[26] Respectful disagreement from a place of commitment to mutual well-being and reciprocity is crucial to alliance. It is, it seems to me, an expression of alliance. One of the things that critics, scholars, audiences, and readers are blessed with is the weapon of critical questioning, and its abdication seems a breech in reciprocal responsibility as potential allies. I'm reminded of the prayer with which Frantz Fanon concludes *Black Skin, White Masks*: "Oh My Body, make of me always a man who questions!"[27]

Critical questioning in the service of the health, empowerment, and balance of both individuals and communities is a sign of respect for the power of poetry—one that honours the integrity of poetic voice; it can also be a gesture of reciprocal responsibility that celebrates how poetry has condoled the critical questioner. Critical engagement, interpretation, and questioning honour the way poetry affects and empowers us. Like Aionwahta's recourse to story in the waterless lake, poetry springs from a well of experiences refracted through talent, inspiration, and imagination to become an offering.[28] This offering is not the straightforward pedantry of commands and instructions, but rather the visceral shock that reawakens our awareness of beauty's persistence within the anguished struggle of existence—it's the unexpected reminder of the mind's inseparability from the heart; it's the unfettered experience of emotions, desires, even thoughts in the fingertips, in the crotch, and in the gut; it's the sound and scent and touch that enable us to more fully inhabit our selves and, in so doing, affirm our kinship with each other and with this Earth. These are among poetry's many gifts, which we can honour through intellectual and emotional engagements that include critical reflection.

When I hear Gregory Scofield read of "maskwa pawing / all his winter hunger" or Kateri Akiwenzie-Damm sing of "thighs / dripping / maple syrup /

between parted lips,"[29] I stand relentlessly embodied, more fully inhabiting my desires and my personhood. When I read Neal McLeod's diagnosis of the strength required "to hold the fire of Gabriel's beach with grace" or Louise Halfe's analogy of a tongue like "a willow whipping...clenched hands" in the struggle to "bury" a "fist,"[30] the veiled connection between weakness and violence is laid bare, along with the persistent capacity of understanding to propel one beyond despair. When I read Joanne Arnott's heartrending condemnation of inequity in "Poverty" or Connie Fife's shattering of neo-liberal illusions of freedom in "Politics,"[31] I am chilled by awareness of my embedded position within a horridly unjust world. Reading these words, I know more fully myself, and I am jarred into recognition of my responsibilities to the people and other-than-human entities around me. Poetry helps me see my world more clearly, not because it tells me what I see, but because it momentarily dissolves the shroud of the quotidian to reveal the persistence of magic and meaning all around me. It unclogs my eyes, ears, and throat so that I experience the world more fully with my whole embodied self. It cleanses these accoutrements by which I am adorned so I am warmed, protected, and expressive of that which truly matters in the core of my being. It allows me to hear more clearly the voices of those I love and of those I've not yet recognized as my kin, and occasionally it coaxes my own voice to song. And for these many gifts I am eternally grateful.

Notes

Although I employ the terms "Writer" and "Reader" in the title, this chapter is concerned with myriad storying relationships: storyteller/listener; sound poet/audience, testifier/witness, etc. Recognizing both the semantic and the affective qualities of words, I choose "Writer-Reader" largely for its alliterative connection to "Reciprocity" and not to limit the possibilities invoked by the focus of this volume—*Indigenous Poetics*. The specific burden of my discussion will be to consider how critical analysis of Indigenous poetry might embody forms of ethical reciprocity that aspire toward alliance.

1 Thomas King, *The Truth about Stories: A Native Narrative* (Toronto: House of Anansi Press, 2003), 29. King's *The Truth about Stories* remains both an oral and a written piece, having been first delivered in 2003 as a series of Massey Lectures and then published by House of Anansi Press later that year. It is available in audio form from the CBC and also in print.

2 Kimberly Blaeser, "Native Literature: Seeking a Critical Center," in *Looking at the Words of Our People: First Nations Analysis of Literature*, ed. Jeannette Armstrong (Penticton: Theytus Books, 1993), 53–54.

3 Lynne Davis, "Introduction," in *Alliances: Re/Envisioning Indigenous-Non-Indigenous Relationships*, ed. Lynne Davis (Toronto: University of Toronto Press, 2010), 5. In her introduction to the recent collection, Lynne Davis identi-

fies three forms of alliance, each governed by different configurations of power. "Sometimes," she writes, "alliances are understood as partners walking side-by-side... each following its own path, with its own laws, customs, and culture, neither interfering in the business of the other... [but coming] together around a specific agenda to accomplish a particular set of goals over a period of time." "A second type of relationship," she continues, "is one of paternalism," in which "non-Indigenous 'partners' may adopt a position of superiority by assuming they know what is best for Indigenous people.... A third stance is one where Indigenous partners provide the leadership, and non-Indigenous people take action in support of the direction that Indigenous people have determined. This is a model that is often found where the assertion of Indigenous self-determination is critical to the Indigenous peoples involved."

The third of these cuts closest to the forms of alliance with which I'm concerned in this chapter, insofar as the interpretive act depends upon (and follows) the creative act. Indigenous poets provide guidance and "leadership" through art, which readers endeavour to "support" through engaged reading strategies. Such readerly efforts at allied interpretation are not immune to the paternalism that plagues Davis's second species of alliance, of course, but by responding to the interpretive cues emergent from the poetry itself, readers can demonstrate a humble commitment to the vision of the writer that might blossom into a form of ethical alliance. One other clarification here is important: while Davis is concerned primarily with alliances between Indigenous and non-Indigenous entities, I want to recognize that the readership for the Indigenous poetry at the heart of this chapter is, of course, not discretely or even primarily non-Indigenous but rather cuts across many identity formulations. Indigenous poetry offers a valuable platform for analyzing modes of alliance within and among Indigenous nations, as well as alliances between Indigenous and non-Indigenous constituencies.

4   See Chapter 17 (Deerchild) in this volume.

5   Lee Maracle, *I Am Woman: A Native Perspective on Sociology and Feminism* (Vancouver: Press Gang Publishers, 1999), 8.

6   Gregory Scofield, "The Dissertation," in *Kipocihkân: Poems New and Selected* (Vancouver: Nightwood Editions, 2009), ll. 8–9.

7   Ibid., II. 12, 15–18.

8   T. S. Eliot, "The Love Song of J. Alfred Prufrock," in *Prufrock, and Other Observations* (New York: A. A. Knopf, 1920), l. 3.

9   For insightful commentary on the complexities of anthologization in Indigenous North American contexts, see Marjory Fee, "Aboriginal Writing in Canada and the Anthology as Commodity," in *Native North America: Critical and Cultural Perspectives*, ed. Renée Hulan (Toronto: ECW Press, 1999), 135–55.

10 Jace Weaver, "Splitting the Earth: First Utterances," in *American Indian Literary Nationalism*, ed. Jace Weaver, Craig S. Womack, and Robert Warrior (Albuquerque: University of New Mexico Press, 2006), 11–13. The literary nationalist movement, spearheaded by Indigenous literary critics like Weaver, Craig S. Womack, and Robert Warrior in what is commonly referred to as

the United States, has emerged over the past decade as a pluralist mode of politically minded critical response to this history of unethical literary criticism conducted largely by non-Indigenous scholars. Cherokee scholar Daniel Heath Justice argues that "Indigenous literary nationalism is a philosophy that places Indigenous intellectual and cultural values at the center of analysis, rather than the margins. It operates with the understanding that Native nations have powerful and sophisticated intellectual foundations, and that these are ideally suited to the study of Indigenous literatures. It's also an avowedly political movement, in that it asserts the active presence of Indigenous values in the study of the literatures of Indian Country, and it sees transformative possibility in studying nation-specific literatures through the critical lenses of their source cultures." Daniel Heath Justice, "Literary Nationalism," in *Daniel Heath Justice—Scholarship*. http://www.danielheathjustice.com/scholarship.html.

11   This, I would argue, is somewhat different from the situation in what is now commonly referred to as the United States, where the field of Indigenous literary studies was deeply influenced early on by settler academics working in mainstream institutions and publishing with mainstream scholarly journals and academic presses. I wish also to recognize at this time the arbitrariness of the imposition of American and Canadian "national" borders on pre-existing/ongoing Indigenous nations whose citizens may or may not self-identify as American or Canadian. I don't intend here to limit the range of national identifiers for Indigenous poets or others or to reify the fictions of Canadian and American nation-states. Rather, I wish to note how the field of Indigenous literary studies developed differently in institutions of higher learning, journals, and publishing houses situated in what is often referred to as the United States than in those situated in what is often referred to as Canada.

12   I must say that many of the poets included in this collection, as well as others, have welcomed me with grace and kindness into their conversations, their laughter, and their lives in ways for which I am forever grateful. I count among my most cherished friends individuals who happen to be Indigenous writers. I recognize, however, that the profoundly supportive community of Scofield's "Tribe" of poets is a space into which I will never insinuate myself.

13   Craig S. Womack, *Red on Red: Native American Literary Separatism* (Minneapolis: University of Minnesota Press, 1999), 75–76.

14   Ibid., 57.

15   Neal McLeod, "Cree Poetic Discourse," in *Across Cultures, Across Borders: Canadian Aboriginal and Native American Literature*, ed. Paul DePasquale, Renate Eigenbrod, and Emma LaRocque (Peterborough: Broadview Press, 2010), 109.

16   Note as you are reading through this section, Porter's use of repetition, cadence, alliteration, imagery, and rhythm. Although Lesley Forrester chose to transcribe Porter's oral performance in a prose style, it could quite easily have been rendered in stanzaic form.

17 Haudenosaunee traditions of condolence delineate the duties of families, clans, and nations to participate in the restoration of balance and well-being to individuals and communities. According to Kanien'kehaka scholar Taiaiake Alfred, "The ritual of condolence is an ancient and sacred custom of my people, the Rotinohshonni. In its structure, its words, and its deep meaning, this ceremony is an expression of the transformative power inherent in many healing traditions." Taiaiake Alfred, *Peace, Power, Righteousness: An Indigenous Manifesto* (Don Mills: Oxford University Press, 1999), xi. "Traditionally," he continues, "the Condolence ceremony represents a way of bringing people back to the power of reason." Ibid., xix. Haudenosaunee is a term of self-definition for the Peoples of Iroquois Confederacy. Rotinohshonni is a Mohawk word meaning "people of the long house." The Iroquois Confederacy is made up of six member nations: the Onondaga, the Mohawk, the Seneca, the Oneida, the Cayuga, and the Tuscarora.

18 Tom (Sakokweniónkwas) Porter, *And Grandma Said... Iroquois Teachings as Passed Down Through the Oral Tradition*, trans. Lesley Forrester (Bloomington: Xlibris Corporation, 2008), 294.

19 Ibid., 293–96.

20 Eduardo Galeano, "In Defense of the Word," in *Days and Nights of Love and War*, trans. Judith Brister (New York: Monthly Review Press, 2000), 191.

21 According to Alfred, "The Condolence ritual pacifies the minds and emboldens the hearts of mourners by transforming loss into strength. In Rotinohshonni culture, it is the essential means of recovering... wisdom." "It is a gift," he continues, "promising comfort, recovery of balance, and revival of spirit to those who are suffering" through a process of "strengthening family ties, sharing knowledge, and celebrating the power of traditional teachings." Alfred, *Peace, Power, Righteousness*, xii.

22 This process accords with Haudenosaunee ethics of non-interference as theorized by Mohawk psychiatrist Clare Brant. In Brant's words, "The ethic of non-interference is a behavioural norm of the North American Native tribes that promotes positive interpersonal relations by discouraging coercion of any kind, be it physical, verbal, or psychological.... A high degree of respect for every human being's independence leads the Native to view instructing, coercing or attempting to persuade another person as undesirable behaviour." Clare Brant, "Native Ethics and Rules of Behaviour," *Canadian Journal of Psychiatry* 35 (August 1990), 535.

23 Relying upon the term "communities" here and elsewhere in this chapter, I'm reminded of Rob Appleford's salient critique of the propensity in my work (and in that of many young scholars of Indigenous literatures) to invoke "the term 'community' in an almost talismanic fashion to justify... political readings of Aboriginal authors without offering justification for the material connection between aesthetic re-presentation in fiction and the political representation the author is assumed to be advocating in aesthetic terms. 'Community,' in these cases, becomes," in Appleford's view, "less a way into a flexible and

responsible critical analysis than a justification for presumptively shoe-horning authors into political models of agency or resistance with which they may in fact have little interest or sympathy." Rob Appleford, "A Response to Sam McKegney's 'Strategies for Ethical Engagement: An Open Letter Concerning Non-Native Scholars of Native Literatures,'" *Studies in American Indian Literatures* 21, no. 3 (Fall 2009): 62. To "presumptively shoe-horn" authors in this fashion is to disregard the cues to criticism embedded within literary art—to ignore, in Blaeser's words, the "critical methods... [that] arise out of the literature itself"—and therefore constitutes an act of critical imposition that, at best, constitutes poor criticism and, at worst, constitutes a breach of ethics. That being said, critics also need to be suspicious of the retreat into author intentionality implied by Appleford's emphasis on the "sympathy" of "authors." Poetry and other literary arts do more than what authors might intend; words resonate beyond the will of their creators—whether due to the limits of language as a representational vehicle, to the potential for authors to fail as well as succeed in the creative process, or to the interpretive possibilities brought to literature by audiences—which means the pursuit of meaning in poetry can't be ethically contained by allegiance to author motives. The key here is attentiveness to words themselves and what they draw forth (at times irrespective of what an author might intend for them to mean). As Appleford makes clear, however, the critic must always "justify" her or his interpretations through attentive analysis of the literary source if she or he wishes to produce a "responsible critical analysis."

24 To put it most simply, the question from critic to poet, "What do you really mean here?" is disrespectful to the complexity of artistic creation because it implies that the matrix of form, content, performance, cadence, rhythm, image, and sound can be distilled into a definitive statement that can do justice to affect and meaning.

25 Gregory Scofield, "A Liberation Through Claiming," in *Masculindians: Conversations about Indigenous Manhood*, ed. Sam McKegney (Winnipeg: University of Manitoba Press, 2014).

26 Robert Warrior, "Native Critics in the World: Edward Said and Nationalism," in *American Indian Literary Nationalism*, ed. Jace Weaver, Craig S. Womack, and Robert Warrior (Albuquerque: University of New Mexico Press, 2006), 179.

27 Frantz Fanon, *Black Skin, White Masks* (New York: Grove Press, 1967), 232.

28 I might add, so does the very best criticism.

29 Gregory Scofield, "Ôchîm ◆ His Kiss," *Love Medicine and One Song—Sâkihtowin-Maskihkiy êkwa Pêyak-Nikamowin* (Wiarton: Kegedonce Press, 2009), ll. 7–8; and Kateri Akiwenzie-Damm, "The Feast," in *Without Reservation: Indigenous Erotica*, ed. Kateri Akiwenzie-Damm (Wiarton: Kegedonce Press, 2003), 24.

30 Neal McLeod, "Words for My Sons," in *Gabriel's Beach* (Regina: Hagios Press, 2008), 104; and Louise Bernice Halfe, *Blue Marrow* (Regina: Coteau Books, 2004), 84.

31 Joanne Arnott, "Poverty," in *Mother Time: Poems New & Selected* (Vancouver: Ronsdale Press, 2007), 23–25; and Connie Fife, "Politics," in *An Anthology of Canadian Native Literature in English* (3rd ed.), ed. Daniel David Moses and Terry Goldie (Don Mills: Oxford University Press, 2005), 502.

Bibliography

Akiwenzie-Damm, Kateri. "The Feast." In *Without Reservation: Indigenous Erotica*, edited by Kateri Akiwenzie-Damm, 24. Wiarton: Kegedonce Press, 2003.

Alfred, Taiaiake. *Peace, Power, Righteousness: An Indigenous Manifesto*. Don Mills: Oxford University Press, 1999.

Appleford, Rob. "A Response to Sam McKegney's 'Strategies for Ethical Engagement: An Open Letter Concerning Non-Native Scholars of Native Literatures.'" *Studies in American Indian Literatures* 21, no. 3 (Fall 2009): 58–65.

Arnott, Joanne. "Poetics of Medicine." Sounding Out: Indigenous Poetics. Trent University, Peterborough, ON, November 5, 2010.

———. "Poverty." In *Mother Time: Poems New & Selected*, 23–25. Vancouver: Ronsdale Press, 2007.

Blaeser, Kimberly. "Native Literature: Seeking a Critical Center." In *Looking at the Words of Our People: First Nations Analysis of Literature*, edited by Jeannette Armstrong, 51–62. Penticton: Theytus Books, 1993.

Brant, Clare. "Native Ethics and Rules of Behaviour." *Canadian Journal of Psychiatry* 35 (August 1990): 534–39.

Davis, Lynne. "Introduction." In *Alliances: Re/Envisioning Indigenous-Non-Indigenous Relationships*, edited by Lynne Davis, 1–12. Toronto: University of Toronto Press, 2010.

Deerchild, Rosanna. "Indigenous Poetry Is Dreaming." Oral presentation at Sounding Out: Indigenous Poetics, Trent University, Peterborough, ON, November 4 and 5, 2010.

Deloria Jr., Vine. "Foreword." In *New and Old Voices of Wah'Kon-Tah*, edited by Robert I. Dodge and Joseph B. McCullough, New York: International, 1985.

Eliot, T. S. "The Lovesong of J. Alfred Prufrock." In *Prufrock, and Other Observations*. New York: A. A. Knopf, 1920.

Fanon, Frantz. *Black Skin, White Masks*. New York: Grove Press, 1967.

Fee, Margery. "Aboriginal Writing in Canada and the Anthology as Commodity." In *Native North America: Critical and Cultural Perspectives*, edited by Renée Hulan, 135–55. Toronto: ECW Press, 1999.

Fife, Connie. "Politics." In *An Anthology of Canadian Native Literature in English* (3rd ed.), edited by Daniel David Moses and Terry Goldie, 502. Don Mills: Oxford University Press, 2005.

Galeano, Eduardo. "In Defense of the Word." In *Days and Nights of Love and War* by Eduardo Galeano, translated by Judith Brister, 169–78. New York: Monthly Review Press, 2000.

Halfe, Louise Bernice. *Blue Marrow*. Regina: Coteau Books, 2004.

Justice, Daniel Heath. "Literary Nationalism." *Daniel Heath Justice—Scholarship*. http://www.danielheathjustice.com/scholarship.html.

King, Thomas. *The Truth about Stories: A Native Narrative*. Toronto: House of Anansi Press, 2003.

Maracle, Lee. *I Am Woman: A Native Perspective on Sociology and Feminism*. Vancouver: Press Gang Publishers, 1999.

McLeod, Neal. "Cree Poetic Discourse." In *Across Cultures, Across Borders: Canadian Aboriginal and Native American Literature*, edited by Paul DePasquale, Renate Eigenbrod, and Emma LaRocque, 109–22. Peterborough: Broadview Press, 2010.

———. "Words for My Sons." In *Gabriel's Beach*, 103–5. Regina: Hagios Press, 2008.

Porter, Tom (Sakokweniónkwas). *And Grandma Said... Iroquois Teachings as Passed Down Through the Oral Tradition*, transcribed by Lesley Forrester. Bloomington: Xlibris Corporation, 2008.

Scofield, Gregory. "The Dissertation." In *Kipocihkân: Poems New and Selected*. Vancouver: Nightwood Editions, 2009.

———. "A Liberation Through Claiming." In *Masculindians: Conversations about Indigenous Manhood*, edited by Sam McKegney. Winnipeg: University of Manitoba Press, 2014.

———. "Ôchîm ◆ His Kiss." *Love Medicine and One Song—Sâkihtowin-Maskih- kiy êkwa Pêyak-Nikamowin*, 10. Wiarton: Kegedonce Press, 2009.

———. "Poetics as Medicine Panel." Sounding Out: Indigenous Poetics. Trent University, Peterborough, November 5, 2010.

Warrior, Robert. "Native Critics in the World: Edward Said and Nationalism." In *American Indian Literary Nationalism*, edited by Jace Weaver, Craig S. Womack, and Robert Warrior, 179–224. Albuquerque: University of New Mexico Press, 2006.

Weaver, Jace. "Splitting the Earth: First Utterances and Pluralist Separatism." In *American Indian Literary Nationalism*, edited by Jace Weaver, Craig S. Womack, and Robert Warrior, 1–90. Albuquerque: University of New Mexico Press, 2006.

———. *That the People Might Live: Native American Literatures and Native American Community*. New York: Oxford University Press, 1997.

Womack, Craig S. *Red on Red: Native American Literary Separatism*. Minneapolis: University of Minnesota Press, 1999.

6

Remembering the Poetics of Ancient Sound kistêsinâw/ wîsahkêcâhk's maskihkiy (Elder Brother's Medicine)

Tasha Beeds

Within a nêhiyaw understanding, stories and, by extension, poetry emerge out of and fall back into the land. The land gives birth to story and reclaims its people in the process. nêhiyawak,[1] poets such as Neal McLeod, Gregory Scofield, Rosanna Deerchild, Louise Halfe, Marilyn Dumont, and Duncan Mercredi have grounded themselves with their nêhiyawak ancestors, territories, and histories despite colonizers' repeated attempts to sever those connections through various government policies designed to assimilate Indigenous peoples. They have followed the echoes of people like Maria Campbell, Freda Ahenakew, Joseph Dion, and Edward Ahenakew, nêhiyawak who were among the first to lay down the pathways between the oral and the written. These writers have "re-fused" traditional European based literary constructs and boxes with nêhiyawiwin (Cree-ness).

In kistêsinâw/wîsahkêcâhk's style, they re-Cree-ate English with nêhiyaw-itâpisiniwin (Cree way of seeing/world view), shape-shifting English textual bodies. From one generation to the next, nêhiyaw writers, storytellers, and poets, draw upon nêhiyaw teachings that our kêhtê-ayak (Old Ones) have held for generations and place them within a contemporary context and medium, showing how nêhiyawi-itâpisiniwin and nêhiyawi-mâmitonêyihcikan (Cree consciousness) are constantly in transition and always evolving to adapt to a generation's place in the world. The âtayôhkêwina, our Sacred Stories, embody nêhiyawi-itâpisiniwin, nêhiyawi-mâmitonêyihcikan, and their transformational nature. At the centre of these narratives is kistêsinâw/wîsahkêcâhk, the powerful being who is our bridge to the rest of Creation.

My journey into the âtayôhkêwina and into the realm of kistêsinâw/wîsahkêcâhk has led me back to my late mosôm (Grandfather), John Beeds. He was the one who taught me, through story, the importance of knowing where I come from. As a child, I spent a great deal of time with him. I remember him telling me to come and sit "back to back" with him on the floor. I can still see the puffs of smoke from his tobacco-filled pipe and feel the soft flannel of his red-and-black shirt. He always had Wrigley's gum tucked into his pocket for me. As we leaned against one another, with him smoking and me chewing gum, he would tell me stories peppered with nêhiyawêwin (the Cree language). From him, I heard the great stories of kistêsinâw/wîsahkêcâhk. From him, I heard how my mosômak (Grand-fathers) were men of the land and how my nôhkomak (Grandmothers) were keepers of it. At the time, I never realized the gifts he was giving me. My mosôm was my first entry point into the âtayôhkêwina, which subsequently led me to one of my greatest teachers, Maria Campbell, and then to the late nêhiyaw writer and Anglican minister Edward Ahenakew. In keeping with the nature of the âtayôhkêwina, I have received differ-ent understandings of these sacred narratives from all three of them, as well as from other nêhiyawak at different time periods in my life. For me, the âtayôhkêwina and kistêsinâw/wîsahkêcâhk have been guides into a deeper understanding of nêhiyawi-mâmitonêyihcikan. Like the various other little sisters and brothers whom he has gifted along the way, he has ê-tawâhikêt, created spaces of possibilities for my scholarship, for myself, and for future generations.

In 1929, Edward Ahenakew published a selection of âtayôhkêwina, which he titled "Cree Trickster Tales" in the *Journal of American Folk-lore*. Ahenakew was born in atâhk-akohp during 1885, a time of great change and upheaval for nêhiyawak. As an Anglican minister grounded in nêhiyawi-mâmitonêyihcikan and nêhiyaw-isîhcikêwina, Ahenakew was one of the first nêhiyaw people to bridge the non-Indigenous world and the nêhiyaw world in terms of his life and in terms of writing and publishing a section of the âtayôhkêwina. Although written in English and published through the lens of an anthropological journal, "Cree Trickster Tales" is a point on a map leading to nêhiyawi-mâmitonêyihcikan and nêhiyawi-itâpisiniwin for those who are looking to find their way to that conscious-ness and awareness.

As a nêhiyaw napêw, an Anglican minister, a writer, a language speaker, and a leader of the people, Ahenakew was an okihcihtâw (a worthy young man/provider) of his era. He drew upon the traditions of the Old Ones within the nexus of Christianity, showing how nêhiyaw culture is living and dynamic. In creating multiple dialogues between our world and English, Ahenakew created new discursive possibilities that we are still learning from. He, like the other kêhtê-ayak of his time, knew future generations of nêhiyawak would adopt new tools and strategies such as reading and writing in English; he also knew we would need to be able to access the âtayôhkêwina through the same means. "Cree Trickster Tales" provides many of us with a starting point to understand the importance of these sacred narratives and a starting point from which to approach our kêhtê-ayak in order to gain more understanding. When I spoke with Maria Campbell, she pointed out how the nêhiyaw words Ahenakew embedded within the English text are maps to further cognizance.[2] kiskinômâsowin: we become our own guides once the âtayôhkêwina are with us. Following the footsteps of kistêsinâw/wîsahkêcâhk, Ahenakew kâ-tawâhikêstamikwayahk, he makes the space and marks the paths for us to follow if we choose to. Just like kistêsinâw/wîsahkêcâhk, he recreates the topography of the English language covering it with nêhiyawi-mâmitonêyihcikan, and creating a space of nêhiyawi-itâpisiniwin—a space the people and beings that are grounded in the landscape will recognize.

As one of our core spiritual beings, kistêsinâw/wîsahkêcâhk carries the âtayôhkêwina. He embodies the narratives, but he does not exhaust all possibilities of them. For nêhiyawak, these sacred narratives demonstrate our relationship to land, articulate a set of laws that govern people, and contain both our spiritual history and the core of our philosophies. They mark wâhkôtowin (kinship/the way we are related to one another and the rest of Creation) and show us what happens when those relationships are out of balance. In addition, our understandings and interpretations weave around these narratives to animate the living present. In her description of the âtayôhkêwina, Maria told me how they are comprised of "interlocking narratives" and how the selection Ahenakew provides us is only a small part of these narratives. We might hear one story and then not hear the rest of it for months or even years. She strongly points out that the âtayôhkêwina cannot be analyzed solely from a non-Indigenous perspective.[3]

Because the âtayôhkêwina are contextual on so many different levels—in nêhiyawi-itâpisiniwin (the Cree way of seeing/world view), the stories are to be heard and understood in relation to one another. It is understood that these stories are told in a series and that they are infinitely organic since there is no end to the connections that can be made between them and the contexts in which the stories are told. There is a further dimension within nistotamowin (the understanding) of the listener and of the teller in light of their life experience and depth of self-awareness. They are understood within the context of kâ-isi-âniskwâtayôhkêtik, the process of connecting the sacred stories together or, as Gregory Scofield described at the Poetics conference, "bundling" those sacred stories together.[4] This process is both highly individualistic and connected to community at the same time. It is up to us as individuals to seek out those who hold the stories to gain the knowledge they contain and to apply it. kiskinômâsowin, we must guide ourselves.

At the centre of the âtayôhkêwina is kistêsinâw/wîsahkêcâhk. Wherever nêhiyawak gather, whether it is around the fire, around the kitchen table, in the bush, or in the centre of the city, he can be found. True to his nature, his ancient power shifted and shaped into the white pages of books. When he is grounded in nêhiyawi-mâmitonêyihcikan, he is just as powerful on the written page as he is through the spoken word. He roams through both media and his energy and spirit continue to illuminate nêhiyawak lives. His role and identity, however, within ê-isi-nêhiyaw-pimâtisitik, the way in which Cree and Métis people live/Cree/Métis culture, has been seriously misunderstood and undermined within the context of Western, particularly Anglo-Canadian, analysis, and narratives. In many ways, the manner in which the Anglo-Canadian world has tried to confine kistêsinâw/wîsahkêcâhk into its language, paradigms, and theories echoes the manner in which it has tried to confine nêhiyawak and other Indigenous peoples. Like Indigenous peoples, kistêsinâw/wîsahkêcâhk has been categorized, constructed, deconstructed, psychoanalyzed, mythologized, anthropologized, and even institutionalized through and by non-Indigenous thought processes. kistêsinâw's/wîsahkêcâhk's true nature and his importance to nêhiyawiwin have been covered with a non-Indigenous ideological blanket of words and concepts.

Many scholars place kistêsinâw/wîsahkêcâhk in a ubiquitous rubric when it comes to Indigenous cultures, making him devoid of any cultural context. Without these cultural contexts, kistêsinâw/wîsahkêcâhk becomes an intellectual toy used to serve a particular agenda. McNeil, citing Doueihi, states:

> In all these theories, the trickster is bounced back and forth, stretched and twisted, so as to fit within the framework staked out by the discourse of domination.... Western culture turns the discourse about the trickster into a discourse by Western culture about Western culture, with the trickster serving only in a nominal function so that the discussion may begin.[5]

kistêsinâw/wîsahkêcâhk has been "bounced," "stretched," and "twisted" to the point where many of us do not even recognize him or his place within wâhkôtowin. In nêhiyawêwin, kistêsinâw/wîsahkêcâhk is our Elder Brother and the sacred narratives he inhabits are our âtayôhkêwina, which are so numerous that they stretch beyond our lifetime. Noah Ratt articulates the limitless nature of them: "When you have white hair, the sacred stories of wîsahkêcâhk will continue, not having been exhausted."[6] Edward Ahenakew's "Cree Trickster Tales" opens a small window into these sacred narratives; it is one in which we may begin to know who kistêsinâw/wîsahkêcâhk is if the window is framed with nêhiyawi-mâmitonêyihcikan. Once we see kistêsinâw/wîsahkêcâhk through this window, all of our senses can tap into him. We can feel his terror as cihcipistikwân (Rolling Head) rolls after him, we can taste that roast duck, and smell his old cisk after he burns it; most importantly, once we start tapping into the stories, we can start to hear the voices of our ancestors and the poetics of ancient sound. We allow the process of mamâhtâwisiwin to take place. We open the door to our relatives—our ancestors, and our Elder Brother kistêsinâw/wîsahkêcâhk—and allow their maskihky to blanket us.

As the bearer of the âtayôhkêwina, kistêsinâw/wîsahkêcâhk guides our path to understanding who we are as nêhiyawak. Through him, we are; through him and his actions, we are able to enter the "storehouse" of memory. Without him, it is very difficult to find our way home, theoretically or spatially. Just as he carried his younger brother on his back while trying to get away from cihcipistikwân,[7] Elder Brother carries these narratives for us while nôtokêw-ahcâk, Old Grandmother Spirit, is the spiritual caretaker of them. kistêsinâw's/wîsahkêcâhk's place in our landscape—spiritually, physically, culturally, and intellectually—cannot be described solely within the framework of a non-Indigenous analysis. His place, however, is fully mapped out through nêhiyawêwin and through nêhiyaw paradigms such as wâhkôtowin. Wheeler explains the connections this paradigm involves:

> In the Cree world, everyone's personal, family, and regional histories interconnect and overlap; all are extensions of the past, and all are grounded in wahkôtowin, kinship/relations. According to nêhiyawiwîhtamawâkan, Cree teaching, etymology, we inherit relationships and obligations from and to the generations behind, among, and before us, to life on this earth as we know it, and to our homelands. Our histories are infused in our daily lives—they are lived experiences.[8]

kistêsinâw's/wîsahkêcâhk's role is understood within this nêhiyaw world view. He is an extension of our past and he reaches into our future. Because he is a part of wâhkôtowin, we have inherited our relationship with him as our ancestors have and as our children will. As nêhiyawak, we have obligations to kistêsinâw/wîsahkêcâhk, as does he to us. We have an obligation to remove the Western ideological blanket that has covered him and replace it with one that has been stitched together with nêhiyawiwin, so we are able to see him as he truly is and see his place within wâhkôtowin.

In the âtayôhkêwina, we are kistêsinâw's/wîsahkêcâhk's little brothers and sisters as are all the birds, insects, animals, stones, and spirit beings; within these Sacred Stories, he is also a son, a brother, a husband, and a father. He has character; he is the full spectrum of Being, both human and spirit. He is who we are with all our faults and strengths. He is also our mediator—kitâsôkaninâw—our bridge between humans and the rest of Creation. The âtayôhkêwina show us how we are related to Creation and they tell of a time when wâhkôtowin was recognized by all beings; all beings also held the knowledge of how to tap into the power, mamâhtâwisiwin, that pulsated through it. mâhtâwisiwin denotes a spiritual energy that is beyond the ordinary. It is like a force that is present in all things and can be accessed in many ways. mamâhtâwisiwin animates wâhkôtowin; however, many of us have forgotten this fundamental principle that is at the heart of nêhiyawiwin.

In her article "We Need to Return to the Principles of Wahkotowin," Maria Campbell speaks of how we no longer know these principles; she critiques that we often focus on "issues external to our culture"; in similar fashion to the way non-Indigenous analysis is superimposed onto Indigenous cultures, so, too, are these issues. Often we focus on everything negative, following the example of the media: the dysfunction, the poverty, the addictions as well as all the things we "don't have" as a people. We "don't have" our language, we don't have enough resources, we don't have enough education, and the list goes on. Because we focus so much on what we "don't have," we forget what we do have and we forget key teachings, too. For instance, in speaking about wâhkôtowin, Campbell states: "Today it is translated to mean kinship, relationship, and family as in human family. But at one time, from our place, it meant the whole of creation. And our teachings taught us that all of creation is related and inter-connected to all things within it."[9] We have to start somewhere in order to remember our relations, and where better to start than with kistêsinâw/wîsahkêcâhk, the one who is our Elder Brother, our first teacher. In this regard, Edward Ahenakew thought far ahead of his time; he knew that we would need direction to find our way back to our teachings from these spiritual and ideological diasporas. The âtayôhkêwina Ahenakew preserved for us—for all of us—is from "our place" and contains these teachings about the spiritual powers that are around us.

The âtayôhkêwina permeate nêhiyaw collective memory through the power of sound. Through orality, these sacred narratives resonate with the voices of nêhiyaw ancestors, creating sound maps that enable generation after generation of nêhiyawak to locate themselves in their identity and to locate themselves within their territories. As McLeod states:

> Through stories and words, we hold the echo of generational experience, and the engagement with land and territory...the "echo" metaphor has often been used by Cree storytellers as a way of describing the past coming up to the present through stories. The late Jim Ka-Nipitehtew, an elder from Onion Lake, said that what he knew was like an "echo of older voices from a long time ago."[10]

The late kêhtê-ayâ Ka-Nipitehtew's description illustrates the nature of the oral tradition. The âtayôhkêwina and âcimowina (historical narratives/daily occurrences/news), once spoken, do not disappear or evaporate into nothingness. Instead, as echoes of voice, they reflect off memory, allowing them to be heard long after they have been spoken. The late Saulteaux kêhtê-ayâ Alexander Wolfe, a keeper of his people's stories, explains: "The oral tradition, in which history is embedded, requires the use of memory. The teachings that instruct a person in their identity, their purpose in life, their responsibility and their contribution to the well-being of others are put in the memory for safekeeping. The grandfathers [and grandmothers] wanted young people to listen, to use their minds to the utmost capacity as a storeroom."[11]

As a "storehouse," the mind acts as a "house of being"[12] for the narratives: the mind has the ability to recall the narratives that provide the paths to identity, purpose, and responsibilities to wâhkôtowin—the paths to being who we are meant to be as nêhiyawak. Wolfe's words also emphasize the importance of listening and remembering. Finally, his analysis of the oral tradition is very similar to German philosopher Heidegger's notion of "language as a house of being." In "Letter on Humanism," Heidegger explores the philosophical underpinnings of the connections between action, accomplishment, language, and Being. He states:

> But the essence of action is accomplishment. To accomplish means to unfold something into the fullness of its essence, to lead it forth into this fullness *producere*. Therefore only what already is can really be accomplished. But what "is" above all is Being. Thinking accomplishes the relation of Being to the essence of man. It does not make or cause the relation. Thinking brings this relation to Being solely as something handed over to it from Being. Such offering consists in the fact that in thinking Being comes to language: Language is the house of Being. Those who think and those who create with words are the guardians of this home. Their guardianship accomplishes the manifestation of Being insofar as they bring the manifestation to language and maintain it in language through their speech.[13]

The words of Heidegger and Wolfe stretch across cultures and time; both are philosophizing the connection between action, the mind, language/words, and Being. Heidegger's analysis can be applied to an Indigenous context and vice versa. The two philosophers provide the opportunity to create a cross-cultural dialogue, which shows that there are overlaps between culturally different knowledge systems.

Within nêhiyawi-mâmitonêyihcikan, the idea of "Being" covers much of the same semantic ground in relation to mamâhtâwisiwin. In *Telling Our Stories*, nêhiyaw oral historian Louis Bird from the Omushkego Nation describes how the kêhtê-ayak in his community believe "the mind is where the spirit lives."[14] mamâhtâwisiwin, as a noun, is the Great Mystery; as a verb, it is the process of tapping into the life force. It also denotes the spiritual power that stretches beyond our own historicity to other times and places. "What already is" for Indigenous peoples are the oral narratives "in which history is embedded." Wolfe speaks of using the mind to its "utmost capacity," recognizing that "thinking accomplishes the relation of Being to the essence of man [and woman]."[15] The mind, through the power of words, taps into mamâhtâwisiwin or "Being" and nêhiyawêwin, language, houses it. The kêhtê-ayâk, like Ka-Nipitehtew, Wolfe, Bird, Ahenakew, and the Grandfathers and Grandmothers before them, were also aware that "those who think and those who create with words are the guardians of this home."[16] In order to access this "home," recognizing the power of words and the importance of listening and remembering are required. Those who do so become the "safe-keepers" of mamâhtâwisiwin, of "Being": these are the kêhtê-ayâk, the oral historians, the storytellers, the artists, the writers, and the poets. This storehouse of memory holding the narratives does not belong to a single individual; instead, this storehouse contains the memories of generation after generation of our people, creating a mindscape of narratives that connect not only to each other, but also to us, embodying wâhkôtowin.

The âtayôhkêwina are living stories animated by the âtayôhkanak that permeate our collective past, present, and future. Through the paths of wâhkôtowin, these powerful narratives bind us to the âtayôhkanak and to our ancestors, so we are never alone and never without guidance. It is through our kêhtê-ayak, our ancestors, the âtayôhkêwina, and kistêsinâw/wîsahkêcâhk that we are able to understand ourselves, our place in the world, and our relationship to each other and other beings. The late William Badger from kâ-pitikonâhk (Thunderchild) is another kêhtê-ayak who bundled his words into English for future generations. In *kâtââyuk: Saskatchewan Indian Elders*,[17] he speaks of a vision he had the morning of the recording of his oral narratives. He states:

When the old people breathe in the wind to speak, good things will be spoken for the future of the young. I could see by this omen that the prayers of the people are being answered and I am thankful for that. As part of what I saw, I could also make out 20 men and 15 women, each wearing a kind of shoulder bag. They moved about on a long and wide plain where they covered the ground, forward and back as though planting something in mid-summer; potatoes and all sorts of vegetables were being harvested from this field. There were Indian people working together, and many other nationalities. I guess this means we are going to be looked upon favorably in the future.[18]

The late William Badger ê-kî-wâpahtihikôsit was shown things by the powers thirty-four years ago. mamâhtâwisiwin, the life force, came into his sight and the sound of it echoes through to us today. By recording this âtayôhkêwin, William Badger shows us how action animates wâhkôtowin. He connects to us, his relations, through this sacred narrative long after his words have been spoken. His gift reflects the very mamâhtâwisiwin that imbues it. His words show how, like kistêsinâw's/wîsahkêcâhk's breath, our breath has the power to kwêskîmot, change the form of the future for the next generation. When we "breathe in the wind," we simultaneously release our prayers and allow yôtin (wind) to come into us; this spiritual action, in itself, is an expression of wâhkôtowin, for we become a part of yôtin and vice versa; we also connect to each other through the echoes of both time and space: ê-âniskwâhkotoyahk, we relate to each other through the wind.

Three generations after William Badger, we are able to relate to him. We are carrying different kinds of "shoulder bags": some of us have pens, paper, and computers in them; others have oral histories; some have medicines and ceremonies, but we are all moving about on this "long and wide plain." The ones who came before us have already covered a great deal of ground. People like Edward Ahenakew have planted seeds. It is up to us to harvest them. We must begin to breathe in the wind to let our sounds echo and let yôtin inside of us in order to speak and write good things "for the future of the young."[19] To help our people now and to help future generations, we must also remember wâhkôtowin and kistêsinâw/wîsahkêcâhk, our guide to our "house of being," the âtayôhkêwina. If we follow kistêsinâw/wîsahkêcâhk through the âtayôhkêwina, we can see how he maps nêhiyawi-mâmitonêyihcikan, the history of our landscape, and all the laws of proper human conduct through wâhkôtowin. His actions create images that indelibly mark our memory. For instance, every time we see the Moon, the Sun, a crane, or a wolf, we see and remember kistêsinâw/wîsahkêcâhk in a way the late kisêyiniw Charlie Burns spoke of. We "hold him in our minds" and he infuses us with maskihky and with mamâhtâwisiwin just as his breath infused the land and animals with life. kistêsinâw/wîsahkêcâhk never left us; he has always been there and he is still there for us...kiskinômâsowin—it is up to us to guide ourselves to him so we can remember and pass on the poetics of ancient sound. kinanâskomitinâwâw for listening.

Notes

This is a revised chapter from my master's thesis, "A Cartography of nêhiyawimâmitonêyihcikan: Cree Consciousness/Thinking: Edward Ahenakew & the âtayôhkêwina (Sacred Stories)," completed in 2010 at the Frost Center for Canadian Studies and Indigenous Studies at Trent University. I would like to acknowledge and thank the Social Sciences and Humanities Research Council and the Gabriel Dumont Institute for supporting my research.

In my understanding of the âtayôhkêwina, one is not supposed to say kistêsinâw's (Elder Brother's) other name, "wîsahkêcâhk," during the summer. Where I come from, it is considered inappropriate to use his name when the snow is not on the ground. Out of respect, I use both names to refer to him; thus, if quoting or reading from this chapter during late spring, summer, or fall, there is the option of using his other name.

1 Although many Indigenous scholars make a distinction between "nêhiyaw" and "Métis," I include both together to recognize the fluid kinship lines and their shared world view. In this chapter, nêhiyawak refers to those who see the world through nêhiyawi-itâpisiniwin, a Cree world view.

2 I visited with Maria Campbell at Gabriel's Crossing during the summer of 2010. Our conversation on the âtayôhkêwina took place on August 10.

3 Maria Campbell, August 10, 2010.

4 During his talk at the Indigenous Poetics conference, Gregory Scofield spoke of how the narratives were like medicine bundles.

5 Elizabeth McNeil, "Trickster Discourse: Mediating Transformation for a New World" (Ph.D. dissertation, University of Arizona, 2003), 196.

6 In November 2008 Neal McLeod and I talked about Noah Ratt's discussion of the timelessness of the âtayôhkêwina while I was writing my master's thesis.

7 Edward Ahenakew, "Cree Trickster Tales," Journal of American Folklore 42, no. 166 (1929): 310.

8 Winona Wheeler, "Reflections on the Social Relations of Indigenous Oral History," in Walking a Tightrope: Aboriginal People and Their Representations, ed. D. T. McNab (Waterloo: Wilfrid Laurier University Press, 2005), 196.

9 Maria Campbell, "We Need to Return to the Principles of Wahkotowin," Eagle Feather News 10, no. 11 (November 2007): 5.

10 Neal McLeod, Cree Narrative Memory (Saskatoon: Purich Publishing Limited, 2007), 6.

11 Alexander Wolfe, Earth Elder Stories (Saskatoon: Fifth House Publishing, 1988), xii.

12 Martin Heidegger, "Letter on Humanism," in *Basic Writings: From Being in Time (1927) to the Task of Thinking (1964)*, ed. D. Krell, trans. F. Capuzzi, J. Glenn Gray, and D. Krell (New York: Harper and Row, 1977), 193–242.

13 Ibid., 193.

14 Louis Bird, *Telling Our Stories*, ed. J. Brown, P. DePasquale, and M. Ruml (Peterborough: Broadview Press, 2005), 44.

15 Heidegger, "Letter on Humanism," 193.

16 Ibid., 193.

17 The proper spelling of katâayuk is kêhtê-ayâk.

18 Saskatchewan Indian Cultural Centre (SICC), *Kâtâayuk: Saskatchewan Indian Elders* (Saskatoon: SICC, 1976).

19 Ibid., n.p.

Bibliography

Ahenakew, Edward. "Cree Trickster Tales." *Journal of American Folklore* 42, no. 166 (1929): 310.

Bird, Louis. *Telling Our Stories*, edited by J. Brown, P. DePasquale, and M. Ruml. Peterborough: Broadview Press, 2005.

Campbell, Maria. "We Need to Return to the Principles of Wahkotowin." *Eagle Feather News* 10, no. 11 (November 2007): 5.

Heidegger, Martin. "Letter on Humanism." In *Basic Writings: From Being in Time (1927) to the Task of Thinking (1964)*, edited by D. Krell, trans. F. Capuzzi, J. Glenn Gray, and D. Krell, 193–242. New York: Harper and Row, 1977.

McLeod, Neal. *Cree Narrative Memory*. Saskatoon: Purich Publishing, 2007.

McNeil, Elizabeth. "Trickster Discourse: Mediating Transformation for a New World." Ph.D. diss., University of Arizona, 2003.

Saskatchewan Indian Cultural Centre (SICC). *Kâtâayuk: Saskatchewan Indian Elders*. Saskatoon: SICC, 1976.

Wheeler, Winona. "Reflections on the Social Relations of Indigenous Oral History." In *Walking a Tightrope: Aboriginal People and Their Representations*, edited by D. T. McNab, 189–214. Waterloo: Wilfrid Laurier University Press, 2005.

Wolfe, Alexander. *Earth Elder Stories*. Saskatoon: Fifth House Publishing, 1988.

7

On Reading Basso

David Newhouse

Wisdom sits in places. It is like water that never dries up. You need to drink water to stay alive, don't you? Well, you also need to drink from places. You must remember everything about them. You must learn their names. You must remember what happened at them long ago. You must think about it and keep on thinking about it. Then your mind will become smoother and smoother. Then you will see danger before it happens. You will walk a long way and live a long time. You will be wise. People will respect you.

—Keith Basso, *Wisdom Sits in Places*

Reading does not consist merely of decoding the written word or language; rather it is preceded by and intertwined with knowledge of the world. Language and reality are dynamically interconnected. The understanding attained by critical reading of a text implies perceiving the relationship between text and context.

—Paulo Freire and Donald Macedo,
Literacy: Reading the Word and the World

Reading the world always precedes reading the word, and reading the word implies continually reading the world…this movement from the word to the world is always present; even the spoken word flows from our reading of the world.

—Paul Freire and Donald Macedo,
Literacy: Reading the Word and the World

Poetics—and particularly Indigenous poetics—has not been a part of my formal education, which has been primarily in the sciences and social sciences. I am more comfortable with the knowledge paradigms and truth traditions embedded in them than I am with the interpretative and hermeneutic underpinnings of the humanities. My comfort was challenged a

73

decade ago when a former colleague here at Trent remarked that "anything can be a text." I realized, in that moment, the limitations of my own education and how narrow it had been. While I had been reading for more than five decades, much of my reading had been confined to the written text. I had not given much thought to how this reading might be extended even though I argued in academic fora for the need to give academic credence to Indigenous oral texts and had taken courses on narrative argumentation at Bard College in upstate New York.

My colleagues in the Trent Frost Centre for Canadian Studies and Indigenous Studies remarked that they knew an Indigenous student had prepared an M.A. thesis without even looking at the name. When queried about this, they spoke of the narrative structure of the argument and the grounding in personal experience; beyond these two characteristics, they spoke of the "feel" of the text.

Their reading involved memory, both individual and collective, as well as expectation. Their reading was shaped by the poetics of our lives and the universe: that mishmash of culture, memory, landscape, and experience. Indigenous poetics is a way of speaking about Indigenous reading, as well as speaking about this mishmash. Indigenous poetics is an inquiry into the nature of the Indigenous universe.

A few years ago, I encountered Alberto Manguel's *A History of Reading* and was struck by the absence of any reference to Indigenous peoples. As I read, I realized that the traditional community I grew up in at the Six Nations of the Grand River had a long history of reading: a tradition in which Speakers read the strings of wampum to recite the Gayanasogowa or Great Binding Law. In fact, I discovered that I was part of a large multigenerational effort to translate the Gayanasogowa and other documents in Haudenosaunee languages into English. This effort, initiated by my great-grandfather Seth Newhouse, was highly controversial and continued in my family until my father, who insisted that the knowledge contained within the documents should be transmitted only in their original languages, stopped it. He would tell us that if we did not know our languages, we would not be able to hear the Creator calling us when we died (apparently the Creator spoke to us only in our original languages, a premise that I found difficult to accept even as a young man) and so would miss our invitation to heaven. I remain convinced that Creation loves a good reading and so perhaps this small piece may proffer an invitation even though it's offered in English.

Every year, I travel along the Mohawk Valley in upper New York state on my way to New York City, the city in the language of my NYC friends. As a child growing up in Six Nations inside the Iroquoian Confederacy, I heard stories of Thayendanegea (Joseph Brant) and his journey to Upper Canada in the early 1780s to look at land for my ancestors. Brant was determined to find a landscape that looked and felt similar to that of the ancestral homelands. The Grand River Valley had this feel. I had always interpreted this story through the lens of cultural comfort, seeing his desire to make those who would move with him feel an immediate sense of comfort and ease. The comfort came from the familiarity of the landscape and the presence of people.

For a decade, I've led a Ph.D. graduate seminar entitled "Indigenous Thought." I use this title to distinguish it from its sister seminar, "Indigenous Knowledge," which is experiential and based upon encounters with lands, Elders, and traditional peoples. My seminar is classroom-based and consists of a series of encounters with written texts, both old and new. The purpose of the seminar is to introduce students to the themes and ideas that Indigenous scholars are writing about. The course texts consist of texts in translation (from the oral to the written and from an Indigenous language to English), as well as academic texts written in standard academic English.

We generally start with the Gayanasogowa (the Great Binding Law) and move to texts such as *Black Elk Speaks, Gaiiwio, Basic Call to Consciousness, The Mi'kmaq Concordat, Eagle Down Is Our Law,* Deskaheh's address to the United Nations, and the writings of contemporary scholars such as Vine Deloria Jr., Emma LaRocque, Howard Adams, Leanne Simpson, Kiera Ladner, Taiaiake Alfred, John Burrows, Gerald Vizenor, and Paula Gunn Allen, as well as young emerging academics who identify as Indigenous. I also try to include scholars who are not of Indigenous heritage or identity and who have lifelong encounters with Indigenous thought, generally through Elders or traditional peoples: Julie Cruikshank, Sarah Carter, and Jim Miller.

For several years, I have included *Wisdom Sets in Places* by Keith Basso. Basso was an anthropologist who has had a twenty-five-year encounter with the Western Apache in their home territory in Cibecue, Arizona. This encounter proved to be profound for Basso. I treat the text as an interesting exercise in translation and transliteration, using it to illustrate the issues involved in the transmission of ideas across cultures and seeing the idea of wisdom sitting in places as interesting. The idea of a storied landscape is not new. There is a vast literature connecting landscapes to stories. The classroom discussion focuses on the landscape, stories, and their meanings. As preparation for the next class, I would ask students to come prepared to tell where wisdom sits at Trent University and the stories that are told to impart this wisdom. My interest focused on the stories and their meanings and the use of stories to impart ethical values and behaviours.

The next week students return to the discussion, perplexed and uncertain. For the most part, they were students who were new to the Trent landscape as this particular class takes place within the first six weeks of term. They were still finding themselves around this new place, sorting out the rules of behaviour, trying to behave well and not embarrass themselves; in short, they were trying to figure out the rules, values, and ethics of Trent academic life, trying to get a handle on the ethos of the place and how it differed from their previous place. They simply did not know the stories. In the midst of one of these conversations, it suddenly dawned on me that they did not know how to "read the landscape." They saw buildings and pathways and beings and tried to connect them using their previous cognitive schema. They also had no memory of the place, encountering it for the first time, and yet no one had taken the time to tell them or show them the memory. I asked them to reflect on the area where they lived recently or grew up and tell me where wisdom sits in those places. They experienced similar difficulties. As the conversation continued, I recalled an old *Star Trek: The Next Generation* episode in which Picard and his crew encounter an alien race that speaks entirely in metaphor. In "Darmok,"[1] Picard struggles with understanding the word "Darmok," uttered over and over again by an alien leader. The meaning escapes him as he has no cultural reference points to use to interpret the term. At the end of the episode, the alien leader and Picard have created a memory and a new phrase in the alien language to describe the site where they had worked together to defeat a common enemy. The moral of the story was that working together creates strength. The students were in the same situation as Picard: struggling with a new landscape and not knowing the stories and meanings attached to it. I saw Keith Basso in a new light: the traditional people who worked with Basso were teaching him how to read. In their view, learning to read was an essential part of becoming wise. My students similarly did not know how to read.

Basso's work contains what I've come to call "an Apache theory of wisdom." According to Basso's understanding of the Apache teachings, every human being has a duty to acquire wisdom (igoyai). Wisdom is a heightened mental capacity that enables one to see beneath the surface of things, to see things and the forces that affect them. It is acquired through conscientious and conscious application of knowledge and deliberate cultivation of the conditions necessary to acquire knowledge. It is also the responsibility of each individual to cultivate the qualities necessary for wisdom: a smooth mind (binin godikooh), a resilient mind (bini gontliz), and a steadiness of mind (bini gonldzi). These qualities of mind are cultivated through a lifelong process of learning the places where wisdom sits. Central to learning to be wise is encountering and coming to know the cultural stories that illustrate ethics and values and the appropriate behaviours necessary for individual and collective survival. In the Apache view, these stories are attached to particular places. Learning them becomes an important part of Apache education. In effect, an educated Apache knows how to read. The Elders who worked with Basso taught him how to read like an Apache, so that he could fulfill his obligation as a human being to become wise.

We tend to think of reading as a private act and the ability to read is widely regarded as one of the foundations of an educated and civilized person. Teaching children to read is considered one of the most important tasks undertaken by the institutions we have built to educate them. An inability to read well is seen as a factor inhibiting the pursuit of a good life and all that it entails. Development of the ability to read is also seen as an important foundation for the life of the mind and scholarship. Learning to read focuses on the printed word, although there have been theories and approaches that focus on reading art, body language, emotions, faces, landscapes, among others. Because of reading's primary focus on printed matter, Indigenous theories have not been explored or articulated. We would not generally conceptualize of Basso as being taught to read by the Apache, nor would we think of what the Apache taught him as reading. I think that what Basso encountered was indeed reading in the sense that reading entails the construction of meaning from symbols, the symbols in this case being features and places in the landscape. Basso recounts a conversation between Lola and Louise that consists entirely of an exchange of place names (Line of White Rocks Extends Up and Out, Whiteness Spreads Out Descending to Water, Trail Extends Across a Red Ridge with Alder Trees). The conversation is about the possible ramifications that might befall a young man who had inadvertently stepped on a snakeskin at a place called Tsi Biyi"itine (Trail Extends into a Grove of Sticklike Tree) if he did not follow the traditional protocols.

Reading also has a performative oral aspect to it. Public reading of texts is one of the important ways in which we transmit our ideas to others. In Basso's case, the reading is both public and oral. One's understanding of the text is demonstrated both through one's recounting of the story and future behaviour.

Linking story and landscape creates a text that can be read, provided that one is taught how to see it; in this way, the Apache Elders taught Basso how to see a text and then how to interpret and construct meaning out of it. Text in this case meant landscape and story. Basso gives a number of examples: the T'iis Cho Naasikaade (Big Cottonwood Trees Stand Here and There) links a stand of cottonwood trees and a story about a woman who forgets her traditional role as mother-in-law and pays a high price for this transgression. The Ndee Dah Naazine (Men Stand Above Here and There) links a bluff and a story about the dangers of acting as an outsider.

The Apache act of reading has an aspect of physical encounter. One has to go out onto the land and encounter the story in the landscape. Learning to read is a guided journey of landscape encounters. Learning to read requires a physical journey and a physical encounter with the landscape, as well as a mental or cognitive encounter. One has to see the place to know the story. Knowing means that one has experienced or encountered it. Basso recounts an encounter with a young woman who has heard the Ndee Dah Nazine and who encounters the place often. She states, as a way of demonstrating her understanding, "I know that place. It stalks me every day."[2] He also tells the story in "Trail of Wisdom" of a conversation between Dudley and Talbert, who has just returned from Trail Goes Down Between Two Hills. Talbert has been acting foolishly at the end of a relationship and the conversation was to see if he had learned the wisdom that resides at Trail Goes Down.

Learning to read becomes a way in which one becomes fully human and fulfills the Apache central imperative of cultivating wisdom. Learning to read is also an act of survival (and perhaps, in the modern context, an act of survivance,[3] to use Vizenor's term). Learning to read becomes the way in which one connects this modern world to the traditional world of our ancestors. Learning to read connects us to their memories, values, and understandings. Learning to read is also a form of spiritual practice involving discipline, conscientiousness, enhanced awareness, and morality. Learning to read brings us to an encounter with the poetics of life and the universe.

I want to turn from the world of the Apache to the contemporary world of students and the question I posed to them: tell me the places where wisdom sits at Trent and the wisdom that is sitting there. My students did not know how to read the landscape in this fashion, nor did I know how to teach them how to read. We simply did not have the institutional apparatus to see the landscape as text, we did not know the various storied spots, we did not even know whom to ask about the text, nor did we know how to ask the questions. Clearly, learning to read required a set of skills and knowledge that we did not have. Furthermore, it required us to see the landscape as text and our relationship to it through a different set of lenses. We were unprepared and we knew it. Learning to read required an entirely new metaphoric universe and cognitive understanding. It was a humbling experience for all of us. We simply did not understand the poetics of our university: the memories, the stories, the narratives linking story to place. Knowledge resided in the classroom and the written texts; wisdom resided elsewhere. We did not know how to convert landscape to story to narrative to wisdom. Perhaps the psychoanalytic tradition of the West might be a tool to render visible the poetics.

The stories contained within the Apache landscape are cautionary tales, tales whose purpose is to illustrate gently, to use a phrase popularized by Neal McLeod, to describe the times after treaty, ê-mâyahkamikahk, "where things go wrong"[4] or "where things went wrong" or what happens when one transgresses their values. They are intended as a guide to living well. Learning to read is more than learning the stories, although they are important. It means learning a set of values and learning that one lives within an ethical universe, where one is expected to behave with respect and responsibility. Learning to read brings the world alive. Learning to read situates humans within the larger universe. It raises a whole series of questions, such as what does it mean to be well read? Does being well read mean that one knows the stories not only of one's family and nation but those of other families and nations? What does it mean to know a story? An interesting question is whether or not being well read is the akin to being wise. Could traditional knowledge holders be considered well read?

The connection between learning to read and cultivating wisdom provides interesting challenges. Wisdom requires the cultivation of the qualities of smoothness, resilience, and steadiness as well as an understanding of the workings of the human mind. Learning to read starts with the telling of story and the telling of the link to landscape. Learning to read is part of learning to be wise.

My students come to the act of reading with a different set of expectations. They engage in reading as a solitary act designed to provide them with information and knowledge that they can then use to advance their own ambitions. Texts are presented in the print form, have authors and editions and copyrights, and are portable (i.e., able to be transported from place to place with relative ease: the new eBook readers permit one to carry thousands of texts in a small compact form, so as long as one has power, one can access them). They do not come to the text with the expectation of becoming wise; the purpose of reading in university education is not wisdom but knowledge. Wisdom comes later and perhaps from a different place.

Learning to read and reading are both private and communal acts in the Apache and university worlds. We read privately and discuss publicly. Public reading—for example, Drew Haydon Taylor reading from one of his books, or the delivery of a keynote address at a conference—is also oral performance, but oral performance of a written text somehow differs from orality, which sees the text emerge from the words as they are spoken (although the text may be present, albeit in a form not normally associated with text). In the "Wisdom of Trails" story, Talbot is expected to demonstrate his reading of the Trail Goes Down Between Two Hills landscape site before Dudley and his friends. Learning to read is also reflective and reflexive. Reading creates us and transforms us. Learning to read is a journey of transformation and discovery. Indigenous learning theory posits that Indigenous learning is experiential and a lifelong journey, one best undertaken in groups and with guides.

The challenge of Indigenous educators, tasked with assisting those who come behind us to live well in the world, is to bring this idea of reading to the table. Reading requires readers. Learning to read requires aspiring to read. Learning to read requires patience and good teachers, as well as openness to the experience of reading and seeing it as exploration rather than burden. It requires a humble ego and courage, both physical and moral, to encounter the unexpected. These qualities, linked to and grounded in traditional values, can be cultivated.

Learning to read also requires an ability to listen to what the text is saying and an ability to listen to what our minds, bodies, emotions, and spirits are saying. Learning to read in an Indigenous sense, if one can universalize from the Apache, is a full body and mind experience. Listening requires stillness, a silencing of the mind or the smoothness that Basso describes. It is impossible to learn to read without learning to be silent. Listening requires patience. Listening requires steadiness of mind, as well as resilience of mind. Learning to read means learning to listen. Learning to listen means cultivating those qualities (steadiness, resilience, smoothness) that the Apache consider essential to wisdom.

Learning to read for the Apache, in Basso's text, is also learning to live in the world. The landscape stories are guides to good behaviour and to the diminishment, not extinction, of risk. They show how to avoid disharmony and how to promote civility and living together.

Reading and learning to read are not simply acts that foster the understanding of the poetics of life; they are acts central to being human and eventually to living well. Reading is more than reading written texts; it is about learning to understand the nature of the world we live within, the entities we encounter, and the development of the morality to live well within it. Reading is an encounter with the poetics of the universe.

In the contemporary world, learning to read is also a post-colonial act (or anti-colonial, if you prefer). It centres Indigenous meanings in the landscapes and renders them visible. Learning to read is an act of reclamation and resistance, as well as an act of affirmation: our stories, our memories, our knowledges are still here, relevant, and alive. Learning to read renders the invisible but often felt poetics of the universe. Learning to read would have allowed my colleagues to articulate the "feel" of the dissertation prepared by an Indigenous student.

Paulo Freire, a Brazilian educator, connects reading with writing and thence to transformation. Reading brings change, or at least the possibility of change. Leroy Littlebear, describing the Blackfoot view of the world, sees a world in constant flux, a world where change is constant, things are in constant movement and able to be transformed in an instance. The ability to read patterns in the flux, like the ability to see the storied landscape, is a key skill for survival.

I want to end with the land search of Joseph Brant. He understood the connection between place, story, memory, and survival. The well-being and survival of his followers depended upon his ability to read well, both in the European sense of written text and in the Indigenous sense of storied landscape text. Brant chose a landscape that was familiar where the old stories might sit well and where new stories might emerge. He understood well the poetics of the universe.

Notes

1 Philip LaZebnik, Joe Menosky, and Gene Roddenberry, "Darmok," *Star Trek: The Next Generation*, season 5, episode 2, dir. Winrich Kolbe (Los Angeles: Paramount Pictures, 1991).

2 Ibid., 57.

3 Gerald Vizenor, *Manifest Manners: Narratives on Postindian Survivance* (Albuquerque: University of New Mexico Press, 1999), 4.

4 Neal McLeod, "Treaties," Indigenous Studies 1000Y lecture, Trent University, Peterborough, 2009.

Bibliography

Basso, Keith. *Wisdom Sits in Places: Landscape and Language among the Western Apache*. Albuquerque: University of New Mexico Press, 1996.

Freire, Paulo, and Donaldo Macdeo. *Literacy: Reading the Word and the World*. New York: Routledge, 1987.

McLeod, Neal. "Treaties." Indigenous Studies 1000Y lecture, Trent University, Peterborough, 2009.

Menosky, Joe, Gene Roddenberry, and Philip LaZebnik. "Darmok." *Star Trek: The Next Generation*, season 5, episode 2, directed by Winrich Kolbe. Los Angeles: Paramount Pictures, 1991.

Vizenor, Gerald. *Manifest Manners: Narratives on Postindian Survivance*. Albuquerque: University of New Mexico Press, 1999.

8

The Pemmican Eaters
Marilyn Dumont

"The Pemmican Eaters," my unpublished fourth poetry collection's title, is derived from John A. Macdonald's moniker for the Métis—"the pemmican eaters."[1]

My intent in this collection is to recreate a palpable sense of the Riel Resistance period in Métis history and evoke the geographical, linguistic/cultural, and political situation of Batoche during this time through the eyes of those who experienced the battles, as well as through the eyes of Gabriel and Madeleine Dumont and Louis Riel.

Gabriel Dumont, Louis Riel's general, is named after his uncle. Gabriel Dumont Sr. lived in the Edmonton area during the late 1800s and early 1900s and was captain of the hunt at Lac Ste. Anne, a Catholic pilgrimage site, once called Manitow Sâkahikan or Spirit Lake by the Cree and Devil's Lake by the missionaries and settlers.[2] My family lineage is from Gabriel Dumont Sr.

In order to situate the poems in my culture, many poems employ elements of the Michif language, which was spoken by my ancestors along with French and Cree. It consists of the Cree language structure with some Saulteaux/Anishnaabe and the use of French nouns and articles, and is thought to have grown out of the wintering camps, where diverse poly-lingual individuals would convene. At one such settlement, Buffalo Lake (Tail Creek), both my Métis paternal and maternal family lines gathered during the winter months. Since language is culture, I have attempted through its minor use to convey Métis beliefs about social relations, the bison and the fur trade economy, spiritual beliefs, the Resistance period, and Rupert's Land.

My attempt in the following lines from "these are wintering words" is to convey that sense of multiplicity of identity as a strengthening rather than a weakening or diluting force in culture:

Metis traders, speak la lawng of double genetic origin   pleasure   doubled
twice the languagetwice the culture mixta not mixed-up, nor muddled   but
completely French,Cree,Ojibway different tongues   buffalo, a delicacy source
language   right from the cow's mouth   mother of all in-group conversation
    wintering camps dispersal   neither Cree, Saulteaux nor French exactly,
but something else   not less   not half   not lacking

One concept that fascinated me in the writing of some of these poems
was the idea of conceptualizing the measurement of territory in order to
fathom its immensity and vastness when it is unfamiliar or foreign. I specu-
late that the explorers of Rupert's Land—in their attempts to comprehend a
land that did not reflect their history, familial, or cultural identity—applied
the American Square Lot Survey System to "tame" the idea of the land to
incorporate it into their cosmology. This system of measurement, attendant
to ownership, was undertaken by the Dominion of Canada when the Métis
had been using the river lot or seigneurial system of New France for half a
century, a system that provided access to both the river and their neighbours. This was a system accepted by the Hudson's Bay Company for its
practical advantages; however, when the American Square Lot Survey System was adopted, the Métis living on those river lots between 1821 and 1869
lost their homelands, and their cultural stories of the land were diluted. In
poems such as "October 1869" and "To a Fair Country," I wrestle with the
ideas of land, measurement, and ownership as evidenced by lines, first from
"October 1869" and then from "To a Fair Country":

October 1869

Did the survey record in its calculations
witness whose lives were fragmented by these precise
coordinates?

could their instruments
determine the number of years
Nault had lived and cleared brush
Harvested firewood on the same land he was now barred from?

Did the surveyor's coordinates record the number of letters, the number of
signed petitions

Did it detect the colourless voices of the Settlers' Rights Association joining in
Louis' protest

Did their instruments detect their words plain as bread "we have not been
consulted in anyway as a people entering into the Dominion"[3]

To a Fair Country

I want to forget a travelling 36 man scrip commission
with 26 speculators
I want to forget their numb greed and narrow vision
I want to forget their dollar an acre thefts

Through my research on the bison and Indigenous conceptions of the
bison's origins, I have crafted poems "Notre Frères," "Li Bufloo," and "You
Wanted to Treat Them as Buffalo" from Gabriel Dumont's perspective and
from stories of the Arapaho, which say that the bison emerged from and
returned to deep bodies of water on Turtle Island. One of the stanzas from
"Notres Frères" reads:

Will Gabriel call, us, his brothers
riding his swiftest buffalo runner
aiming Le Petit
pulling the universe in their sway
the Milky Way—dust of buffalo spirits passing

Or lines from "Li Bufloo," Mitchif for bison:

We came from the buffalo wallows
bowls in the earth hollowed out
by the backbones of our greater ones
those who have returned now,
through those same curves in the earth

Although most of the poems in "The Pemmican Eaters" are written
in free verse, I have also experimented with writing in traditional form,
poetry written using words that adhere to a certain measure in accent or
syllable count and follow patterns of rhyming. One of the more familiar
forms is the sonnet or sestina. The impetus for exploring traditional form
stems from my teaching of poetry and attempts to have students listen to
the language and cadence in their poems. I discovered that one way was to
have students write a sestina, a villanelle, or a pantoum and, through the
process of replicating sound as well as sense in the creation of a poem, learn
about this fundamental relationship in the craft of poetry.

In specific poems such as "Fiddle Bids Us Dance," the sestina form was
used to capture the steady cadence of the fiddle while step-dancing, while
the pantoum form employed in "Notre Frères" conveys a sense of the eternal universe with its recurring pattern of lines.

Fiddle Bids Us Dance

The first high call of the fiddle bids us dance
Baits with its first pluck and saw of the bow
Reels us, feet flick-fins to its lure and line
Steady second fiddle stoking the fire below
our red river jig and step-dance will witness
that we long kissed this earth with our feet

that we long kissed this earth with our feet
before the surveyors executed their dance
of lines and stakes at the corners to witness
the Dominion's decree to leave just fiddle and bow
and no quarter sections to bury our relatives below
because we resisted the government's line

Notres Frères

We were born beneath the water
in the darkest depths of the lake
We rise, our hooves rumbling
spewing lake water, muzzles dripping

in the darkest depths of the lake
Will Gabriel call, us, his brothers
spewing lake water, muzzles dripping
pulling the universe in our sway

One of the challenges for a writer who produces a book once every seven years doesn't need is another layer of perception with which to craft and winnow lines of poetry. However, I discovered in the process of attempting to recreate an historical time period convincingly that I needed to immerse myself in the geographical setting, social, economic, and political forces of the time by researching and reading every historical memoir and every recognized historical study of western Canada and of the Métis in the fur trade.

I have been working intermittently on this collection for seven years despite the added complication of historical research to the practice of writing poetry. I have been challenged by conveying a Métis perspective through Michif and daunted by my own historical legacy, but I have grown in my craft and deepened my sense of identity as a Métis.

Notes

1 Bob Beal and Rudy Wiebe, *War in the West: Voice of the 1885 Rebellion* (Toronto: McClelland and Stewart, 1985), 9.
2 E. O. Drouin, *Lac Ste. Anne Sakahigan* (Edmonton: Editions De L'Ermitage), 1973), 5.

3 Joseph Howard, *Strange Empire: Louis Riel and the Métis People* (Toronto: James Lewis and Samuel, Publishers, 1974), 117.

Bibliography
Beal, Bob, and Rudy Wiebe. *War in the West: Voice of the 1885 Rebellion*. Toronto: McClelland and Stewart, 1985.

Drouin, E. O. *Lac Ste. Anne Sakahigan*. Edmonton: Editions De L'Ermitage, 1973.

Howard, Joseph. *Strange Empire: Louis Riel and the Métis People*. Toronto: James Lewis and Samuel, Publishers, 1974.

9

Cree Poetic Discourse

Neal McLeod

Introduction

In many Indigenous studies departments throughout Canada, the discipline has been put into the category of social science. Such an approach, while effective on some levels, does narrative violence to the integrity of Indigenous narrative knowing. By narrative violence, I mean that Indigenous narratives are sanitized and there is a conceptual shift that often takes the vitality away from Indigenous life-worlds. Within the United States, writers such as Robert Warrior, Paula Gunn Allen, and many others have encouraged the use of literary paradigms to examine Indigenous knowledge; they have also, in large part, resisted the narrative violence inflicted upon Indigenous knowing in the academic institutions within Canada.

Thinking poetically involves moving away from the epistemological straitjacket and the colonial box that the social sciences have often placed on Indigenous narratives. Thinking poetically gives us a space to recreate, although imperfectly, the narrative thinking of the greatest of our kêhtê-ayak (Old Ones) and our storytellers. This metaphorical discourse, composed of symbolic and poetic descriptions of the world and our experiences, saturate and permeate Cree narrative memory. I call this way of understanding the world through sound Cree poetics: Cree poetics link human beings to the rest of the world through the process of mamâhtâwisiwin, the process of tapping into the Great Mystery, which in turn is mediated by historicity and wâhkôtowin (kinship). Louise Halfe's poetic interpretation of the classical Cree story cihcipistikwân (Rolling Head) exemplifies the idea of Cree poetics.[1] Halfe's poetic discourse embodies and is part of what I call a "body poetic," which connects our living bodies to the living Earth around us.

Narrative Violence of Conventional Academic Discourse

Academia has also, in many ways, become an extension of the colonialism of Indigenous peoples and the subordination of Indigenous narrative knowing. This colonialism is done tacitly, and many people who criticize it are dismissed as "radicals." Consequently, they are excluded from the old boys' academic clubs, which are often exceptionally incestuous. Many adherents of the conventional academic disciplines pretend to be leading experts of Indigenous cultural and knowledge ways, which has been a particular problem in fields such as history and anthropology.

Vine Deloria Jr., perhaps more than anyone, radically questioned the epistemological and narrative violence inflicted upon Indigenous peoples. He radically critiques the racism and colonialism in the academy, as well as the culture of tokenism. What made Vine Deloria Jr.'s critique of Western representations of Indigenous knowing so radical and effective was the fact that he did not care about the manufacturing of Indigenous knowledge within the academy. Ironically, he was hired because he radically attacked the status quo and grounded his position as a lawyer and social activist. While Vine Deloria Jr. broke a great deal of ground conceptually, his position was like all positions—fundamentally limited because he did not make many culturally specific references within his work. In many ways his work was a "negative sculpting" of what Indigenous knowledge was not in relation to Christianity, modernity, and colonialism. By negative sculpting, I mean the way in which Deloria defines what Indigenous knowledge is not, as opposed to what it is.

Our narratives have been guided and dissected by academia; what is needed now is a new wave of writing and a new wave of Indigenous scholarship. As contemporary Indigenous scholars, we need to ground our discourses in cultural-specific metaphors and ground ourselves in the languages of the ancient pathways of Indigenous thinking. In essence, we need to build the "positive space" of Indigenous knowledge. Writers such as Vine Deloria Jr. were and are important because they were grounded in their communities and cultures; however, contemporary Indigenous scholarship must be one of cultural specificity. nimosôm (my grandfather), John R. McLeod, a pioneer in the development of Indian control of Indian education, once said that he wished for the "creation of an Indian-controlled institution where the finest Indian thinking could occur." He thought poetically about our traditions by immersing himself in the stories, languages, and ceremonies of the kêhtê-ayak. Part of this attempt to think poetically involved radically rethinking Christianity— just as Deloria did before him.

ê-ânisko-âcimocik: Connecting Through Storytelling

ê-ânisko-âcimocik, literally translated, means: "they connect through telling stories." The central strand in which Cree poetic discourse flourishes and continues is through the connection of contemporary storytellers and poets to the ancient poetic pathways of our ancestors. By drawing upon the epic and traditional narratives of our people, we can ground ourselves in cultural-specific references and linguistics anchors, allowing us, in turn, to resist the onslaught of modernity and colonialism, which, while related, are not the same.

One of the key components of Indigenous studies involves the use of names. Names define and articulate a place within society and the world. Indigenous names are absolutely essential for the description of Indigenous realities. In order to describe this reality, we need words to shape and interpret it. For instance, we need to be able to name the process of poetry. In Cree, I would say that this process could be described as mamâhtâwisiwin (the process of tapping into the Great Mystery), which is mediated by our historicity and wâhkôtowin (kinship). Because of this connection to other generations, there emerges an ethical dimension to Cree poetic discourse, namely, the moral responsibility to remember.

One of the challenges of linking the old narrative memory is to keep the language and understandings inherent therein. My great-grandfather, kôkôcîs, Peter Vandall, noted the importance of language and the need to preserve it in order to maintain ties between generations:

> êwako aya, tâpiskôc ôki anohc, namôya tâpsikoc kiskinahamâtowin ôki nêhiyâsisak, mitoni nitawêyihtamwak nêhiyawak kahkiyaw, tâpiskôt otawâsimisiwâwa môniyaw-kiskêyihtamowin kit-âyayit.[2]
>
> It is that, for instance, the young Crees of today do not seem to want education. All of the Crees really want their children to have White-Man's knowledge.

nicâpan (my great-grandfather) contrasts the Western and Cree modes of education, and laments the way in which many Crees have seemingly turned their backs on our narrative traditions. He describes how many have absorbed the epistemological and narrative violence inflicted upon our rich traditions. The consequence of this absorption is that we often do not value our traditions, turning instead to Western models and frameworks. It is precisely this internalization of colonialization that Vine Deloria Jr. radically attacked as well. In contrast, nicâpan notes the importance of having dignity and pride in our narrative traditions:

> êkwa namôya êkosi ta-kî-itôtahkik osk-âyak. ka-kî-kiskêyihtahkik ôma ê-nêhiyâwicik, êkwa onêhiyâwiwiniwâw anima namôya kakêtihk ê-itêyihtâkwaniyik.

Now, the young people should not do that. They should know that they are Cree, and that their Cree-ness means a great deal.[3]

It should be noted that nicâpan uses terms like "seems like" and "it appears" to describe the way in which many people, especially young people, have turned their backs on ancient Cree poetic pathways: the way in which kêhtê-ayak transmit culture through stories and narratives. Such a narrative strategy allows people to change their behaviour but still save their honour in the process. It also invokes the power of ancient Cree poetic pathways as a way of restoring the dignity of his people, especially the younger ones. Within this process, there is a struggle to preserve a narrative genealogy, which differs from the trajectories of English-speaking scholarship and mainstream literatures. Our ancient poetic pathways are not a mimicry of colonial narrative structures but grounded in our own traditions and world views.

mamâhtâwisiwin: Cree Poetic Process
Poetic thinking involves dreaming, relying on the visceral, like a painter or jazz musician. A poetic way of thinking urges us to radically rethink the surface of things, like a dreamer. Such thinking allows us to bring back the words and the depth of the Great Mystery that the kêhtê-ayak have already charted.[4] In a way, thinking poetically is radically historical and does not mean the "narrative space" is ordered chronologically. Poetic thinking involves the bending of time to a single point of consciousness. That is why Vine Deloria Jr., in *God Is Red*, so aptly noted that much Indigenous thinking is in terms of space instead of time.[5] mamâhtâwisiwin, the Cree poetic process, is mediated not only by historicity but also wâhkôtowin, including our kinship to the land. The process of mamâhtâwisin involves spirituality and the belief that reality is more than what we understand on the surface.

The term "ê-mamâhtâwisit," the verb form of mamâhtâwisiwin, means he or she is "spiritually gifted." It could also be translated perhaps as "they know something that you will never know." Once I asked my friend, the late Edward Caisse from Green Lake, Saskatchewan, about a line from *Pulp Fiction*: "she is a funky dancer." He said, "ê-mamâhtâwisimot" or "she/he knows something that you will never know" (by the way she dances). Sometimes old Cree words become toys for anthropologists and other cultural tourists, but it should be noted that these terms and ideas have great relevance today. For instance, one Cree term for "computer" is mamâhtâwisi-âpacihcikan, which could be rendered as "the powerful machine."

ê-mâmâhtâwisit wisâhkêcâhk is a common expression within Cree stories. It means that kistêsinâw, our elder brother, "has the ability to tap into the Great Mystery." Because of this ability, kistêsinâw was the first ceremonialist, trying to link living beings in this dimension to the force of life beyond our conscious reality. In the process, wîsahkêcâhk transformed the world, made it safe for humans, and gave names and shapes to Creation.

In Louise Halfe's powerful book, *The Crooked Good*, the narrator ê-kwêskît (Turn Around Woman) talks about the origin of stories and the source of poetic insight as "[t]he gifted people of long ago, *kayâs kî-mamâhtâwisiwak iyiniwak*."[6] She adds, "They never died. They are scattered here, the everywhere, somewhere, they know the language, the sleep, the dream, the laws these singers, these healers, *âtayôhkanak*, these ancient story keeper."[7] Just like nôhtokwêw âtayôhkan (the Old Grandmother Spirit) keeps the stories, the mamâhtâwisiwak, the poetic dreamers, keep ancient poetic pathways.

In *The Crooked Good*, Halfe discusses the classic Cree narrative "Rolling Head" and reframes it by retrieving the feminine voice, which has often been written over, spoken through, through the sound of colonial imagination. In this work, Cree poetic memory is essential to the process of retrieving the hidden and submerged female perspective.

ê-kwêskît notes that she is a "dreamer."[8] She adds, "I dream awake. Asleep, the day was the story."[9] Part of the process is tapping into the Great Mystery, creating pathways for other dreamers. "The story" is always open and open to re-examination: "So, every day, I am born."[10] What Halfe means by this statement is that she can always add more to her journey through life and her poetic pathway.

Embodied Understanding

All poetic pathways are "embodied understandings" and are the poet/dreamer's location in understanding the world and reality. In many ways, this idea is similar to Gadamer's notion of *Urteil* ("the original place").[11] Through an embodied sense of awareness, one is about to link one's own experiences with a larger narrative structure. Through this embodied understanding, one is able to expand one's own understanding and also, in a small way, the larger collective memory.

Often this embodied memory involves everyday experiences and events. Stories are not abstract and cut off from the living world around, but completely enmeshed in the concrete world of sensations and physical connections. Embodied memory is the connection to sensations of the body, and also the connection to the sensations of the land.

Marilyn Dumont's poem "âcimowina" in *A Really Good Brown Girl* is an interesting example of this living memory. She does not describe the stories of her grandmother directly, but rather the sensations that emerge from the concrete world. She opens her poem by making the stories (âci-mowina) of her grandmother embodied:

> my grandmother stories follow me,
> spill out of their bulging suitcases
> get left under beds
> hung on doorknobs.[12]

The stories exist within her living place, her house, and are around her in all of the daily sensations, such as "their stories smell of Noxzema, mothballs and dried meat."[13] The sensation of smell is indeed one of the strongest forms of awareness that we have. She also describes the stories in terms of medicines that are found around her house:

> their Polident dentures in old cottage cheese containers
> Absorbine Junior, Buckley's and "rat root" take over my bathroom
> counters[14]

By drawing upon Dumont's description and words, we can immerse ourselves in the embodied elements of her grandmother's stories. This poetics of embodiment, of wâhkôtowin is also found in various treaty narratives wherein concepts such as forever (in terms of how long the Treaties would last), which sound very distant and abstract within the English narrative, are rendered poetically embodied through the discourse of traditional knowledge keepers. The well-respected Jim Kâ-Nîpitêhtêw recited the classical Cree phrasing of this:

> hâw, êkos êkwa, êkw ôma k-ês-âsotamâtakok, kâkikê, iskoyikohk pîsim ka-pimohtêt, iskoyikohk sîpiy ka-pimiciwahk, iskoyikohk maskosiya kê-sâkikihiki, êkospî isko ka-pimotêmakan ôma k-ês-âsotamâtân.
>   Indeed, thus now the promises which I have made for you, forever, so long as the sun shall cross the sky, so long as the rivers shall run, so long as the grass shall grow, that is how long these promises I have made to you will last.[15]

Forever, then, is understood in relation to the concrete, living Earth and we come to understand its meaning through our connection to these elements.

Central to an embodied, poetic understanding of the world is what I would call "poetics of empathy," which could be translated into Cree by the term wâhkôtowin (kinship/relationships). Through relations, we are able to create the web of understanding of our embodied locations, and extend it to a wider context of collective historicity and through a poetics grounded in dialogue and an open-ended flow of narrative understanding. A poetics of wâhkôtowin and empathy are key to a thorough engagement with history. These concepts are at the heart of Louise Halfe's *The Crooked Good*. In her book of poetry, Halfe radically questions the way in which cihcipiscikwân (Rolling Head) has been told and urges us to recover the hidden female voice, which has been shattered and altered by colonialism and Christianity. Describing this reimagining of the narrative mapping, she states: "The story gnawed, teased our infinite heavens."[16]

In the disseminated versions, the Rolling Head is portrayed as a disembodied woman who has been unfaithful to her husband and who, in turn, has been beheaded. She is also portrayed as a mother who pursues her children and scares them in her pursuit. What is missing in these accounts is the empathy that we could feel for the mother, as well as the embodied understanding of her voice and position within the narrative.

Empathy to cihcipiscikwân dramatically enlarges our understanding of the narrative and also moves to correct some of the extreme distortions caused by Christianity, such as the limitation of the role of women, which has often accompanied the colonization of Indigenous women and peoples. Halfe's radical reinterpretation brings back lost elements through narrative imagination, while recreating and redrawing ancient themes and ancient poetic pathways. cihcipiscikwân's following and attempt to recover her sons marks the land and sky in the same way that wîsâhkêcâhk did. Thus, cihcipiscikwân is a dreamer and ancient Cree poet.

Halfe describes the loss of cihcipiscikwân and, in particular, the destruction of their home: "Their home eaten by fire."[17] The home has been altered and destroyed by a series of factors, not simply because of Rolling Head's infidelity. Another key factor intimated by Halfe is the fact that the husband has been away a great deal on hunting trips. Rolling Head, through the named narrator of ê-kwêskît and Rib Woman, regains her character and point of view. The reshaped narrative gives her position form and embodiment. Halfe notes that cihcipiscikwân "dig[s] through *okiskêyihtamawin*—her knowledge / sad and lonely / more than her bitter medicine."[18] cihcipiscikwân is portrayed as having lost a great deal—the father has pushed things beyond livable limits. By presenting the narrative in this manner, we are empathetic to cihcipiscikwân. We feel her pain and sorrow.

cihcihpiscikwân: The Rolling Head Narrative

To understanding the innovative way in which Louise Halfe has opened the interpretation of the Rolling Head narrative, it would be helpful to examine the narrative in some detail through an intra-textual dialogue. Cree poetic consciousness rests on the notion that a narrative can never exhaust its possibilities as there are always new embodiments and interpretative locations.

The conversation and dialogue between these interpretative locations and interpretative embodiments also enriches the conversation.

Each telling of a story is an embodiment: by telling I mean in both oral and written forms. Each understanding is, in turn, embodied. Thus, our understanding of poetic narrative pathways is an occasion of speaking and, in turn, an occasion of understanding. Each occasion of speaking/ telling accounts for variations within the narratives and helps to explain differences between different accounts. The versions of narratives that have been committed to writing in various forms do not represent the totality of the speaker/teller, nor does it represent the totality of the possibilities of the narrative within a larger context. The occasion of speaking/telling, the demands of the audience, and the time in which the story is communicated alter the way in which the story is presented and indeed understood.

An interesting element in the occasion of speaking/telling of the various versions of the cihcihpiscikwân âtayôhkêwin (sacred story) is that one can analyze the narratives in the light of Christian influence. By examining the most "complete" version of the narrative, that of Edward Ahenakew, the existence of the snake as a lover of wîsakêcâhk's mother is most striking.[19] A superficial reading would make it appear that the snake is perhaps a Christian influence, especially because Edward Ahenakew was an Anglican priest. What makes this hypothesis more plausible is that the Alanson Skinner text, recorded earlier, does not have the Trickster's mother's lover as a snake. Instead, the lover is simply in human form.[20] It should be noted that there is considerable overlap between the Plains Cree and the Plains Ojibway.

Skinner's representation of the lover in human form is also questionable because "The Rolling Head"/"the Flood" cycle is scattered throughout Skinner's collection in fragments. From this we can presume, apart from many of the narratives being summaries, that the stories would also have been told during shorter sessions. Thus, one of the ways in which we can account for the differences between these two representations is related to issues of transcription and also to the fact that Edward Ahenakew was a cultural insider, a Cree from the Sandy Lake reserve. He represented the narratives himself and not through the distorting lens of an outsider anthropologist.

Another argument that the snake is a pre-Christian element is that the Leonard Bloomfield version, which was recorded in the 1930s (a few years after the Ahenakew version), also has the lover as a snake.[21] The decisive counter-evidence that the lover of cihcipiscikwân was not a human but a snake is in the Bloomfield version: the storyteller consciously juxtaposes his version of Creation with the Christian Creation story. This juxtaposition would seemingly imply that he was extremely conscious of any Christian influence that may have been operative in the Cree world at the time.

The motif of the snake figures strongly within Cree narrative traditions. Louise Halfe's interpretation of the narrative opens us to non-Christian interpretations of understanding this central figure within the narrative of cihcipiscikwân and a return to older ways of understanding snakes. For instance, there is a story told to me by Charlie Burns of kâ-monakos, which is also the origin story for the place name of maskihkiy âstôtin/ Medicine Hat.[22] Within the narrative, the Crees are surrounded by the Blackfoot, and kâ-monakos calls upon his helper, the snake, to create a tunnel through which the Crees can escape. Thus, in this story, the snake is a helper and not an evil entity as in the Christian framework. Understanding this allows us to be more empathetic to Rolling Head's lover and also, in turn, to Rolling Head.

Toward a Critical Cree Poetic Consciousness

Cree narrative memory is essentially open-ended, and different elements of a story can be emphasized during a single performance, which can be characterized as the "occasion of speaking/telling." In other words, there can never be a "complete" authoritative performance of a narrative because the audience and the demands of the occasion will always vary. Furthermore, a narrative can never be fully exhausted because the dynamics between the teller and the listener will also vary: the story will always be understood in slightly different ways, depending on the experiences of the people in the group listening. Such open-endedness with the Cree poetic consciousness is the foundation of critical thinking. I would argue that Cree poetics is a first-order act of theory and critical thinking. The storytellers, kâ-mamâhtâwis-iwak, engaged in this process, open up new possibilities of narratives in a variety of ways: new ways of interpreting old narratives in light of new experiences, recovery of old voice echoes suppressed by colonialism, and new understandings of narratives due to intra-narrative dialogue (ânisk-wâpitamâcimowin: "the act of inter-textual connecting"). This model of critical consciousness reframes the notion of theory. Instead of theory being abstract and detached from concrete experience, theory (critical poetic consciousness) emerges out of concrete situations and through conversation and the storyteller. In this way, then, our Elders and storytellers could be thought of as theorists and critical thinkers.

It is important to remember that Indigenous poetic consciousness does not simply involve a glorification of tradition, but rather a radical questioning of tradition, albeit one that is grounded in it. This is perhaps one of the most important contributions of Louise Halfe's book, *The Crooked*

Good. The title itself reminds me of another of the core elements of Cree poetic thinking. Good and evil are not binary opposites but exist in all possibilities, all moments, and all beings. As Derrida has pointed out, the West has done epistemological violence to itself by thinking in terms of binaries, which distort a more holistic understanding of reality. This epistemological and narrative violence has, by extension through colonialism, been inflicted upon Indigenous peoples and their narratives and texts. Interestingly, the old narrative of cihcipiscikwân is described as a "nightmare"[23] or an embodiment of trauma, which has occurred collectively through colonization, but has also occurred existentially through the choices that we make in our daily lives.

In *The Crooked Good,* Louise Halfe helps us move beyond an essentialized understanding of the narrative of cihcipiscikwân. She moves toward an organic understanding of the story, and links a contemporary understanding to a past understanding, as evidenced in the last page of the book, where the narrator ê-kwêskît's words exist side by side with those of Rolling Head.[24] Through this intra-narrative dialogue, the ancient story develops new layers, and organically grows through the activity of narrative imagination. Narrative imaginations expand the interpretative possibilities of the sacred story and, in turn, the interpretative possibilities of the present moment and present reality. The narrative layering of the story engages our state of being embodied in a collective poetic pathway, allowing us to critically think of this positioning and, finally, to think of possibilities to reshape this embodied present. The central character, cihcipiscikwân, embodies this state of critical poetic consciousness: "*cihcipistikwân* stretches through her watery sleep / Phantom arms. Feels...where does the gathering of the self begin?"[25]

mistasiniy: Linking to Ancient Poetic Pathways in My Own Work

In my own writing as a poet, I have drawn heavily upon older Cree narratives. In particular, I have learned a great deal from Charlie Burns, storyteller from nîhtâikihcikanisihk ("where there is good growing"), my reserve, the James Smith Cree reserve in northeastern Saskatchewan. In particular, I remember one story, the story of mistasiniy, which I included in my book *Cree Narrative Memory.* In my book *Gabriel's Beach,* I rendered the narrative in the following way in excerpted form:

mistasiniy
a boy was in a travois
wood cut earth
makes marks
tâpiskoc nêhiyawâsinahikan

like Cree writing, syllabics
pulled from sun
paths opened up
no light, and lets sun fall
through new cracks
napêsis with kôhkom
passing through prairie
travois holding baby body
loses in the pathway
paths of heard voices

boy was found
by a mosâpêw
buffalo bull
old, body cut
paths across prairie
his old body
memories of clustered
sun's passing
he sheltered the boy
from the wind
sâpowâstan, blowing through

another bull
younger challenged him
did not want
the orphan boy in the camp
he came from those
killed the buffalo, he said
the fought, raced
and the old buffalo won
keep the boy, and sheltered him
like trees hiding the earth
from open suspicious sky

as time gathered
created words and lost others
the boy was told
that he had to go home
mosôm buffalo gave stories
like body held memory
his body moving
ê-waskâwît

people in the boys camp
knew he was coming back

awa ê-kî-kôsapahtat
performed the ceremony
opened ground and sang songs
he came back, came home
but as he left
grandfather turned into stone.[26]

mistasiniy (the Grandfather stone) was destroyed in 1966 because two major waterways were to be joined in Saskatchewan. There was a great campaign by many to try to save the stone or move it, but, regrettably, these efforts were not successful. The narrative embodies the notion of wâhkôtowin as the stone embodies the relationship that people have with the buffalo. In addition, the narrative also marks the importance of adoption and the way in which we can raise children, who may not be ours biologically.

I adopted my son, Cody McLeod, and made sense of my adoption through thinking about the mistasiniy. I wrote a poem about my understanding of the older narrative and linked the older story organically to my life:

meditations on paskwa-mostos awâsis

Buffalo Child
I remember
when you came to me
vulnerable, shy
unprotected from prairie wind
sickly, dry pasty skin
tired of open spaces
valley loses shelter
trees wind
through the end

Buffalo Child, paskwa-mostos awâsis
wakes the prairie grass
promises of his grandfather
you give your hide
your house of being
sit on open prairie
heavy and old standing earth
broken by dynamite
tears the line of old relationship
but the ancient stone
becomes my body

Buffalo Child
paskwa-mostos awâsis
rock has fallen

clipped from valley's embrace
but the story lives through
this boy
his body becomes
his ancient stone

I took a boy in
like Old Buffalo Grandfather
as I tried my best to guide him
I thought of this story often

our bodies tattooed
with lands memories
with land speak, askiwêwin
even though the stone is gone
the story lives on
old stories give our bodies shape
and guide the path of sound
like trees guiding the wind[27]

I understood that my son Cody was a living embodiment of that story, and that the kinship tie to him had been marked in the land by mistasiniy. These old stories mark our bodies with meaning and live on within us, despite colonial encroachments such as the destruction of the stone. This poem is also an example of the organic nature in which old narratives become alive through our lives and experiences. Cree poetic consciousness radically questions the way in which the West has framed "history" in progressive and teleological terms. Rather, narratives are alive and embodied in the moment and historicity of our understanding, never fixed and always changing organically, like the colours and shapes in the sky, like the folds and contours of water on lakes.

Conclusion

Cree poetic discourse is an ancient activity, stretching back to the beginning of Cree consciousness and ceremonies. mamâhtâwisiwin, "tapping into the Great Mystery," describes this process within the Cree language. If we are to move toward Indigenous studies as a unique discipline, with its own intellectual and narrative trajectories, we must draw upon conceptual frameworks within Indigenous languages and cultures. Cree poetic discourse connects to old voice echoes—to the stories and embodied experiences of the ancestors. Through our dialogue with these older stories (âniskwâpitamâcimowin), pathways of understanding are re-travelled and indeed expanded. These poetic pathways are embodied and emerge from a concrete, tactile engagement with the world.

Not only do the ancient poetic pathways become embodied, they also, through the process of âniskwâpitamâcimowin, of inter-textual narrative interchange, allow us to see beyond the contingencies of the present. In turn, this critical Cree consciousness allows us to reimagine narratives, and to envision and imagine new possibilities for the future. Cree poetic discourse is profoundly grounded in land and territory and ancestral knowledge. At the same time, contemporary poets, writers, and contemporary storytellers extend Cree poetic discourse into the present.

Notes

1   Louise Halfe, *The Crooked Good* (Regina: Couteau Press, 2007).

2   Peter (kôkôcîs) Vandall, "Being Cree," in *wâskahikaniwiyiniw-âcimowina: Stories of the House People*, ed. and trans. Fred Ahenakew (Winnipeg: University of Manitoba Press, 1987), 36.

3   Ibid.

4   Willie Ermine, "Aboriginal Epistemology," in *First Nations Education in Canada: The Circle Unfolds*, ed. Marie Battiste et al. (Vancouver: UBC Press, 1995).

5   Vine Deloria Jr., *God Is Red: A Native View of Religion* (Golden, CO: Fulcrum, 1972).

6   Halfe, *The Crooked Good*, 3.

7   Ibid.

8   Ibid., 4.

9   Ibid.

10   Ibid.

11   Hans-Georg Gadamer, *Truth and Method* (New York: Seabury Press, 1960).

12   Marilyn Dumont, "âcimowina," in *A Really Good Brown Girl* (London: Brick Books, 1996), 70.

13   Ibid.

14   Ibid.

15   Jim (pimwêwêhahk) Kâ-Nîpitêhtêw, "The Pipestem and the Making of Treaty Six," in *ana kâ-pimwêwêhahk okakêskihkêmowina*, ed. and trans. Freda Ahenakew et al. (Winnipeg: University of Manitoba Press, 1998), 13.

16   Halfe, *The Crooked Good*, 22.

17   Ibid., 26.

18   Ibid., 16.

19   Edward Ahenakew, "Cree Trickster Tales," *Journal of American Folklore* 42, no. 166 (October–December 1929): 309–53.

20   Alanson Skinner, "Plains Ojibway Tales," *Journal of American Folklore* 32, no. 124 (April–June 1919): 280–305.

21   Leonard Bloomfield, *Plains Cree Texts* (New York: G. E. Stechert, 1934).

22   Charlie Burns, "kâ-monakos." This story was told orally to me many times since 2000.

23   Halfe, *The Crooked Good*, 20.

24 Ibid., 124.
25 Ibid., 19.
26 Neal McLeod, "mistasiniy," in *Gabriel's Beach* (Regina: Hagios Press, 2008), 36–37.
27 McLeod, "meditations on paskwâw-mostos awâsis," in *Gabriel's Beach*, 38.

Bibliography

Ahenakew, Edward. "Cree Trickster Tales." *Journal of American Folklore* 42, no. 166 (October–December 1929): 309–53.
Bloomfield, Leonard. *Plains Cree Texts*. New York: G. E. Stechert, 1934.
Deloria Jr., Vine. *God Is Red: A Native View of Religion*. Golden, CO: Fulcrum, 1972.
Dumont, Marilyn. "âcimowina." In *A Really Good Brown Girl*. London: Brick Books, 1996.
Ermine, Willie. "Aboriginal Epistemology." In *First Nations Education in Canada: The Circle Unfolds*, edited by Marie Battiste and Jean Barman, 101–22. Vancouver: UBC Press, 1995.
Gadamer, Hans-Georg. *Truth and Method*. New York: Seabury Press, 1960.
Halfe, Louise. *The Crooked Good*. Regina: Couteau Press, 2007.
Kâ-Nîpitêhtêw, Jim (pimwêwêhahk). "The Pipestem and the Making of Treaty Six." In *ana kâ-pimwêwêhahk okakêskihkêmowina*, edited and translated by Freda Ahenakew and H. C. Wolfart, 106–19. Winnipeg: University of Manitoba Press, 1998.
McLeod, Neal. "mistasiniy" and "meditations on paskwâw-mostos awâsis." In *Gabriel's Beach*, 36–37, 38–39. Regina: Hagios Press, 2008.
Skinner, Alanson. "Plains Ojibway Tales." *Journal of American Folklore* 32, no. 124 (April–June 1919): 280–305.
Vandall, Peter (kôkôcîs). "Being Cree." In *wâskahikaniwiyiniw-âcimowina: Stories of the House People*, edited and translated by Fred Ahenakew, 36–37. Winnipeg: University of Manitoba Press, 1987.

Poetics of Place

10

"Bubbling Like a Beating Heart": Reflections on Nishnaabeg Poetic and Narrative Consciousness

Leanne Simpson

The river that runs through the city I live in is called the Otonabee. The river runs through Kina Kitchi Nishnaabeg-ogamin[1] from the Trent River (which we call Zaagaatay Igiwan because it is shallow)[2] into Rice Lake (known to us as Pimaadashkodeyong, which means the "moving across the prairie" and refers to the practice of burning to maintain the tall grass prairie beside the lake).[3] In and around Peterborough (Nogojiwananong, the place at the rapids), the name "Otonabee" is spoken every day by those of us living in the city—for example, the Best Western Otonabee Inn, Otonabee Meat Packers, Otonabee Animal Hospital, and so on. Thousands of times a day, the word "Otonabee" is spoken by people who have no idea what the word means, and who are ignorant of both the history of this Michi Saagiik Nishnaabeg land they live on, and our contemporary Michi Saagiik Nishnaabeg presence. This process is repeated all over Canada every day, and represents the disappearance of Indigenous presence.

If you look up "Otanabee River" in Wikipedia, the site will tell you that the river is called Odoonabii-Ziibi or the Tulibee River.[4] But there is no reference to where that translation comes from. I asked my Elder Gdigaa Migizi, from Waawshkigaamang, what the word "Otonabee" means in Nishnaabemwin.[5] He began by telling me that the first part means "heart" from the word ode, and that the word odemgat means boiling water because when water boils, it looks like the bubbling or beating of a heart. He then explained that Otonabee is an anglicized version of Odenabi, meaning the river that beats like a heart in reference to the bubbling and boiling waters of the rapids along the river.[6]

After I left Doug's house, I began to think what the word ode means to me as a Michi Saagiik Nishnaabeg woman. I thought of how Odena means "city" in our language, or the place where the hearts gather. I thought about how Ode'min Giizis is June or the Moon when the heartberries (strawberries) are ready. I pictured those odeminan or heartberries and their runners connecting the plants in a web of interrelationships, much like cities. I then remembered that according to Nishnaabeg Elder Basil Johnston, Odaenauh refers to nation, so our conceptualization of nation is an interconnected web of hearts.[7] On a deeper philosophical level, that heart knowledge represents our emotional intelligence, an intelligence that traditionally was balanced with physical, intellectual, and spiritual intelligence to create a fully embodied way of being in the world. Emotional intelligence or presence on its own, however, is a vital force in Nishnaabeg consciousness because, according to Nishnaabeg Elder Jim Dumont, our word for truth, (o)debwewin, literally means "the sound of the heart" (with "we" being the stem for "sound").[8] Truth for Nishnaabeg people, then, is a personal concept based in love and the raw resonance of emotion. And this is just the beginning of the cultural meaning around ode. There are songs, teachings, stories, and ceremonial meanings that deepen these basic understandings.

My point in writing this is that the word "Otonabee" is heard or read differently by Canadians and Nishnaabeg peoples. When I hear or read the word "Otonabee," I think "Odenabe" and I am immediately connected to a both a physical place within my territory and a space where my culture communicates a multi-layered and nuanced meaning that is largely unseen and unrecognized by non-Indigenous peoples. I am pulled into an Nishnaabeg presence, a decolonized and decolonizing space where my cultural understandings flourish. I am connected to Nishnaabeg philosophy and our vast body of oral storytelling. I am pulled into my Michi Saagiik Nishnaabeg lands and the beating-heart river that runs through it. My consciousness as a Michi Saagiik Nishnaabeg woman, my poetics as a storyteller and a writer, come from the land because I am the land. Nishnaabemwin seamlessly joins my body to the body of my first mother; it links my beating heart to the beating river that flows through my city. Just as the word "odenabe" pulls me inward, I want my writing and my creative work to do the same thing for others—to pull people into my consciousness as a Michi Saagiik Nishnaabeg woman. I want to pull people into a Michi Saagiik Nishnaabeg–constructed world, even if only for a few seconds.

"Houses of Ancient Sound"

When I brought my two children into the world, I became very focused in thinking about how to make the Nishnaabeg world a better place for them—a place where their identities were not under constant scrutiny, a place where they knew how to speak their language, a place where they had opportunities to practise their spiritual and cultural beliefs, a place where ultimately they could have autonomy and self-determination over their lives and the lives of their families. I had a vision for my family.

By the time my eldest son was two, he had taught me the power and importance of storytelling. As I put my academic life officially on hold, I became engaged in telling oral stories several times a day, first to Nishna and then to both Nishna and my daughter Minowewebeneshiinh. Over the past five years, it has become one of the most consistent and powerful tools my partner and I have in terms of imparting Michi Saagiik Nishnaabeg Gikendaasowin (knowledge, information, and the synthesis of our personal teachings), inaadiziwin (way of being), and ishitaawin (culture, teachings, customs, and history) to our children.[9]

At first it started out with simple Dibajimoowinan—personal narratives and stories about my own family's history and my own experience. Then I was forced to get more creative as I had to create stories that addressed particular situations my kids were facing. I also began changing the endings of my life stories to what I wished had happened instead of what had happened as a way of envisioning a more positive future. I did this as a teaching tool to impart to them a vision of the world where problems and conflicts could be solved in an equitable and just manner through patience, negotiation, listening, and visioning.

By the time Nishna was four or five, we were also spending hours a day reading books. While I appreciated the growing body of Indigenous children's literature, I was also interested in telling them our oral body of stories—those sacred Aadizookaanan, which we tell only in the winter. I began taking them to events and ceremonies in my community so they could hear Edna Manitowabi or Gdigaa Migizi tell these stories. The more they heard, the more they wanted to hear. I was struck by how they listened closely to these stories while they played, telling them and retelling them when the opportunity arose.

As my children and I connected with other Nishnaabeg families in our community, my mama colleagues and I started Nishnaabeg Bimaadiwiwin,[10] a series of culturally based programs for families that involved Nishnaabemwin Saaswaansing (language nest) on the land teachings and a performance group. We began to seek out written accounts of these sacred to fill out our curriculum. But the textualized versions of these were often riddled with problems. I found it difficult to see Michi Saagiik Nishnaabeg values embedded in them—gentleness, the demonstration of non-authoritarian power, respect for individual difference, and non-interference. Instead they were laden with Judaeo-Christian moralistic teachings, punitive acts, objective truth, and violence[11]—a layer that I had not experienced in the presence of Elders and oral storytellers. In response, I began taking the narrative structure and retelling the stories to my children in a way that was completely informed by my own interpretation of Michi Saagiik Nishnaabeg culture, in a way that was aligned with our Creation stories. I began telling these stories to my classes at the university and the children in the language nest.

Neal McLeod, in *Cree Narrative Memory: From Treaty to Contemporary Times*, writes that storytelling is a visionary process because it challenges us to rethink, reorder, and reimagine the world. It challenges us to revitalize the processes that enable other realities to come into existence. He writes that storytellers have a dual responsibility to: (1) the past—*remembering* the stories, histories, and lifeways that made our ancestors they peoples they were, and also to (2) the future—to create the social space where these new and imagined worlds can exist, even if only for seconds or moments. The listeners have the responsibility to be fully present in those moments of reimagination, to not only collectivize this consciousness but to embody the transformative energy so that, as McLeod writes, "Their bodies become houses of ancient sound."[12] Our bodies collectively echo the sounds of our ancestors, the sounds of the land, and (o)debwewin, the sound of our hearts.

Contemporary Indigenous storytelling in its variety of formats— whether it is performance (theatre, spoken word, music, performance art), film and video, literature, or oral storytelling—plays a critical role in rebuilding a culturally based artistic renaissance and nation-based political resurgences because it is a primary way we can collectivize alternative visions for the future. By collectivizing I mean not just sharing these visions with the broader Indigenous community, but also nurturing and deepening relationships with others in our community. Douglas Cardinal writes that "Aboriginal peoples live in a dream state of vision. As Native Peoples we are trained to bring dreams up into reality, into the real world. As a Native person, I am trained to bring out people's visions. I am a dreammaker trained to make people's dreams a reality. I am totally involved in a dream in making. It is a way for you to view yourself."[13] Although visioning is often a solitary process, part of making dreams and visions a reality is growing our collective base.

Creation as Resistance and Resurgence

Many Nishnaabeg Elders have told me that nearly everything you need to know to live a good life in this world comes from our stories of Creation and recreation. In one part of an Aandizokan about Creation, Gzhwm[14] Mndoo engages in a creative, artistic process to create the first human. Our Elders teach us that we are to insert ourselves into these stories,[15] so in this case, Gzhwm Mndoo was engaged in creating me, Betasamosake.[16] The creative process was long and difficult, and Gzhwm Mndoo is at once an engineer, designer, researcher, and artist. The task required patience, persistence, tenacity, and perseverance, but in the end Gzhwme Mndoo lowers the most beautiful creation to the Earth in a nest of the most complete, all-encompassing, accepting love.

Inserting oneself into this Aandisokaanan tells us a great deal about Nishnaabeg poetic and narrative consciousness. It tells us that we are not to experience these stories at arm's length, but that this consciousness is highly personal and highly contextual. In essence, it tells us we are all both storytellers and story-makers because once we have received the gift of a story, it becomes our responsibility to engage with it until the meaning has been embodied and becomes part of our own (o)debwewin.[17] It is the responsibility of the listener to interpret that story in a way that is meaningful in his or her own life and experience, and then carry that story forward in an embodied manner. In order to embody the vital and layered meanings of Nishnaabeg poetics and narrative consciousness, we need to be fully present in mind, body, and spirit; we need to be connected to our culture, our lands, and our language.

In the next part of this Aandisokaanan, Gzhwe Mndoo places a hand on my forehead and imparts all of the knowledge Gzhwe Mndoo learned and used in constructing the world into my forehead. The knowledge is so vast that it spills out of my head into my entire body.[18] To me, this means that we each embody all of the creative energy that went into making the universe; that to access this unfathomable body of knowledge, we need to align ourselves with our original teachings and use our full bodies to engage the knowledge. We have within ourselves, at this very time, all the knowledge we need to vision and create better realities for our communities. My body is a house of ancient sound; it is a house of ancient creative power that first visioned our world. Our responsibilities as storytellers to both the past and the future come from our Creation stories.

Meaning, Engagement, and Nishnaabeg Presence

Creation stories have taught me a lot about how to interpret and understand our Aadizookaanan and Michi Saagiik Nishnaabeg Gikendaasowin. They have taught me that meaning is layered, nuanced, emergent, and dynamic in Nishnaabeg poetic and narrative consciousness. Interpreted through the lens of lived experience, meaning for a particular story might change throughout one's life. My understanding of our Creation stories has shifted since I first heard them as a young person, then during pregnancy, then as a nursing mother, and now as a mother, but the stories are also understood in the context of my Nishnaabeg name, doodem,[19] paawaamin,[20] and my own personal gifts and lived experience.

Some constructed meanings will be shared among groups of people, while others might never resonate with individuals. Interpreted through individual contexts such as visions from ceremony or dreams, the meaning of our stories is highly personal, and it requires our full presence and engagement—spiritually, emotionally, physically, and intellectually—over time to carry the meaning through our lives and to embody it.

When we engage in creative processes and its simplest form, this is making—the making of a painting, a play, a story, a pair of moccasins, a garden, a ceremony, even a meal—and we align ourselves with the creative forces of the cosmos. Making is the base of our culture. Making is regenerative and ensures more diversity, more innovation, and more life. In essence, Indigenous societies were and are societies of doing, societies of presence. In the space of the colonized, society is a culture of *absence* because consumer culture requires both absence and want to perpetuate itself. Without want, consumer culture simply cannot exist. By becoming makers we disconnect ourselves from being consumers engaged in the corporate-capitalist empire, and we become producers of not just things but of our own meanings. We become makers of our own visions. The process of creation then becomes extremely important within Nishnaabeg consciousness—*how* we engage, our ways of making, learning, and creating are embedded within a larger epistemological framework that values emergence, vision, flux, and dynamic relationship with both human and non-human entities. This process is necessarily emergent because it is impossible for humans to predict the outcome once the spiritual world has been mobilized through ceremony or prayer.

This has always stood out for me in my work with Nishnaabeg knowledge holders. Meaning comes from the context rather than the content. Knowledge holders spend a great deal of time setting up the conditions for engagement rather than trying to predict or control the outcome. Ultimately we access knowledge through the quality of our relationships and the personalized context we collectively create—the meaning comes from the context and the process, not the content.[21] Similarly, Sákéj Youngblood Henderson says the meaning comes from the *performance* of our culture[22] and, of course, Gerald Vizenor communicates this by writing that the meaning is in the telling, the meaning is in the presence, our individual and collective presence—creation as presence.[23]

While this was clear to me within an Nishnaabeg context, it was reinforced when I launched my edited book in 2008, *Lightening the Eighth Fire: The Liberation, Protection, and Resurgence of Indigenous Nations.* To me, the book represented a complex set of relationships I had developed and nurtured with each of the contributors to pull the book together in a way that made sense. I relate to those relationships, to those people, and to the knowledge they embody in a stronger way than I related to the text. When I look at the book, I think of the process of making the book rather than the content captured on its pages.

Writing for My People

In oral contexts, the dynamic relationship between the storyteller and the listeners is an important part of the creative process. As the audience interprets and reacts to the story in their personalized ways, the dynamics of the relationship shifts and feeds back on itself. It is often difficult to predict what will emerge out of the process, and indeed that in and of itself is a grounding aspect of the process. Often an oral storyteller can read how the audience is reading and interpreting the story and has the ability to react accordingly.

This is far more difficult in written work because the relationship between writers and readers is one that is separate in time, space, and context. I think my best writing, perhaps, is in the projects that I engage in for Nishnaabeg audiences, primarily because I do not have to explain the cultural iconography, Nishnaabeg semiotics, metaphor, and theoretical underpinnings of our narrative traditions, not to mention the humour imbued within our stories. This explanation is an enormous process and a burden carried by Indigenous artists, intellectuals, knowledge holders, and Elders. To me, this seems like an imposition on my intellect and creativity because my focus is shifted from *doing* and *living* to *talking about* or *explaining*.

I have recently begun to write creatively, moving away from academic writing and non-fiction writing because I have grown tired of explaining. I felt the need to create a space for myself to vision and to live, where my primary pursuit was *doing or making stories* grounded in contemporary Nishnaabeg ontologies and animating contemporary Nishnaabeg poetic and narrative consciousness rather than writing *about* those things. In making that decision, I realize that ultimately I have chosen to write for a Nishnaabeg audience because I assume that potential readers will have a fairly intricate understanding of Nishnaabeg history, our ways of being, our oral traditions, and at least a rudimentary understanding of

Nishnaabemwin. I am assuming this audience will have the ability to read Nishnaabeg semiotics, metaphor, and oral literary references within our own shared cultural understandings. When a black bear appears in one of my stories, I am assuming that reader connects this with our Bear teachings, ceremonies, and our songs, rather than interpreting the bear within the shared meaning of Canadian and Western culture.

Monique Mojica recently confirmed my thinking on this in comments she made during a lecture on her artistic process. She was speaking about her collaboration with a Kuna painter and a discussion they had regarding Kuna aesthetics in visual art. I was stunned while listening to her because the theoretical underpinnings of Kuna aesthetics were the very same principles that underlay Nishnaabeg aesthetics, poetics, and our storytelling traditions. Mojica talked about four foundational elements—duality/perception, abstraction, metaphor, and multi-dimensionality.[24] Nishnaabeg stories are not told "straight on." When a traditional storyteller tells a story, the story is slowly revealed to the listener in the space between the teller and the listener. It is told through the duality of our world view and through different perceptions. Abstraction assists this process by referencing other oral and natural elements. Our languages are metaphorically dense, leading Mojica to comment that "we are governed by poets," creating stories within stories, and the full philosophical and metaphorical meaning of the stories sink in after the narrative elements have been processed. Indigenous peoples live in a multi-dimensional space; we are conscious of the process of telling stories on the beings we are speaking about, which gives rise to the seasonality of story within Nishnaabeg culture.

The intellectual in me was so excited to hear Mojica pull these theoretical underpinnings out in the open. The storyteller in me knew that these characteristic were always inherent and expressed so readily in the oral and written work of Indigenous storytellers. Western literary traditions and theories don't always fit our work because so many of us are operating from a different core way of being in the world.

Performance for Our Peoples

I was reminded of this last spring, when our local Ode'min Giizis festival[25] brought Nishnaabeg performance artist Rebecca Belmore to Peterborough to participate in "Mapping Resistances,"[26] an international exhibit of Indigenous performance art curated by Wanda Nanibush. Belmore's piece engaged her full body as knowledge as she performed her artistic intervention in a well-known central location in downtown Peterborough.[27] I was an audience member in her performance, which followed my participation in "Mapping Resistances" as storyteller.

Belmore's presence was a political, intellectual, spiritual, and emotional innovation strategically designed to infuse a colonial space with non-authoritarian power, presence, and connection. The audience gathered at Price Chopper, a grocery store in downtown Peterborough. The entrance to Price Chopper faces a large parking lot, and along the sidewalk is a long, large brown concrete wall. The audience gathered across the street facing the wall. After a short while, Belmore and two other people—a Nishnaabeg woman and a white man with a trumpet dressed in historic British military costume—drove a black pickup truck, which was blaring classic rock music, up onto the sidewalk. Belmore got out of the truck and methodically place four purple pillows on the sidewalk with four Ancestors (rocks) on each purple pillow. She then proceeded to unload several single-litre plastic bags of milk and lined them between the pillows. When the milk was lined up, she aggressively (and violently) ripped open each bag with her teeth and poured the milk into a large bucket. Then she took a long paint roller and began to paint three large Xs on the brown concrete wall. The other Nishnaabeg women methodically washed each one off with a garden hose, while the military man played sad music on his trumpet. This went on for several minutes. Presencing and erasing. Presencing and erasing. Presencing and erasing. Presencing and erasing. Eventually, the three packed up their belongings, hosed off the sidewalk, and left in the black truck.

While the performance itself was dense with references to the other performance art and the work of the other artists participating in "Mapping Resistances," it also strongly utilized Nishnaabeg metaphor. Colonizers have taken our land, our sustenance and—through the processes of capitalism, industry, and manufacturing—have used that (represented here by milk) to erase us. The idea that colonialism has taken away our sustenance and used it to oppress us is particularly relevant to Michi Saagiik Nishnaabeg people because the Crown insists we "lost" our "rights to hunting and fishing" under the terms of the Williams Treaty, rights that were protected in several of the treaties we made in the time leading up to that agreement. Our parents and grandparents were forced to fish at night, and to eat squirrels and groundhogs in order to survive the loss of sustenance. The idea that our women were made to feel ashamed of their ability to breastfeed (an act that provides our children with their first teachings about treaty-making)[28] and encouraged to rely on mass-produced formula is another example of taking our sustenance and oppressing us with it. I clearly remember Belmore's mouth during the performance while she ripped open the plastic bags of milk, an image in sharp contrast to glancing down at a child gently latching on to my nipple. Belmore's performance is a

metaphor for the humiliation that is the result of the loss of self-determination, and it is embedded with cultural meaning.

While witnessing the piece, however, I felt far from humiliated. It
was an extraordinarily meaningful experience in my life, one that I have
thought of almost every day since it happened. During the performance I felt powerful, free, and inspired. I felt proud of who I am. Belmore
drew me into a decolonizing space that made my presence and attention
focused completely. I lost sense of time and space. I was transported into a
world that Belmore as the artist/storyteller had visioned—a world where
Nishnaabeg flourished and where justice prevailed, a world where my voice
and my meanings mattered. She created a world where it was safe to be
angry, sad, and powerful and to voice those emotions. Downtown Peterborough, like any other occupied space in the Americas, is a bastion of colonialism as experienced by Nishnaabeg people. But for twenty minutes in
June, that bastion was transformed into an alternative space that provided
a fertile bubble for envisioning and realizing Nishnaabeg visions of justice,
voice, presence, and resurgence.

Her performance reminded us that we as Nishnaabeg people are living
in political and cultural exile. It disrupted the narrative of normalized
dispossession and intervened as Nishnaabeg presence—not as a victim
but as a powerful, non-authoritarian Nishinaabekwewag power. Belmore's
performance was liberation from within, and I am reminded of her (my)
presence and her (my) power because she has altered the landscape in my
memory and in the memory of everyone who witnessed her performance.
I say "liberation from within" because the outside colonizing society didn't
necessarily shift. The shift came from within Belmore, and then from
within me. Nishnaabeg and Indigenous artists like Belmore interrogate
the space of empire and envision and perform ways out of it, even if the
performance lasts only twenty minutes. It is a way out of it; it is one more
stone thrown in the water. It is a glimpse of a decolonized contemporary
reality; it is a mirroring of what we can become.

Ultimately Belmore reminded me that we as artists and writers have
the power to create decolonized spaces of resurgence within our own communities. We have the power to vision alternative realities and responses
to empire. We have the responsibility to collectivize these visions in order
to bring those dreams of our ancestors into realities. When we engage in
our own culturally based poetics and narrative consciousness, we can, to
a greater degree, create healing spaces for our peoples—spaces where, for a
few minutes, we can experience the love, the connection, and the liberation
that our ancestors are so desperately trying to bring into the contemporary
realities we face as colonized peoples. Artistic expression melts the bars

of occupation and frees both our minds and our hearts to connect to the emergence Gzhwm Mndoo set in motion when this world came into existence. Our bodies, hearts, and minds house the visions for new realities. "Making" or engaging in artistic pursuits aligns us with our creative energy of our Origin stories, thereby liberating new realities and new possibilities.

Notes

This chapter is based in part on an excerpt from Leanne Simpson, *Dancing on Our Turtle's Back: Stories of Indigenous Recreation, Resurgence, and a New Emergence* (Winnipeg: Arbeiter Ring Publishing, 2011).

1 This means "the place where we live and work together," and is the traditional name for Michi Saagiik Nishnaabeg or Mississauga territory, the southeastern part of the Nishnaabeg nation. Simpson, *Dancing on Our Turtle's Back*, 14.

2 Gidigaa Migizi (Doug Williams), Waashkigaamongki (Curve Lake First Nation), July 15, 2010.

3 Gidigaa Migizi (Doug Williams), Waashkigaamongki (Curve Lake First Nation), January 13, 2012; for a slightly different spelling, see Rick Beaver, Alderville First Nation, October 2008; and Ruth Clarke, *To Know This Place: The Black Oak Savana/Tallgrass Prairie of Alderville First Nation* (Alderville First Nation, ON: Sweet Grass Studios, n.d.), 200.

4 "Otonabee River," Wikipedia, http://en.wikipedia.org/wiki/Otonabee_River.

5 Ojibwe language.

6 Gidigaa Migizi (Doug Williams), Waashkigaamongki (Curve Lake First Nation), July 15, 2010.

7 Basil Johnston, *Anishinaubae Thesaurus* (East Lansing: Michigan State University Press), 178. Johnston uses his own orthography, the reasons for which and his orthographic approach are explained in the introduction to *Anishinaabae Thesaurus*.

8 Jim Dumont, Trent University Elders' Conference, Peterborough, February 2010.

9 Wendy Makoons Geniusz, *Our Knowledge Is Not Primitive: Decolonizing Botanical Anishinaabe Teachings* (Syracuse: Syracuse University Press, 2009), 11.

10 This was started with the support of Marrie Mumford and Indigenous Performance Initiatives.

11 For examples, see Dorothy M. Reid, *Tales of Nanabozho* (Toronto: Oxford University Press, 1963); Emerson Coatsworth and David Coatsworth, comps., *The Adventures of Nanabush* (Toronto: Doubleday Canada, 1979).

12 Neal McLeod, *Cree Narrative Memory: From Treaties to Contemporary Times* (Saskatoon: Purlich Press, 2007), 100.

13 Douglas Cardinal and Jeannette Armstrong, *The Native Creative Process* (Penticton: Theytus Books, 1991), 108.

14 I am using the verb "Gzhwm" rather than "Gchi" because, according to Gidigaa Migizi, Gzhwm represents awe, warmth, love, total acceptance, protection,

and understanding rather than an authoritarian Creator that is imbued with fear and punishment. Gidigaa Migizi (Doug Williams), Waashkigaamongki (Curve Lake First Nation), July 15, 2010.

15 Jim Dumont was the last Elder to share this teaching with me at the Trent University Elders' Conference, Peterborough, February 2010.

16 Betasamosake is my traditional Nishnaabeg name and it means "walking toward women."

17 Jim Dumont teaches that one cannot repeat a story until it becomes part of their debwewin.

18 Jim Dumont was the last Elder to share this teaching with me, at the Trent University Elders' Conference, Peterborough, February 2010.

19 Clan

20 Spirit-helper or guide

21 Leanne Simpson, "The Construction of Traditional Ecological Knowledge" (Ph.D. diss., University of Manitoba, 1999).

22 Sákéj Youngblood Henderson, *First Nations Jurisprudence and Aboriginal Rights* (Saskatoon: Native Law Centre, 2006).

23 Gerald Vizenor and Robert Houle, Pine Tree lecture, Trent University, Peterborough, February 19, 2010; Gerald Vizenor, *Fugitive Poses: Native American Indian Scenes of Absence and Presence* (Lincoln: University of Nebraska Press, 1998).

24 Monique Mojica, Nozhem First Peoples Performance Space, Trent University, Peterborough, September 22, 2011.

25 Ode'min Giizis festival is an annual multi-disciplinary arts festival organized by Mississauga artists. It takes place in June, or Strawberry Moon (Ode'min Giizis), in Peterborough and is a collaboration of local, national, and international artists in various disciplines.

26 Wanda Nanisbush, "Mapping Resistances" with Rebecca Belmore, Robert Houle, James Luna, Tanya Lukin Linklater, Archer Pechawis, Leanne Simpson, and Doug Williams, June 18–19, 2010, Peterborough. This exhibition was put together as part of the Ode'min Giizis festival and in commemoration of the twentieth anniversary of the Oka Crisis.

27 Belmore's performance took place as part of the Ode'min Giizis festival's "Mapping Resistances," Peterborough, June 19, 2010.

28 Explained to me by Edna Manitowabi, Peterborough, September 2001.

Bibliography

Cardinal, Douglas, and Jeannette Armstrong. *The Native Creative Process.* Penticton: Theytus Books, 1991.

Clarke, Ruthe. *To Know This Place: The Black Oak Savanna/Tallgrass Prairie of Alderville First Nation.* Alderville First Nation, ON: Sweet Grass Studios, n.d.

Coatsworth, Emerson, and David Coatsworth, comps. *The Adventures of Nanabush: Ojibway Indian Stories.* Toronto: Doubleday Canada, 1979.

Genuisz, Wendy Makoons. *Our Knowledge Is Not Primitive: Decolonizing Botanical Anishinaabe Teachings*. Syracuse: Syracuse University Press, 2009.

Henderson, Sákéj Youngblood. *First Nations Jurisprudence and Aboriginal Rights*. Saskatoon: Native Law Centre, 2006.

Johnston, Basil H. *Anishinaube Thesaurus*. East Lansing: Michigan State University Press, 2007.

McLeod, Neal. *Cree Narrative Memory: From Treaties to Contemporary Times*. Saskatoon: Purich Press, 2007.

Nanibush, Wanda, with Rebecca Belmore, Robert Houle, James Luna, Tanya Lukin Linklater, Archer Pechawis, Leanne Simpson, and Doug Williams. "Mapping Resistances" exhibit, Ode'min Giizis festival, Peterborough, June 18–19, 2010.

"Otonabee River." Wikepedia. http://en.wikipedia.org/wiki/Otonabee_River.

Reid, Dorothy M. *Tales of Nanabozho*. Toronto: Oxford University Press, 1963.

Simpson, Leanne. "The Construction of Traditional Ecological Knowledge: Issues, Implications, and Insights." Ph.D. Diss., University of Manitoba, 1999.

———. *Dancing on Our Turtle's Back: Stories of Indigenous Recreation, Resurgence, and a New Emergence*. Winnipeg: Arbeiter Ring Publishing, 2011.

Vizenor, Gerald. *Fugitive Poses: Native American Indian Scenes of Absence and Presence*. Lincoln: University of Nebraska Press, 1998.

Vizenor, Gerald, and Robert Houle. Pine Tree lecture. Trent University, Peterborough, February 19, 2010.

11

Getting (Back) to Poetry: A Memoir
Daniel David Moses

1.

As a kid, I wasn't much interested in poetry as such.

The words, if I can separate them out, that must have meant the most to me, that added meaning to my world, that made my reality most real then, that first decade or so of my life, were the language that was used in church. The forms that language took, the songs of praise and celebration, the prayers, the year's round of liturgy, those exotic, fantastic stories from the King James Bible (all these years later, I have yet to meet a shepherd or encounter, despite my family name, a talking burning bush), made God, etc., seem self-evident. The aesthetic richness, the whole emphatic style of the experience, as well as the warmth of the communal gathering— although I didn't come to entertain such ideas about causes and effects/ affects till much later— made me feel good, made me feel more real, so I was more than willing to go along carelessly, probably thoughtlessly, with the crowd.

Then the bishop patronized me.

I'd spent the time—weeks? months?—preparing for my confirmation ceremony, memorizing, of course, but also trying earnestly to understand the ceremony. It had to do with the church my parents belonged to and took me to every Sunday; it had to do with the meaning of our lives on this Earth and after. I was a worker, growing up then on a farm, which made me a good student, even in Sunday school, maybe especially there, since already at that age, twelve—was it a case of me being precocious or there being slim pickings among the adult congregation?—I was already running a Sunday school class, telling the little ones the stories, getting them to at least feel their import.

Perhaps it was slim pickings, since I don't recall such a class for the intermediate kids, except the one that was leading me to my confirmation.

I'd expended all that effort, getting ready to take that next step in my growing up, and then, at that moment in the ceremony that should have given public recognition to my individual self or soul, the bishop got my name wrong.

I whispered to the man leaning above me in his purple stole and surplice, with all the urgency a polite twelve-year-old dared, that my name was not Daniel *Donald* Moses but Daniel *David* Moses. How had it happened? Daniel David Moses, a name with Old Testament heft, and the man had not been able to announce it right once.

And David, my middle name, was also my father's first name, which added to its biblical weight that of a legacy and my love for the man.

That leader of the Anglican church grinned down into my oh so serious, bespectacled nearsighted hazel eyes, at my round brown visage—I picture us freeze-frame still, face to face across the altar rail—and confided with a whisper and a crinkle of amusement in the corner of his eye (I imagine it looked from the congregation like a fatherly interaction) that he thought it wouldn't matter, that God would know the difference.

While the bishop got on with the (I now have to assume) chore of bringing the rite to its conclusion in that brick church on the Six Nations reserve, I went back down the steps and sat in the pew next to the other few candidates, bowed my brush cut, and took no comfort from his reassurance of God's omniscience.

I must have been feeling angry and perhaps insulted and, I would guess, resentful, though what good those emotions did me, officially only at that moment an adult member of the congregation, I don't know. "He's just too lazy to fix it," I would have told myself if I'd dared articulate my emotions. Or maybe too proud to admit he screwed up. Or maybe he just doesn't really care about the ceremony. Or us kids.

Or, I might also add, if I had at that age more of a sense of the history of our Mohawk-led community, the name Thayendanegea, Joseph Brant, Aboriginal United Empire Loyalist and missionary (1742–1807), whose name was not yet taught in our schools. I had to learn it later on my own and of the history of our little "mission church" the Anglican diocese oversaw from its seat in London, Ontario. I might also have wondered, "Maybe he just doesn't want to be bothered with us Indians." But the kid I was then knew, even without those contexts, that there was something important about the words of the ceremony, something essential about speaking them right, even if some of those words were only my own name. Was it the measured and musical way the words of the hymns and stories, the prayers, came together inside my head and moved me, lifting my body up, out of its weight, its singularity and into the community of celebrants, of worshippers?

I suppose now that the kid I was had already had those few epiphanic moments that had kept me interested in continuing to accompany my folks to that same old church. I remember in one such moment I was kneeling in a pew halfway up the aisle, all alone (perhaps not an accurate memory), the sun filtering in through St. Peter's modest frosted-glass pseudo-Gothic arched windows like gold, the grain of the pew's pinewood like reality's fingerprints. The kid I was then knew a mystery worthy of respect and practice when he'd experienced it.

Were the bishop and I not singing from the same hymnal?

The unarticulated emotions, that confusion, unexamined, slowly subsided, and when those feelings were gone, in that calm, so was any will or willingness to believe in·the specifics of the church. I can say now that the metaphors of the bible and the liturgy, without the wishing effort on my part, no longer connected to the reality of my lived experience. I gave up my Sunday school class and started to resist the weekly church attendance, to my parents' puzzled chagrin. I didn't explain, though. I don't know if I would have been able to at the time. I don't recall ever being asked for an explanation. And it's still part of my ritual with my mother when I'm visiting her. "Do you want to come to church with me?" "No, thank you." "I'll pray for you."

But my connection to and certainty about the forms of language used in the church's ceremonies and events, words and sentences that were measured and musical, songs and stories, and my love for the community those ceremonies created and served, remained in me, with me, without any sure direction or context.

2.

"Like fish in water" is the simile that still suggests for me our quotidian relationship with language. Language is invisible, almost intangible, perhaps delicious, and as we move through it and its currents, they also move us. It's a tool we use to do the things that make up our social discourse, it's the agreed-upon code of our attempts at communication, and mostly we don't—and don't need—to pay it much heed.

When our attention does get drawn to its existence by, for instance, the making of a pun, most folks by reflex apologize for playing around with it. "Pardon the pun," they say, often when they're not even making one, even when the play on words they're making draws additional attention, focus, to the shifty complex meaning of what they're saying. The reflex apology comes up as if they're sure that they're somehow doing wrong, overstepping, maybe because we're not supposed in polite society to mark or remark upon language's eddies and undercurrents, its dark knots or dead spots, its irrationalities and awkwardnesses, the places where it's less than clear, unfathomably deep or stub-a-toe shallow, where it verges into the nonsensical. Notice how children or the inebriated or the artistic aren't so apologetic, are allowed or encouraged to take liberties with words—dumb or mistaken or silly can be fun! Language isn't perfect, though we want it to be water or air, though we long for it to be fire or earth, to be the quintessence of our existence.

I've been so insistently using "we" in the hope that you'd be able and willing to politely follow along, to be swept up in my poet's quotidian dilemma, my love-and-hate but mostly love relationship with language.

I suspect you've seen how we who find ourselves this involved with words behave, at once resisting the work, claiming to have writer's block, muttering of our hatred and disgust for the effort, then diving in and—some of us—disappearing from our families and friends for days, weeks, some even, the stories go, forever.

Is all this largely mental anguish worth it? Isn't such an unworldly, wordy rapture about to go out of style along with religion? But even scientists admit to resorting to language when a coefficient just isn't enough.

3.

How did I come, by the age of twelve and a bit, back in probably 1964, the shards of my Christian faith sharp around my feet, a broken crystal ball? How did I come to still be, after my not quite fatherly interaction with the careless bishop, in love with this present but ineffable thing called language? Why was I so sure about it, so adamant about its continuing value? Was I feeling lost and desperate to grab hold of just anything? Unlikely.

Thanks to my mission church upbringing, I can still name my growing up on the Six Nations reserve on a farm, despite the chores, perhaps because of the proximity of nature—I had fields and woods, streams and hills, swamps and frog ponds, and a swimmable stretch of the Grand River as my world—as my own bit of Eden. That church metaphor still rings true.

My mother, since the death of my father, has a number of times said she was sorry that she and my father had been unable to give me the better things in life, hadn't somehow prepared me well enough for the world, which puzzles me because it seems that they did provide the essentials. I grew up well fed, our food often farm fresh, surrounded by a big and complex family. It extended on both sides from what I now recognize as the luxury of living and nearby grandparents through aunts and uncles—who worked in factories, as nurses, as bureaucrats, as symphony musicians—to dozens of far-flung first cousins. I grew up with stability, since my parents, who were together, parted only by death, for over sixty years, as I was growing up, never communicated to us kids, me and my one sister, any of the struggles they had, eking out a living in the delimited economy an Indian reserve in Canada at that time allowed. And those few of my relations who had dealt with residential school—Granma, my grandmother on my mother's side, for instance, the one who did Indian crafts, beadwork and leatherwork, made rag rugs, and started her own craft store—never talked about it, only took steps to help others avoid the place.

With all the physical and emotional practicalities taken care of, I was not the sort of youth who, even when feeling lost, would have learned anywhere the option of despair when something as attractive but intangible as the Holy Trinity followed Santa Claus and the Easter Bunny into the trash. I was the sort of youth who did have the spiritual need, perhaps as an alternative to or extension of my church-induced habit of faith or perhaps as an expression of simple curiosity for the unusual, the imaginative, the extraordinary. Science and science fiction and horror magazines supplemented the meagre portions of such fare English classes were supplying me.

And I was a reader, despite the presence of the television, that new black-and-white moving picture machine, lately arrived in my family's living room, with its Sunday offerings of *The Ed Sullivan Show*, *The Wonderful World of Disney*, and, of course, on some other day, *The Lone Ranger*, the only show with a real Indian on it. And that Indian, Harry Smith, one of the show's principals (better known in the wider world as Jay Silverheels), was actually one of the Smiths who lived over on Sour Springs Road, friends of my Grandpa George, so, despite the wooden (the unavoidable adjective) acting of the show, we did watch it. How had I become that reader? How had I first come to know anything, beyond the animal reflex of learning to speak it, about language? One Sunday ceremony a week is not sufficient cause for the reading effect—and in most cases probably has the opposite result.

Sometime earlier on, I'd had the dubious experience of being, for probably a year, under the care of an optometrist, who believed, perhaps applying some Protestant spiritual rigour to the weaknesses of the flesh, that the only way to improve my weak eyes was to give them a workout, so he prescribed lenses that gave me something less than adequate vision. Bodybuilding for the eyeballs? He also forbade more than an hour of television per day since (I'm not sure he was wrong) that seemed to him to be lazy looking. The doctor's regimen resulted in my eyesight getting alarmingly worse quickly and in my parents finding me another doctor. But I theorize that I had used my non-television time that year to develop the reading habit.

And then there was my first teacher, Mrs. Minnie Green, who ruled, with a yardstick and a black leather barber's strop, over one room, Six Nations School Number Four, a white-painted clapboard building with a green-shingled roof and forest-green trim and tall windows on its east and south faces, the better to capture the winter sun, since the place was heated by an iron pot-bellied wood-burning stove. It was located on Fifth Line, a field's width east of its intersection with Seneca Road. My younger sister and I walked or rode our bikes to that school, which comprised six grades. I'd be surprised if there ever were more than thirty pupils.

With Mrs. Green patrolling the aisles in her cotton-print dress, cardigan, and black sensible shoes, we got down to a lot of memory work: "Thirty days has September, April, June, and November...," repetition, "Thirty days has September...," spelling tests, times tables and, for our reading, we learned with (this one detail makes it all so completely another era) Dick, Jane, little Sally, and Spot. And there had to be work we could do on our own while Mrs. Green shifted her attention from one to another of the grade groups those aisles separated.

If you were able to get your work done before she had time to get back to check your accomplishment, you were permitted—it felt like a reward—to go quietly to the tall grey cupboard, if you hadn't already done so, in the room's shadowed southeast back corner and open its creaky doors and choose a book from what passed for The Library. Over the six years, I read every one of them at least once, though the few I might name hesitantly now—*Winnie the Pooh*, *Treasure Island*, *The Water Babies*?—don't include much of what I understood then as poetry, except for one example, which I will come to shortly.

Still, I suspect my first encounter with, say, "Kubla Kahn" by Coleridge and with the sonnet "On First Looking into Chapman's Homer" by Keats ("Then felt I like some watcher of the skies / When a new planet swims into his ken; /... Silent, upon a peak in Darien") occurred near that cupboard door. My one clear memory of a book from that cupboard comes from my discovery there of an edition of *Gulliver's Travels*. It both astounded and intrigued me since it must have been over a thousand pages. The bible had been the only book I'd seen to that point in my life that was an actual tome. I had probably also seen some Disney bowdlerization of the *Gulliver's Travels* story and so had no idea it might have originated in something so big and grown-up. Reading that book and finishing it (yes!), even though I'm pretty sure I didn't understand a lot of it, became my first great accomplishment as a reader.

There was one exercise—probably in grade four or five, judging from my memory of the row I sat in then, closer to the windows and the southern exposure—that tested our understanding of grammar. We parsed sentences on the page. This is the noun (straight underlined in black), this is the verb (underlined with a squiggly line), this is the subject (circled in red), this is the object, this is the adjective, this is the adverb. Even when there were words we didn't know meanings for, this exercise showed us how the English language worked, how sentences were supposed to fit together, how things got said. Meaning was manageable.

We were taught, it seems to me now—or maybe it was just how the farm boy I was then, with tractors and harrows, balers and combines in my head, was able to comprehend it—to approach language like it was a machine, all gears, levers, and pulleys. It seems that our study of language as machine allowed me to think language's parts were easily discerned and described, that their functions and applications, as long as they were kept clean and well greased, would be clear and run efficiently.

Mrs. Green did give me nearly perfect marks on such tests, so I had reason to feel for quite a while that I knew it all, at least as far as language was concerned.

And as a reward, we were all allowed to do art in the afternoon on Fridays.

Included in the memory work for Mrs. Green were a few poems from one of those library books, *Flint and Feather*, poetry by Emily Pauline Johnson, memory work that was more remarked upon since the poet Pauline Johnson (1861–1913) was and is the one famous cultural personality from our community's history (none of our families had any tales about encountering, say, Coleridge or Keats, or even E. J. Pratt). She was the lone artist featured in the cycle of stories our annual Six Nations Indian Pageant then presented to the wider public. The remaining six characters, all men, were chiefs, warriors, and prophets.

Pauline, though described romantically by lady biographers as the daughter of a Mohawk chief and a Victorian Englishwoman, was, as far as we were concerned ("halfbreed" not being part of our vocabulary and despite the context of our remembered tradition of matrilineal descent), a Mohawk woman who, back in the old days, had gone into the world outside of the reserve—the outline of her life's journey suggested by the names Toronto, London (the one in England), New York, and Vancouver—and had become, through the force of her personality and the glamour of her exotic parentage, our first known poet. But whatever her reputation out there in Canada (which has lately been revived in universities by feminist and/or Aboriginal scholars after some slight diminution mid-twentieth century), as far as we were concerned, she was always from here, she was always one of our own. I have portions of at least two of the poems still by heart: "The Song My Paddle Sings," a rousing lyric about the ecstasy of canoeing, and "Lullaby of the Iroquois,"[1] which, with a simple tune, became part of the repertoire of the student choir I was part of, once I'd moved on from Number Four for grades seven and eight in Central School in the village of Ohsweken.

But the prominence her myth and work enjoyed in our community was also manifested in Chiefswood, a mansion in design, certainly if not in size, that stood, slightly dilapidated but still a recognized historical site, in the trees above the flood plain of the Grand River just down around the bend and across the wide lazy current from where my own family lived.

Even so, the idea that one might write poetry, let alone become a poet like Pauline when one grew up, was not something anyone, let alone the farm boy I was, would have been encouraged to consider. It might have been a question, by then, of the practice being seen as woman's work, since we'd had over two centuries of living literally surrounded more and more by the newcomers. We had tended to emphasize more the masculine face of our culture for them—our warriors and lacrosse players and steelworkers. But more likely it was just being practical. My Grandma Bee, my father's mother, a retired schoolteacher, who with one hand expressed admiration for Pauline's poems and her approval of my piano lessons, with the other held my wrist and attention to warn "You'll be poor" when I started to indicate my inclination toward the arts, toward somehow becoming a writer.

My response was playfully practical. Pencil and paper, I suggested, are just not that expensive. I think I can manage. This was clearly decades before computers and word processing came into the picture.

4.

All these years later, I hold on to this memory as if it was some goofy kind of prophecy.

During most of my youth we lived in a nearly hundred-year-old frame house on a hill. A distance from the road, hidden behind two barns, it was sheltered by pine and maple windbreaks and a big old poplar tree. The rumble of trains passed in the night to the north, so far off through the bush and across the river, that it was a sort of island existence. No one but family and the neighbours, it seemed, noticed us up there.

So when old friends of my parents, folks from when they were first married, a young couple living for a short time in the city of Toronto, found us there, came to visit, it was strange, a rare thing. They were strangers to me (they were white but that wasn't at issue), and I felt a bit shy, even though I was entering my adolescence, perhaps had already had my encounter with the bishop. (A cousin one Christmas about then, noting my growth, asked teasingly, "Dan, how come you're getting so tall?" The perfect reply danced off my lips: "The urge to rise above it all.")

The adults sat visiting in the sun on the unsheltered cement porch. Perhaps it was one of the first warm days of spring. I was introduced, then hung back to listen, seen but not heard. My mother turned, trying to draw me out or into the conversation. "But Dan, what do you want to do?" She was talking about my life. With sudden appropriate—but under-rehearsed—musical comedy hand gestures, perhaps something I'd seen Jimmy Durante do in an old black-and-white movie on TV, I found myself exclaiming, "I want to sing! I want to dance!" Ha-cha-cha-chaaa!

I avoided making a serious response in front of those strangers, made the adults laugh, but also provided for myself a fleeting realization. I *did* want to, metaphorically at least, sing and dance. My growing fascination with the arts wasn't something I could take so lightly much longer.

A new school friend was so enthusiastic over one particular poem we were studying in class. This must have been grade ten. It was a work with a regular structure, end rhymes, an established rhythmic pattern. I'm imagining something by Poe, but only because I know I definitely already knew some of his short stories from my explorations of the horror genre. That poem's formal perfection, my friend was certain, must take a genius to achieve.

I, with my language-as-machine prejudice, wasn't nearly as impressed. "It's just a trick," I declared. "Anybody could do it."

Was I just being contrary or was I trying to impress him, the new kid in the class, one of the few in the room who, like me, wasn't a long-time resi-dent of Caledonia and hadn't gone through primary school with the rest?

"Bet you couldn't," he smiled.

"How much?"

Over the following weekend I wrote a little ballad based—perhaps my friend chose the subject—on the Rapunzel ("Let down your hair!") story. End rhymes and an almost consistent rhythmic pattern allowed me to win the wager, proving that at least that part of poetry didn't take a genius. In the process, however, I developed a suspicion that something else was going on in poetry, something I sensed between the lines, a something else that I was intrigued by and to which I started trying to pay attention. Just how do you figure out figures of speech?

So it has to have been then, in the middle of my high schooling, grade eleven (we still had thirteen grades then), shortly after the Rapunzel poem wager, long after the bishop had left my spirit in the lurch, that I finally started to act on my interest, started making the decisions that would edge my education in the direction of writing. Training in the other arts wasn't an option, despite the academic bent of the school I attended, in our curriculum.

It didn't occur to me to seek out extracurricular possibilities out there on the reserve or in the adjoining small towns. Despite my schoolteacher grandmother's hobby of oil painting—she turned out renditions of land-scape photos taken from calendars—the visual arts didn't appeal to me, perhaps because her use of grids to transfer the images to canvas made the process seem primarily an exercise in geometry. And despite years of lessons with one of our church's ministers (they come and go) and then with one of my aunts, my piano performances proved, I suspect, mechanical at best. Any dexterity I might have been achieving mentally wasn't getting expressed by my fingers on the keys. I was clumsy, vibrating with adolescent energy and probably just too impatient to practise enough to get better when I knew I could be reading, say, an Arthur C. Clarke science fiction novel.

It occurs to me now that those years of music lessons, though they didn't produce a musician, did shape my sensibility, did open up the way I approach language. I do hear, behind the sense it makes, sounds that remind me, if I try to describe it, of the vocabulary we use for music. Beats, rhythm, refrains, rhymes, themes, harmony, melody, might be description or metaphor about either of these arts, the way I feel them. Language, in the music of poetry, succeeds at not only being literal. I look at my stanzas and realize that, mostly, they're not like prose paragraphs, containers for meaning or ideas, but like bars in music, measures of time and emotion.

To move in the direction of writing, I chose to take all three of the languages available, English, French, and Latin. (I also chose the available math courses, which, with my mental dexterity, promised marks to maintain my average.) The experience of comparing and contrasting the three languages over three or four years, even if I never really became fluent in either the living French or the dead Latin, allowed me to start to step back and see English more clearly as a separate material thing.

Learning to speak any of the traditional languages our family's mixed heritage suggests—Delaware, Mohawk, Tuscarora, or Cayuga, just to go back to my grandparents' generation—was not a possibility then. (I've been told, not without some sense of worry by my mother, that some of the schools at home do teach a couple of languages by immersion now. "What will they do when they have to go off reserve?") Scattered words from probably the Mohawk language came into the conversations of my parents' generation, words used mostly for effect, swearing, or teasing.

The phrase "gitgit ota" comes to mind and I believe it's Mohawk because sometime in the last five years I heard those words again, an unexpected pleasure, in a film from France about colonial North America, the words used by a Mohawk warrior character expressing his opinion of an English ally: the words mean "pig shit."

Even practical back then, my family, apparently on both sides, had taken English on as our first language at least two generations back, so I have a feeling toward it of entitlement, not of colonization. I feel ownership. This is my native language.

This means I can, for instance, attend a reading of Canadian and British poets and be surprised, disappointed, and even offended, having been told the Brits are prizewinners, at how lazy and conventional the work of the UK folks seems in the context of the work of the Canadians. The Brits may have started the English language, but they certainly don't seem to be taking very good care of it.

Why we were reading aloud in grade thirteen English, I don't know. Had the teacher not had time to prepare his lesson? It seems like something that should have occurred much earlier in our education. But there we were, in turn reading sections from the novel our class was studying. Was it Alan Paton's *Cry, the Beloved Country*?

I do remember that when my turn came, I got so involved in the story that by the time I finished my section, my voice had deepened, was about to break. I was moved and, from the fleeting glances I shared with other students in the class, momentary surprise, embarrassment, I could see they were too. I was so surprised by the power the words had over the emotions of my fellows and myself that I still remember the moment. You spend three or four years trying to be cool and suddenly you're sharing anguish over a story about the injustice of racism on the other side of the world. What was that about?

Rather than discount the experience, I got more intrigued. Speaking the words, getting them and their emotions back from the page, out of storage, became something I valued.

As I learned about the roots of some English words in Latin, about the different ways English and French used those roots, and about the different ways the sentences in the three languages were structured, my assumptions about how one might make sense of things were shaken and stirred.

Translating the senator Cicero and the warrior Julius Caesar, one after the other, a speech followed by a memoir, gave me an example, in an entirely different context, of what the word "style" might mean. I hadn't quite understood before.

The study of poetry in Latin also showed me where the practice of prosody, which on rare occasions I was dealing with in my English classes, probably had its origins. I wonder now if it was a rarely taught subject because neither the teachers nor the curriculum really had any confidence in its efficacy, even though it had the weight of tradition.

Poems structured with a recognizable rhyme scheme, for instance, seemed to me to be using a clear characteristic of the English language, rhyming words, as an obvious way of manufacturing poetry, drawing attention to the words, focusing meaning in the language in a credible way.

But the effort to detect, say, the pattern of the dactylic hexameter or spondees or of the iambic pentameter as some sort of support for sense struck me as not so obvious, as rather dull and mostly beside whatever point the poem might be making. You would think such analysis of the abstract event of language would have appealed to me with my trusty old assumption of language-as-machine, but by the time I was looking at Latin, I had moved beyond that image. It didn't fit with what I was experiencing on language's more organic ground.

Prosody that developed to create poetry in other tongues—Latin, Italian—carried forward through history by the artist servants of the church and state and claimed its ground in English cultural convention apparently in the age of the Renaissance, ended up feeling to me like an awkward imposition, if not imperial colonization, especially since folks had been doing it for hundreds of years. I did understand that Latin could use such patterning to shape poetry since the language's meaning relied more on the cases of words than on their order. (A rusty effect, inverting the accepted English word order to achieve a rhyme, can still get a smirk at the expense of such meter-minded efforts.) And efforts to use meter and rhythm as the final arbiter of poetry in English no longer really seemed credible to me. It all just made poetry seem more like a problem in a slippery kind of math, not a way to get at an emotive or moral truth.

On the other hand, most of the so-called free verse we found in our curriculum didn't impress me either, but I didn't know enough about poetry or language yet to figure out why. I suspect that only about that time had I really, for instance, come to appreciate the relative merits of something as basic and essential to good writing as the active voice.

Our teachers didn't help much either, since by that point they had moved with relief beyond the mechanics to encouraging us to find the meanings of poems. "What is the poet trying to say?" they would ask in all sincerity, even though I'm sure even then I wanted to point to the words on the page, which seemed perfectly articulated to me. All of this made me uncomfortable and I'd come to suspect the study of English as effect/affect was the wrong way to learn about writing as cause.

But I swallowed my dissatisfactions and, like my teachers and the curriculum, put up with prosody.

Looking ahead, I found a way to continue my poetry/language education at York University, where I was able to take writing workshops, to learn to do by doing. It might not have been the most efficient use of my time, but I was also, I now realize, learning about and acclimatizing myself to the foreign customs of Downsview, Ontario, Canada, and of the culture of the university, none of which I'd had much experience with, living on

the reserve. We had had, while I was growing up, for a few years, a graduate student anthropologist renting a room with us, but she hadn't shared
information about the U of T with ten-year-old me.

I studied screenwriting and short fiction as well, but it was the poetry
and playwriting, words written to be spoken, where I found most of my
passion focused. I tried to take in what was offered by my poet professors,
the inscrutable Frank Davey and the entertaining Irving Layton. My aesthetic, such as it was, was too old-fashioned for (I'm now guessing) post-
modernist Professor Davey to be much interested in encouraging and I was
too male to get much of Mr. Layton's focused attention (I've been informed
he ended up marrying one of my classmates).

But some not-English course I took—perhaps the college tutorial, a
humanities course called "What Is Truth?"—brought the book *Love's Body*
by Norman O. Brown to my attention. Although I look at the book now and
see it described as an extension of Freud's ideas into Western civilization's
politics, economics, philosophy, and literature, and have even encountered
folks who dismissed it as the work of a Communist, at the time, what I
took from it was that the power of poetry in English was more efficiently
got at if one were aware of and using verbs and metaphors connected to our
physical experience, to our lived lives. I started being aware of the level of
abstraction of words, starting trying to make my diction more evocative of
the concrete and the sensual.

At UBC next, I was scheduled to study with Pat Lowther, a poet who
was then beginning to receive recognition for her spare, imagistic, gently
musical poems. But after two classes, she disappeared. It turned out that
her husband, another not-as-successful poet, had murdered her. Although
that drama happened at a distance, although another instructor was found
for our class, the vague threat that one might get killed on account of
poetry (I didn't yet have access to additional details, adultery for one, that
would come out at the man's trial) must have been what put me into a
minor philosophical panic. I got so obsessed about the difference between
facts and truth, I started writing poems that expressed only that to which
I felt I could attest. The poems were as truncated as haikus but with none
of their power—which isn't all that great anyway in English. The work was
so frustrating, the replacement instructor, I suspect, would have failed me.
He didn't include me on the guest list for a special reading and dinner with
W. S. Merwin, the renowned American poet, but not knowing there was
such a list, I went happily along with the rest to the event anyway.

I got out of my philosophical quandary, somehow laughing it off,
through watching Orson Welles's ironic documentary—it was a new
release at the art cinema just off campus at the time—*F Is for Fake.*

I also like the motto I found somewhere during this time in the work of Marshall McLuhan: Art is anything you can get away with.

And this was probably when I started counting syllables as a practical alternative to traditional Western prosody if the evidence of the poems in my thesis is to be trusted. (Hey, I note now, William Carlos Williams didn't think the iamb fit with American speech rhythms. Why not just extend his suspicions north of the border?) But maybe it would be more truthful to say I just couldn't be bothered with all that metering when syllables felt like real things to me and, as far as I could tell, the rhythm ended up being taken care of by the sense and the emotions of the poem. Concise and precise diction equalled musical, equalled poetic for me (metaphors are also in there somewhere).

As I was finishing up my work for my degree, a new style of poem starting coming to me, lyrical, simple, sometimes playful stuff I was just writing for myself and not for school. I continued working on those poems for a couple or three years afterward while I lived again with my parents on the reserve and worked for the Woodland Cultural Centre as a researcher, visited, for a summer, my UBC friends in NYC, and finally moved to Toronto.

The one rule I set myself, after all those years in the polysyllabic world of university culture, was that I couldn't use any word in those poems of more than two syllables without first checking out its meaning in a dictionary. I no longer wanted to take any truth for granted or from habit. In the process, I found mostly the simpler words did the poetic job. I didn't need to sound English to write poetry.

And those were the first poems, despite words like "cumulus," that got published consistently by the little magazines, that eventually, thanks to bill bissett's blewointmentpress, became my first book, *Delicate Bodies*, that seemed to represent with some clarity what I guess I'd call my poetic voice and my particular poetics.

I'll end this with the first poem from that first book.

Song in the Light of Dawn[2]

Fish. My eyes were sleepy
fish and in the overcast
world the road to work was mud.
Then something near a pond

turned my head. A black bird's
banded wing made the perfect
lure, the gay colour a hook
without hurt, a blushing

wash. Now further on on
this shoulder of the high
way even the gravel and
asphalt greys overflow

their textures. They're so clear
I feel more than awake. Oh
to stay and swim in them here
would be—would be enough.

Notes

1 E. Pauline Johnson, *Flint and Feather: The Complete Poems of E. Pauline John-son (Tekahionwake)* (London: Hodder and Stoughton, 1912).
2 Daniel David Moses, *Delicate Bodies* (Vancouver: blewointmentpress, 1980).

Bibliography

Johnson, E. Pauline. *Flint and Feather: The Complete Poems of E. Pauline Johnson (Tekahionwake)*. London: Hodder and Stoughton, 1912.
Moses, Daniel David. *Delicate Bodies*. Vancouver: blewointmentpress, 1980.

12

Kwadây Kwańdur—Our Shagóon

Alyce Johnson

Place names hold significant value when an Indigenous language communicates narrative poetics filled with songs and stories onto cartographic maps. Place-based narratives denote embedded meanings such as directionals and verb-based instructions that a language provides for spatial dimensions and measurements within landscaped knowledge.[1] In the Yukon, the Southern Tutchone language holds dimensions that measures time, projects space, socializes people, identifies place, and narrates practice. In Southern Tutchone epistemology, the term "Kwadây Kwańdur" translates into "long-ago story," a time that narrates a geography of spatial world stories, which Tlen and Moore term "place-based narratives." These narratives demonstrate movements on the land.[2] Southern Tutchone ontology derives from an understanding of a time when animals and humans interchanged and interacted within both worlds spatially. Kwadây Kwańdur stores a memory of how "Crow Made the World"[3] as he flies a creation of northern landscapes. Our Shagóon—*our history*—narrates and frames our philosophy of Kwadây Kwańdur, when Kitty Smith uttered this oral memory: "That Crow, he does everything. Teaches everything."[4] Crow teaches us to dance a landscape pedagogy filled with memories as we sing the songs of our ancestors.

Social enactment of storied songs and ceremonies ingrains pedagogy filled with a collective, spatial reflexivity—a look back into a landscaped past to know our narrative futures. Essential to this understanding is that we belong to the trails that memory ancestors and, in turn, features knowledge of this landscape through narrative genres of stories, songs, dances, and ceremonies. One of these indicators is language, which Tlen and Moore note as "spatial expressions...[that] have essential narrative functions."[5] In its many forms, language has the ability to contextualize K'àma Dzêa (Ptarmigan Heart's) narrative realities along with its power to shape the future through Southern Tutchone cultural expressions, which become a living genre and a spatial memory.

Kwadây Kwańdur as Our Shagóon[6]

Through the lens of oral traditions, dimensions become more complex yet cohesive as they interconnect Southern Tutchone ontology and epistemology. Kwadây Kwańdur shares poetic dimensions that we know are fixed in time, place, and people; a spatiality of oral traditions, in Western ideology, fails to perceive our ontology or world view as Indigenous knowledge. From a Kaajèt perspective, my perception of Kwadây Kwańdur conveys this perception of worlds passed on that localizes Southern Tutchone to named landscapes. As a place, K'àma Dzêa (Ptarmigan Heart) overlays a landscape of Indigenous knowledge and narrative memory, a storied geography of experiences and pedagogy of teachings told and retold within a narrative paradigm.

This breadth allows for a greater understanding of our narrative past as Julie Cruikshank describes "the relation between mobility and connection to land deepened as I recorded stories of lives where a single year could often be mapped as a travel narrative."[7] In her elaboration of how Athapaskan peoples adapt to the interface between two cultures as the Alaska Highway moved through the Yukon region following trails, Cruikshank elaborates further that "ethnographers have repeatedly documented the ability of Athapaskan Indians to adapt to the changing conditions of life, and nowhere is this clearer than in Southern Yukon."[8] Southern Tutchone trails have always brought in shared Indigenous philosophies as well as new ideologies, and with changing world views and evolving languages come new ways of thinking and knowledge, but also opportunities for our communities to grow into our pasts.

In essence, Neal McLeod encapsulates what it means for Indigenous researchers to share our identities in a past and present context that defines our identities through oral traditions. He demonstrates this understanding with his elaborations of Cree-ness as a consciousness of place and peoples uprooting Western ideologies: "Great stories challenge the status quo."[9] Challenging academic boundaries creates not only a level of discomfort within academia, but also within our communities, which necessitates research expansions and extensions.[10] Words hold a power; therefore, we come to know from Kwadây Kwańdur—from a place in the past—to share stories with our futures with powerful words of knowledge. It is a constructing of Kaajèt and Aguna minds.

However, Elders are concerned about this lack of knowing our traditions because Western ways reshaped our world views and we failed to practise it or remember its importance. These clan responsibilities require commitment to ensure that our children grow into strong ways. In order for our children to grow up with clan minds, we must map them with stories and teach them Kwadây Kwańdur pedagogy and narrative genres embedded in a landscape of memories, for the land retains a spatial memory of ancestral languages.

To encapsulate how Kwadây Kwańdur intersects the past into futures, we must understand the poetic words of Dakwàkàta,[11] Mrs. Annie Ned, in *Life Lived Like a Story*:

> Long time ago, what they know, what they see, that's the one they talk about, I guess. Tell stories—which way you learn things. You think about one your grandma tells you. You've got to believe it, what Grandma said....Old-style words are just like school.[12]

As indicated in Mrs. Annie Ned's dialogue, it is critically important that the stories remain fixed and that as storytellers, we not delineate or sway from it as their truths. A storytelling method fixes these memories to "think" about and "believe" in the ways of our ancestors. To counteract further impeding Western ideologies requires us to adhere to Southern Tutchone Elders' knowledge stored in poetic forms of stories and songs. Becoming a "critical storyteller" functions as a counter-narrative, which Patricia Settee elaborates and shares as Indigenous pedagogy and cultural teachings that counter the master narrative.[13] This process requires a memory that stores this information, a training ground for Indigenous storytellers to challenge our notion of spatial memory beyond cartographic definitions into a poetic past.

One of the challenges that I face as a member of a Kaajèt–Crow clan was the reality that as long as we do not share long-ago stories, we tend to forget the roots from which Kwadây Kwańdur grounds our identities. In a search for how oral traditions function as part of identity requires a narrative lens as a method of retaining this memory from many generations past. When asked about stories, some Southern Tutchone Lhù'ààn Mân Kéyi Elders did not remember them, and I cannot recall the details of stories that Shadazhan Mą (Singing to Herself), our late mother, Jessie Johnson, told me; therefore, collective narrative memory requires more than that of Elders alone as McLeod indicates in *Cree Narrative Memory*. It requires a closure between the gaps of clan generations as well as a method to retain this information. Part of that memory has been geo-spatially stored as oral history when "memory is the core of oral history, from which meaning can be extracted and preserved."[14] Returning to this knowledge means that memory allows us to recall and live the narratives as truth.

To gain this knowledge means a return not only to the practice of old-time stories, but also to research storage forms to retrieve this knowledge. It is a responsibility to adhere to our higher laws. Catharine McClellan elaborates how children grew up following instructions and that "what the old people had to say was a prime source of knowledge."[15] To gain knowledge is to listen carefully to the stories and glean the best from the wisdom of the storytellers. For instance, when McClellan asks a Tlingit man about stories, he kept "thinking, thinking, all the time" to remember the stories told a long time ago and could not sleep for days.[16] What he shares is the depth one can draw from memory as one retrieves stories, as in this case when he searches his mind to recall and step back in time to meet a present need.

Stories recited and memorized convey places that travellers either followed or located within a shared language that communicates knowledge. McClellan demonstrates that

> Older natives memorized the information so well that when they had to go places they had never been before, they still could recognize the landmarks and get to where they wanted to go. Text by Athapaskan Elders demonstrate again and again how thoroughly the landscape was recited in oral tradition.[17]

Kwadây Kwańdur is an oral tradition that language fuses as memory to places. Language also contains directionals within a language to provide a spatially imagined landscape as a place-based narrative that landmarks the landscape.[18] Landscape pedagogy provides a real yet imaginary lens that enables the storyteller to convey spatiality to the listener or learner while simultaneously affirming places in narratives.

Kwadây Kwańdur as an Interactive K'ènji (Place)

Understanding oral traditions from within a clan system requires an understanding of spatiality of time in place and people within geography of spaces, a term that I have come to understand as a geo-spatial theory of place in a multi-dimensional sense. The land holds many layers of stories, not only in time, but also with peoples who occupy that time and space in a past, present, and future context. Indigenous languages enable this multi-dimensionality to merge cohesively into each generational experience; however, without a language, we detract from its nuances. When orality and text intersect in narratives, Cruikshank notes that "Yukon elders address this conjunction of place, space, and time explicitly when they speak about where they have lived and traveled," particularly when songs explain social and cartographic intersections with Mrs. Annie Ned's "You don't know this place, so I am going to sing it for you."[19] Through the tertiary lens of

Indigenous educators who refer to narrative as storytelling and pedagogy, the teaching method that Mrs. Annie Ned shares becomes an Indigenous reality into a narration of her life experiences and interactions as her binding roots of knowledge. Words intermesh into Indigenous knowledge of places, times, peoples, and landscapes when life narratives orally share this social reality beyond an explanation of a past.

Through an interactive process, life storyteller engages his or her audience to situate them into stories within contexts, geography, spirituality, presences, pedagogy, interrelationships, and spatiality. This multi-layered interconnectedness between ontology and narratives transferred through a life history paradigm is evident in Gengenbach's *Binding Memories*. She writes that "Over and over, I heard that it was women who not only brokered such boundaries in the course of their life but were responsible for maintaining the intergenerational chain of transmission by handing these stories down to daughters and granddaughters."[20] On a recipient level, the accounts of Yukon Elders that Cruikshank interviewed bring deeper meanings into her research: "converging accounts (that) helped me to appreciate how meanings of northern landscapes continue to be shaped by culture, gender, age, and historical circumstances by the teller."[21] Narratives function to retain a spatial memory that is important to social cohesion and to link a past to a future as well as storyteller to recipient in a temporary kinship relation of a Kwadây Kwańdur ontology. Southern Tutchone Elders elaborate on kinship relations with animals to establish interconnections to other spatial worlds.

In a Kwadây Kwańdur narration of spatial life histories, these stories remain an essential part of Southern Tutchone societies. Language is that critical intersection that Mele Estella Tupou Raikai interconnects to Mi'kmaq land values and principles merge past into present.[22] Further to Raikai's analysis of the Mi'kmaq language as a life-giving force, Jon Rehyner and Edward Tennant interconnect Indigenous ontologies as a strong connection to epistemology: "each language carries with it an unspoken network of cultural values," which links with socio-linguistic expressions that communicate Indigenous values and principles.[23] With the continuous discussions on language loss, academic researchers stress that the English language continues to lose the cultural values embedded in an Indigenous language.[24] One of the issues is the transferability from an Indigenous language to English when one understands that meaning is lost through modification and translation.[25]

The stories in a language become even more precious while we face the challenges of Western impositions.[26] Basil Johnston measures this loss: "As rich and full of meaning as may be individual words and expression, they embody only a portion of the entire stock and potential of tribal language, wisdom, and intellectual attainment."[27] However, on a cartographic note, English maps modify the landscapes to the degree that place holds a foreign value as it layers Indigenous territories with another narrative memory described in English.

One recent narrative memory of the Yukon landscape was the finding of Kwädäy Dän Sinchi (long-ago person found): an Indigenous person found in one of the receding glacial systems in the Yukon proves that the oral traditions predate written history. Cruikshank shares Kitty Smith's narrative of *Falling Through a Glacier* and he was renamed Kwädäy Dän Sinchi (long-ago person found).[28] Stories validate spatial memory in a measurable dimension of time as it travels through generations of knowing. Kwadây Kwańdur links back to Creation stories of "How Crow Made the World," kinship relations in "The Girl Who Married the Bear," stories of Asuya, the Giant Beaver Man, or "The Man on the Moon" figure. These spatial narratives frame a pedagogy of teachings that Tlen and Moore qualify as place-based narratives.[29] Kwadây Kwańdur embodies a pedagogy that is more than a place; it is a way of place-knowing and a call for a return to long-ago stories.

Connecting storytelling to social worlds, the Southern Tutchone interrelationship with animals shaped a perceptual understanding that this land also shares other spatial worlds. Southern Tutchone narratives exemplify Creation in "How Crow Made Light," all of which McClellan retains as oral history records in her many years of investing into our future memory.[30] To teach us about our collective consciousness and social reliance upon one another, I remember this story, which Shadazhan Mą told me of how two orphans saved our people from starvation. These pedagogical narratives infuse Southern Tutchone with a language of spatial worlds in the dimensions of past, present, and future. Language is not only a socializing factor that carries into each generation, but also a geographical indicator that locates Southern Tutchone to their regions. Narrative genres require a memory of practised traditions to retain them with a shift toward narrative paradigms that centralize the tenets of Indigenous poetics.

From a position of dialogic Kaajèt, singing and dancing to Southern Tutchone narrative poetics demonstrate that there is no division between ontology and epistemology in a world of narrative genres. Kwadây Kwańdur is a way of life before first contact with non-Indigenous peoples. The twenty-first century continues with Western ideology hampering traditional practices whereby we no longer tell these stories, and Elders have difficulty remembering them (personal dialogue) for few request this geo-spatial memory. As Indigenous peoples, we must position ourselves from within an ontology that teaches these epistemologies and change the methods within Indigenous research paradigms. Our traditional protocols require that strength in us to forge ahead in history and to live it as an Indigenous past, a method of sharing oral traditions in our present time.

Growing Up Kaajèt—Crow Clan

Clans have a significant role in Indigenous societies. In Southern Tutchone ontology, it begins with the mothers whom Kaajèt and Aguna name into futures, as in the case of K'àma Dzêa (Ptarmigan Heart), as an embodiment of traditions from a clan ontology based upon traditional methods of growing into a landscape epistemology or teachings from the mother's clan. In this context, I perceive myself as belonging to a family of Crow members from my mother's stories, which are based upon my relations and have a common ancestor from a poetically defined narration of "Crow Made the World."

Stories, songs, dance, and ceremonies are clan-specific, providing communicative expressions of experiences as one grows into a Kaajèt ontology with an epistemology that teaches them their responsibilities as clan or family members. Growing up Kaajèt is to grow into pedagogy, into teachings rooted not only to peoples but also to history attached to places of experience, and narrative genres hold powerful symbols of greater responsibility. Genres belong to clans or families that identify themselves through symbolic icons such as ts'urk'i (crow/raven), which represent Kaajèt as belonging to the Crow family, and agäy (wolf) for Wolf members.[31] Through Indigenous names genres come alive, transferring through women narratives and the practices of gifting names.

The concept of geo-spatial narrative is not broadly defined, nor is it a cohesive elaboration to include a naming ceremony interconnected to place names within Indigenous research beyond kinship relations or genealogy, which Linda Tuhiwai-Smith refers to as "personal names that many people carried."[32] Continuing with the significance of names and the need to bring a sociality of narratives closer to our understandings of its functions, Cruikshank deliberates on the Crow-Wolf sociality of family relations. She does so to make this distinction: "It immediately situates everyone, since kinship affiliations can be determined immediately by answers to simple questions like "Who is your mother?" or where names are clan-owned property, "What is your Indian name?"[33] While we share our Indigenous stories, we must understand this geo-spatial pedagogy in order to know it within our social realities and to preserve it as living genres. As long as the discourse continues to define Indigenous pedagogy as knowledge, research will continue to refine the conceptual perceptions of oral traditions as languages transform narratives into poetic forms. Narratives and oral history retain this landscape pedagogy and push the master narratives to its periphery, centralizing Indigenous knowledge as its core.

Language shapes epistemology; therefore, it outlines our relationships with peoples and the lands from within a linguistically defined philosophy. Language is a key factor that constitutes my Kaajèt identity to understand what Á Maata Lena Johnson means to be "planted here like a forest tree."[34] This metaphor communicates a deeper meaning, translating experiences into another layer of language that conveys the essence of how she is rooted with the land by likening herself to the life of a "tree." Although she spoke those words in 1977, over thirty years ago, they continue to live within the memories of those who shared that event. Words, whether uttered, sung, storied, or celebrated, remain alive spatially through a language of narrative genre: "There was a special regard almost akin to reverence for speech and for the truth."[35] Words have the power to image life narratives of the past while contextualizing stories and songs into present and future realities. These performances in narratives travel from the present into the past with a fluidity that marks a significant trail worthy of discoursing into futures.

In Southern Tutchone traditions, songs performed at a potlatch become a collective narrative ceremony whereby the collective agreement of giving Southern Tutchone names determines one's route in life of either Kaajèt or Aguna. Oral history and narrative poetics determine how place names celebrate individuals who carry the names. Kaajèt narratives begin this Kwadây Kwaṅdur trail as a living genre by gifting a landscape name that contains a geo-spatial memory for it is in a time-past, yet in a constant-present, with knowledge for future spaces when Kaajèt children carry names of our ancestors' landscaped experiences. My journey into this geo-spatial trail is also a "coming-to-know," which educator and Tewa Gregory Cajete shared as an Indigenous quest to relearn our histories.[36] Growing up as a Kaajèt brings the concept of "homelands" closer to this place as an important part of our Shagóon.[37] That knowledge deepens as I travel this trail. I continue to grow into this knowing as a responsibility toward our history as our Shagóon, a sharing of poetic narrations that define my Kaajèt roots.

Languages share a multi-dimensionality of worlds in place as kwädäy kwänjē (old words).[38] As a Kaajèt making my narrative memories, I have circled backward to my trails and to a place in my geo-spatial past to know our Shagóon. This time of knowing our geo-spatial narratives has entered upon me—a reality that I must continue to journey, making my future Kaajèt even more important to name their narratives. To understand the poetics of songs and stories conveyed in a language, Á Näya Joe Johnson shared that "The language is just like that. They use it for a map."[39] The

Elders' collective statements forefront their knowledge of language as an important part of one's socialization of place and knowledge of landscape features as Á Näya Joe Johnson closes his fingers to indicate the closeness in this relationship between language and landscape.

One Kaajèt song that continues landscaped narratives is the song "Little Arm Tatäy," which geo-visually sings of Jimmie Johnson as he walks around the bend into the *atäy* (a pass between two mountains) that leads toward K'àma Dzêa. His landscape experiences in the early twentieth century provide a visual image of him crossing the frozen lakes while walking trails that Southern Tutchone no longer traverse. To understand the narrations of this song, one must know the language or be instructed about how the words evoke a memory of Tsäyda Tà. Within songs and dances is embedded a poetry of the landscapes of time and place, a living genre performed of a memory foregone yet constant and present.

In *Our Voices: Native Stories of Alaska and Yukon*, Ruppert and Berner share Mrs. Annie Ned's spatial memory of how stories function within clan genres:

> I'm going to put it down who we are. This is our *Shagóon*—our history. Lots of people in those days, they told their story all the time. This story comes from old people, not just from one person—from my grandpa, Hutschi Chief; from Lebarge Chief; from Dalton Post Chief. Well, they told the story of how first this Yukon came to be.

> This is our *Shagóon*. *Kajìt* me—that's Crow: *Ts'ürk'i*. Wolf people they call *Agünda*; wolf (the animal) is called *ägäy*. Hutschi Chief was *Kajìt*, and Big Jim was *Agünda*.[40]

This birthing into a clan with loyalties is one to which clan members inherit clan narratives. Loyalties define the relationships of peoples from both clans through stories that Kaajèt and Aguna pass on to each generation. As Mrs. Annie Ned indicates, clan training of stories come at an early age: "Since I was ten, that's when I got smart. I started to know some things."[41] Growing into a clan genre begins early in spatial memory and is entrenched into our Shagóon.

Á Näya Joe Johnson reiterates this relationship with the lands that hold both inanimate and animate narratives in a geo-spatiality that covers landscape knowledge: "everything had a spirit like trees, animals, and you got to respect it. And that is what you call traditional knowledge. You have to respect."[42] Elders' words hold powerful directives to remind us that it is time to listen and to learn what it means to memory: "the language helps you to remember,"[43] and that "You're brought up...your education is you memorize everything. You put it in here, you don't forget it."[44] In this

acknowledgement of his learning experiences, he forefronts memory retention while acknowledging its loss in a new world of technology that changed
our memories, and English, which helped us to forget our traditional ways.

While faced with critical issues of language loss and cultural impositions, these external devices nonetheless necessitate that their utilization
retain this landscaped memory. For instance, Cruikshank acknowledges
one of these glacial stories[45] with Tlen's citation of "The Giant Worm" in
the Donjek glacial system.[46]

As Kaajèt, the stories reinforce our knowledge of place-based protocols when we visit specific sites on the land, for their experiences differ
from ours and necessitate our construction of knowledge. In 2007, I had
an opportunity to attend a gathering with Elders, Kluane First Nation
employees, and Parks Canada at the Bighorn, the intersection between the
Steele and Donjek glaciers where this story retains a landscape law of "The
Giant Worm."

Á Mąya Margaret Johnson shared the story of my Á Tàya[47] Jack Allen.[48]
Jack Allen warned a non-Indigenous individual about not cooking bacon
grease one morning, but he did not heed the warning and lost his life in
a glacial surge. Dire consequences ensue if traditional pedagogies are not
adhered to or followed precisely. She spoke to me about the mountain
called Méddhį Daada (Owl Mountain), which holds this story as it faces
the intersection of these two glacial systems merging in Dan Zhùr Chù (the
Donjek River), which reminds us to adhere to our narrative laws embedded in Kwadây Kwańdur as Cruikshank, McClellan, and Tlen remember.[49]

A disregard for and disrespect of landscape pedagogy concerns Elders
today when the higher laws of the land do not hold this same place value.
Pedagogy holds symbolic value when these stories of place share a knowledge that we neither practise nor believe because Western impositions have
set in new ideologies of narrative pasts as "myths."[50] As a clan member, I
enter Kwadây Kwańdur as a dialogic Kaajèt—one who speaks from within
my clan and does not represent how other Kaajèt perceive their respective
worlds. It is a reconstruction of my identity and journey without a name
and no grounded trail in life.

The right to claim legitimacy to public performances and storytelling
stems from clan protocols. This entitlement to narratives within traditional knowledge is what Á Näya Joe Johnson called "a living heritage."[51]
Cruikshank connects Mrs. Annie Ned's landscaped narratives with a parallel kinship of peoples and places "that even selection of a clan name is
linked with a particular location: a second song was sung there."[52] Easterson exemplifies this process: "each moiety has established its claim to
particular crests (Wolf of Crow), songs, names or dances.... By keeping

the moieties of Wolf and Crow, it was believed that society would remain intact surviving through time."[53] Songs belong to clan members and convey interrelationships with the land as well as other peoples. Protocols strictly detail the responsibilities of maintaining these narratives. In her interconnections between "place, kinship and ideas about personhood," Cruikshank forefronts kinship, and "membership is inherited from one's mother."[54] As a ceremonial practice, potlatch narratives fuse memory of growing up Kaajèt or Aguna, and are a performance of power.

Cruikshank clearly demonstrates this power in her work with the late Angela Sidney, while as a researcher she deepened her understanding of oral traditions: "the central thesis guiding her [Sidney's] work was that while oral tradition can indeed broaden our understanding of the past, it tells even more about the present."[55] The element of shared spaces of discourses becomes a collaborative process whereby Elders share their knowledge, exerting their stories as a right to share and speak from within languages of meaning. In a social context, Cruikshank's use of life stories as a methodology to examine clan narratives not only expounds those interrelationships between Southern Tutchone and Tlingits, but also forefronts oral traditions as a method of knowledge retention, spatial memory, and narrative genres.[56] To gain in-depth knowledge correlates the multi-dimensionality of oral traditions as they traverse through time and space with a people's mobility on the land and intersecting worlds.

Tan Kwa Gà—Trails Intersect Kwadây Kwańdur

Narrative songs foreground memory of life story experiences.[57] Life story incorporates the spatial narrations of Elders sharing their life experiences when Grace Johnson's "fascination with glaciers grew from their persistent and puzzling appearances in life stories."[58] In a public performance of this song, "Jimmie Johnson," we create a visual world that discursively provides a geo-spatial imaging of one of our ancestors walking in a life story. To understand how songs converge upon narratives into knowledge of our Shagóon, we must look through the lens of our ancestors' memories.

In *Potlatch: The Southern Tutchone Way*, Easterson provides a tertiary lens of the past: "Jimmie Johnson from Burwash Landing was a 'big man' who, according to elder Grace Johnson, had made a potlatch for his living mother."[59] When Grace Johnson shares this story of our Jimmie Johnson, she talks about one of our leaders in the context of a "big man," someone who is of great importance. Through this tertiary lens of our Elders, I begin to perceive his life story. In interpretation, it means that his leadership skills preceded him as a well-known person. These Kaajèt narratives become part of places and spaces in people's lives and express the narrative genres.

This power in a language has the ability to move from space to place with the individuals who contain and carry that knowledge as experience and memory. Spatially narrated stories, through the stored records of Kwadây Kwańdur, research projects, and oral history enable a people to enter and revisit a past to live this genre. In storied narratives, trails play a significant role in Lhù'ààn Mân Kéyi that connects social alliances with other nations. With first contacts, trails provided an entry into this region. Trails not only brought in peoples but also their languages, knowledge, and diseases, thus creating social chaos and disorder. English became our community's main language of communication and disrupted our social systems.[60] New trails into Lhù'ààn Mân Kéyi brought in a host of social issues, political infrastructures, foreign ideologies, and displaced philosophies that require a return to Kwadây Kwańdur as a place-based philosophy.

Our Elders stress the importance of knowing one's narratives, as well as the responsibility of being a Kaajèt member. Á Maata Lena Johnson and Á Näya Joe Johnson discuss how language as a map signifies the importance of knowing because we need to remember places. Geographical spaces function not only on maps, but also within narrative genres to indicate cultural expressions, which Tlen and Moore have advocated as place-based narratives.[61] Cruikshank's elaborations forefront the importance of landscape knowledge, which connects language to culture: "Through words the landscape is fashioned into a world of manageable, human proportions."[62] Narratives as a storytelling genre indicate a familiarity with the environment, and language portals that ontology through time with each telling of one's life narrative. Southern Tutchone place names function as linguistic and geographical indicators to express a people's interactions as well as to validate lands and resources as important to their sustenance and social interactions. Collective, narrative memory initiates landscape pedagogy shaped within languages in places that name experiences. In a language, place names signify a peoples' landscape pedagogy rooted to an Indigenous knowledge.

Á Tsy Copper Lily Johnson talks about the names: "Pack around someone's name; She's the one who made the song."[63] To understand the use of metaphorical words in poetic terms, one must understand what she means with "pack around someone's name" when she referred to Southern Tutchone individuals who carry the names of their family members. In the knowledge that K'àma Dzêa's name is being packed around through times, spaces, places, landscapes, and peoples, this "pack[ing] around someone's name" becomes a living genre as well as a "place-based narrative" socially constructed in the Southern Tutchone language.[64] It is the multi-functional duality within names that metaphors place, and the spaces in which growing up Kaajèt are a narrative and poetic reality.

Narrative Poetics and Realities

Oral history has multiple functions, and documenting place names is only one method of Indigenous knowledge retention. It digitizes memories of long-ago places and peoples. It holds languages that express and communicate movement in narrative genres and memories of place-knowing. In their work with Southern Tutchone and Kaska Dena language groups, Tlen and Moore identify an important feature of language communication when the landscape grounds narratives into cultural knowing.[65] Tlen and Moore elaborate that verb-based language, as opposed to noun-based English, use directionals that locate nouns as subject or object placed in deictic directionals from the speaker or narrator to the listener.

For instance, Á Näya Joe Johnson, in describing where my cabin is located at Tl'äw K'à Chù (Duke River), uses both gestures and directionals that position the cabin's location within this region.[66] Although Elders do not speak of a directional specifically, his declaration that "the language is 100 percent right" equates and transfers to the underlying meanings of how languages convey and gesture a landscape of motion expressed within narrative that is geographically specific. In their discussion of decolonizing Indigenous research, Bartlett et al. encourage the use of Indigenous languages for understanding life stories: "the Algonkian language is *process/oriented verb-based*, whereas Eurocentric language is *subject/oriented noun-based*."[67]

Elders know traditions in ways that we now seek, and research reports and leadership meetings frame the discussion of their traditional knowledge. This extract from *Traditional Knowledge Research Guidelines*[68] from the Council for Yukon First Nations Elders' consultation reiterates this need for cultural preservation: "traditional knowledge is first to me you have to respect Elders...because it's very, very strict spiritual life."[69] With each generation, part of that past knowledge is lost as it strips another layer of present knowledge from our future knowledge. As part of this consultation with Yukon Elders, their knowledge transfers into digital format for storage retrieval. Clan memory holds the sacred laws to which Southern Tutchone must adhere and teach.

Conclusion

With shifting paradigms in Indigenous research becoming more inclusive of knowledge constructed on the basis of a collective consciousness, Indigenous researchers create spaces within narrative genres to express their respective realities rather than separate disciplines within the academy. Western ideologies and philosophies conflict with Indigenous consciousness of place. This intersection creates a space whereby a (re)creation of dialogic encounters ensues through the cross-weaving of those encounters and extends into spaces to emerge from within those dichotomies. It then creates a space to look within those spaces reflexively, externalizing internal reviews of one's position within research.

A conceptual formulation of how a geo-spatial philosophy interconnects a holistic ecological relationship within a Kwadây Kwandur epistemology initiates a discourse between Indigenous philosophies of place with an intersection between cartography and iconography. As a Kaajèt and Indigenous researcher involved in the Southern Tutchone language, these types of discourses continue to remain contentious and persist as a colonialist discourse, which requires expansion into Indigenous mapping philosophies. A return to Edward Glave's 1890 words reiterates Tlen and Moore, and Burenhult and Levinson's conceptual elaborations and linguistic inquiries of place:[70]

> The Indian names of the mountains, lakes and rivers are natural landmarks for the traveler, whoever he may be; to destroy these by substituting words of a foreign tongue is to destroy the natural guides...another very good reason why these should be preserved is that some tradition of tribal importance is always connected with them. These people have no written language, but the retention of their native names is an excellent medium through which to learn their history.[71]

When Indigenous knowledge constructs from a heritage speaker's knowledge, those who grow up in a first language before being exposed to the English language possess language in ways that other learners do not experience.[72] English does not provide this "sense of place," which Basso describes in an Apache context and, as Huggins, Huggins, and Jacobs note, becomes more of a "sense of displacement."[73] Despite increased use of the English language and issues of language loss in Canada, place names remain a constant presence on Kluane First Nation's electronic maps; however, Western cartographic maps do not reflect this overlay while names such as K'àma Dzêa remain constant with the practice of naming children after landscape features as physical inscriptions. As long as maps do not reflect Indigenous names, they lose important philosophical features within narratives of place.

Á Näya Joe Johnson's understanding of landscape language elaborates on Burenhult and Levinson's conceptualization that "place names are one of the most conservative elements in a language, surviving even repeated language shifts."[74] Despite a decline in speakers of an Indigenous language, narratives in Southern Tutchone will continue to communicate the philosophy of place in ways that English fails to capture as it isolates words from the nuances embedded within narrative forms. Indigenous researchers raise many issues within academia; however, one critical difference between Indigenous and Western knowledge is that non-Indigenous outsiders lack certain philosophical boundaries that cannot be crossed, sacred knowledge that must be withheld, or information to which others are not privy.[75]

Speaking as a Kaajèt who grew up in this area, this access of information allows for an in-depth engagement with the Elders for knowledge acquisition and accumulation while following Kaajèt laws. John W. Frieson defines an oral tradition as one that is "evoked in the consciousness of the participants."[76] They hand over their concerns to those willing to not only listen, but to act upon the broader issues that affect our futures. As Mrs. Annie Ned advises, "This is our *Shagóon*—our history.... Not *you* are telling it: it's the person who told you that telling you the story."[77] This consciousness of my reality stems from Kaajèt knowledge from a position of Kwadây Kwańdur life narration:

> Finally we come to human beings themselves. They too were first created by Crow according to accounts given by all three tribes. The Tagish say that this was one of the last things he did. He made them of cottonwood bark and then divided them into Crow and Wolf moieties, saying "You are going to be on my side—Crow. An on the other side of the campfire—you are Wolf people. You marry each other."[78]

Clan protocols ensured social cohesion with shared resources and intermarriages between clan systems, ingraining social responsibilities; however, maps do not indicate any Kaajèt or Aguna genres. Traditional laws require these genres to be passed on to successive generations of children, storytellers, and researchers through creative methods of documentation. This lack requires a need to retain stories as Archibald indicates that one must take the oral traditions to teach spiritual practices without breaking our traditional laws.[79] The grave messages about the English language overshadowing the decline of Indigenous languages make clear the need for Indigenous genres to remain alive for future references, purposes, and retention.

Notes

1 Daniel Tlen and Patrick Moore, "Indigenous Linguistics and Land Claims: The Semiotic Projection of Athapaskan Directionals in Elijah Smith's Radio Work," *Journal of Linguistic Anthropology* 17, no. 2 (2007): 266–86.

2 Daniel Tlen, *Kluane Southern Tutchone Glossary English to Southern Tutchone* (Whitehorse: The Northern Research Institute, 1993), 7; Tlen and Moore, "Indigenous Linguistics and Land Claims," 282.

3 Julie Cruikshank, *Life Lived Like a Story: Life Stories of Three Native Elders* (Vancouver: UBC Press, 1990), 179–83.

4 Ibid., 183.

5 Tlen and Moore, "Indigenous Linguistics," 267.

6 This excerpt of Mrs. Annie Ned's stories is from James Ruppert and John W. Berner, *Our Voices: Native Stories of Alaska and the Yukon* (Lincoln: University of Nebraska Press, 2001).

7 Julie Cruikshank, *The Social Life of Stories: Narrative and Knowledge in the Yukon Territory* (Vancouver: UBC Press, 1998), 17.

8 Julie Cruikshank, "The Gravel Magnet: Some Social Impacts of the Alaska Highway on Yukon Indians" (paper presented at the Alaska Highway Conference, Fort St. John, June 18–20, 1982), 173.

9 Neal McLeod, *Cree Narrative Memory: From Treaties to Contemporary Times* (Saskatoon: Purich, 2007), 99.

10 Sandy Grande, *Red Pedagogy: Native American Social and Political Thought* (Lanham: Rowman & Littlefield, 2004).

11 Cruikshank does not use this term. This is Mrs. Annie Ned's Southern Tutchone name.

12 Cruikshank, *Life Lived Like a Story*, 267.

13 Patricia Settee, "Pimatisiwin: Indigenous Knowledge Systems, Our Time Has Come" (Ph.D. diss., University of Saskatchewan, 2007), 124–25.

14 Donald Ritchie, *Doing Oral History: Exploring Indian Reality* (Markham: Octopus, 1992), 19.

15 Catherine McClellan, "My Old Peoples Stories: A Legacy for Yukon First Nations, Part I: Sourthern Tutchone Narrators," *Occasion Papers in Yukon History* 5, no. 1 (2007): 67, http://www.tc.gov.yk.ca/pdf/mcclellan_opyh_5(1).pdf.

16 Ibid.

17 Catherine McClellan, "Before Boundaries: People of the Yukon/Alaska" (paper presented in Whitehorse, 1989), 6.

18 Tlen and Moore, "Indigeneous Linguistics and Land Claims."

19 Cruikshank, *Do Glaciers Listen? Local Knowledge, Colonial Encounters & Social Imagination* (Vancouver: UBC Press, 2005), 66.

20 Heidi Gengenbach, *Where Women Make History: Women as Makers and Tellers of History in Magude, Mozambique* (West Sussex, UK: Columbia University Press, 2005), 60, http://www.gutenberg-e.org/geh01/geh08.html.

21 Cruikshank, *Do Glaciers Listen?*, 52.

22 Mele Estella Tupou Rakai, "A Neutral Framework for Modelling and Analysing Aboriginal Land Tenure Systems," *Technical Report* no. 277 (2005): 99, http://gge.unb.ca/Pubs/TR227.pdf.

23 Jon Rehyner and Edward Tennant, "Maintaining and Renewing Native Languages," *Bilingual Research Journal* 19, no. 2 (1995): 279, http://jan.ucc.nau.edu/~jar/Main.html.

24 Jo-Ann Q'um Q'um Xiiem Archibald, *Indigenous Storywork: Educating the Heart, Mind, Body, and Spirit* (Vancouver: UBC Press, 2008); J. Edward Chamberlain, "From Hand to Mouth: The Postcolonial Politics of Oral and Written Traditions," in *Reclaiming Indigenous Voice and Vision*, ed. Marie Battiste (Vancouver: UBC Press, 2000); Cruikshank, *The Social Life of Stories*; Eugene A. Nida, *Language Structure and Translation* (Stanford: Stanford University Press, 1975); Tlen and Moore, "Indigenous Linguistics."

25 Nida, *Language Structure and Translation*, 91.

26 Winona L. Stevenson. "Decolonizing Tribal Histories" (Ph.D. diss., University of California, 2009), 9.

27 Basil Johnston, "One Generation from Extinction," *Native Writers and Canadian Literature* no. 124–125 (1990): 10–15, http://cinema2.arts.ubc.ca/units/canlit/pdfs/articles/canlit124-Generation.(Johnston).pdf.

28 Cruikshank, *Do Glaciers Listen?*, 55, 246.

29 Tlen and Moore, "Indigenous Linguistics."

30 McClellan, *My Old People Say.*

31 Cruikshank, *The Social Life of Stories*, 14.

32 Linda Tuhiwai Smith, *Decolonizing Methodologies: Research and Indigenous Peoples* (New York: Zed, 2001), 15

33 Cruikshank, *The Social Life of Stories*, 22.

34 Andrew Hume, "Johnson Tells Inquiry: I Feel Like I Was Planted Here," *Whitehorse Star*, June 3, 1977.

35 Johnston, "One Generation from Extinction," 12.

36 Gregory Cajete, *Native Science: Natural Laws of Interdependence* (Sante Fe: Clear Light Publishers, 2000), 80.

37 Ruppert and Berner, *Our Voices*, 187; Tlen and Moore, "Indigenous Linguistics," 35; Terry N. Tobias, *Chief Kerry's Moose: A Guide to Land Use and Occupancy Mapping, Research Design, and Data Collecting* (Vancouver: Union of Indian British Columbia Chiefs' Ecotrust Canada, 2010), 35, http://www.ubcic.bc.ca/files/PDF/Tobias_whole.pdf .

38 Tlen, *Kluane Southern Tutchone Glossary*, 8.

39 Joe Johnson, focus group interview with Southern Tutchone Lhù'ààn Mân Kéyi Elders by Alyce Johnson, August 24, 2009, a videography research project, Kluane First Nation Chief and Council Chambers, Burwash Landing, Yukon.

40 Ruppert and Berner, *Our Voices*, 193.

41 Ibid., 193.

42 Johnson, focus group interview, August 24, 2009.

43 Margaret Johnson, personal discussion, 2004.

44 Johnson, focus group interview, August 24, 2009.

45 The term "knowledges" pluralizes individuality as a collectivity as Elders bring their narratives into a collective narrative that remembers places, spaces, and peoples.

46 Daniel Tlen in Cruikshank, *Life Lived*; Cruikshank, *Do Glaciers Listen?*, 4. Frederick Schwatka (1891) also validates a similar story, which is in Arland S. Harris, *Schwatka's Last Search* (Fairbanks, AK: University of Alaska Press, 1996).

47 Ätäya translates into my maternal "uncle."

48 Margaret Johnson, interview by Alyce Johnson, personal discussion at Bighorn, Kluane National Park, Burwash Landing, Yukon, 2004. Curtis Carlick,
my grandson, received this name from my mother in 1997.

49 Cruikshank, *Do Glaciers Listen?*; McClellan, *My Old People Say*; Tlen, *Kluane
Southern Tutchone Glossary.*

50 Marcia Pablo, "Preservation as Perpetuation: Native Voices," *American
Indian Quarterly* 25, no. 1 (2000): 18–20, http://muse.jhu.edu.cat1.lib.trentu
.ca:8080/journals/american_indian_quarterly/v025/25.1pablo.pd; Stevenson,
"Decolonizing Tribal Histories."

51 Kluane First Nation, "Land Claims Negotiations," main table, transcriptions
SR234-18, 2001/113, cassette 2/3, September 25, 1997, transcription review by
Alyce Johnson (Burwash Landing: Kluane First Nation, 1997).

52 Cruikshank, *Life Lived*, 348.

53 Mary Easterson, *Potlatches: The Sourthern Tutchone Way* (Vancouver: Copy
Copy, 1992), 4–5.

54 Cruikshank, *Do Glaciers Listen?*, 68.

55 Cruikshank, "Glaciers and Climate Change," 56.

56 Cruikshank, *Life Lived Like a Story.*

57 Cruikshank, *Do Glaciers Listen?*

58 Ibid., 51.

59 Easterson, *Potlatches*, 5.

60 Kenneth Coates, "Indian Participation in the Economy," a draft discussion
paper prepared for the Yukon Economic Development Strategy Fall Conference, Whitehorse, 1986; Cruikshank, "The Gravel Magnet"; Tlen and Moore,
"Indigenous Linguistics."

61 Tlen and Moore, "Indigenous Linguistics."

62 Cruikshank, *Life Lived Like a Story*, 354.

63 Kluane First Nation, undated transcripts: Jessie Joe and Copper Lily Johnson,
transcribed by Alyce Johnson, 2004, 10.

64 Tlen and Moore, "Indigenous Linguistics," 282.

65 Ibid., 267.

66 Joe Johnson, personal discussion, 2009.

67 Judith G. Bartlett et al., "Framework for Aboriginal-Guided Decolonizing
Research Involving Metis and First Nations Persons with Diabetes," *Social
Sciences and Medicine* 65 (2007), 2375, http://www.elsevier.com/wps/find/
homepage.cws_home.

68 For additional information on this Elders' workshop, review the Council of
Yukon First Nations guidelines at this link: http://www.northerncontami
nants.ca/done/index.html.

69 Lena Johnson, in *Traditional Knowledge Research Guidelines: A Guide for
Researchers in the Yukon. A Report* (Whitehorse: Council for Yukon First
Nations, 2000), 8.

70 Tlen and Moore, "Indigenous Linguistics"; Niclas Burenhult and Stephen Levinson, "Language and Landscape: A Cross-linguistic Perspective," *Language Sciences* 30 (2008): 135–50, http://www.sciencedirect.com.

71 Edward Glave, cited in Julie Cruikshank, "Legend and Landscape: Convergence of Oral and Scientific Traditions in the Yukon Territory," *Arctic Anthropology* 18, no. 2 (1981): 79.

72 Maria Polinsky, "Heritage Language Narratives," in *Heritage Language Education: A New Field Emerging*, ed. Donna Brinton et al. (New York: Routledge, 2008), 149–63.

73 Keith Basso, *Wisdom Sits in Places: Landscape and Language among the Western Apache* (Albuquerque: University of New Mexico Press, 1996); Judith Huggins, Rita Huggins, and Jane M. Jacobs, "Kooramindanjie: Place and the Postcolonial," *History Workshop Journal* 39 (1995): 167.

74 Joe Johnson, focus group interview with Southern Tutchone Lhù'ààn Mân Kéyi Elders by Alyce Johnson, August 24, 2009; Burenhult and Levinson, "Language and Landscape," 138.

75 Martin Ball, "People Speaking Silently to Themselves: An Examination of Keith Basso's Philosophical Speculations on Sense of *Place* in Apache Cultures," *American Indian Quarterly* 26, no. 3 (Summer 2003): 460–78; Cruikshank, "Glaciers and Climate Change"; Rupert Ross, *Dancing with a Ghost: Exploring Indian Reality* (Markham: Octopus, 1992).

76 John W. Frieson, "The Function of Legends as Teaching Tool," *Interchange* 30, no. 3 (1999): 307.

77 Ruppert and Berner, *Our Voices*, 193.

78 McClellan, "My Old Peoples Stories," 93.

79 Archibald, *Indigenous Storywork*.

Bibliography

Archibald, Jo-Ann Q'um Q'um Xiiem. *Indigenous Storywork: Educating the Heart, Mind, Body, and Spirit*. Vancouver: UBC Press, 2008.

Ball, Martin W. "People Speaking Silently to Themselves: An Examination of Keith Basso's Philosophical Speculations on Sense of *Place* in Apache Cultures." *American Indian Quarterly* 26, no. 3 (Summer 2003): 460–78.

Bartlett, Judith G., Yoshitaka Iwasaki, Benjamin Gottlieb, Darlene Hall, and Roger Mannel. "Framework for Aboriginal-Guided Decolonizing Research Involving Metis and First Nations Persons with Diabetes." *Social Sciences and Medicine* 65, no. 12 (2007): 2371–82. http://www.elsevier.com/wps/find/homepage.cws_home.

Basso, Keith. *Wisdom Sits in Places: Landscape and Language among the Western Apache*. Albuquerque: University of New Mexico Press, 1996.

Burenhult, Niclas, and Stephen Levinson. "Language and Landscape: A Cross-linguistic Perspective." *Language Sciences* 30, nos. 2 and 3 (2008): 135–50. http://www.sciencedirect.com .

Cajete, Gregory. *Native Science: Natural Laws of Interdependence.* Sante Fe: Clear Light Publishers, 2000.

Chamberlain, J. Edward. "From Hand to Mouth: The Postcolonial Politics of Oral and Written Traditions." In *Reclaiming Indigenous Voice and Vision*, edited by Marie Battiste, 124–41. Vancouver: UBC Press, 2000.

Coates, Kenneth. "Indian Participation in the Economy." A draft discussion paper prepared for the Yukon Economic Development Strategy Fall Conference, Whitehorse, 1986.

Council for Yukon First Nations. "Traditional Knowledge Research Guidelines: A Guide for Researchers." Whitehorse: Council for Yukon First Nations, 2000. http://www.northerncontaminants.ca/done/index.html.

Cruikshank, Julie. *Do Glaciers Listen? Local Knowledge, Colonial Encounters & Social Imagination.* Vancouver: UBC Press, 2005.

———. "Glaciers and Climate Change." *Arctic* 54, no. 4 (2001): 377–93. http://pubs.aina.ucalgary.ca/arctic/Arctic54-4-377.pdf.

———. "The Gravel Magnet: Some Social Impacts of the Alaska Highway on Yukon Indians." Paper presented at the Alaska Highway Conference, Fort St. John, June 18–20, 1982.

———. "Legend and Landscape: Convergence of Oral and Scientific Traditions in the Yukon Territory." *Arctic Anthropology* 18, no. 2 (1981): 67–90.

———. *Life Lived Like a Story: Life Stories of Three Native Elders.* Vancouver: UBC Press, 1990.

———. *The Social Life of Stories: Narrative and Knowledge in the Yukon Territory.* Vancouver: UBC Press, 1998.

Easterson, Mary. *Potlatches: The Southern Tutchone Way.* Vancouver: Copy Copy, 1992.

Frieson, John W. "The Function of Legends as a Teaching Tool." *Interchange* 30, no. 3 (1999): 305–22.

Gengenbach, Heidi. *Where Women Make History: Women as Makers and Tellers of History in Magude, Mozambique.* West Sussex, UK: Columbia University Press, 2005.

Glave, Edward. "Our Alaska Expedition." *Frank Leslie's Illustrated Newspaper 70* (November 22, 1890). Cited in Julie Cruikshank, "Legend and Landscape: Convergence of Oral and Scientific Traditions in the Yukon Territory." *Arctic Anthropology* 18, no. 2 (1981): 67–90.

Grande, Sandy. *Red Pedagogy: Native American Social and Political Thought.* Lanham: Rowman and Littlefield, 2004. http://www.gutenberg-e.org/geh01/geh08.html.

Huggins, Judith, Rita Huggins, and Jane M. Jacobs. "Kooramindanjie: Place and the Postcolonial." *History Workshop Journal* 39, no. 1 (1995): 165–80.

Hume, Andrew. "Johnson Tells Inquiry: I Feel Like I Was Planted Here." *Whitehorse Star*, June 3, 1977.

Johnson, Joe. "Discussions at K'àma Dzêa. Kluane First Nation Traditional Territory." Site Visitation Notes. Burwash Landing: Kluane First Nation, 2004.

————. Focus group interview with Southern Tutchone Lhù'ààn Mân Kéyi Elders by Alyce Johnson, August 24, 2009, a videography research project, Kluane First Nation Chief and Council Chambers, Burwash Landing.

————. Kluane First Nation Land Claim Negotiations: Main Table. Transcriptions: SR234-18. 2001/113. Cassette 2/3, 4. Transcription review by Alyce Johnson. Burwash Landing: Kluane First Nation, September 25, 1997.

Johnson, Lena. A focus group interview with Southern Tutchone Lhù'ààn Mân Kéyi Elders, August 24. A videography research project. Burwash Landing: Kluane First Nation Chief and Council Chambers, 2009.

————. Discussions at K'àma Dzêa. Notes. Burwash Landing: Kluane First Nation, 2004.

————. In *Traditional Knowledge Research Guidelines: A Guide for Researchers in the Yukon*. A Report. Whitehorse: Council for Yukon First Nations, 2000, 8.

Johnson, Margaret. A conversation with Alyce Johnson. Personal communication, Burwash Landing, 2005.

————. Discussions with Alyce Johnson at K'àma Dzêa. Personal communication, Burwash Landing, Kluane First Nation, 2004.

————. A focus group interview with SouthernTutchone Lhù'ààn Mân Kéyi Elders, August 24. A videography research project. Burwash Landing: Kluane First Nation Chief and Council Chambers, 2009.

Johnston, Basil. "One Generation from Extinction." *Native Writers and Canadian Literature* 19, no. 199 (1990): 10–15. http://cinema2.arts.ubc.ca/units/canlit/pdfs/articles/canlit124-Generation(Johnston).pdf.

Kluane First Nation. Land Claim Negotiations: Main Table. Transcriptions: SR234-18. 2001/113. Cassette 2/3. September 25. Transcription review by Alyce Johnson. Burwash Landing: Kluane First Nation, 1997.

————. Undated transcripts of Jessie Joe and Copper Lily Johnson. Transcribed by Alyce Johnson, 2004, 10.

McClellan, Catherine. "Before Boundaries: People of the Yukon/Alaska." A conference paper. Whitehorse, 1989.

————. *My Old People Say: An Ethnographic Survey of Southern Yukon Territory*, Parts 1 and 2. Ottawa: Canadian Museum of Civilization, 2001. Originally published by National Museums of Canada, Ottawa, 1975.

————. "My Old Peoples Stories: A Legacy for Yukon First Nations. Part I: Southern Tutchone Narrators." *Occasional Papers in Yukon History* 5, no. 1 (2007). http://www.tc.gov.yk.ca/pdf/mcclellan_opyh_5(1).pdf.

McLeod, Neal. *Cree Narrative Memory: From Treaties to Contemporary Times*. Saskatoon: Purich, 2007.

Nida, Eugene A. *Language Structure and Translation*. Stanford: Stanford University Press, 1975.

Pablo, Marcia. 2000. "Preservation as Perpetuation: Native Voices." *American Indian Quarterly* 25, no. 1 (2000): 18–20. http://muse.jhu.edu.cat1.lib.trentu.ca:8080/journals/american_indian_quarterly/v025/25.1pablo.pd.

Polinsky, Maria. "Heritage Language Narratives." In *Heritage Language Education: A New Field Emerging*, edited by Donna Brinton, Olga Kagan, and Susan Baukus, 149–63. New York: Routledge, 2008.

Raikai, Mele Estella Tupou. "A Neutral Framework for Modelling and Analysing Aboriginal Land Tenure Systems." *Technical Report* no. 227. University of New Brunswick, 2005. http://gge.unb.ca/Pubs/TR227.pdf.

Reyhner, Jon, and Edward Tennant. Maintaining and Renewing Native Languages. *Bilingual Research Journal* 19, no. 2 (1995): 279–304. http://jan.ucc.nau.edu/~jar/Main.html.

Ritchie, Donald. *Doing Oral History: A Practical Guide Using Interviews to Uncover the Past and Preserve It for the Future.* New York: Oxford University Press, 2003.

Ross, Rupert. *Dancing with a Ghost: Exploring Indian Reality.* Markham: Octopus, 1992.

Ruppert, James, and John W. Berner. *Our Voices: Native Stories of Alaska and the Yukon.* Lincoln: University of Nebraska Press, 2001.

Settee, Patricia. *Pimatisiwin: Indigenous Knowledge Systems, Our Time Has Come.* Ph.D. diss., University of Saskatchewan, 2007.

Smith, Linda Tuhiwai. *Decolonizing Methodologies: Research and Indigenous Peoples.* New York: Zed, 2001.

Stevenson, Winona L. "Decolonizing Tribal Histories." Ph.D. diss., University of California, 2000.

Tlen, Daniel. *Kluane Southern Tutchone Glossary English to Southern Tutchone.* Whitehorse: Northern Research Institute, 1993.

Tlen, Daniel, and Patrick Moore. "Indigenous Linguistics and Land Claims: The Semiotic Projection of Athapaskan Directionals in Elijah Smith's Radio Work." *Journal of Linguistic Anthropology* 17, no. 2 (2007): 266–86.

Tobias, Terry N. *Chief Kerry's Moose: A Guide to Land Use and Occupancy Mapping, Research Design, and Data Collecting.* Vancouver: Union of Indian British Columbia Chiefs' Ecotrust Canada, 2010. http://www.ubcic.bc.ca/files/PDF/Tobias_whole.pdf.

13

"Pimuteuat/Ils marchent/They Walk": A Few Observations on Indigenous Poetry and Poetics in French

Michèle Lacombe

Many Indigenous poets from a wide group of First Nations in Quebec are publishing in French, although in this chapter I limit myself to work by Innu poets Joséphine Bacon and Rita Mestokosho. My interpretation of a few of their poems draws further attention to their writing, but also introduces several issues concerning the readership for Indigenous poetry written in French. Briefly, I address the difficult question of translation and self-translation, whether from Indigenous languages to French or from French to English; I consider the nature of recent collaboration between Indigenous and non-Indigenous writers using French; I comment on linguistic challenges facing Indigenous poets educated in French (whether or not they attended residential school); and I translate a few words from Mestokosho and Bacon as well as by francophone scholars who speak to the critical reception of Indigenous creative writing in that language. In the process, I turn to the metaphor of walking to suggest the continuous and discontinuous movement between ancestral understandings based in Indigenous languages and cultures and the coexistence of such knowledge with European languages and urban cultures.

My title is inspired by two passages. The first is the opening lines of Louise Halfe's *Blue Marrow*:

The walk began before I was a seed.
My mother strung my umbilical cord in my moccasins...

Soon the mountain too had feet...
âstam, she said [come, come here].[1]

The second is from the title and opening line of Joséphine Bacon's poem "Pimuteuat" (They Walk), from which I quote later in the chapter.[2] In both cases, I read these poems as referring not only to the ancestors' life on the land, and to changing circumstances that have affected the speaker, but also to walking as a contemporary metaphor for poetic movement. Words that walk—whether in referential, metaphorical, translated, spoken, or dialogical language—point in a number of different directions that are more or less accessible to the reader, depending on her or his own experiences and language skills. Indigenous poetics allows for a wide range of linguistic, formal, and rhetorical strategies, realigning the contemporary poetic voice with older forms of storytelling. For me, the rhythms of the poetic foot, sometimes moccasined and sometimes not—rhythms associated with the heartbeat, with human breath, and with dancing in Indigenous and other languages—are embodied in "words that walk."

When Armand Garnet Ruffo toured Australia in 2003, together with Indigenous writers from across Canada who had been invited by the Canada Council to participate in an exchange with Indigenous writers from Australia, the list of those from Canada included only one name that he didn't recognize—Rita Mestokosho, an Innu poet from Ekuanitshit (Mingan) in northeastern Quebec. Given that many Innu communities' experiences of residential schools included being taught in French, it is not surprising that Mestokosho's second language (after Innu) is French rather than English. And because the Indigenous writers from Canada and Australia who first met as part of this exchange spoke little, if any, French, Mestokosho read from her work in Innu. Ruffo comments on the irony that "'one of our own' stood on the periphery of our literary family" in a collective speaking tour meant "to forge links with other Indigenous writers."[3]

An example of forging links with other writers is found in the 2008 anthology *Mots de neige, de sable et d'océan*, in which Mauricio Gatti brings together French-language work by Wendat, Innu, Atikamekw, Anishnaabe, Wabanaki, Amasigh, Kabyle, Ma'ohi, and Kanak Indigenous writers from Quebec, Algeria, Morocco, French Polynesia, and New Caledonia, many of whom are not familiar with English-speaking Indigenous writers from former colonies in their part of the world. Tomson Highway's French-language preface to this book opens with the following words: "C'est toujours un défi d'écrire dans une langue qui n'est pas sa langue maternelle. C'est toujours un défi de *devoir* écrire dans une langue qui n'est pas sa langue maternelle" (It is always challenging to write in a language other than one's mother tongue. It is always challenging to *have* to write in a language other than one's mother tongue).[4] A fluent speaker of French, Highway celebrates Indigenous literature in all of its manifestations.

The usefulness of the 2008 Wendake workshop at which Highway spoke, which brought together Indigenous writers from Quebec and "la francophonie" and led to the publication of Gatti's anthology, inspired Heather MacFarlane, Jennifer Andrews, and me to produce a special section of *Studies in Canadian Literature* on "Indigeneity in Dialogue: Indigenous Literary Expression Across Linguistic Divides." In Wendake Heather and I witnessed the convergence of shared perspectives on "Indigenous world views, experiences of European colonialisms, patterns of resistance, and interest in how oral literatures relate to writing" despite the differences in former French colonies from various parts of the world where Indigenous authors now publish in French and sometimes also in their original languages. We felt that if "it was possible to organize internationally focused initiatives such as the gathering in Wendake, surely it must be possible to foster similar exchanges between French- and English-speaking Indigenous writers not separated by oceans."[5] While French-English language barriers are difficult to overcome at gatherings, the work of translation cannot help but facilitate dialogue between Indigenous poets in Canada. That said, translation undertaken by Innu poets themselves, while preferable, is not always possible, and in any case, their priorities as writers may lie elsewhere. And while academics (especially those who, like me, do not speak an Indigenous language) can play a useful role in promoting the work of translation, we remain primarily literary critics rather than translators.[6] For its part, government advocacy for translation of Indigenous literature is not as high profile as the translation of Canadian literature—two categories that some readers view as overlapping—although the Canada Council has supported such efforts.

Tomson Highway reminds us that it is possible to write in Cree—he has published many of his own plays in that language, as well as in English, for instance—but that the readership for Cree publications remains small, something that French-Innu bilingual texts such as Josephine Bacon's book of poems aim to address. Saskatchewan writer Freda Ahenakew, for example, has translated and edited bilingual books of stories and speeches. Highway's parents did not speak English, and he explains that when he writes, the voices come to him in Cree, and the words are transcribed into English and sometimes into French on his keyboard in a painful, difficult process that he describes as simultaneous translation: "Je les entends dans ma langue maternelle, mais leurs mots doivent sortir en anglais sur l'écran de mon ordinateur" (I hear them in my mother tongue, but their words are screened into English on my computer's monitor). Highway speaks of similarities between languages such as Innu and Cree, and of how words spoken in northern Manitoba and Saskatchewan belong to the same family as "ceux de Maliotenam, de Mashteuiatsh, de Wemotaci et de Ekuanit-shit." He insists that Cree is the funniest of languages: "La langue cri est beaucoup plus drôle—cent fois plus drôle!—que la langue anglaise, que je trouve trop lourde." For him, English comes from the head and Cree from the body, from the Earth. When prompted, he playfully suggests that French, for its part, comes from somewhere in between.[7] Cree poets from western Canada tend to write in English and sometimes in Cree, while Innu poets from Quebec tend to write in French and sometimes in Innu. During group discussion at the Sounding Out Indigenous poetics conference organized by Neal McLeod and that led to the publication of this book, Louise Halfe indicated that she had met Mestokosho, and that she, too, recognizes the similarities between Cree and Innu words. But for those readers of Halfe and Mestokosho who do not speak an Indigenous language, translation between French and English remains important. And for Indigenous poets from Quebec such as Huron-Wendat writers who did not grow up speaking either Huron or English, translation from the French is vital for their work to achieve wider circulation.

Mauricio Gatti, who has edited the first anthology of Indigenous authors from Quebec, *Littérature amérindienne du Québec: Écrits de langue française*, explains in his introduction that his use of the adjective "francophone" does not necessarily refer to an Indigenous writer whose mother tongue is French or who is French-identified, but rather to someone who expresses himself in that language at least some of the time. His anthology includes selections from twenty-eight Innu, Algonquin, Cree, Huron-Wendat, Atikamekw, Mohawk, and Métis writers of stories, poems, novels, theatre, and life-writing. Gatti sees francophone Indigenous writing from the 1960s and earlier as emphasizing protest, testimonial, and historical narrative, and recent literature as increasingly focused on poetics and creativity. He suggests that the readership for and research on this work remains in a preliminary stage in Quebec.[8] A second book based on Gatti's Ph.D. dissertation, "Être écrivain amérindien au Québec: Indianité et création littéraire," looks at European influences on Indigenous literature, but also conceives of French-language Indigenous writing on its own terms. Gatti is interested in questions of production and reception as well as definitions of who is an Indigenous author.[9] The book's two long chapters address questions of identity and contexts for the emergence of writing in French. The section on identities discusses tradition and modernity, the Indian Act, manifestations of colonialism, and issues of authenticity.

The section on contexts for writing considers the relationship of orality to writing and the vitality of creative writing in a world characterized by the urgent need for political intervention.

Gatti's comments about Rita Mestokosho suggest that living, speaking, and writing in Innu, in her home community of Ekuanitshit (Mingan), shapes her being and her writing as a poet. He notes that she thinks in Innu and translates her thoughts into French. He cites Matimekosh community member Lisa-Marie Gabriel on Innu people's complex relationship with language; he also compares their use of French to that of "minority context" writers such as Acadian and Franco-Ontarian poets, and to poetry by recent immigrants who write in French. Gatti sees similarities between Innu writers' French language use (including what I would call reserve French) and that associated with contemporary Québécois youth, who speak and understand several registers of French, including standard international French with a Quebec accent and the urban working-class dialect known as *joual*.[10] In my experience, educated French youth sometimes consciously and playfully mix English words into spoken French, referred to as *franglais*, and in this sense their language no less than their culture is characterized by what post-colonial theorists refer to as hybridity and French critics as *métissage*. Their Facebook French also frequently resembles spoken French, but in Quebec as elsewhere, written French— with the exception of joual literature in the 1960s or dialogue in novels— remains more formal and grammatically correct.[11] For many Indigenous writers and especially for poets, I might add, the influence of French teachers in residential school, combined with sensitivities in Quebec about the difference between supposedly "superior" European and "inferior" North American French, leads them to adopt a more formal language. Facing Eurocentric prejudice that to this day still assumes they are incapable of abstract thought or a sophisticated style, they sometimes feel constrained to mimic conventional poetic, grammar, diction, and verse forms in order to be heard at all. My sense is that there is still an expectation that in order to be taken seriously as poets, Innu poets' French language use and literary experimentation—while original, innovative, and inclusive of Innu words—must in style and grammar be consistent with the usages of Québécois poets who define the norm.

When it comes to a sense of place, Gatti makes comparisons with Quebec immigrants and with other francophone communities, at the same time that he references the sense of home of both rural and urban Innu writers, as well as overlap between these, citing Innu historian Jean-Louis Fontaine, author of a book on Innu rituals and beliefs in the early seventeenth century, among other texts.[12] Gatti also invokes Drew Taylor's book

Funny You Don't Look Like One, which is about cultural stereotyping based on physical traits such as dark hair, eyes, and skin, in his own observations about how Mestokosho's appearance appeals to Europeans and Québécois who identify such features with misguided notions of exotic, "authentic" Indians. He goes on to suggest that it is the community of Indigenous writers that is best positioned to speak to the Indigenous identity of its members in the face of such stereotypes in the culture at large.[13] In this context Gatti speaks of the important relation between individual and collective expression in Innu writing as exemplified in Mestokosho's work.[14] Access to publishers, critical reception of their work, and participation in national and international poetry festivals or conferences are also mentioned; here, exchanges between Indigenous and other writers, both mainstream and marginalized, at once depend on and enhance cross-cultural dialogue.

Gatti cites poets such as Louise Halfe and Kateri Damm, among others, concerning some of the challenges facing Indigenous writers.[15] He concludes that Indigenous writing is slowly becoming visible compared to better-known English, French, and "immigrant" writing. He reminds us of the pluralism of Indigenous writing in French, his chosen focus. Were we to compare French and English literature based on similar languages such as Cree and Innu, it would be interesting to revisit the impact of Anglican and Catholic missions, given that these two denominations were both active in Saskatchewan Cree and Quebec Innu country. In particular, Catholic Oblate missionaries' mixed legacy included the compilation of dictionaries, sermons, and other proselytising tools in both Cree and Innu. The French-Swiss Oblate missionary Louis Babel (1826–1912), for instance, spent his life among the Innu from 1866 onwards. Manuscript versions of his Innu language texts are in the Oblate Archives in Ottawa, while the University of Manitoba archives hold documents pertaining to the Catholic Oblates among the Cree. Unlike Cree, which uses syllabics, and unlike the double-vowel system used in Anishinaabemowin orthography, Innu-Aimun (due to the French influence) primarily uses Roman orthography, although there are variations within its transcription.[16] Diane Boudreau, to my knowledge the only other person besides Gatti to publish a monograph on Indigenous writing in Quebec, briefly discusses the nineteenth century in her 1993 book *Histoire de la littérature amérindienne au Québec*, mentioning the influence of clergy and their collaborative work on Indigenous language dictionaries, but she stresses Abenaki more than Innu contexts.[17]

In contrast to the situation in western Canada, one interesting development in books of poetry by Indigenous authors recently published in Quebec has to do with the emergence, in francophone publishing circles, of co-publications, collective work, and side-by-side edited volumes in which

Indigenous poets and non-Indigenous poets encounter or talk about each other's work. Perhaps this is influenced by the fact that unlike other provinces, Quebec carries an extra layer of political and cultural identification for many of its inhabitants for whom it is the heartland of French Canada, if not of the Quebec "nation." Such co-publication projects entail awareness, on the part of their editors and contributors, of the complex dialogue (or lack of dialogue) between federal, provincial, and First Nations representatives in the Quebec context. Besides foregrounding literary expression, these side-by-side editions of Euro-Canadian and Indigenous writing serve to sensitize a francophone readership about the legitimacy as well as the particular perspectives of Indigenous literary voices that all too often have been overlooked or distorted in the midst of ongoing French-English political and linguistic debates. This complicated, frequently chilly cultural climate is not unrelated to age-old debates, alluded to above, about whether formal French or local colloquialisms are more suitable in Quebec literature. As mentioned, like the role of residential school, this climate may contribute to many Indigenous authors' use of what is perceived as "proper" French. However, it also leads to new forms of cross-cultural dialogue, while providing Indigenous authors with additional publication venues.

In 2010, the Quebec quarterly poetry magazine *Exit: revue de poésie* (no. 59), for instance, devoted half of its space to Indigenous writers. In this issue the magazine's editor, the Quebec poet and critic Stéphane Despatie, borrows the title of his introduction to the issue from the 2008 book of poetry by the Huron-Wendat poet Jean Sioui, *L'avenir voit rouge* (The Future Sees Red). Despatie opens with the following questions:

> Est-ce que la poésie est toujours clairvoyante ou bien est-elle parfois trop centrée sur elle-même pour voir le reste et s'intéresser aux autres? Est-elle tendue vers l'avenir, attachée au passé ou bien ficelée sur le dos de l'instant présent? Peut-être marche-t-elle en équilibre sur un fil de fer qui passe au-dessus du temps, mais au milieu des drames comme de la beauté.[18]
>
> (Is poetry always clear-sighted, or is it sometimes too inwardly focused to recognize the balance and take interest in others? Is it stretched to the future, attached to the past, or strung up on the present moment? Maybe it is a balancing act, walking that high-wire line floating above the present, in the midst of drama no less than of beauty.)

The section on Indigenous poets, entitled "Dialogue," is introduced by Jean-François Létourneau, and includes work by Joséphine Bacon and Rita Mestokosho as well as twelve other poets, spanning several generations, whose work appears in magazines and sometimes in book form. Létourneau's introduction to the section begins with the following unattributed quotation:

"Marcher, c'est caresser le pays avec ses pieds" (To walk is to caress the land with one's feet). He views the issue and its contents as an open invitation "à la découverte de l'autre en soi, à l'exploration du territoire rêvé et réel afin de colmater la brèche qui nous sépare du pays sur lequel nous marchons, chaque jour de nos vies" (to the discovery of the other within oneself, the exploration of landscapes real and imagined, so as to breach the divide that separates us from the land upon which we walk, each and every day of our lives).[19]

Reviewing the *Exit* volume under the title "Debout après la folie" (Still standing after the craziness), the Quebec novelist Louis Hamelin, a frequent commentator on Indigenous writing, illustrates ongoing prejudices and stereotypes evident in some reactions to Innu singer-songwriter Kathia Rock's electric dance moves at a barbeque attended by beer-swilling Québécois. After invoking earlier responses to the Oka Crisis and Meech Lake, Hamelin underscores how poetry publications "proposent de commencer à rebâtir, en jetant, entre le rêve et les communautés réelles, des passerelles tissées d'images patients et de mots fragile, comme autants d'arc-en-ciel au milieu d'une embellie" (suggest that we start rebuilding, interjecting gateways—woven of patient images and fragile words—between living communities and the dream, like so many rainbows in a clearing sky).[20] For Hamelin, twenty years or so after Oka, and in the wake of a much older set of injustices and prejudices, a new kind of poetic voice and dialogue, one no longer preoccupied primarily with the decolonization of the Québécois imagination, is slowly beginning to emerge in Quebec, even as it remains difficult to circumvent the sexualized and objectifying gaze of those segments of the public and the journalistic profession who are more interested in spectacle than in poetry.

Véronique Audet's book about Innu music, *Innu Nikamu—L'Innu Chante: Pouvoir des chants, identité et guérison chez les Innus*, which mentions Innu poets and novelists, also helps to counter uninformed audience and media responses to Indigenous songwriting and public performances by Innu artists in Quebec. Audet describes the lengthy, introspective, and consultative process by which Kathia Rock took up the traditional Innu hand-drum associated with male singers, eventually using it in performances for diverse audiences—a move not without controversy in certain segments of her community. She discusses the struggles and contributions of many Innu musicians from the 1950s to the present, and includes a CD compilation of representative performers in her book. Popular artists such as Quebec singer-songwriter Chloé Sainte-Marie have helped Innu poets and musicians reach a wider audience, and Audet lists Sainte-Marie's renditions of Innu songs in her bibliography. In albums such as *Je Marche à toi* (I walk to/toward you), for instance, Sainte-Marie offers her version of the Innu songs "E pamutelan epeikussian/Promenade Solitaire Innu"; she also draws attention to the poetry of Joséphine Bacon by setting it to music.

In a recent anthology of creative writing featuring work by Indigenous and non-Indigenous poets and the collaboration of an Indigenous and a mainstream publisher, a CD is also included with the book. This compilation, *Les Bruits du monde (livre-disque)* [People Sounds/World Sounds (a sound-book)], was co-published in 2013 by the Institut Tshakapesh in Mani-Utenam and Mémoire d'encrier in Montreal.[21] This is only the latest of a number of anthologies that bring together the work of Indigenous and Québécois poets, a phenomenon that merits further comment. On the one hand, there is much more such cross-cultural collaborative work taking place between Innu and Euro-Canadian poets in Quebec, largely edited by non-Indigenous people. On the other hand, examples of co-publications that bring together French-speaking and English-speaking Indigenous poets and writers in Canada are to my knowledge still non-existent, although my research does not extend to Inuit work. In considering the perspective of cross-cultural publications in Quebec, I turn to one of the first and most influential of these, the book *Aimitiau! Parlons-Nous!*, edited by the writer and critic Laure Morali, who pairs up fifteen Indigenous and non-Indigenous poets invited to engage in poetic dialogue.

Morali, who, like Gatti, immigrated to Canada and settled in Quebec some years ago, is a well-known poet and editor who also has done much for the world of Indigenous writing in French. The Innu word *aimitau* [*sic*] means "she/he reads it," while *Parlons-Nous* can be translated as "let's talk to/of one another." In the words of Innu poet Joséphine Bacon, "Kashikat ishinakuan tshetshi mamu aimiaku tshetshi nishtuapetamaku tan mamu e ishinikashiaku—Aujourd'hui, il est important de se parler pour que nous sachions comment, tous ensemble, nous nous appelons" [Today, it is important to talk to one another so that together we can discover how we are named].[22] Morali's book has led to new books of poems by Mestokosho and Bacon, also co-written with non-Indigenous poets. The exchange of poems between José Acquelin and Joséphine Bacon in *Aimititau!* led to the publication of their book *Nous sommes tous des sauvages* [We are all savages] in 2011. According to Louis Hamelin, in the afterword entitled "Développement sauvage,"

> Nous n'avons pas affaire, dans ce livre, malgré les apparences, à une simple suite de poèmes croisés. On pourrait d'ailleurs se demander à quoi rimerait une telle démarche: une vraie correspondence dans le régistre poétique est-elle seulement possible? Il n'y a pas, ici, d'échange au sens strict, dynamique du terme, et si les textes se répondent, c'est presque toujours indirectment, chacun dans son style, sur des ponts qu'il revient en grande partie au lecteur de tisser.[23]

(Appearances notwithstanding, we are not dealing with a simple suite of crossed poems in this book. Indeed, we might ask ourselves what such a move would rhyme with: can a true correspondence even exist in the poetic register? Here is no exchange in the strict, dynamic sense of the term. If texts answer one another, it is almost always indirectly, each in its own style, and across bridges spun mostly by the reader.)

I do not agree with Hamelin's commentary on these two poets when he sets up what I see as a binary opposition and contrast between Acquelin's "pensée ludique" and love of paradox and the invocation of "pensée traditionelle" and spirituality in Bacon.[24] In my view, Bacon's work, while it reflects traditional Indigenous knowledge, is also characterized by language play and a philosophical understanding of paradox.

The flourishing of literary friendships, intertextual exchanges, and poetic experiments emerging from *Aimititau!* is also evident in the publication of *Uashtessiu/Lumière d'automne* (Autumn lights) by Jean Désy and Rita Mestokosho, who first met at the *Aimititau* book launch in the Innu community of Mashteuiatsh—they each had been paired with another poet in Morali's book. *Uashtessiu* is epistolary poetry (correspondence or letters in the form of poetry, sometimes presented as call and response). At times lyrical and at other times more pointed, it takes the form of a poetic conversation between an Innu poet who lives in her First Nations community on the lower north shore of the St. Lawrence, and a French-Québécois poet and medical doctor who practised in the Mingan area and whose summer camp in that region is near her reserve. Both are seasoned travellers and cultural ambassadors with an abiding sense of their own home-place and the need to protect it from environmental threats. Reading this exchange, I am struck by how much common ground appears in their poetic dialogue spanning the seasons from spring to winter. Désy contributes the prologue contextualizing the exchange, Mestokosho the epilogue in the form of a prayer; in between, reading each other's letter-poems sparks further work, and also gives voice to his hopes of their once again crossing paths.

Despite common interests, however, I also note differences that disturb. Désy expresses his love of the land and his visceral experience of the seasonal extremes on the rivers that flow into the St. Lawrence, at the same time that he wishes to partake of an Innu world view that—however different from his own—he tends to universalize. Mestokosho, for her part, while reminding us that "la poesie instaure un langage universel" (poetry inaugurates a universal language)[25] firmly insists both on particularity and on a greater measure of collective autonomy for her people, as well as solidarity with those who are not Innu when it comes to defending Innu territory and the Innu language. If the book traces the trajectory of each poet's day to day thoughts and activities through the seasons by means of the cross-fertilization of their poetic exchanges over time, it also offers new and exciting work by Mestokosho, some of it in Innu. The fact that these lines written in Innu are not always rendered into French is somehow—at least for me—reassuring. The francophone reader can still follow pathways from one poet's words to another, witnessing thoughts and feelings whose voicing is sometimes heated, sometimes lyrical, sometimes ironic, and always engaging. The generous, hard work of friendship here reminds me of Joséphine Bacon's own teasing and caustic comments about friendship in an exchange with Chloé Sainte-Marie on the occasion of a group reading that included poetic tributes to Bacon and other poets.[26]

While Désy sticks to French, Mestokosho liberally sprinkles a few English as well as Innu words into her text. My sense is that in this book Mestokosho, while still employing formal French, fortuitously turns to free verse and the epistolary format to introduce more fluid and colloquial speech rhythms into her poetry. Here is a quote from her poem "On the Road Again 2"[27] from the spring segment of the book. The English title of this poem, like its French body, belies its Innu cultural knowledge and spirit:

Je crois bien
sur la route, sur la mer—
sur mes pieds
je scrute mes pas
qui avancent et reculent
par l'eau salée
par les rivières dénudés
par le gravier du coin
par les sentiers de mon coeur
mais surtout
c'est mon âme
qui sourit depuis ce matin

je crois bien
que le poème est la survie
de nos âmes nomades... [28]

(Well do I believe[29]
on the road, on the sea
on my feet
scanning my feet
moving back and forth
by salt water

by denuded rivers
by banked gravel[30]
by the pathways of my heart
above all
my soul
smiling since morning

Well do I believe
that the poem is survival
of our nomad souls…)

Flying, swimming, walking, dancing, riding, driving—these activities have, like dreaming, long functioned as inspiration and metaphor for poetic movement; in Indigenous world views, they also possess specific resonances associated with the land, the animals, and their spirits. I am especially interested in the ways in which this passage from Mestokosho's poem invokes the vocabulary of walking (including paths, roads, tracks, and traces). She brings together images from land and water and the space in between in ways that resonate for me as someone who grew up in northeastern Quebec, loving its saltwater tide pools in summer and frozen beaches in winter. Mestokosho's work also suggests the ties between the contemporary poet and her ancestors, at the same time that the vitality of traditional homelands and Indigenous languages, while beleaguered, do not keep the poet from pleasurably navigating modernity and playing with an acquired language that has its uses.

In this recent work, Mestokosho builds on her earlier prose poem "La Vie d'un Innu" (The Life of an Innu) from her first collection *Eshi Uapataman Nukum/Recueil de poèmes Montagnais*. The title of this collection translates into French as "Comment je perçois la vie, grand-mère" and into English as "How I see life, grandmother."[31] In this volume, the prose poem "La Vie d'un Innu" speaks of the anticipated meeting of several converging life paths in Innu country:

Dans la vie d'un Innu, il y a deux chemins se défilant devant lui. Le premier est tracé par des pas d'hommes qui ont passé avant lui, ce chemin est lourd car il est profond en peines et en joies aussi. Il prendra ce chemin pour évoluer dans l'environnement où il vit.

L'autre chemin est invisible. Il est tracé par la lumière de la vie. Il peut y accéder par la force de son Mistapéo. Ces deux chemins sont reliés quelque part dans le monde où nous vivons et dans le monde des esprits où nous voyageons par nos rêves.

Quand les deux chemins se rejoindront à ce moment-là, l'Innu se retrouvera lui-même.[32]

(In the life of an Innu, two roads unwind before him. The first is outlined by the footsteps of men who have come before him; this road is hard as it is deep with sorrow and with joy also. He will take this road to evolve in the environment in which he lives.

The other road is invisible. The light of life shows us its traces [tracks]. He can find it by means of his Mistapéo.[33] These two roads join up, somewhere in the world in which we live and in the spirit world where we journey in our dreams.

When these two roads come together, at that moment the Innu will once again find himself.)

Mestokosho's efforts to save the Romaine River from the planned construction of a hydroelectric dam reflect this vision and inspire her poetic work. The Romaine is one of those rivers, like that in her home community, whose estuaries are so lyrically represented in the collection co-written with Jean Désy, and whose lifeblood, as a salmon river, her people depend on. In a January 2010 interview with Christophe Premat, Mestokosho states that on the heels of Morali's project, her next publication project was inspired by her concern about the Romaine, and that the nine-month epistolary exchange grew out of that as well as out of the importance of cross-cultural communication in books such as Aimititau.[34]

In this sense Mestokosho's contributions to collaborative work such as Aimititau and Uashtessiu/Lumière d'automne are consistent with the perspectives of grandmothers and grandfathers associated with her first collection Eshi Uapataman Nukum. Here are the opening words in her entry for Aimititau:

Je t'écris cette lettre pour te parler de la rivière Romaine, celle que j'aime comme ma grande soeur ainée millénaire. Cette rivière est la route qu'empruntaient mes grands-parents pour retourner chez eux. Et chez eux c'est le territoire traditionnel, celui qu'on veut inonder. J'en pleure intérieurement. Car la rivière, c'est le bonheur des Innus. Le saumon y vit encore aujord'hui. Il nage en toute liberté, et c'est à nous de le défendre, de le protéger....[35]

(I am writing this letter to talk to you of the Romaine River. I love her as I love my millenarian older sister. This is the route that my grandparents took to go back home, and it is their traditional homeland that would be flooded. It makes me cry inside. The river represents happiness for the Innu.

Salmon still live there today, swimming freely. It is up to us to defend the salmon, to protect it....)

Mestokosho insists that she did not choose poetry as a vocation, but rather that it chose her. She also finds it more useful than political speeches for defending environmental causes closely allied to Innu people's traditional homelands, although she also works as a councillor for her Innu nation. She adds that she hopes to find allies in other local populations, and is grateful that she can express herself in French, allowing her to translate the import of this battle (traduire le sens de ce combat).[36]

Joséphine Bacon's bilingual Innu-French book of poems *Bâtons à message/Tshissinuashitakana* (Message Sticks) also reflects an understanding of the place of ancestral knowledge in contemporary contexts, although her quiet words leave as much room for a sense of loss and deep sadness as they do for her a sense of continuity, hope, and advocacy in poems such as "Le Nord m'interpelle/ Niepuatik" Tshiuetin" (The North Calls Me), or in her poems about the barricades at "Rapide Lake."[37] Published in 2009, this was Bacon's first book of poems, winning the Montreal People's Poetry Award. For me, Bacon's poem "They Walk," which I cite below, has several meanings. It honours the ancestors as well as those living Innu and Naskapi elders who remember walking over a thousand kilometres overland by snowshoe every year. Families (including young children) paddled and portaged, and also walked from the North Shore of the St. Laurence River to the interior of Nistassinan, all the way to Ungava Bay in what is now Nunavik, following caribou herds and engaging in other seasonal activities, including visits to fur trading posts. Bacon also alludes to the different, postmodern experiences of nomadism, a central metaphor in Innu literature and in the lives of contemporary urban authors and residential school survivors such as herself. Here is the short title poem from Bacon's book in its entirety, given by the poet in French and Innu, followed by my translation from the French:

Ils marchent
sans courbure,
attentifs
aux sons de la neige
sous la raquette

des bâtons
à message
les attendent
au milieu du lac gelé.

Pimuteuat
Shutshi-pimuteuat
natutamuat
tshikashameuat tshetshi
mamakushkahk

tshissinuatshitakana
pakushenitamuat
tekushinitaui
tetau-taushkum.[38]

(They walk
unbending
heeding
the sounds of snow
under their snowshoes

message
sticks
await them
in the middle of the frozen lake.)

The message sticks in her lyric are inseparable from the walking, and both are born of the land and the seasons, intimately tied to knowledge of the darker side of life as well as to love and beauty. Elsewhere, Bacon recites that "Mon peuple est rare, mon peuple est précieux comme un poème sans écriture" ("My people are rare, my people are precious like a poem without writing").[39]

Bacon's friend Laure Morali offers a brief biography and character sketch of the poet in her afterword to the book. Born in 1947 on the road between Betsiamites and Ungava, and orphaned at the age of three, in 1951 Bacon left her home community of Pessimit (not far from Tadoussac) to go to residential school at Mani-utenam (now known as Mani-utenam/ Uashat [Sept-Îles]). She remained there until the age of nineteen, never losing her language. In residential school, the nuns misheard her Innu name Pipin (dragonfly) as the French nickname Bibitte (bug). Morali states that the dragonfly is the housekeeper of Papakassik (Caribou Master)[40] as she cleans the caribou's bones. Utsheu, the fly, is always the first to show up in the shaketent.[41] Bacon has kept the nickname Bibitte. In contrast to Morali's expansiveness, many of Bacon's poems are brief and understated, if not cryptic, in their quiet allusions, such as the following:

Je me suis faite belle
pour qu'on remarque

la moelle de mes os,
survivante d'un récit
qu'on ne raconte pas.

Niminunakuitishun
nuash nishkana tshetshi uapatakaniti
tshetshi pishkapatakaniti
nin eka nita
tshe tipatshimikauian.[42]

(I made myself a beauty
to render noteworthy
my bones' marrow
the survivor of a story
we do not tell.)

According to Morali, when the young Joséphine arrived in Montreal pregnant with her first child after leaving residential school, her hunter friend gave her a baby beaver named Fidel, and this beaver lived in her apartment for three months, eating the furniture. Bacon still lives in Montreal, travelling to Innu country; she has produced documentary films about Innu elders, their language, and their stories. She says that she writes on scraps of paper in both French and Innu, and is forever losing poems written on bingo sheets, cigarette packages, envelopes, restaurant menus, and paper napkins, so she gives them to her friend Laure Morali for safe-keeping.[43] Morali's evocation of the author–editor relationship, and of the relationship between the oral tradition and writing, is reminiscent of Lee Maracle's piece "I Want to Write" in *I Am Woman*:

> Scribble...scribble...scribble...I gathered up a host of paper napkins, brown bags and other deadwood paraphernalia on which I had scribbled the stories that people gave me. Scribbled sitting in the back of buses, inside grungy restaurants and in the audiences of great gatherings. Typed out the scribbles between the demands of young children and worked them up for publication until finally they made their way to the printer.
>
> On all these scraps are written the stories of people of my passion.[44]

For Bacon and Morali, the friendship between the author and "keeper" of these "scraps" of paper speaks to the ambiguous, sometimes contradictory, and always complex role of the editor and the archive in the worlds of academia and publishing, hinting at the life of the spoken word and the silences that circulate outside these frames of reference.

. The title of Bacon's book, which I translate as "Message Sticks," alludes to an important element in Innu systems of signification derived from the culture of *nutshitmit* (the interior lands, the country, hunting territory) as outlined by the author in the preface to her book:

> *Tshissinuatshitakana*, les bâtons à message, servaient de points de repère à mes grandparents dans le *nutshimit*, à l'intérieur des terres. Les Innus laissaient ces messages visuels sur leur chemin pour informer les autres nomades de leur situation. Il plantaient deux morceaux de bois d'épinette blanche, plus ou mois courts, l'un à l'oblique de l'autre. Un bâton penché très pres du sol contre un bâton vertical signifiait la famine, et son orientation désignait, comme une boussole, le térritoire où ils se rendaient. Les *tshissinuatshitakana* offraient donc des occasions d'entraide et de partage. À travers eux, la parole était toujours en voyage.[45]

> (*Tshissinuatshitakana*, message sticks, were points of reference for my grandparents in *nutshimit*, in the interior of the country. The Innu left these visual messages on their path to inform other nomads of their situation. They would place in the earth two pieces of white spruce, more or less short, at an oblique angle from each other. A stick bent close to the earth against a vertical stick meant famine, and its direction signified, like a compass, the territory where they were going. Message sticks thus represented occasions for mutual aid and sharing. Through them, speech was always travelling.)

She adds that "les ainés se sont tus, nous laissant l'écho de leur murmure" (the Elders fell silent, leaving us with the echo of their murmurs),[46] but goes on to say that the publication of her book led her back to these Elders and to the children who represent the journey's continuation. Bacon concludes her preface by citing the following lines from one of her poems:

> Mamu uitsheututau aimun tshetshi pimutataiaku,
> pimipanu aimun anite etaiaku,
> mititatauat tshimushuminanat tshetshi eka unishiniaku,
> aimitutau tshetshi minuiniuiaku.

> Accompagne-moi pour faire marcher la parole,
> la parole voyage là où nous sommes,
> suivons les pistes des ancêtres pour ne pas nous égarer,
> parlons-nous...[47]

> (Come with me so speech can walk
> Speech travels there where we are
> Let us follow the paths of the ancestors so that we do not become lost
> Let's talk...)

Like Mestokosho, Bacon continues the work of these elders, and her poetry plays its part in this, while belonging in the world of French language writing as well.

Some might argue that there is a time lag between Indigenous poetry emerging in English and later in French, not unlike the time lag between the emergence of "mainstream" Canadian and Indigenous poetry. Certainly English-language Indigenous poetry became known, at least among Canadian readers, much later than did poetry by Canadian poets such as Duncan Campbell Scott. And it would appear that French-language Indigenous poetry became known by Québécois readers much later than did English-language Indigenous poetry in other places. Well-known writing by non-Indigenous authors such as Louis Hamelin, who has written fiction about Indigenous peoples, also risks displacing the work of Indigenous writers themselves—much as a similar phenomenon took place at an earlier moment in English Canada. However, the time-lag scenario is partly misleading, given that Indigenous literature, like the oral tradition itself, has been around forever. What is unmistakeable, though, is the lack of a level playing field for Indigenous poets. This problem is compounded for Indigenous poets who write in French, to the extent that their numbers are smaller, and also that markets for their work—at least in Canada—are much more limited. Mestokosho published her first work with Les Éditions Piekuakami in Mashteuiatsh. Ironically, it is in French-speaking Europe, more than at home in Canada, that readers know and value her work.

More recently, Melina Vassiliou, a young Innu poet, published her first book *Fou, Floue, Fléau/Nin Tshishe Ishkuess* with the *Institut culturel et educatif montagnais* in Sept-Îles. There are no easy solutions to this dilemma of how or even whether to access mainstream publishers and wider circulation in Canada or abroad, any more than there is much control over how work by so-called "exotic Indians" is read by Europeans. Despite important work by scholars and editors such as Mauricio Gatti and Laure Morali, the relative dearth of critical commentary by Indigenous academics in French, compared to analysis by Indigenous scholars in English-speaking Canada, is also discouraging, although that, too, is starting to change alongside the growing presence of Indigenous youth at university. Institutional structures, however, especially in post-secondary education, are slow to change. Perhaps in time it will be easier for Indigenous as well as other scholars to take up the challenge of helping to publicize the work of francophone Indigenous poets; at the moment, their work is featured at spoken word and music festivals in Montreal, such as the annual festival organized by Terres en vue/Land InSights [*sic*] for National Aboriginal Day, as well as in Wendake and Mani-utenam.

Despite the linguistic constraints that limit dialogue between anglophone and francophone Indigenous poets, or the complexities of organizing events that would bring them together, I am heartened by imagining what unrecorded conversations between Cree and Innu poets might be like; hope arises from such imaginings. At the same time, I am grateful for the tremendous gifts, as well as the hard work and engagement of Cree and Innu poets such as Louise Halfe, Rita Mestokosho, Joséphine Bacon, and Mélina Vassiliou, to mention only a few whose work is still relatively accessible to those who read only English or French. I believe that their voices need to be more widely heard. For this reason, if for no other, their work could benefit from translation into French and into English and vice versa, despite the inevitable limits built into the art of translating between and across European and Indigenous languages and cultures. As we go to press, Phyllis Aronoff's *Message Sticks/Tshissinuatshitakana*, a "Bilingual Innu-aimun-English translation," has just been published by Tsar Books/Coach House in Toronto (2013). This is a very positive development indeed. However, I find myself wishing that Aronoff had included her own translator's comments as well as translating Bacon's and Morali's preface and afterword. Did she, like me, simply translate the French versions of the poems into English and, if so, what available sources if any—other than the author's glossary—were consulted for meanings in Innu? It would be useful to have the translator briefly address some of these questions in the book.

In my case, because I limited myself to a few short passages from Bacon and Mestokosho for this chapter, I did not approach the poets for assistance. Rather, after translating a few of Bacon's poems, I consulted with an Innu student in my Indigenous women writers' course who is a fluent speaker and who has studied the language at university level. Mary Janet Hill is familiar with Sheshatshiu Labrador dialect rather than Pessamit dialect (although she did obtain further assistance from her mother, who knows several dialects). Needless to say, I learned more about Bacon's skill in two languages from sitting down and talking with Mary Janet than from any other research process. In the course of our conversations—Mary Janet speaks no French and I speak no Innu—we both made new discoveries when comparing our readings—hers translated into English from the Innu, mine translated into English from the French. My initial sense that Bacon's words point to spiritual meanings was reinforced, at the same time that I was struck by significant differences in the French and Innu versions given by the poet. In the end I decided to stay with my original translations and decision to place all three versions on the page. The ironies, inequities, and advantages of bilingualism (or multilingualism) in the lives of Indigenous peoples, in contrast to Canadian experiences of linguistic diversity, are suggested by the pregnant silences as well as the "words that walk" in books by Innu poets.

Notes

1 Louise Bernice Halfe, *Blue Marrow* (Regina: Coteau, 2005), 1–2.

2 Neal McLeod reminds me that this Innu word for walking is similar to the Cree expression "wîsahkêcâhk ê-pâh-pimohtêt" (he was always walking). In a poem using a similar expression on pp. 22–23, Bacon gives the following wording for "Les anciens marchaient sans cesse" [The old ones walked ceaselessly]: "Tshimushuminanat nekanat/nanitam aiatshipianat."

3 Armand Ruffo, "Afterword," in *Indigeneity in Dialogue: Indigenous Literary Expression across Linguistic Divides/L'autochtonie en dialogue: l'expression littéraire autochtone au-delà des barrières linguistiques*, special section/dossier special, *Studies in Canadian Literature/Études en littérature canadienne* 35, no. 2 (2010): 111. Note that the French used the word *montagnais* (mountaineers or mountain people) to refer to Innu people, a term that some members of the Innu community still use to refer to themselves. Innu-Aimun is spoken by many people of all generations in several of its dialects. In Labrador English tends to be the second language, while in Quebec French is the second language, although some Innu speak all three languages, as well as being familiar with Cree.

4 Tomson Highway, "Préface," in *Mots de neige, de sable et d'océan: littératures autochtones*, ed. Mauricio Gatti (Wendake: Les Éditions du CDFM/Hurtubise HMH, 2008), 7. All translations from the French in this chapter are my own, and I assume full responsibility for any errors in these translations.

5 Michèle Lacombe, Heather MacFarlane, and Jennifer Andrews, "Introduction," in *Indigeneity in Dialogue: Indigenous Literary Expression across Linguistic Divides/L'autochtonie en dialogue: l'expression littéraire autochtone au-delà des barrières linguistiques*, special section/dossier special, *Studies in Canadian Literature/Études en literature canadienne* 35, no. 2 (2010): 5.

6 I am of French (Acadian and Québécois) and Maliseet (Malécite) background; my father's French-Métis ancestors lived on the south shore of the St. Lawrence River in Quebec and both sides of the Saint John River, spanning what is now the state of Maine and the province of New Brunswick. My mother's ancestors were Acadians living in Nova Scotia and New Brunswick, and French living in Isle Verte, an isolated island in the St. Lawrence River. My childhood in the late 1950s and 1960s was spent in Sept-Îles, near the Innu community of Uashat/Mani-utenam, where my father worked as a schoolteacher. I speak my French mother tongue fluently, but English (in which I was always schooled) long ago became the language in which I write.

7 Tomson Highway, "Préface," 7–8 passim.

8 Mauricio Gatti, *Littérature amérindienne du Québec: Écrits de langue française* (Montréal: Hurtubise HMH, 2004), 18–23, 20–25 passim.

9 Mauricio Gatti, *Être écrivain amérindien au Québec: Indianité et création littéraire* (Montréal: Hurtubise HMH, 2006), 18–23.

10 This term for urban working-class speech is derived from the slang word based on the local pronunciation of *cheval*, which is French for "horse."

11 Gatti, *Littérature amérindienne*, 108–13.

12 Ibid., 119.

13 Ibid, 139–40.

14 Ibid., 146.

15 Ibid., 159–74 passim.

16 See the Babel entry in vol. 14 of the *Dictionary of Canadian Biography* (Toronto/Quebec City: University of Toronto Press/Laval University, 2000), http://www.biographi.ca/009004-119.01-e.php?&id_nbr=7183. See also the Oblates of Western Canada Fonds, University of Manitoba, http://umanitoba .ca/libraries/units/archives/collections/rad/oblates.html. (It should be noted that Albert Lacombe, the Oblate missionary to the Cree and Blackfoot and compiler of a Blackfoot dictionary, is no relative of mine.) The Innu have produced their own website for providing access to French, English, and Innu language tools. See http://www.innu-aimun.ca/modules.php?&lang=English and http://www.languagegeek.com/algon/naskapi/inlnu.html.

17 Diane Boudreau, *Histoire de la littérature amérindienne au Québec* (Montréal: l'Hexagone, 1993). Like José Mailhot, an ethno-linguist who is knowledge-able about Innu stories and dialects and who has published anthropological research about the Innu oral tradition, Boudreau emphasizes traditional story-telling. However, she argues for the re-appropriation of missionary, govern-ment, and ethnographic writing, and the countering of their distortions, in new essays, poems, plays, short stories, and novels by Indigenous authors. She reads Indigenous literature as resistance writing, speaking of it as polymorph-ous, hybridized, and "invented." She also compares traditional "tribal" cul-tures from Africa and America, suggesting that "invented" traditions emerge as one of several strategies for cultural survival. See pp. 15–17, 100–101.

18 Stéphane Despatie, "L'avenir voit rouge," *Exit: revue de poésie* no. 59 (2010): 2.

19 Jean-François Létourneau, "La poésie amérindienne," *Exit: revue de poésie* no. 59 (2010): 52, 54.

20 Louis Hamelin, "Debout après la folie," Le Devoir.com, July 12, 2010.

21 Véronique Audet, *Innu Nikamu—L'Innu Chante: Pouvoir des chants, identité, et guérison chez les Innus*. Québec: Presses de l'université Laval, 2012, 180–86.

22 Joséphine Bacon, in *Aimititau! Parlons-nous!* Montréal: Mémoire d'encrier, 2008. For the meaning of *aimitau*, see *Supplément au Dictionnaire Montag-nais-français*, http://www.innu-aimun.ca/modules/vocab/files/Supplement_ English.pdf.

23 Jean Hamelin, "Postface: Développement sauvage," in Joséphine Bacon and José Acquelin, *Nous sommes tous des sauvages* (Montréal: Mémoire d'encrier, 2011), 69.

24 Ibid. As I did not encounter this new publication until the summer of 2012, after Sounding Out had been submitted, there was no time to comment on it further.

25 Christophe Premat, "Entretien avec Rita Mestokosho, écrivaine de langue innue," mardi 19 janvier 2010, *franska institutet*, http://www.franskaspraket .eu/spip.php?article9.

26 See http://www.youtube.com/watch?v=RYRe-Y3w3Ko for a powerful dual language poetic interchange between Joséphine Bacon and Chloé Sainte-Marie, in which Sainte-Marie reads out place names in Innu followed by Bacon's rendition of these in French. This reminds me of the untranslated incantatory invocation of Innu names for the Caribou Master and some of the other Masters associated with different animals on page 38 of her book of poems. In this clip, we are also privy to off-stage banter between Bacon and Sainte-Marie.

27 The Innu word for "on the road" is *meshkanat*—see *Innu Aimitu*.

28 Rita Mestokosho, in Jean Désy and Rita Mestokosho, *Uashtessiu/Lumière d'automne* (Montréal: Mémoire d'encrier, 2010), 22.

29 "I guess" would be another translation.

30 "Corner stones" would be another translation.

31 A Swedish publisher advertises a new English-Innu-French edition as slated for publication in Stockholm in 2011; I have not yet been able to access this book. It is listed as *How I See Life, Grandmother—Eshi uapataman nukum— Comment je perçois la vie, grand-mère*. Stockholm: Beijbom Books, 2011.

32 Rita Mestokosho, *Eshi Uapataman Nukum/recueil de poèmes Montagnais* (Mashteuiatsh: Éditions Piekuakami, 1995), 19.

33 Innu scholar Jean-Louis Fontaine reminds us that Mistapéo is the guiding spirit in the shaketent ceremony, as well as the one who guides the master spirits of the different animals, occupying a very important role in the life of Innu hunters and their families. This term also refers to a person's guiding soul-spirit. See Fontaine's *Croyances et rituels chez les Innus 1603–1650* (Québec: Les éditions GID, 2006), 33.

34 Premat, n.p.

35 Rita Mestokosho, in *Aimititau! Parlons-nous!*, ed. Laure Morali (Montréal: Mémoire d'encrier, 2008), 37.

36 Premat, n.p.

37 Joséphine Bacon, *Bâtons à message/Tshissinuashitakana* (Montréal: Mémoire d'encrier, 2009), 28–29, 102–3.

38 Ibid., 16–17.

39 Ibid., 7.

40 Missionaries, anthropologists, and Innu all recognize how the life of the Innu was and is centred around the caribou as a vital source of food, clothing, and spiritual sustenance. Communicating with the caribou spirit, who is the master of those animals, whether through shaketent, drumming, singing, prayer, or reading bones, reflects the importance of reciprocity in human relationships with the animals who sustain the hunter's family and the community's life. The Makushan is a communal feast held to thank the Caribou Master; this ritual is also tied to the maintenance of social relations in the community. The ritual consumption of caribou bone marrow is an important component of the Makushan.

41 Laure Morali, "Postface" to *Bâtons à message/Tshissinuashitakana* (Montréal: Mémoire d'encrier, 2009), 136.
42 Bacon, *Bâtons à message*, 82–83.
43 Morali, "Postface," 136.
44 Lee Maracle, *I Am Woman: A Native Perspective on Sociology and Feminism* (Vancouver: Press Gang, 1996), 3. I am grateful to Lee Maracle for reminding me of this at the Sounding Out conference.
45 Bacon, *Bâtons à message*, 7.
46 Ibid., 8.
47 Ibid.

Bibliography

Bacon, Joséphine. *Bâtons à message/Tshissinuashitakana*. Montréal: Mémoire d'encrier, 2009.

Bacon, Joséphine, and José Acquelin, *Nous sommes tous des sauvages*. Montréal: Mémoire d'encrier, 2011.

Boudreau, Diane. *Histoire de la littérature amérindienne au Québec*. Montréal: l'Hexagone, 1993.

Despatie, Stéphane. "L'avenir voit rouge." *Exit: revue de poésie* no. 59 (2010): 3–4.

Fontaine, Jean-Louis. *Croyances et rituels chez les Innus 1603–1650*. Québec: Les éditions GID, 2006.

Gatti, Mauricio. *Être écrivain amérindien au Québec: Indianité et création littéraire*. Montréal: Hurtubise HMH, 2006.

Gatti, Mauricio, ed. *Littérature amérindienne du Québec: Écrits de langue française*. Montréal: Hurtubise HMH, 2004.

———, ed. *Mots de neige, de sable et d'océan: littératures autochtones*. Wendake: Les Éditions du CDFM/Hurtubise HMH, 2008.

Halfe, Louise Bernice. *Blue Marrow*. Regina: Coteau, 2005.

Hamelin, Louis. "Debout après la folie." Le Devoir.com, July 12, 2010.

Highway, Thomson. "Préface." In *Mots de neige, de sable et d'océan: littératures autochtones*, edited by Mauricio Gatti, 7–10. Wendake: Les Éditions du CDFM/Hurtubise HMH, 2008.

Lacombe, Michèle, Heather MacFarlane, and Jennifer Andrews. "Introduction." *Indigeneity in Dialogue: Indigenous Literary Expression across Linguistic Divides/L'autochtonie en dialogue: l'expression littéraire utochtone au-delà des barriers linguistiques*. Special section/dossier special, *Studies in Canadian Literature/Études en literature canadienne* 35, no. 2 (2010): 5–12.

Létourneau, Jean-François. "La poésie de Rita Mestokosho." *Littoral* no. 4 (automne 2009).

———. "La poésie amérindienne." *Exit: revue de poésie* no. 59 (2010): 51–55.

Maracle, Lee. *I Am Woman: A Native Perspective on Sociology and Feminism*. Vancouver: Press Gang, 1996.

Mestokosho, Rita. *Eshi Uapataman Nukum/recueil de poèmes montagnais*. Mashteuiatsh: Éditions Piekuakami, 1995.

Mestokosho, Rita, and Jean Désy. *Uashtessiu/Lumière d'automne*. Montréal: Mémoire d'encrier, 2010.

Morali, Laure, ed. *Aimititau! Parlons-nous!* Montréal: Mémoire d'encrier, 2008.

Morali, Laure, and Rodney Saint-Éloi, eds. *Les bruits du monde (livre-disque)*. Mani-utenam/Uashat/Montréal: Institut Tshakapesh/Studio Makusham/ Mémoire d'encrier, 2013.

———. "Postface." In *Bâtons à message/Tshissinuashitakana*. Montréal: Mémoire d'encrier, 2009.

Premat, Christophe. "Entretien avec Rita Mestokosho, ecrivaine de langue innue." Mardi 19 janvier 2010. *franska institutet*. http://www.franskaspraket .eu/spip.php?article9.

Ruffo, Armand. "Afterword." *Indigeneity in Dialogue: Indigenous Literary Expression across Linguistic Divides/L'autochtonie en dialogue: l'expression littéraire autochtone au-delà des barrières linguistiques*. Special section/ dossier spe- cial, *Studies in Canadian Literature/Études en literature canadienne* 35, no. 2 (2010): 110–13.

Sioui, Jean. *L'Avenir voit rouge*. Trois-Rivières: Écrits des Forges, 2008.

Vassiliou, Mélina. *Fou, Floue, Fléau/Nin tshishe ishkuess*. Sept-Îles: Institut cultu- rel et éducatif montagnais, 2008.

Vollant, Florent. "Kamanitushit/Faire Appel aux Esprits/Appealing to the Spirits." Translated by Marie-France et Danielle Madge. *Littoral* no. 4 (automne 2009).

White, Marie. "Wendake Creates First Ever Native Literature Gathering." *Wind- speaker*, October 1, 2008.

14

Through Iskigamizigan (The Sugar Bush): A Poetics of Decolonization

Waaseyaa'sin Christine Sy

Biindigenh (Come In)
maadjiimaadiziwin: at the sugar bush[1]

> this is not a jazz tune
> rap, rock, or riff;
> the tat-a-tapping of
> cedar sticks knocking.
this is the rhythm & go of
mashkikimakwe ziigwaning
(mother earth at spring),
the creaking of mitigag (trees)   sway
the cawing of aandegag (crows) caw   caw
the cracking of mikwam (ice) to & fro
crunchy goon (snow) and drip-
to-the-drop of wiishkaabaaboo
maple sap, sugar water flow
> this is not the push
> & pull of pen on paper,
> the push and pull of
> poles harvesting rice
> or fish, not a tradi-
> tional or jingle, this is the
long time gather and haul
of sugar water, maple sap
wiishkaabaaboo,
the stand up and walk
visit and talk, boiling
and toiling in Her ziigwan
manidoowin (spring ceremony),

this is the all night&day sifting
of nibi, lifting herself up
to new life in trees,
   we don't even have to say please
this is Us, cajoling her
with love into sweet life
ziinzaabaakwad, maple sugar

This spoken word poem—the knowledge that it conveys, the aesthetics, and the pedagogical rational imbedded within it—represents the experiences and knowledge embodied through my personal decolonization process as Ojibway Anishinaabe ikawe (being who is capable of creating a separate new person who separates from her; she is woman).[2] I began this process in 1995, the moment I learned about colonization in Canada and began to learn about its relationship with Indigenous peoples historically and in the present. My short history is testimony to the powers of colonization: being raised in my white Canadian biological, step-, and adopted family and socialized by white-dominated institutions based on a Canadian value system allowed such a truth—that I did not know about colonization until I was told about it; I did not know I was colonized until I was told about it. Since that time I've been on a constant circular path of learning, praxis, and practice. It's important to note that this decolonization process has primarily occurred and continues to occur within my homelands, Gichi Gamingoong (the Great Lakes). I've been focusing on decolonizing and Anishinaabe-izing my relationship with mashkikimakwe (i.e., Mother Earth)[3] with serious focus, time, and commitment over the last four years. This has been done specifically within the homelands of my relatives, the Michi Saagii Anishinaabeg (Mississaugi Anishinaabeg) with the guidance and teaching of Elder Doug Williams of Curve Lake First Nation.[4] This poem reflects my relationship with iskigamizigan—the sugar bush at the time of harvesting maple sap and making maple sugar.[5] The knowledge reflected through it is the result of my engagement with intentionally reclaiming Anishinaabewiziwin—all the elements that make up Anishinaabe life—for the purposes of self-preservation, raising my child in the best possible way in preparation for her adult life within a contemporary colonial society, and for the purposes of maadjiimaadizwin (keeping the Anishinaabe lifeline going through the generations).

I wrote this poem on commission for Match-e-be-nash-she-wish Band of Pottawatomi Indians of Michigan and created it with the energy, spirit, and beats that I've come to know are characteristic of iskigamizigan specifically, and Anishinaabe life, generally.[6] In exchange for creating it, I received a pound of ziinzaabaakwad (maple sugar), a brain-tanned deer hide, and a CD on ash basket making—all made by Pottawatomi Anishinaabeg and non-Pottawatomi in and around Match-e-be-nash-she-wish.[7] I've performed her as spoken word in several venues, including two important Indigenous-oriented endeavours in Nogojiwanong (mouth of the river; Peterborough, Ontario)—the Sacred Water Conference and TRACKS.[8] "maadjiimaadiziwin: at the sugarbush" is situated here with some of her social history and my history with personal decolonization as an entry point into my discussion of the poetics of decolonization. Biingdigenh, come in!

Toward an Anishinaabe Gendered Poetics of Personal Decolonization

Upon reading "maadjiimaadiziwin: at the sugarbush," the reader may readily recognize the Anishinaabe knowledge she conveys and/or her aesthetics. In addition, they may also generate various interpretations based on a growing Indigenous literary criticism.[9] What is not so easily engaged with, but has been fundamental to her creation, is the personal decolonization process that allows her to exist. Decolonization, generally, may be understood as a process and event that includes both resistance against colonization and the reclamation of Indigenous lifeways.[10] Lee Maracle, Wendy Makoons Geniusz, Waziyawatin, and Michael Yellowbird, as well as Eric Ritskes, identify personal decolonization as a necessary process in liberation *from* colonization as well as liberation *toward* a new reality where Indigenous life, according to Indigenous terms, is affirmed and recreated.[11]

Indigenous critical and creative scholars illuminate the relationship between personal decolonization and literary expression in varied ways. For example, Sto:lo writer Lee Maracle utilizes literary art forms and critical praxis to name and interrogate colonialism and resist it within a framework of personal decolonization.[12] Cherokee literary critic Daniel Heath Justice illuminates the relationship between decolonization and literary expression in terms of theory and practice. Specifically, he elucidates Indigenous literary nationalism with what he refers to as a decolonizing imperative, stating:

> Literary expression is an extension of living peoplehood, in all its complex, contradictory, vexed, and difficult realities. To live is to challenge the erasure rhetorics of colonization—so too is to tell stories, to write, to make films, to imagine possibilities of a life lived otherwise. This is the heart of what I have elsewhere called the *decolonization imperative*, "the storied expression of continuity that encompasses resistance while moving beyond it to an active expression of the living relationship between the People and the world." The decolonizing imperative of Indigenous literary expression actively reflects our *lives*, not our deaths.[13]

Whereas Maracle utilizes literary expression in *I Am Woman* to examine the colonial conditions of her context and history, identifying this as a part of a three-step process in her own personal decolonization, which includes decolonizing the feminine,[14] and Justice names the decolonizing imperative of Indigenous literary nationalism, non-Indigenous writers also identify a relationship between literature and decolonization.

As Anishinaaabe ikawe who writes creatively to express the implications of my own decolonization and reclamation, the questions about a poetics of decolonization that emerge in an interview between non-Indigenous writers Shawn Rhodes and Tim Lilburn resonate with my own reflections.[15] Some of the explicit and implicit questions they ask that may apply to the consideration of an Indigenous poetics of decolonization include: How was this poem produced? What is the environment or geography it comes from? What is the significance of the language being utilized/not utilized here?

Where Rhodes is concerned with how colonization affects non-Indigenous poetics, and where Indigenous poetics clearly renders colonial affects, I am concerned with how decolonization affects Indigenous poetics. I'm interested in reading or knowing about the decolonization in Indigenous literature. What kind of psychic, emotional, spiritual, physical, reflexive work, and/or building of social relations went into creating this piece of literature (or any creation, for that matter)? I ask these questions not as interrogation or demand for accountability or truth-telling but rather because I think that the declaration of and discussion of a personal decolonization process will be generative for our literatures and for our lived realities.

My sense is that such a path may invite further participation and increased consciousness and action toward that end. It may further the theorizing of Indigenous poetics as they are being newly created or in our engagement with the history of our written literatures. It will contribute to strength-building in our continued resistance against colonial implications and contemporary neo-colonialism as it is occurring today. It will contribute to the maintenance of our momentum or increase it in our abilities to regenerate our Indigenous lives. In addition, I'm concerned in the work of a personal decolonization in its ability to establish dialogue in Indigenous reader–writer relationships. How can a poetics of decolonization inform an Indigenous reader? In turn, how does an Indigenous reader, within the realm of his or her own consciousness of colonization or decolonization, impinge on the literature? As we reclaim our Indigenous consciousness (through decolonization), how will this shape an Indigenous literary criticism? I sense that it will also serve the relationship between Indigenous writer and non-Indigenous reader by reducing the potential for cultural voyeurism or tourism through reading. A poetics of personal decolonization grounds the writing and the reading in a political reality of colonization and decolonization.

In this chapter, I share aspects of my own decolonization as it has unfolded over the past twenty years. In reviewing creative visual and literary work I've produced over the past fifteen years as a part of this process, it's evident that my relationship with aki (the land), specifically iskigamizigan, has operated greatly as a place through which to decolonize. It has become a place to tether my reclamations of Anishinaabe-ness and to ground my relationship with the world as ikawe. The literary expressions I included here reveals a significant, continually shifting temporal, imagined, ceremonial, and actively physical relationship with iskigamizigan.[16] Over the years, my relationship with this place has been one of several in the natural world through which I've begun returning to myself.

In Anishinaabemowin, "returning to myself" is known as biskaabiiyin and it refers to the reclamation aspects of Indigenous self in decolonization.[17] Biskaabiiyin, then, is the Anishinaabe (nation-specific) concept for understanding decolonization and is the starting point through which I understand my changing relationships to self, land, language, and the world. Through dibaadjimowin (a personal storytelling process) around the literary pieces I've selected, a sketch emerges revealing the work of and/or pivotal points in personal decolonization that may occur through return to place. What follows is a story of personal decolonization through the reclamation of Anishinaabeg language, erotica, and ways of knowing, told through story, poetry, and prose. What it yields is an Anishinaabe ikawe poetics of decolonization.

Reclaiming Anishinaabemowin (Language): A Short Dibaajimowad (Personal Story)

It was during my early twenties when I first learned that I belonged to a language other than English. Being raised with my white Canadian biological and stepfamily and immersed in white Canadian social institutions (e.g., public school system), dignified knowledge about what it meant to be Indian, Aboriginal, or Native, let alone Anishinaabe, was mostly unavailable to me until I reached university. To my father's credit, he did what he could to undo negative messages I received in the world about being "Indian." The best memory I have of this was an exchange shortly after I started elementary school: "I hate being an Indian," I said, to which he replied, "Don't you dare. You see all this land here? This is all yours. It was stolen from you. But don't you worry because one day it's going to come back full circle." He also gave me stories about my mother that told truths of her shortcomings and her strengths; stories of how they met and stories of her birthing experience; stories of when she was "here" and "away"; and he often declared the limitations he had in his own ability to teach me about who I was as Indian, assuring me that I would find out as I got older. "You'll find people to teach you who you are, Chrissy-Ann. All of that will come." he would say.

I don't remember the exact circumstances of when I first learned that Anishinaabemowin was also my language. I do remember connecting with a maternal aunt, in Winnipeg, Manitoba, in the spring of 1996, a few years after my mother's passing, and learning that my mother stopped speaking Anishinaabemowin when she was hospitalized for tuberculosis in a sanatorium. Upon her release, my aunt says that my mom would speak only English and never spoke Anishinaabemowin again. This story of cultural extinguishment and assimilation angered me and this anger motivated me to begin learning my language.[18]

My first Anishinaabemowin ekinomaaget (Anishinaabe language teacher) was Mary Beaver from Batchewana First Nation (located around Bawating, Sault Ste. Marie). She taught language classes weekly at the Sault Ste. Marie Indian Friendship Centre and I attended weekly. My purpose was to undo colonization. As it turns out, I've developed a practice or habit that looks like this: as soon as I discover that something of my Anishinaabe lifeline has been disrupted or interfered with due to colonialism, I make an effort to reclaim it. While anger at the idea of my mother's experience in the sanatorium fired me up to learn my language, it was Mary's teaching and the social atmosphere that kept me going. Anger quickly turned into appreciation, connection to the group, and attachment. Years later, after studying the language formally at university, even more powerful meanings were made: Anishinaabemowin could explain the world to me in a way that made sense, that resonated with my insides, and that illuminated the world in a way that English and Western socialization did not. Anishnaabemowin illuminated the world in a life-giving manner.

Reclaiming my language, or beginning to reclaim it, contributed to a (re)ordering of myself with Creation from Indian to Anishinaabe. This return didn't manifest itself in terms of my relationship with iskamizigan until spring 2001 when, sitting in a shared art studio with a group of non-Indigenous women friends, I was inspired to create an image of the sap inside of maple trees. Drawing on what I had recalled from my language classes with Mary, I named this in Anishinaabemowin without the use of a dictionary or reference to notes. I called the sap, ziisbakodeaboo—sugar liquid—and named my oil pastel interpretation the same. While I've learned that the accurate word for maple sap is wiishkaabaaboo, I think that the first act of renaming something in Anishinaabemowin and to do so by retrieving a word that has become embodied is a sacred, powerful act. To have the desire to do so is the first step.

I recall being particularly thrilled with having this Anishinaabe understanding of something real and physical—this language, these words. I was thrilled to be able to articulate something of the world around me in Anishinaabemowin. I held this joy quiet within me as I wasn't sure it would be meaningful to them. To pull an ancestral word out of my body in the act of naming something was humanizing, or rather Anishinaabe-izing. It was an unforgettable experience of what I have now come to know as an act of resistance, reclamation, and continuance.[19]

Iskigamizigan and the Erotic
In May 2003, a year after my daughter was born, I returned to university to continue learning Anishinaabemowin. In a seminar on Indigenous orality and literature, I was introduced to two Indigenous authors, Dene author Richard Van Camp and Anishinaabe author of mixed ancestry, Kateri Akiwenzie-Damm. The themes of sexuality running through Van Camp's *Angel Wing Splash Pattern* and the subject of erotica in Akiwenzie-Damm's *Without Reservations: Indigenous Erotica* shifted my experience of self as an Indigenous woman in relationship with the world. These texts compelled my amazement, a kind of shame, and left me perplexed. Amazement because I was reading Indigenous emotional, sensual, embodied life force for the first time. Ashamed because why didn't I know of this sooner? "This" being *our* sexuality and sensuality, *our* way of writing our life force. Perplexed because while women's studies as a discipline grounded me in theoretical understandings of women's sexuality, sexual oppression, and sexual liberation, it was the theories of white women's lives—not Indigenous women's lives and relationships—I was being taught. I was not being taught about the possibility for full Indigenous life, including the erotic, in these classes.

Van Camp introduced raw expressions of the erotic in youth as well as traditional oral erotic story in *Angel Wing Splash Pattern* that affirm the erotic in the lives of Indigenous elderly.[20] Akiwenzie Damm's *Without Reservations: Indigenous Erotica* and her article, "Erotica, Indigenous Style" theorized my feelings of shame for not knowing us or myself in a distinctly Anishinaabe erotic way and validated my question: Why did I not know this?[21] Emerging from Akiwenzie-Damm's observations that there was an absence of Indigenous peoples' intimate, romantic, and sexual literary expressions, *Without Reservations* speaks directly from and to her theory that this absence is the result of colonization. Specifically, residential schools operated to disrupt existing genders, gender relations (including intimate, views of gendered selves), and gendered behaviours, and supplanted this with a rigid heterosexual system grounded in Christian views of good and evil.[22] She states that the absence of Indigenous erotic life in literature is the result of concerted efforts to silence our erotic voice, our aliveness.[23]

Also compelling was how these texts introduced me to the emotional, sensitive, sensual worlds of Indigenous men and two-spirit sexuality. Having been raised in a hetero-patriarchal world where women are objectified and marginalized for the sake of men's interests (interests that are also shaped by patriarchy) and where feminism in the early 1990s taught me to recognize this social organization, my own agency and desire for full life on my own accord taught me to resist patriarchy and disrupt it, to work toward its transformation. These texts introduced me to the worlds of men and disrupted a colonial heterosexual, gender-rigid view of the world.

Van Camp and Akiwenzie-Damm's writing gave me permission to expect something more than the colonial Canadian definitions of gender and relationship had to offer: love, or at least intimacy, in all its forms, between Indigenous peoples. In this new reality of possibility and permission, I was inspired to explore my own erotic poetic voice as Anishinaabe woman. In the following poem, I turn once again to Anishinaabemowin and ishkigamizigan-as-place to explore this voice:

ziisaabaakodenibi
in the cold
there,
a fire burns,
sweetness trickles.
you take me there
to them,
mitigag,   maple trees

working for sugarwater,
ziisaabaakodenibi
.   you are,
tapping for flow
you say,
slow and sure
sweet water comes
you say,

sugarwater clear
flows from out
out

slow the drip
caught with a tip
of finger

hotskin sweet
licktreat
sugarwater clear
sweetness on your skin
you share
sweetness
on my tongue

then the fire
and the wait,
long simmer,
slow bubble
boiling to dark,
thick, sweet.

cooled
and sugared lips
now,
licked soft sticky
now,
in the cool
and hot
out there[24]

Here, my relatively non-existent relationship with the sugar bush interestingly found its way into my creative thinking and exploration of erotic
Anishinaabe woman's voice. Also interesting is how continuity, as Justice discusses in the decolonizing imperative, is evident through my use of Anishinaabemowin, beginning with my use of the word "ziisaabaakodenibi" as
a title. The word differs from the first word used in my painting, "ziisbakodeaboo" and shows shifting understanding and use of the language in a
reclamation process. Finally, paired with the permission and possibility to
write erotically in a distinctly Anishinaabe-meaningful way was a developing consciousness of heterosexual privilege and oppression of Indigenous
sexuality. In this context, I intentionally erased a heteronormative construction of the erotic as a way to create imaginative space for other gendered and
relational possibilities that exist in Anishinaabe worlds. In my own lived
and literary decolonization process, I am concerned with (1) having space
to decolonize and reclaim Anishinaabe life; (2) articulating this process
creatively and meaningfully; and (3) ensuring that I am divesting of my

own privileges as a cis-gendered (I identify with the gender I was ascribed at birth based on my sex), heterosexual woman (who behaves in queer ways)[25] while simultaneously creating literature that generates imaginative space (not exclusive, status quo space) that is accountable to colonialism and the regeneration of new realities.

Anishinaabe Knowledges: Paawaanhjigenhgoon (Dreams)

As in "ziisaabaakodenibi" the imaginative realm figures greatly in the production of any literature. A unique feature in its creation is found in the possibility and permission that other Indigenous writers generated for me to explore my own erotic voice. This idea of permission is not meant in the sense of the permission a parent gives to a child, an MNR officer gives to an Anishinaabe person, an Indian agent gives to an Indian, but rather I mean it in the sense of permission that is generated when realities, rules, or social norms are constructed to benefit a certain group and Indigenous writers dismantle this by creating new realities with words. This prompts the question: What else is possible for our poetics? What exists in our neo-colonial realities that needs to be dismantled so that we may feel liberated to engage new imaginary space? A short prose piece I wrote in 2010 called "(Seal) Women & Sugar Water" suggests that the sources of our literary expression may be a site for possibility.

Anishinaabe peoples obtain knowledges from multiple sources and methods: observations, reflections, intuition, sleeping, ceremonies, fasting, and dreaming, to name a few. Historically, we housed these knowledges in birchbark scrolls, artisan work (e.g., beading, quillwork, etc.), petroglyphs, pictographs, petro forms, sacred songs, and aadisookanan (sacred stories). In turn, these are also sources for public or private reading, interpretation or recital, and application. In the spirit of Creek literary critic Craig Womack's critique of essentializing and creating hierarchies of knowledge—that being the valuing of such forms of knowledge as ceremonial knowledge above academic knowledge—I agree with his assertion that we obtain our knowledges from academia as well.[26]

That being said, Western education institutions typically portray the knowledges taught and generated in their institutions as hegemonic—as though they are the only knowledges—or as superior. When there is reference to forms of knowledges not generated in the Western academy, such as Indigenous knowledges, they are portrayed as inferior or invalid. It's only recently that through the advocacy of Indigenous peoples and allies that Western universities and colleges have created Indigenous studies departments within their institutions and, more recently, have begun to acknowledge the validity of Indigenous knowledges.[27]

The present discussion on paawaanhjigegoon (dreams) as knowledge is significant in illuminating personal decolonization as it considers how Indigenous peoples may be conditioned to value a dominant colonial education system and epistemologies (methods of knowing) and/or not even realize that we have our own knowledges systems, ways of educating, or ways of knowing. As my own consciousness in this area began to shift to become more aware of Indigenous knowledges and ways of knowing, and as this was affirmed by Indigenous leaders, artists, and scholars, I began to be more readily engaged with our own epistemologies. As I became more engaged meaningfully in Anishinaabe methods and to make meaning in knowledge that has come to me through our sources, my ability to use our methods and make interpretations has strengthened. For example, in terms of my dream knowledge, I am less likely to doubt when certain knowledge comes to me than I may have been in my earlier years. Most significant is that the ease with which I now engage with the knowledge in my dreams in physical reality has increased. For instance, I accept certain paths presented to me through dream time (i.e., certain gifts that have been given to me, messages about my relatives, etc.) and allow their knowledge to influence my decisions or interpretations of events.

Below, I've included a short prose piece on the feminine nature of the sugar bush work. The following short prose is generated from a dream I had in 2010 during a time when I was reflecting about ininaatigag (maple trees)—their behaviours, the contexts of their behaviours, what was readily observable to me, and what was not observable. It's important to note that Anishinaabe epistemologies are based on rigorous methodologies and methods. James Dumont discusses the intentional nature and methods manifested in ceremonial ways that are applied to invoke knowledge through dreaming.[28] Indeed, my lived experience in seeking knowledge through fasting has required intensive, long-term planning, discussion, preparation, and social support. It's important to note that the dream knowledge expressed here wasn't obtained through such rigorous methodology but was gifted to me during a time of significant reflection. Also important is that this dream is not the only one that has given me insight into iskigamizigan.

(Seal) Women & Sugar Water

This is how it must be to be inside ininaatig, inside ziisaabaakode nibi when it's getting ready to run. Cold, pure, clean, cold. Smooth running. Fast running. More than smooth, fast. Light, very light. It's very light in here. Cold but not intolerable, not miserable, not *I wish I was warm* kind of cold. More like an *I have arrived. I am ready. This is what creation put me here to do* kind of cold. People are coming, it's time, I'm getting excited, energetic, getting happy kind of cold.

There are many women here. Older, experienced, sure, confident. No time to worry about you, gotta go with the flow kind of women; *if you want to learn just watch and learn and do it* kind of women; *no nonsense, got no time for trepidation, we're getting the job done* kind of women; *love to be here, love to have fun, this is gonna be good* kind of women. I gotta step up if I want to keep up to these women kind of cold.

Clear cold. Clarity cold. Blue tinge bright light, tiny, tiny crystals, snowflaky float about, microscopic crystal float, light blue bright light cold. Breaking through the surface, scratchy, barky, grey cold, beautifully textured, protector bark, straight bark, rough bark man tree bark. *Breaking through to the outside is going to have to happen at some point* kind of cold. And round, round we go. Circulating sap is a clear fast excited fun sugar water circulation.

Anticipating slight resistance because the surface is frozen but nothing that a little bit of exertion, movement, and friction can't handle. Second thoughts won't help, don't help, in this situation. Doubt, colonizing doubt, isn't ininaatig, isn't ziisaabaakode nibi. Maple tree sugar, maple tree sap, sugar water women know what they're supposed to do: pick up speed, don't panic, be sure, move straight, be flexible, agile, stay focussed, move through the resistance. move.

Paawaanhjigegoon, if engaged and accepted as Anishinaabe forms of knowledge gifted to us during our sleep time, may provide nuances into a situation that a person is considering. In this case, the paawaanhjige that informed this prose validated a question I had about the feminine forces of the sugar bush and the gendered nature of the work. It also provided insight into some of the conditions of this gendered work. Finally, my dream also presented a problem that was not readily understood, but over time, in dialogue with other Indigenous knowledge holders and reflection, is slowly revealing possible interpretations.

Conclusion

In making the statement "biindigenh" I invited readers to "come in," to enter into a poetic space that expresses a "sticky and sweet strand / of Anishinaabe life / in Anishinaabe land." I invited readers to engage with this consciousness as I have come to know it and interpret it through iskikamizigan. By elaborating on this space through sharing my personal relationship with the production of this poem, the places she was produced, and the social relations that informed her production, as well as her own social history in this world, I have shared a process of personal decolonization. While Indigenous writers have formulated relationships between colonization, decolonization, and literary expression in various ways, and while non-Indigenous writers are creating a poetics of decolonization, my contribution in revealing nuance in this relationship is to flesh out a gendered and Anishinaabe nation-specific poetics of personal decolonization.

By engaging my literary production over the years and revisiting memories, I am able to trace my own personal decolonization and, in turn, identify points in this process that have been key to me as Anishinaabe ikawe in my homeland. As a next step in a collective decolonization (resistance, reclamation, regeneration) process, the contours of an Anishinaabe ikawe poetics of decolonization may include and expand on—but of course not be limited to—reclaiming, embodying, and employing Indigenous languages in our present creative contexts; (re-) imagining Indigenous erotic life and relationships; and immersing ourselves in our own methods of knowledge production or research queries, and manifesting this knowledge or answers through our literary expressions.

These are some of the explicit points of an Indigenous poetics of decolonization. However, the implicit that exists here, but which has not been set out as a point of examination or discussion, include the significance of land/place and social relationships. Indeed, from an Anishinaabe world view, there is much to be discussed about these foundational aspects of decolonization. By naming a return to Indigenous relationship *with* land (whether it be real or temporal) as I have through iskigamizigan, and the regeneration of social relationships within a kinship network (either real as in the exchanges around "maadjiimaadizwin: at the sugar bush" or imagined, as is the case of "ziisaabaakode nibi"), as foundational in my own personal decolonization and literary expression, I hope not to suggest rigid prescriptions in decolonization but points of possibility for personal decolonization. From here, literary expression of personal decolonization may generate an urban poetics of decolonization that regenerates or re-envisions what a relationship with land or social relationships may look like and what such praxis or practice may produce. The point is to inscribe contemporary Indigenous poetics with the work of decolonization so that we may reduce cultural voyeurism or tokenism and even prompt critical praxis in a non-Indigenous audience; prevent the recreation of a new kind of romantic Indian, the romantic Indigenous person (in this case the one who has either been untouched by colonization or hasn't had to do any decolonizing process in generating an Indigenous literature); and nurture the personal in decolonizing practice. Finally, a poetics of decolonization that attends to those sites where we have been impacted by colonization will contribute to the production of a dynamic, generative, and compelling literature.

Glossary

aadizookaanan: sacred stories

aandeg(ag): crows

aki: land

anangoonhsag: stars, constellations

Anishinaabe(g): the name of the Indigenous Nation who consider the Great Lakes Region home after migration from the Atlantic Coast; there are multiple translations for this word; however, my understanding is "the good being" or "the good beings"; the Anishinaabeg Nation is made up of the Ojibway, Odawa, Pottawatomi, and Mississaugii.

Anishinaabe'aadiziwin: Anishinaabe culture

Anishinaabemowin: Anishinaabe language

Anishinaabewiziwin: all the elements that make up Anishinaabe life

asemaa: tobacco used as medicine in ceremony; in this case reference to petition spirits and give thanks to the spirits and gizhewe manidoo (the great, kind mystery; the Creator)

biboon: winter

biindigenh: come in

biskaabiiyin: returning to my Self

dibaadjimowin: the art of telling a personal story

Gichi Gamigoong: the Great Lakes

giigoonhsag: fish (pl.)

giikendaasowin: the art of knowing, research

goon: snow (on the ground)

ikawe: she is woman

ininaatig(ag): man tree(s), maple tree(s)

iskigamizigan(ing): the place where sap is boiled, the sugar bush at the time of boiling sap

ishkode: fire

maadjiimaadiziwin: moving life, connected, through the generations

maashkikimakwe: Mother Earth

manidoowin: the art of being with spirit; ceremony

manidooyag: spirits

manoomin: rice

Match-e-be-nash-wish: is the name of Pottawatomi community and is formerly known as powerful bird rises or leading bird of strength; it has local community meanings as well that refer to the veracity of the People and also refers to the Crane Clan, a predominant clan in the area.

Michi Saagii: one of the Nations within the Anishinaabeg Nation; refers to the people who live at the mouth of rivers

miijim: food

miinawaa: and

minobimaadizwin: the art of living the good life

Nogojowanong: where the river meets the lake; river mouth; Mississaugi Anishinaabeg place name, which is now popularly known as Peterborough, Ontario

odjig: fisher
ogimaa: chief, leader
Ojibway: one of the Nations within the Anishinaabeg Nation
paawaanhjige(goon): dream(s)
pane shenaa: forever and ever; this is a phrase that comes from the Match-e-be-
nash-she-wish Pottawatomi
Pottawatomi: the keepers of the fire; a Nation within the Anishinaabeg Nation
waaseyaa'sin: glowing rock
w'dinawemag: our relatives
wiin: our
wiishkaabaaboo: maple sap
ziigamide: maple syrup
ziigwan(ing): late spring; in the spring
ziinzaabaakwad: maple sugar
ziisaabaakodenibi: maple sap, sugar water (earlier form in learning)
ziisbaakodeaboo: maple sap, sugar water (earlier form in my learning)

Notes

1 This is a shortened version of the original poem.
2 Helen Roy, *Introduction to the Sound Based Method of Understanding Anishi-naabemowin: Understanding All the Sounds That Are Heard* (Canton, MI: Niish Ishikoden Productions, 2012), 107.
3 For a more nuanced cultural, social, and linguistic discussion of mashki-kimakwe, please see Margaret Noori, "Comets of Knowledge," in *Centering Anishinaabeg Studies: Understanding the World Through Stories*, ed. Jill Doer-fler, Niigaanwewidam James Sinclair, and Heidi Kiiwetinepinesiik Stark (East Lansing: Michigan State University Press, 2013), 36, 56.
4 Michi Saagii Gichi Piitzijid Gidigaa Migizi (Mississaugi Elder Doug Williams) of Waawshkigemonki (Curve Lake First Nation) discerns between Michi Sagiig (Mississauga) and Michi Saagii (Mississaugi) as being adjective and noun, respectively. He indicates that he prefers Michi Saagii be used in nam-ing his people in writing. Personal communication, Kinomaagewaabkong (Peterborough Petroglyphs), August 30, 2103.
5 Pashkdinong and ninaatgokaaning are two names that also mean "maple bush" where the first is the place name for what is now known as Gore Bay, Ontario, and the latter is used in reference to the ecological place of maple bush. Mary Grace Peltier, "Zhiishiigwaaning Nango Enji-zhinkaadge/How Sheshegwaning Got Its Name," in *Gechi-Piitzijig Dbaajmowag: The Stories of Our Elders, A Compilation of Ojibwe Stories, with English Translations*, ed. Alan Corbiere (Manitoulin Island, ON: Ojibwe Cultural Foundation, 2011), 63–63. I include this here to show the nuanced understanding Anishinaabeg have about places and how this is revealed through language.
6 Match-e-be-nash-she-wish means "powerful bird rises" or "leading bird of strength." For further elaboration, refer to glossary. Personal communication, Gun Lake Tribe Historian Kevin Finney, September 12, 2013.

7 Generating more material exchange in my social relations is important to me. I see it as a way to decrease dependency on a monetary system that has been a part of colonizing Indigenous peoples and key in creating a system of dominance in Indigenous–settler relations, as well as between Indigenous Nations and nation-states. For more on the problem with money and the problem of negotiating Indigenous poverty, the market, and pursuit of wealth, see Taiaiake Alfred, *Peace, Power, Righteousness: An Indigenous Manifesto* (Don Mills: Oxford University Press, 1999), 114–19.

8 First envisioned by Curve Lake First Nation Elder Dorothy Taylor, the purpose of the Sacred Water Gathering is to restore the sacred relationship between humanity and the water. Sustainable Peterborough, http://sustainablepeter borough.ca/sacred-water-gathering-may-8th-9th-10th-2013/; and TRACKS (Trent Aboriginal Culture, Knowledge, and Science is a summer youth outreach program meant to promote ongoing interest in and linkages between Indigenous cultural knowledges and Western science. Trent University, http://www.trentu.ca/ies/tracks.php.

9 In the case of Indigenous literary criticism, I make reference to Craig S. Womack, *Red on Red: Native American Literary Separatism* (Minneapolis: University of Minnesota Press, 1999); Armand Garnet Ruffo, ed., *(Ad)dressing Our Words: Aboriginal Perspectives on Aboriginal Literatures* (Penticton: Theytus Books, Ltd., 2001); Craig S. Womack, Daniel Heath Justice, and Christopher B. Teuton, eds., *Reasoning Together: The Native Critics Collective* (Norman: University of Oklahoma Press, 2008); Paul DePasqualie, Renate Eigenbrod, and Emma LaRocque, *Across Cultures/Across Borders: Canadian Aboriginal and Native American Literatures* (Peterborough: Broadview Press, 2010); Qwo-Li Driskell et al., eds., *Queer Indigenous Studies: Critical Interventions in Theory, Politics, and Literature* (Tucson: University of Arizona Press, 2011); Mark Rifkin, *The Erotics of Sovereignty: Queer Native Writing in the Era of Self-Determination* (Minneapolis: University of Minnesota Press, 2012); and Keavy Martin, *Stories in a New Skin: Approaches to Inuit Literature* (Winnipeg: University of Manitoba Press, 2012).

10 Waziyatawin and Michael Yellow Bird, eds., *For Indigenous Minds Only: A Decolonization Handbook* (Santa Fe: School for Advanced Research, 2012).

11 Lee Maracle, *I Àm Woman: A Native Perspective on Sociology and Feminism* (Vancouver: Press Gang Publishers, 1996); Wendy Makoons Geniusz, *Our Knowledge Is Not Primitive: Decolonizing Botanical Anishinaabe Teachings* (Syracuse: Syracuse University Press, 2009); Waziyatwain and Yellow Bird, *For Indigenous Minds Only*; and Eric Ritskes, "What Is Decolonization and Why Does It Matter?", *Intercontinental Cry: Essential News and Film on the World's Indigenous Peoples*, September 21, 2012, http://intercontinentalcry .org/what-is-decolonization-and-why-does-it-matter/. On the recreation of Indigenous lifeways, Leanne Simpson provides examples of what this might look like through storytelling. As an example, see her recreation of a sugar bush story in *Dancing on Our Turtle's Back: Stories of Nishinaabeg Re-creation,*

Resurgence, and a New Emergence (Winnipeg: Arbeiter Ring Publishing, 2011), 74–81, 83. On the need to engage in a more thoughtful process of determining between maintaining tradition versus recreating Indigenous lifeways to meet a present, Tara Williamson poses a number of case-specific questions in "Of Dogma and Ceremony," *Decolonization: Indigeneity, Education & Society*, August 16, 2013, http://decolonization.wordpress.com/2013/08/16/of-dogma-and-ceremony/.

12 Maracle, *I Am Woman*.

13 Daniel Heath Justice, "A Relevant Resonance: Considering the Study of Indigenous National Literatures," in *Across Cultures/Across Borders: Canadian Aboriginal and Native American Literatures*, ed. Paul DePasqualie, Renate Eigenbrod, and Emma LaRocque (Peterborough: Broadview Press, 2010), 66.

14 Maracle, *I Am Woman*, xii.

15 Shawn Rhodes, "A Poetics of Decolonization: An Interview with Tim Lilburn," *Fiddlehead* and *The Malahat Review*, Friday, October 26, 2012, http://fiddleheadwest-malahateast.blogspot.ca/2012/10/a-poetics-of-decolonization.html#more.

16 I have produced a comprehensive body of artistic expression about iskigamizigan, including visual art, spoken word (recording), and written prose, song, and poetry. I have included only four pieces here: two poems, one short prose, and one dibaadjimowin.

17 Geniusz, *Our Knowledge Is Not Primitive*, 9. Geniusz discusses the word "biskaabiiyaang" to refer to "returning to ourselves." I have written "biskaabiiyin" to reflect the first person. Also, Elder Doug Williams shares that this work refers to coming out of a dark place into an opening. Personal communication, Curve Lake First Nation, July 2011.

18 I think it's important to indicate that extinguishment and assimilation is my interpretation. I don't know what my mother was feeling or thinking while hospitalized, nor do I know the conditions she lived in while in the sanatorium or how she negotiated those conditions. I do wonder if she had been provided with medical treatment in Anishinaabemowin, would she have continued speaking her language? If so, how would retention of her language have influenced her life, her sense of self, or her sense of self in relation to the world?

19 Editorial constraints prevent me from including this oil pastel drawing in this chapter.

20 See "How I Saved Christmas" and "Why Ravens Smile to Little Old Ladies as They Walk By" in Richard Van Camp, *Angel Wing Splash Pattern* (Wiarton, ON: Kegedonce Press, 2002), 24–26, 78–100.

21 Kateri Akiwenzie-Damm, "Erotica, Indigenous Style," in *(Ad)dressing Our Words: Aboriginal Perspectives on Aboriginal Literatures*, ed. Armand Garnet Ruffo (Penticton: Theytus Books, 2001), 143–51; and Kateri Akiwenzie-Damm, *Without Reservation: Indigenous Erotica* (Wiarton: Kegedeonce Press, 2003).

22 Akiwenzie-Damm, "Erotica, Indigenous Style."

23 Ibid.

24 Interestingly, three years after writing this poem, I learned that the sugar bush was a site of romantic hetero exchange, and maple sugar was often used as treats for "sweethearts." See Lucy Eldersveld Murphy, "To Live among Us: Accommodation, Gender, and Conflict in the Western Great Lakes Region," in *Native Women's History in Eastern North America Before 1900*, ed. Rebecca Kugel and Lucy Eldersveld Murphy (Lincoln: University of Nebraska Press, 2007), 368–414.

25 By "behave in queer ways" I mean I conform to my heart and the practical necessities dictated through my relationship with the land (i.e., harvesting berries, hauling sap through snow, paddling/poling canoes or boats, essentially moving my body in all kinds of ways in spaces that are often restricted and require ease of movement and mobility). By conforming to my heart and my relationship with the land, I have found that my behaviour tends to differ from contemporary stereotypical Anishinaabe women's behavioural expectations, such as wearing skirts to ceremony or harvesting medicines. My heart and relationship with land do not prevent me from honouring the ways of others, but they do require me to be discerning in those ceremonial activities I partake in and to be respectful of the ways people carry out their ceremonies when I am personally invited. They also require me to consider how much of my heart knowledge and practical knowledge I am willing to suspend in order to have particular community relationships.

26 Craig Womack, "Theorizing American Indian Experience," in *Reasoning Together: The Native Critics Collective*, ed. Craig Womack, Daniel Heath Justice, and Christopher B. Teuton (Norman: University of Oklahoma Press, 2008), 353–409.

27 As an example, Trent University in Peterborough, Ontario, acknowledges the validity of Indigenous knowledges as a means to understand the world. Trent University, "Vision for Trent University," April 30, 2010, http://www.trentu.ca/planning/visionrenewal/.

28 Jim Dumont, "Journey to Daylight Land," *Laurentian Review* 8, no. 2 (1976): 31–43.

Bibliography

Alfred, Taiaiake. *Peace, Power, Righteousness: An Indigenous Manifesto*. Don Mills: Oxford University Press, 1999.

Akiwenzie-Damm, Kateri, ed. *Without Reservation: Indigenous Erotica*. Wiarton: Kegedonce Press, 2003.

———. "Erotica, Indigenous Style." In *(Ad)dressing Our Words: Aboriginal Perspectives on Aboriginal Literatures*, edited by Armand Garnet Ruffo, 143–51. Penticton: Theytus Books, 2001.

DePasqualie, Paul, Renate Eigenbrod, and Emma LaRocque. *Across Cultures/Across Borders: Canadian Aboriginal and Native American Literatures*. Peterborough: Broadview Press, 2010.

Driskell, Qwo-Li, et al., eds. *Queer Indigenous Studies: Critical Interventions in Theory, Politics, and Literature.* Tucson: University of Arizona Press, 2011.

Dumont, James. "Journey to Daylight-Land." *Laurentian Review* 8, no. 2 (1976): 31–43.

Eldersveld Murphy, Lucy. "To Live Among Us: Accommodation, Gender, and Conflict in the Western Great Lakes Region, 1760–1832." In *Native Women's History in Eastern North America Before 1900: A Guide to Research and Writing,* edited by Rebecca Kugel and Lucy Eldersveld Murphy, 368–414. Lincoln: University of Nebraska Press, 2007.

Geniusz, Wendy Makoons. *Our Knowledge Is Not Primitive: Decolonizing Anishinaabeg Botanical Knowledge.* Syracuse: Syracuse University Press, 2009.

Justice, Daniel Heath. "A Relevant Resonance: Considering the Study of Indigenous Literatures." In *Across Cultures/Across Borders: Canadian Aboriginal and Native American Literatures,* edited by Paul DePasqualie, Renate Eigenbrod, and Emma LaRocque. Peterborough: Broadview Press, 2010. *The Malahat Review,* October 26, 2012, http://fiddleheadwest-malahateast.blogspot.ca/2012/10/a-poetics-of decolonization.html#more.

Maracle, Lee. *I Am Woman: A Native Perspective on Sociology and Feminism.* Vancouver: Press Gang Publishers, 1996.

Martin, Keavy. *Stories in a New Skin: Approaches to Inuit Literature.* Winnipeg: University of Manitoba Press, 2012.

Rhodes, Shawn. "A Poetics of Decolonization: An Interview with Tim Lilburn." *Fiddlehead* and *The Malahat Review,* October 26, 2012. http://fiddleheadwest -malahateast.blogspot.ca/2012/10/a-poetics-of decolonization.html#more.

Rifkin, Mark. *The Erotics of Sovereignty: Queer Native Writing in the Era of Self-Determination.* Minneapolis: University of Minnesota Press, 2012.

Ritskes, Eric. "What Is Decolonization and Why Does It Matter?" *Intercontinental Cry: Essential News and Film on the World's Indigenous Peoples,* September 21, 2012. http://intercontinentalcry.org/what-is-decolonization-and-why-does -it-matter/.

Roy, Helen. *Introduction to the Sound Based Method of Understanding Anishinaabemowin:Understanding All the Sounds That Are Heard.* Canton, MI: Niish IshikodenProductions, 2012.

Ruffo, Armand Garnet, ed. *(Ad)dressing Our Words: Aboriginal Perspectives on Aboriginal Literatures.* Penticton: Theytus Books, 2001.

Simpson, Leanne. *Dancing on Our Turtle's Back: Stories of Nishinaabeg Re-creation, Resurgence, and a New Emergence.* Winnipeg: Arbeiter Ring Publishing, 2011.

Trent University, "Vision for Trent University," April 30, 2010. http://www.trentu .ca/planning/visionrenewal/.

Van Camp, Richard. *Angel Wing Splash Pattern.* Wiarton: Kegedonce Press, 2002.

Waziyatawin, and Michael Yellow Bird, eds. *For Indigenous Minds Only: A Decolonization Handbook.* Santa Fe: School for Advanced Research, 2012.

Williamson, Tara. "Of Dogma and Ceremony." *Decolonization: Indigeneity, Education & Society,* August 16, 2013. http://decolonization.wordpress.com/2013/08/16/of-dogma-and-ceremony/.

Womack, Craig S. *Red on Red: Native American Literary Separatism*. Minneapolis: University of Minnesota Press, 1999.

———. "Theorizing American Indian Experience." In *Reasoning Together: The Native Critics Collective*, edited by Craig Womack, Daniel Heath Justice, and Christopher B. Teuton, 353–410. Norman: University of Oklahoma Press, 2008.

Womack, Craig S., Daniel Heath Justice, and Christopher B. Teuton, eds. *Reasoning Together: The Native Critics Collective*. Norman: University of Oklahoma Press, 2008.

15

The Power of Dirty Waters: Indigenous Poetics

Niigaanwewidam James Sinclair

> *For our ancestors to have created a language that is at the same time simple in structure and construction, rich and complex in range and depth of meanings, and musical and moving is extraordinary.*[1]
>
> —Basil Johnston

"Winnipeg" is a Cree and Anishinaabe word derived from wiinad-, meaning "dirty" or "muddy," and nibiing, meaning "waters."[2] The original phonetic pronunciation was likely Wînipêk or Wiinabik. It is used to describe Lake Winnipeg, a shallow body of water over 24,000 square kilometres in the centre of what is now the province of Manitoba. Of course, Cree and Anishinaabe communities had used the word for years before the arrival of Europeans, but the first phonetic recording was "Ouinipigon" in 1734 by French explorer Pierre Gaultier de Varennes, Sieur de La Vérendrye. This later morphed into "Ouinipique" "Ouinipeg," and "Winipic" over the next century.[3] The infamous 1817 Selkirk Treaty entrenched the name, dividing the territory, "beginning on the western shore of the Lake Winnipic, otherwise Winnipeg...."[4] Settlers named the urban development in and around Upper Fort Garry Winnipeg and, in 1873, it was incorporated as a city.[5] The rest, as they say, is history.

Documenting "historical names and places of the Canadian Northwest" in 1885, Charles Napier Bell wrote that Lake Winnipeg "is so called because during certain summer months the water of the lake is tinged with a green color, owing to the presence of a vegetable growth which abounds in parts of the lake. It is a minute needle-shaped organism, about half an inch in length, sometimes detached and sometimes in clusters and at times the water is almost as thick as peasoup."[6] Anyone who has visited the lake, particularly during the summer, knows what Bell is describing—algae. In Anishinaabemowin we call it ataagib. Lake Winnipeg has had wide-ranging algal blooms for a long time. Examining lakebed fossils in fact, University of California paleontological researcher Dr. Wayne Fry discovered that certain species can be traced to the ancient Lake Agassiz, an almost 500,000 square kilometre glacier that melted thirteen thousand years ago, carving out land and water formations that covered much of North America (like Lake Winnipeg).[7] Ataagib, therefore, is Manitoba's oldest inhabitant.

For those unfamiliar, algae are prominent in most waterways and are critical to the span and life of the environment. Produced by nutrients found in water, these autotrophic, plant-like organisms are distinct to an area, taking on the makeup of its surrounding environment. Embodying photosynthetic mechanisms that absorb light and release entities like compounds and oxygen, they are both independent and interdependent parts of an ecosystem. They are essential contributors in aquatic food chains, providing food and shelter for insects and zooplankton, which are consumed by amphibians, animals, birds, and eventually humans. In other words, ataagib are living beings that have unique relationships with other aquatic entities. They give water life.

We can learn a lot from ataagib. For instance, algae are so intricately tied to the forces in their environment that they respond to the most subtle of changes. The addition of nutrients, like phosphorous and nitrogen, result in an almost immediate production increase that can quickly saturate the water and—coupled with a shallow, muddy bottom—result in a filamentous blue-green formation. Over time and once widespread, this kind of algae can overwhelm an ecology, producing toxins that suffocate aquatic life, a barrier that prevents light from entering the water and the growth of bacteria and parasites. This formation happens organically but rarely, occurring most often because of groundwater pollution via chemical and agricultural fertilizer runoff, fossil fuel burning, marshland destruction, and deforestation. Algae can then cause sickness, skin rashes, mutation, and even death to those who come in contact with it. To remain at safe, ecologically productive levels, algae rely on a delicate balance of nutrient introduction, water flow, and the needs required by their living network.

With one of the largest drainage systems in North America (Figure 15.1), it should come as little surprise that algae is produced in such high abundance in Lake Winnipeg. Covering parts of four provinces, four states, and over a dozen major urban centres, this watershed spans over 1 million square kilometres and affects more than 5 million people. Water runoff from these sources is consistent and constant, flowing into several major tributaries that lead into the lake, including the Red River, Winnipeg

Figure 15.1   The Lake Winnipeg watershed

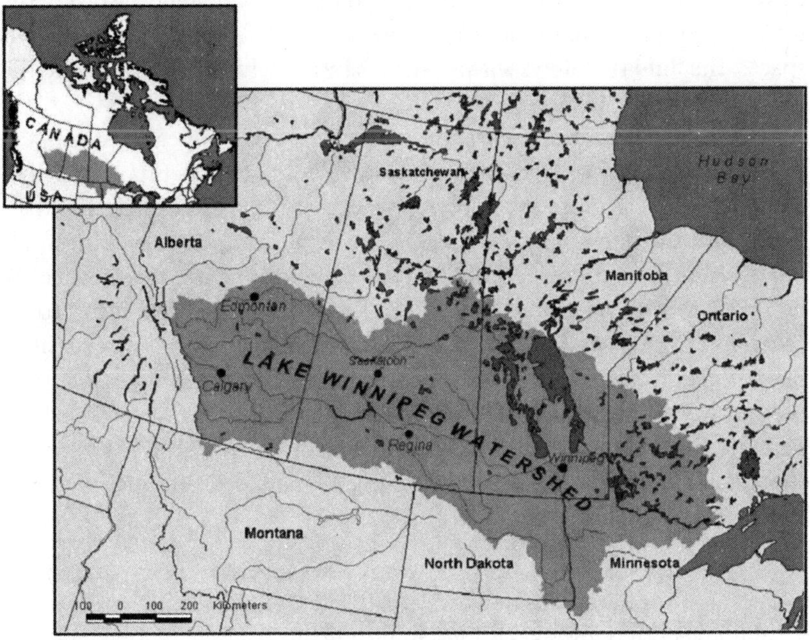

Source: "About the Lake: Watershed." Lake Winnipeg Research Consortium Inc.,
http://www.lakewinnipegresearch.org/aboutlake.html.

River, and Saskatchewan River. Once the water enters, there is one primary
exit point, the northeast Nelson River flowing into Hudson Bay (which is
regulated by multiple hydroelectric dams). In other words, a lot flows into
Lake Winnipeg from a multitude of directions and much less leaves, moving slowly and sporadically when it does.

Anishinaabe and Cree communities knew that the "muddy" or "dirty"
waters of Lake Winnipeg are due to ataagib, algae produced by multiple
rivers and runoff points. These communities named the lake because of
its appearance and the ecological network in which it operated. Keeping
this in mind, it is logical that the plural form for water—nibiing—is used.
It also makes sense that Cree and Anishinaabeg stories of Lake Winnipeg
describe muddied beings (like Wolverine and Nanabush) who travel from
faraway places to wash themselves in the lake, marking the water forever
in the process.[8] Algae not only describe multiple tributaries that become
"dirty waters," but also how the lake is produced by its watershed. In other
words, everything that flows off the rocks, seeps through the soil, and
interacts with animals, plants, and humans along the way eventually forms
part of the Lake Winnipeg aquatic community. "Winnipeg" is therefore a

name that introduces one to a series of relationships that culminate in the ecosystems, entities, and life within the lake and, ultimately, the rest of the world. It serves as a reminder that while water bodies may be autonomous spaces, the fluid that flows within them is intimately and deeply tied to life cycles throughout the globe.

This is hardly rocket science, but today's Lake Winnipeg illustrates the sad reality of algal overproduction, with blooms exponentially swelling alongside increased use of fertilizer, the destruction of forest and marsh-lands, and the burning of fossil fuel. This is nothing short of an unfold-ing disaster. In the summer of 2003, two Lake Winnipeg beaches had to be closed due to the discovery of *Escherichia coli* (*E. coli*) and algal toxins that had infected sand and local fauna. Satellite images showed that algal blooms encompassed the northern basin and were spreading throughout the south. Commercial fishers reported high densities of algae in fishing nets and a dramatic decrease in healthy catch. In June 2011, Eric Rumble of *Canadian Geographic Magazine* pronounced that Lake Winnipeg is "sicker than the Great Lakes in the 1960s," writing:

> The sources are obvious and are massive in scale: the rise of industrial farm-ing and livestock production, a hydroelectric dam network on northern Manitoba's Nelson River that has limited natural nutrient outflow since the mid-1970s, widespread depletion of the watershed's marshlands, plus a deluge of sewage, fertilizers and detergents from growing towns and cities.[9]

As reported by the Lake Winnipeg Foundation, "About 8,000 tonnes of phosphorus enter the lake each year but only about 2500 tones flow out. The rest accumulates in the lake."[10] The delicate aquatic ecology of Lake Winnipeg is flooded, under constant attack, and very, very sick.

In January 2005, a research body called the Lake Winnipeg Stewardship Board (LWSB) presented a report entitled *Our Collective Responsibility: Reducing Nutrient Loading to Lake Winnipeg*, which offered recommenda-tions in thirty-two areas to repair the damage. As Bill Barlow, chair of the LWSB, states: "The message from the Lake is clear. Nutrient loads on the rivers feeding the lake must be decreased to a point where natural bal-ances in the lake can be re-established. The key for the protection and rehabilitation of Lake Winnipeg is through the sustainable management of its watershed. That is the task."[11] In other words, we need to stop filling the groundwater with fertilizer and soap, polluting the atmosphere with our cars, destroying marshlands for houses, and clear-cutting trees for urban sprawl. We need to take responsibility *for our lives*. Today, obstacles to the LWSB plan continue, including costs, lack of political will, and difficulty in convincing those throughout the watershed that the plan is worth supporting. While there has been some improvement, it is not known how long it will take to reverse some effects.[12] "[T]he frame of reference for crafting an appropriate remedy," Rumble states, "hasn't existed before."[13] Meanwhile, algal blooms continue to grow and "dirty waters" threaten to become "death waters."[14]

This was foreseeable, for the processes that create Lake Winnipeg are embedded in its very name. Embodied within "Winnipeg" are explanations for how "dirty waters" are formed, how beings like ataagib are born, and how an ecosystem operates. The word is metaphor, metonymy, and synecdoche all at once; the description mirrors its meaning. Winnipeg is a sign of connection, collaboration, and a process where forces—good and bad—come together to form relationships in a local and global context. It is an acknowledgement of the mobility, fluidity, and power of water to generate relationships that resonate throughout the world. "Winnipeg" is a remarkable word, one that not only embodies a place, but also its makeup and how it interacts with the world. All of us who employ this term are provided with an opportunity to learn this every time it's used.

However, Winnipeg most of all is a gift—an offering that aims to understand the knowledge within "dirty water," the world, and life. Given by our ancestors and forged via experience and history, the word is evidence that we don't need to invent sites where meaningful and sustainable relationships can be forged—models are right in front of us. Stopping to consider the power within words like Winnipeg, one quickly gets a sense of a world with many sentient, subjective, and even competitive parts. It illustrates how we are surrounded by entities offering us chances to form independent and interdependent ties with them—and a living network. It also gestures to a world made up of balance and powers that throw this balance out of sync. In other words, we don't need cellphones, the Internet, or Facebook to show us how we are all connected; earth, wind, and "dirty waters" demonstrate this to us already (and do it far better). Understanding this is not easy; it's difficult, intellectual work—like trying to form a relationship with knowledge itself. This is a process requiring time, care, and consideration about geography, philosophy, and science all at the same time. Winnipeg offers these kinds of gifts; it is a word that gestures to processes on how we can forge a collective and sustainable home. It is also a critical and creative expression of power and understanding—a song, story, and *poem* all at one.

Winnipeg is reflective of a praxis called *Indigenous Poetics*, an ethic and action residing within Indigenous expressions that mark our presence as members of intellectual and expansive cultures and communities. My colleague Neal McLeod and those putting together this collection are ambitious in trying to encapsulate this power. As I have illustrated, this praxis is embedded within the language, stories, and names our ancestors handed down to us. Within these words reside not only our cultural and spiritual inheritances and legacies but also our intellectual and narrative traditions. Indigenous poetics are critical gestures of articulation and voice, words that create and define us. They are offerings of relationship given to beings throughout Creation to share space and time with us, and maybe even some food. They represent an ongoing commitment to tie our world together and contribute to it via the methods we've been given in this life and the next. In other words, Indigenous poetics are the intricate and intellectual acts of gifting words full of breath, rhythm, and expression in the hopes that they will be accepted in a world constituted by language.

The beautiful and provocative power of Indigenous poetics is found in the words, blood, and water that flow through Indigenous bodies, minds, and mouths. It resides in the expressions Indigenous peoples use in political and social spaces and times we inhabit, and in the songs and stories we share in communities we encounter. These are not figments of our distant cultural past, forever lost in the enduring stereotype of disappearing peoples, nor are they in the vague and empty shells of anthropological recordings or New Age how-to manuals. Indigenous poetics can be found in lodges and living rooms, backwoods and boardrooms, cities and classrooms. It can be uncovered in the everyday expressions of Indigenous peoples living their lives: in parents explaining the world to their children; in students writing essays; in learners speaking their ancestral languages. This life force can be heard, as Okanagan poet Jeannette Armstrong explains, in the "land" that

> holds all knowledge of life and death and is a constant teacher. It is said in Okanagan that the land constantly speaks. It is constantly communicating. Not to learn its language is to die. We survived and thrived by listening intently to its teaching—to its language—and then inventing human words to retell its stories to our succeeding generations. It is the land that speaks N'silxchn through the generations of our ancestors to us. It is N'silxchn, the old land/mother spirit of the Okanagan People, which surrounds me in its primal wordless state.[15]

Here in Manitoba, Lake Winnipeg is speaking. Through "wordless" words of ataagib, sickness, and a water filled with toxins, she is telling us that human selfishness is making her, and all of our relatives who depend on her, sick. In other words, we are hurting ourselves. We must listen to her or we will die.

Listening to the world is not just about the ecology and environment. It is to engage with it completely. In Indigenous societies, for example, we have medicine people who interact with the universe using dreams and sacred plants, women who communicate with water, men who forge relationships with fire, and many more engagements too numerous to recount. Indigenous poets do this work with language, gesture, and thought. This is a mobile, constant job, done from place to place and time to time. Indigenous poets perform acts similar to singers in ceremony, forming vibrations and rhythm from their hearts and throats that remind us we are part of a moving and powerful world, one in which we can join in and dance to at any time. They teach with words, rhythm, and tone, inviting us to listen, watch, and join in. Through gifts of sound they provoke waves of movement, silence and stillness, and forge balance, illustrating how we live in an ordered universe constituted by language. Indigenous poets do this all the time in standoffs, wars, and books. They interact with the world we know— and those we don't—and open doorways of possibility. Like our ancestors who gave us gifts like Winnipeg, Indigenous poets give us words that not only describe the world but embody the tools necessary for us to live in it.

One of the most powerful ways Indigenous poets have done this work is by engaging the complicated role of English in Indigenous lives. As one of the greatest living Indigenous poets today, Acoma Pueblo writer Simon Ortiz writes:

> Since colonization began in the 15th century with the arrival of the Spaniard priest, militarist, and fortune and slave seeker upon the shores of this hemisphere, Indian songmakers and story-tellers have created a body of oral literature which speaks crucially about the experience of colonization. Like the drama and the characters described above, the indigenous peoples of the Americas have taken the languages of the colonialists and used them for their own purposes. Some would argue that this means that Indian people have succumbed or become educated into a different linguistic system and have forgotten or have been forced to forsake their native selves. This is simply not true. Along with their native languages, Indian women and men have carried on their lives and their expression through the use of the newer languages, particularly Spanish, French, and English, and they have used these languages on their own terms. This is the crucial item that has to be understood, that it is entirely possible for a people to retain and maintain their lives through the use of any language. There is not a question of authenticity here; rather it is the way that Indian people have creatively responded to forced colonization. And this response has been one of resistance; there is no clearer word for it than resistance.[16]

These are complex matters. English, of course, has been used as a tool to both dominate and oppress our communities and our lives. There are forces within the syntax and semantics of this language that suggest its incommensurability with Indigenous expressions, discourses, and cultures. Translatability is a constant concern, with English terms never quite representing the meaning Indigenous language speakers articulate. Still, Indigenous poets work tirelessly with English to ascertain its value, relevance, and meaning in Indigenous lives. They resist not only the ongoing colonization of the Americas through language and discourse but the assumption that Indigenous cultures and communities are passive victims in a linguistic genocide. Even those like Ortiz—a fluent speaker of Acoma—attempt this work today, suggesting that there are cultural and ideological possibilities in English, regardless of such historical and discursive baggage. Like the work performed by narrative traditions of the past, Indigenous poets are speaking lives into being.

Indigenous poetics begins with the principle that our poets are not only our creative guides but our staunchest political and pedagogical intellectuals, advocates, and activists. They bravely engage such difficult struggles as found in our relationships with non-Indigenous peoples, spirits, animals, the sky, the Moon, the Sun, alcohol, Christianity, residential school, love, and who we are as members of the human race. They resist things like imperialism and invasion, but in such a way that creates and resiliently asserts presence in the universe—what Ortiz calls "struggle."[17] Indigenous poets struggle like a swimmer who fights against water but also moves with it, creating ripples and waves that emanate outward and back again. They embody what Robert Warrior calls "intellectual sovereignty," an "intellectual and critical praxis" centred not only on Indigenous cultural and political traditions but the "tensions, differences, and processes" embedded within current, everyday reality.[18] Indigenous poetic artists who practise intellectual sovereignty combine elements from incorporeal and corporeal ceremonial and everyday life to gesture to ways in which we can form and inform our cultures and communities through our words.

I am proud that we are honouring Indigenous poetic traditions in this book. Thinking just of the formative Indigenous poets who have shaped my intellectual journey, so many names come to mind. I think of past voices like Pauline Johnson (Tekahionwake), Wayne Keon, and Marvin Francis; living icons like Lee Maracle, Marie Annharte Baker, and Gerald Vizenor; and contemporary artists like Gregory Scofield, Kateri Akiwenzie-Damm, and Rosanna Deerchild. I hear and read new and vibrant Indigenous voices like Katherena Vermette, Christine Sy, and hip-hop artist Wab Kinew. Many more could be mentioned here and even more are coming. My six-year-old daughter, who loves the rhythm of song, language, and movement, wants to be a poet. There may be no more important community of Indigenous thinkers and writers than our poets, for they are the creative and critical voices forging paths for us to walk, run, and even dance on.

During the symposium that resulted in this collection, poet Duncan Mercredi (another living icon and—no surprise!—from Manitoba) shared a concept he utilizes in his writing called "writing in a tree."[19] "Writing in a tree," as I understand it, is about fostering words through their growth from seed to sapling to maturity, multiple rings of development, ties with forces like wind and rain, and ability to adapt and resist storms, infection, seasonal cycles. It is to carry them, work with them, and help them resiliently continue to grow and bud, even when parts die and fall away. It is not to assume that we own language. It is to know that we are only a participant in its energy, a relation, a cousin that visits and shares tea, drinking in its power. "Writing in a tree" is to examine the beauty inherent in the universe's microcosms—like seeds or words—and try to understand the macrocosmic possibilities in all things. It suggests that struggles to live, grow, and speak are long-standing practices that continue life and may even be—dare I say it—"essential" parts of Indigenity. "Writing in a tree" is a powerful and poetic pedagogy: it certainly explains how our ancestors struggled to make homes in harsh circumstances and alongside other beings. It also articulates how our cultures and communities endure after centuries of invasion and assault. It explores the potential in resistance, the beauty in cultural contact with others, and concepts like autonomy and self-determination. It does all of this and more. "Writing in a tree" suggests that Indigenous cultural change can be cyclical, resilient, and like wildfires—a process that is as much about the devastation of forests as the growth formed after the fire. And, within a tree, what is it that sustains, flows, and is the single most important substance for growth? Water.

It might just be that water forges a critical and creative ethic embedded in Indigenous poetics and this is evidenced in Manitoba and its writers. The waterways that make up the Lake Winnipeg watershed and lead to it have been the home of Indigenous cultures and communities from time immemorial. They have shaped our existence and have been sites of activity, change, and struggle as ancestors of communities now known as Anishinaabe, Assiniboine, Cree, Dene, Inuit, Métis, Oji-Cree, and Sioux inhabited, migrated to, and settled throughout lands known originally as Manitowapow. Travelling by canoe, shoreline, and on foot, people made communities, held ceremonies in sacred spaces, and forged relationships among themselves and with beings throughout the environment. They learned from and with this world via the water, establishing traditions that continue today. Formed much like the algae that form "dirty waters," these peoples were created from their relationships with one another, etching their thoughts, experiences, and ideas about life in this place in oral and written expressions that changed and adapted with the environment over time. Of course, alphabetical writing was imported to Manitowapow by

Europeans, but the stories and names forged by inheriting and producing knowledge existed long before newcomers arrived. Adapting forms like *gikinoo'amaage-asin* (petroforms) and *wiigwaasabakoon* (birchbark scrolls) to other forms of text has resulted in an extraordinarily rich body of literature produced by Indigenous storytellers, writers, and poets in Manitowapow since time immemorial.[20]

This narrative tradition is encapsulated within the very word "Manitowapow," a name that originates within the water en route to Winnipeg. Originating in the Cree and Anishinaabe terms manitou (manitow in Cree, spirit or mystery) and wapow (sacred water, or water that is spoken for), these sounds emerge at the Narrows within Lake Manitoba, where waves resonated against the rocky shores of Manitou Island. These were thought to be sacred beats that resonated like waves of turbulence throughout Creation and formed all beauty, definition, colour, and meaning. Winnipeg has been created by this mystery water, this motion formed from the breath emerging from the water. It is the culmination of the network of relationships in which beings made and continue to make homes (which did not cease when the Europeans arrived). Winnipeg is also illustrative of a web of connections that has continued regardless of the increasing "dirtiness" or "muddiness" of the water, even if it has become deeply challenged. Manitowapow, Winnipeg, and ataagib are all signs of ourselves and our experiences, words, and ever-changing knowledge of this place.

It is my hope that we recognize the responsibilities of our gifts; that we listen to the Earth, the water, and engage the work Indigenous Poetics gesture us towards. It is my hope that by doing this we can understand more completely the power of the universe and how it is constituted by language. Indigenous poetics is not a new expression; it is an ongoing and lived praxis of which we can all be a part. We only have to interact with our narrative traditions, try to understand our inheritances, and express our experiences with a living universe as resilient, capable, and dynamic Indigenous peoples and we can encapsulate some of its power. The rest, as they say, is history.

Miigwech.

Notes

1 Basil Johnston, *Anishinaubae Thesaurus* (East Lansing: Michigan State University Press, 2006), vii.

2 John D. Nichols and Early Nyholm, *A Concise History of Minnesota Ojibwe* (Minneapolis: University of Minnesota Press, 1995), 96, 120. Some, like Pat Ningewance in *Talking Gookom's Language: Learning Ojibwe* (Lac Seul, ON: Mazinaate, 2008), 272, cite the plural of nibi to be nibiin. This is interestingly reflected in the different recordings throughout time and space cited by

Bell (see endnote 3). I would also like to say gichi-miigwech to Neal McLeod, who shared with me that in Cree wînipêk comes from the stem wîn, meaning "dirty" and pê, meaning "water."

3 Charles Napier Bell, *Some Historical Names and Places of the Canadian Northwest: A Paper Read Before the Society on the Evening of 22d January, 1885* (Winnipeg: Manitoba Free Press, 1885), 2–3. According to Bell, "Ouinipigon" morphed into "Ouinipique" in 1742 (recorded by colonial official Arthur Dobs), "Ouinipeg" in 1757 (Louis-Antoine, Comte de Bougainville), and "Winipic" in 1789 (Sir Alexander Mackenzie).

4 Alexander Morris, *The Treaties of Canada with the Indians of Manitoba and the North-west Territories: Including the Negotiations on Which They Were Based, and Other Information Relating Thereto* (Toronto: Belfords, Clarke & Co., 1880), 13.

5 "Who Named the North-Land?" *Manitoba Free Press*, August 19, 1876, 3. Scottish and Métis legislator James McKay decided on the name.

6 Bell, *Some Historical Names*, 3.

7 Wayne L. Fry, "An Algal Flora from the Upper Ordovician of the Lake Winnipeg Region, Manitoba, Canada." *Review of Palaeobotany and Palynology* 39 (1983): 313–41.

8 Louis Bird, *Telling Our Stories: Omushkego Legends and Histories from Hudson Bay* (Toronto: University of Toronto Press, 2005), 73–78. My Anishinaabe colleague Leanne Simpson tells a story in a new manuscript called "The Gift is in the Making" about how Nanabush fell into a marsh and, embarrassed, washes himself in Lake Winnipeg, which dirties its water and gives the lake its name. I say miigwech to Leanne for sharing this with me.

9 Eric Rumble, "Blue-Green Algae Plague Lake Winnipeg" *Canadian Geographic Magazine*, June 2011, http://www.canadiangeographic.ca/magazine/jun11/lake_winnipeg_algae.asp.

10 The Lake Winnipeg Foundation is "an independent, non-profit, charitable ENGO of citizen volunteers dedicated to finding solutions to the problems causing deterioration in the Lake Winnipeg ecosystem" and can be accessed at www.lakewinnipegfoundation.org/.

11 Lake Winnipeg Stewardship Board, *Reducing Nutrient Loading to Lake Winnipeg and Its Watershed: Our Collective Responsibility and Commitment to Action*, December 2006, ii, http://www.lakewinnipeg.org/web/downloads/LWSB_December_2006_Report_3.pdf.

12 Lake Winnipeg Stewardship Board, *Manitoba's Progress Towards Implementing Recommendations of the Lake Winnipeg Stewardship Board*, December 2009, http://www.gov.mb.ca/waterstewardship/reports/misc/lake_winnipeg_stewardship_board_report_on_progress.pdf. In this report the LWSB reports that "the Province has made significant progress in implementing the recommendations. Of the 135 individual recommendations, progress on nine (6.5 percent) was rated as "Excellent." Progress on seventy-nine (59 percent) of the recommendations was rated as "Satisfactory," thirty-eight (28 percent) as "Marginal," and nine (6.5 percent) as "Unsatisfactory" (iv). It also, however, states that "[s]ince the resources required to fully implement all the

recommendations simultaneously are enormous and likely beyond the capacity of the Province alone, it was expected that completion of some recommended actions would be delayed" (iv).

13 Rumble, "Blue-green."

14 "Algae Blooms Mar Lake Winnipeg Beaches," *CBC News Manitoba*, July 27, 2010, http://www.cbc.ca/news/canada/manitoba/story/2010/07/27/mb-lake-winnipeg-algae.html. In this report Al Kristofferson of the Lake Winnipeg Research Consortium states there is "no evidence current levels are declining."

15 Jeannette Armstrong, "Land Speaking," in *Speaking for the Generations: Native Writers on Writing*, ed. Simon Ortiz (Tucson: University of Arizona Press, 1998), 176.

16 Simon J. Ortiz, "Towards a National Indian Literature: Cultural Authenticity in Nationalism," *MELUS* 8, no. 2 (Summer 1981): 7–12.

17 Ibid., 11–12.

18 Robert Warrior, *Tribal Secrets: Recovering American Indian Intellectual Traditions* (Minneapolis: University of Minnesota Press, 1995), 115–22.

19 This is, of course, my interpretation of Mercredi's presentation. Any errors are my own.

20 For more on this, see Niigaanwewidam James Sinclair and Warren Cariou, eds., *Manitowapow: Aboriginal Writings from the Land of Water* (Winnipeg: Highwater Press, 2012).

Bibliography

"About the Lake: Watershed." Lake Winnipeg Research Consortium Inc. http://www.lakewinnipegresearch.org/aboutlake.html.

"Algae Blooms Mar Lake Winnipeg Beaches." *CBC News Manitoba*, July 27, 2010. http://www.cbc.ca/news/canada/manitoba/story/2010/07/27/mb-lake-winnipeg-algae.html.

Armstrong, Jeannette. "Land Speaking." In *Speaking for the Generations: Native Writers on Writing*, edited by Simon Ortiz, 7–12. Tucson: University of Arizona Press, 1998.

Bell, Charles Napier. *Some Historical Names and Places of the Canadian Northwest: A Paper Read Before the Society on the Evening of 22d January, 1885*. Winnipeg: Manitoba Free Press, 1885.

Bird, Louis. *Telling Our Stories: Omushkego Legends and Histories from Hudson Bay*. Toronto: University of Toronto Press, 2005.

Fry, Wayne L. "An Algal Flora from the Upper Ordovician of the Lake Winnipeg Region, Manitoba, Canada." *Review of Palaeobotany and Palynology* 39, no. 1 and 2 (1983): 313–41.

Johnston, Basil. *Anishinaubae Thesaurus*. East Lansing: Michigan State University Press, 2006.

Lake Winnipeg Stewardship Board. *Manitoba's Progress Towards Implementing Recommendations of the Lake Winnipeg Stewardship Board*, December 2009. http://www.gov.mb.ca/waterstewardship/reports/misc/lake_winnipeg_stewardship_board_report_on_progress.pdf.

————. *Reducing Nutrient Loading to Lake Winnipeg and Its Watershed: Our Collective Responsibility and Commitment to Action*, December 2006, ii. http://www .lakewinnipeg.org/web/downloads/LWSB_December_2006_Report_3.pdf.

Morris, Alexander. *The Treaties of Canada with the Indians of Manitoba and the North-west Territories: Including the Negotiations on Which They Were Based, and Other Information Relating Thereto.* Toronto: Belfords, Clarke & Co., 1880.

Nichols, John D., and Early Nyholm. *A Concise History of Minnesota Ojibwe.* Minneapolis: University of Minnesota Press, 1995.

Ningewance, Pat. *Talking Gookom's Language: Learning Ojibwe.* Lac Seul, ON: Mazinaate, 2008.

Ortiz, Simon J. "Towards a National Indian Literature: Cultural Authenticity in Nationalism." *MELUS* 8, no. 2 (Summer 1981): 10.

Rumble, Eric. "Blue-Green Algae Plague Lake Winnipeg." *Canadian Geographic Magazine*, June 2011. http://www.canadiangeographic.ca/magazine/jun11/ lake_winnipeg_algae.asp.

Sinclair, Niigaanwewidam James, and Warren Cariou, eds. *Manitowapow: Aboriginal Writings from the Land of Water.* Winnipeg: Highwater Press, 2012.

Warrior, Robert. *Tribal Secrets: Recovering American Indian Intellectual Traditions.* Minneapolis: University of Minnesota Press, 1995.

"Who Named the North-Land?" *Manitoba Free Press*, August 19, 1876, 3.

16

A Poetics of Place and Apocalypse: Conflict and Contradiction in Poetry of the Red River Resistance and the Northwest Resistance

Jesse Rae Archibald-Barber

Introduction

The Red River Resistance (1869–70) and the Northwest Resistance (1885) were pivotal events in Canadian history, when the Métis and several First Nations defended their lands against western expansion.[1] These martial conflicts were widely documented in historical texts, but they were also represented in the poetry of the era, as writers on both sides struggled to articulate a sense of national identity. Literary depictions can be seen in poems by Louis Riel, Charles Mair, Kate Simpson Hayes, Isabella Valancy Crawford, and E. Pauline Johnson. Riel wrote several poems that represented Métis perspectives, which stand in opposition to the English Canadian perspectives in poems by Mair, Hayes, and Crawford. They were all writing for a sense of place and belonging, asserting their right to claim the land, though from sharply differing viewpoints. However, between these positions, Johnson was unique at the time for her attempt to reconcile the differences through a consideration of both sides.

The poetics of place in these poems involves the issue of homeland and how identity is connected to it, and this is not without conflict and contradiction. From an Aboriginal perspective, the losses of lands and sovereignty are among the main causes of protest and resistance as the colonial displacement of Aboriginal cultures suppressed their historical identities. Indeed, from the English Canadian perspective, establishing a sense of homeland was supported by the aggressive dismantling of Aboriginal

nations. Consequently, the depiction of these conflicts in the poetry reinforced division between peoples, and because of this, the poetics of place in
the context of the two Resistances conveys a heightened motive for revenge
from both sides—revenge for the loss of warriors, soldiers, and land in
previous conflicts.

In their attempts to resolve the contradictions within their own positions, the poets often turned to apocalyptic imagery. However, while the
use of apocalyptic imagery is powerful, it can also be a deceptive rhetorical
device. The English Canadian poets used the notion of the apocalypse to
legitimate the process of colonization and the displacement of Aboriginal
cultures as part of a larger and inevitable cycle of history, thereby mitigat-
ing their own involvement. The use of apocalyptic imagery by Aboriginal
poets is equally problematic; however, their use is based less on legitimiz-
ing the conflicts and more toward transcending the desire for revenge to
reach a place where reconciliation can begin.

Western Expansion and the Red River Resistance: Louis Riel and Charles Mair

Known more as a political figure, Riel nonetheless left behind a large volume
of creative writing, mostly written in French and Michif.[2] Poetry gave him
an outlet to express his political aspirations, religious visions, and personal
experiences, and his poems offer a variety of forms, such as lament, com-
plaint, narrative, parody, allegory, and religious consolation. One of Riel's
most common topics is loss, including the loss of innocence, ways of life,
and vocations, which he expresses in elegies on exile, homeland, loved ones,
and even on his own death. Despite this remarkably elegiac tone, though,
Riel had a powerful sense of faith that gave him the inspiration to act politically, especially when it came to the independence of the Métis Nation.

The poem "La Métisse" (Métis Girl) (1870) expresses the territorial
conflicts at Red River as Riel attempts to consolidate a Métis nationalist
consciousness in resistance to the displacement of the way of life they had
established over generations. The poem represents the political divisions
of the period and recounts several events, including the main skirmish at
Fort Garry; the raid on Dr. Schultz's house, which led to the capture and
imprisonment of forty-eight Canadians; and the journey of a delegation
to Ottawa to petition for provincehood. The speaker is a young girl, who
expresses her pride "[d]'appartenir à cette nation" (to be part of the Métis
Nation). She affirms that the Métis already have an established heritage,
and she also celebrates the distinction of her people as the reviled Other of
western Canada:

Mais vous pouvez voir déjà leurs destins
Être haïs comme ils sont les honore.
Ils ont déjà rempli de grands desseins

(The Métis already follow a clear path
To be so hated is their worthy prize
They already boast a glorious past)[3]

The speaker takes pride in the difference her people gain by being "hated" because it eliminates any doubt about their distinctiveness as a people and as a nation: "Vit les Métis triompher à genoux" (A kneeling race lifted its triumphant arms). The speaker also expresses the Métis's right to protect their homeland, as she describes the defense of Fort Garry, where "[h]uit cents métis [...] [a]vec autant d'amour que de vaillance [...] [d]e leur aider à garder leurs foyers" (eight hundred strong... valiantly defended their country... so that their humble homes might be preserved). Overall, the poem conveys the success of the Red River Resistance. Indeed, for a short time, the Métis succeeded in securing the territory. However, Riel's depiction of the Resistance met with harsh criticism from many English Canadians, particularly from Charles Mair, who was affected by Riel and the Métis on a personal level during the raid on Dr. Schultz's house described in the poem.[4]

Charles Mair, according to Fred Cogswell, was an English Canadian nationalist, whose "Eastern prejudices" "certainly did much to precipitate the Red River Rebellion."[5] Mair was a poet and a political agent: politically, he did reconnaissance for the Canada First Party, formed a year after Confederation; as a poet, he wrote eulogistic descriptions of the Red River settlement and the surrounding prairies: "there is, in truth, a prospective poetry in the soil here—the poetry of comfort and independence."[6] In this way, he promoted English Canadian settlement of the area. However, Mair drew animosity from the Red River locals for his insulting descriptions of Métis women in private letters that had been leaked to the *Toronto Globe*.[7] Moreover, Mair's negative attitude toward the Métis, shared by the Canada Firsters and by Dr. Shultz, whose local paper advocated annexation to the Dominion, added to the Métis's fears that the federal government was about to displace them from their homelands. Subsequently, in 1869, while returning from his honeymoon, Mair was denied entry to Fort Garry, which had come under control of Riel and his provisional government with the Declaration of the People of Rupert's Land.[8] Mair was fiercely defiant, though, for when his group was forced to sign a document of surrender, Mair refused and demanded that they "fight to the death."[9] Nonetheless, Mair was imprisoned with the rest of his party in Fort Garry and was sentenced to be executed. However, Mair escaped and led a series of expeditions to retake the fort, all of which failed until the Canadian government sent troops. These failed attempts, along with the threat against his own life, family, and friends, and the loss of his property and creative work, fuelled Mair's resentment of Riel and the Métis, which he expressed in his poetry.

In "The Last Bison" (1890), Mair brings together many of the nineteenth-century assumptions about the vanishing Indian, the idea that Indigenous cultures would soon disappear from the land.[10] More than this, the poem provides Mair with a vehicle to channel his hatred of the Métis. Distinctly Romantic in imagery and style, the poem takes place in an aesthetic refuge, with the poet alone in nature, "'twixt dreams and waking," "change and mutability."[11] The land is empty and peaceful, with no sound but the "rustling leaf." The speaker muses in a pensive repose and envisions an ideal nature until he is suddenly "startled" by a "mighty bison." The majestic beast first appears like an apparition of the "fancy," but becomes all too real when it lets out a terrifying roar, but "no voice replie[s]!"—the land is empty of all but the bison and the poet. Mair takes this sense of isolation and loss to an extreme level as this particular bison is "the last survivor of his clan!" Indeed, because it is bleeding from a mortal wound, it will soon die, marking the end of the entire species.

With the intense finality of the event, the poet becomes overwhelmed by a metaphysical connection with the bison: "He seemed to pour his mighty spirit out / As thus he gazed, till my own spirit burned" and "[g]ave to that glorious attitude a voice, / And, rapt, endowed the noble beast with song." Through this metempsychotic transference from the animal to the human, the poet taps into the memory of the species and recalls the symbiotic relationship between the bison and the First Peoples:

> I grew, and with my kindred ranged
> Their realm stupendous, changeless and unchanged,
> Save by the toll of nations primitive,
> Who throve on us, and loved our life-stream's roar,
> And lived beside its wave, and camped upon its shore.[12]

Cutting through the entire continent, the bison herds once existed as an ever-flowing stream, along which several Indigenous peoples developed their civilizations and thrived. Mair characterizes them as possessing a natural innocence, for killing bison at this time was a "blameless strife," done out of "claims of hunger, not of greed." Moreover, prior to colonization, there was no mournful sense of loss as death was not an end of life to be lamented, but a "fulfillment" of a greater "fate." In other words, transcending contradiction, the "mutability" of nature functioned as part of an eternal cycle, "changeless and unchanged."

Hence, Mair idealizes the Plains Indian relation to the bison and the land with a Romantic sense of their unity within nature, but while the Métis also based their culture on the buffalo hunt, Mair initially blames them for the destruction of the life source of an Indigenous culture. Indeed, Mair historically locates the point at which the land and the bison became doomed when "the red man mixed his blood / With paler currents." The speaker condemns the Métis as a people who hunt the bison solely for commercial gain and not "the simple needs of men":

> Then arose a race—
> The reckless hunters of the plains—who vied
> In wanton slaughter for the tongue and hide,
> To satisfy vain ends and longings base.

The bison have existed throughout the rise and fall of cultures over centuries on the Great Plains. However, with the loss of the bison, a primary historical link with an Indigenous way of life has been forever broken. According to Mair, because of the emergence of the Métis Nation, that which was seemingly endless and recurring has disappeared irrevocably into the past. Hence, we see depictions of empty lands and the disappearance of the Native inhabitants, but this time Indigenous peoples are idealized, while degrading descriptions are deflected onto the Métis—from Mair's perspective, because the Métis are the racial result of colonial and First Nations contact, they have a negative effect on the stability of the land, belonging in neither Indian nor Canadian space.

Riel, of course, reacted to Mair's negative perception of the Métis as the cause of the downfall of the land with his own negative view of the English Canadian. Riel wrote a poem lampooning Mair being scolded by the postmaster's wife; he also wrote letters clarifying the dignity of the Métis in Red River.[13] However, a look at an earlier poem on a previous conflict reveals a more deeply rooted animosity and disturbing basis for both Riel's motives and forms of consolation. In "Le chat et les souris" (The Cat and the Mice) (1864–65), Riel consolidates his people's resolve in opposition to English Canadian expansion. The poem presents a rather simplistic allegory of military conflict, but it contains a question, a message, and a justification for action. Most importantly, at the heart of the poem, Riel uses the memory of dead ancestors and lost lands as a motivation to overcome the fear of death in combat:

Pour que de son amorce
　　La peur ébranlât moins les coeurs,
Chacun devait de plus penser à ses malheurs
Aux parents massacrés, à ces chères victimes
Dont les cruelles morts étaient autant de crimes
Qui criaent la vengeance.
[...]
　　　　　　　　　Aux souris la victoire
Resta, non pas sans morts pourtant, mais avec gloire.
Elles purent au moins savourer une fois
Les joies de la vengeance. Et sous leurs petits toits
Les neveux bien longtemps en surent la mémoire.[14]

　　　　　　(To lessen the onslaught
Each time fear reared its riven head,
Each would remind himself of ills befallen him,
Of parents massacred, of dear ones made victim,
Whose cruel deaths were suffictint [sic] indictment.
They cried vengeance.
. . . .
The mice, their ranks thinned, finally claim victory,
A galling taste though not without some glory.
They at least have the consolation, the sweet taste
Of revenge. They can cling to the memory
And to future generations recount the tale.)

Significantly, the poem demonstrates how Riel turns the threat of military conflict into a motivating vengeance, using the memory of the loss of land, friends, and kinfolk as fuel to overcome the fear of one's own death when defending the Métis Nation and ensuring its continuing existence.

The Northwest Resistance and the Cycle of Revenge: Hayes, Crawford, and Johnson

From the battle at Seven Oaks to the 1869 resistance at Red River, the divisions were clear and positions were taken.[15] Red River—the junction of the fur trade, the first farming settlement, and the portal to the West—has a history filled with racial conflict, struggles over the land, and the establishing of national identities.[16] Indeed, for Riel, his political success at Red River soon met with personal grief, given his exile from the country, as the feelings of displacement and alienation he felt metaphorically as death in earlier poems became all too real after Red River. However, Riel had a chance to redeem himself and his people over a decade later during the Northwest

Resistance. After the Canadian government had established its authority in Red River, many Métis resettled in areas around the Saskatchewan River. At the same time, the Canadian government continued to push further west. Riel returned to Canada in the summer of 1884 to lead the Métis along with Gabriel Dumont, and, together with several Cree, Blackfoot, Blood, Peigan, and Saulteaux nations, again attempted to establish an independent nation against Canadian expansion.

Although there were English Canadians who sided with the Métis, many officials responded aggressively with military force, and the response by many writers was equally aggressive in poetry, especially in poems that lament the loss of soldiers in battle. For instance, in "Riel" (1895), Kate Simpson Hayes, like Mair, sees the Métis as an aberration: "And o'er this lovely prairie land there fell / The blight of a proud heart's unrest: Riel!"[17] She rejects the pride in the Métis nationalist stand as she asserts that the "dying moans" and "new-made mounds" are ultimately the fault of Riel's overreaching pride. She further expresses anger at Riel for the soldiers' deaths in the conflict, and in turn rejoices at the defeat of the Métis, voicing the Canadian victory as "a British cheer / That ends in a wild wail! / From wigwam hear the swell / In that deep cry of anguish and reproach: Riel!" For Hayes, the "British cheer" becomes the primary expression to atone for the loss of English Canadian soldiers in battle.

This attitude is also found in the poem "Songs for the Soldiers" (1885) by Isabella Valancy Crawford, in which she uses the battle cheer as motivation to maintain the ongoing defence of Canada as a way to console the loss of English Canadian troops. However, unlike Hayes, Crawford does not mourn the fallen soldiers but glorifies them: "If songs be sung let minstrels strike their harps / To large and joyous strains":

> So let her chant
> The paeans of the dead, where holy Grief
> Hath, trembling, thrust the feeble mist aside
> That veils the dead, and in the wondrous clasp
> Of re-possession ceases to be Grief.[18]

Like Riel, but from the opposing side, Crawford uses the process of mourning to transform "Grief" into something beyond itself. To dwell on a lament for the fallen soldiers who died defending the country's cause would be to remain in a "feeble mist," which would dishonour their sacrifices. Rather, Crawford "chronicle[s] the heroes" and honours the particular deaths of "Brown, Moor, and Fitch" not with anguish, but with resolve for the victory that their lives and deaths secured:

> The day they made that bold burst at Batoche,
> And with their dead flesh built a wall about
> Our riving land.

The macabre garrison imagery is striking, but Crawford emphasizes their gruesome deaths in order to elevate their sacrifices to the highest level of national and religious purpose as they died defending the "the sacred towers of Home." Reinforcing the English Canadian perspective, Crawford condemns the Métis cause and turns the martial death cries into a celebration of the defence of the "nation's pride." Hence, we see how both sides of the conflict use the defeat of the other to console the loss of their own soldiers, mirroring each other's revenge while exclaiming their own right to victory and the safety of their homes.

On a more personal level Crawford further divides her poem into consolations for the mother, the wife, and the lover. The loss of a son, husband, or lover to war cannot be fully reconciled with the blaring trumpets of patriotic fervour. Thus, Crawford addresses each woman's grief and tries to reach the hearts of the English Canadian people in an attempt to strike a balance between remembrance and glorification so as not to exploit the sacrifices for political or ideological gain. However, while her series of vigils and consolations may embolden the resolve of English Canadian mothers, wives, and lovers, she avoids any consideration of the loss of Métis and First Nations families. This irony can be located in Crawford's use of high rhetoric: in the poem, she praises the "glory on the sword" that defends "the dear lines that map the nation out upon the world," which is ironic because it was not the Métis who "[b]eat at the wall" of the Dominion as they were the ones encroached upon in lands they had lived on for generations. More strikingly, Crawford frames the entire conflict with a compressed apocalyptic image that simultaneously deifies the Canadian deaths, yet dwarfs the great historical consequences that come with the defeat of one culture over another:

> Give them such breasts
> As hold immortal fires, and they shall fly,
> Swept with our little sphere thro' all the change
> That waits a whirling world.[19]

Crawford's method of consolation here reinforces the status quo of the era. In other words, while much of her poetry, like Mair's, contains an inherent Romantic lament for the loss of an Indigenous past, she nonetheless overlooks the Métis losses. She reinforces divisions between English Canadians and the Métis by overlooking their losses at the expense of glorifying her own.

However, while the lyrics from opposing Métis and English Canadian perspectives console one side to the exclusion of the other, Mohawk-English poet E. Pauline Johnson was unique in her time as her poetry conveys a much more balanced attitude toward the Northwest Resistance than many of her contemporaries. In "A Request" (1886), Johnson switches between Métis and English Canadian sympathies throughout the poem, encouraging an understanding of both sides. The poem is an address to the Woman's Auxiliary of Missions of the Church of England in Canada. In it, Johnson advocates a mutual respect and healing process, encouraging the English Canadian women to consider the grief of the Indian mothers:

O Indian mother, list'ning for the coming of your son
Who left his home a year ago to fight the Volunteers,
To meet his death from British guns, his death song British cheers.[20]

The speaker refers to the cheers of victory in poems such as those of Hayes and Crawford that rejoice at the death of the Métis warrior. In this way, Johnson takes their words and uses them against them. Indeed, Johnson considers the English Canadian soldier's mother who "listen[s] for his tread," for mothers on both sides wait "[f]or footsteps of the boy who left but nevermore returns."

What is interesting here, perhaps because Johnson is writing from a distance about another Indigenous culture, is that the speaker does not pass judgment or place blame on either side—"'Tis not my place to question"—but rather asks that the Women's Auxiliary send missionaries to help alleviate the scarcity and famine that resulted from the fighting. Struggling to find a sense of humanity in the midst of conflict, Johnson sees that it is no longer an issue between two opposing nations, but that there is a need for personal dignity and freedom from suffering. However, Johnson's double perspective tends to complicate her critical reception as she bases her petition on the responsibility the women have as Christians to send the missionaries: "And, perhaps, beyond the river brink the waves of death have laved, / The jewels in your crown will be the Indian souls you've saved." This plea, taken one way, is disturbing in light of the historical outcome of the assimilation and removal policies of the reserve and residential schools system. Taken another way, the speaker is also asking that the Canadian mothers live up to their own Christian ideals. Either way, Johnson's point addresses the collective trauma that comes with being torn from place—and, as we have seen in previous poems of the era, this trauma is the root of the impulse to retaliate and defend one's lands.

The difficulty of Johnson's negotiation is even more apparent in "A Cry from an Indian Wife" (1885). The speaker finds herself in an ambiguous position, between cultures, confronting the possible loss of her husband in the Resistance: "My heart the target if my warrior falls." She is divided in her sympathies between a peaceful surrender to the Canadian government, or the continuing resistance against western expansion to preserve First Nations and Métis cultures. At first she tells her husband to take his "tomahawk" to "drink the life-blood of a soldier host," but then just as quickly holds him back:

> Go; rise and strike, no matter what the cost.
> Yet stay. Revolt not at the Union Jack,
> Nor raise thy hand against this stripling pack
> Of white-faced warriors, marching West to quell
> Our fallen tribe that rises to rebel.[21]

She does not want to lose her closest loved one, or see the "young and beautiful and good" Métis defeated, but neither does she want to see the loss of the English Canadian boys. Hence, she does not blame the individual English Canadian soldier, but rather:

> Curse to the fate that brought them from the East
> To be our chiefs—to make our nation least
> That breathes the air of this vast continent.

One may criticize Johnson's indecisive political position here toward the Métis resistance, but such criticism does not take the whole poem into consideration. Johnson is trying to make a point: in addition to her fears of her own loss, the speaker tells her husband to think of the English Canadian mothers and maidens who will lose their husbands, sons, and lovers: "Ah, how her white face quivers thus to think, / *Your* tomahawk his life's best blood will drink." Johnson attempts to put both sides into perspective in the poem as the speaker fantasizes about the feelings of the English Canadians. Furthermore, it is not just the death of an individual that must be consoled as the conflict involves a multitude of people on both sides, including entire families, communities, and the nations themselves.

Ultimately, however, as Emma LaRocque comments, "even though Johnson clearly feels conflicted between the two sides, she supports the Indian finally on the basis of land rights."[22] The defeat of the Métis was tied historically with the displacement of First Nations peoples, for the entire conflict comes on the heels of the collective death of the buffalo and the collapse of several Great Plains cultures. These issues still resonate today, as Métis and First Nations peoples continue to defend their sense of place within Canada.

Johnson's speaker appears to foresee the consequences of these conflicts as she goes back and forth between the desire for revenge and the need to transcend it in order to end the suffering. Despite her indecision, she intimately considers each side respectively, developing a sense of the other's loss. Indeed, although she appears to be ambiguous, indecisive, and contradictory, the speaker's position gives her the ability to empathize with individuals on both sides. Hence, Johnson shows that while the fear of death does not end the fighting, but rather gives further motive for vengeance, there is still more to life than making the Other suffer. Nonetheless, Johnson makes another problematic statement at the end of her poem, when she offers a kind of bittersweet consolation for the defeat of the Métis Nation: "perhaps the white man's God has willed it so."

The Apocalyptic Resolution: Johnson, Mair, and Riel

To make some sense of Johnson's problematic statement, it is helpful to return to the apocalyptic image in Crawford's poem—the image of the "whirling world." It is a powerful notion, but it is also deceptive, for this kind of trope is really a rhetorical device that poets use to cancel out any of the contradictions that they cannot resolve in their poems—in Crawford's case, the fact that the victory cheers mean the defeat of the Métis, without consideration of their loss. The image of the "whirling world" allows Crawford to absorb the loss of Aboriginal cultures into the greater cycles of history, and it also absolves her own society's role in that loss as it implies that Canadian and other Western cultures will one day end as well.

The significance of Johnson's critique becomes even more clear when we return to our analysis of Charles Mair's poem and his use of the death of the last bison as a metaphor for the disappearance of Indigenous cultures. Mair makes an extreme use of the apocalyptic consolation as the speaker expresses "Sorrow [...] o'er man's decay": "For here, but yesterday, the warrior dwelt / Whose faded nation had for ages held, / In fealty to Nature, these domains." The speaker envisions an idyllic past that was "[o]nce resonant," where "happy offspring roved." However, the speaker laments their disappearance, for they have "[a]ll vanished now!":

> With them had fled
> The bison-breed which overflowed the plains,
> And, undiminished, fed uncounted tribes.
> . . . .
> Endless and infinite – vast herds which seemed
> Exhaustless as the sea. All vanished now!
> Of that wild tumult not a hoof remained
> To scour the countless paths where myriads trod.[23]

The images of sublime abundance turn to elegiac themes of exile and scarcity as he paints a picture of the aggressive extirpation of the bison from their last refuge:

> ...scattered! Meagre bands, in wild dismay,
> Were parted and, for shelter, fled away
> To barren wastes, to mountain gorge and glen
> A respite brief from stern pursuit and care,
> For still the spoiler sought, and still he slew us there.

The strong use of compression in the poetic sequence allows Mair to diminish Native loss and overlook colonial presence as the "virgin air and waters" are somehow "[i]nviolate still!" Mair's political bias against the Métis underlies the contradiction here as the setting of the poem, the refuge of the dying bison, is the same place where the Northwest Resistance occurred. Diminishing the Métis loss of homeland, Mair ends his sweep of history anticlimactically as all the violent conflicts from the Spanish Conquest to Frog Lake fall into "forgetfulness" as a "chuckling wrong" and "weary clangour."

Mair has focused his view on the Métis resistance as a terminal point of Canadian history. As we saw, the bison's song suggested that the Métis were responsible for the downfall of the land. However, Mair now takes things a step further: even though he is an English Canadian, he goes on to demonize the effect that British colonialism has had on what he sees as a more noble and romanticized Indigenous condition: "we flourished, and our name / Prospered until the pale destroyer's concourse came":

> Then fell a double terror on the plains,
> The swift inspreading of destruction dire—
> Strange men, who ravaged our domains
> On every hand, and ringed us round with fire;
> Pale enemies, who slew with equal mirth
> The harmless or the hurtful things of earth
> In dead fruition of their mad desire:
> The ministers of mischief and of might,
> Who yearn for havoc as the world's supreme delight.

Mair ends up blaming English Canadian expansion, along with the Métis, for the destruction of the bison and an idealized Indigenous past. He further focuses his blame on the unfettered consumption of natural resources, not just for the extinction of the bison, but for the eventual demise of all natural life:

> perished in the swelling sea
> And stayless tide of an encroaching power
> Whose civil fiat, man-devouring still,
> Will leave, at last, no wilding on the earth
> To wonder at or love!

The depth of Mair's nihilistic view is shocking as he depicts nineteenth-century Canadian western expansion as indifferent to the destruction its growth causes and oblivious to how this will even lead to the downfall of Western civilization.

Mair works with the conceit that the same ambition that leads to a civilization's success can also lead to its ruin. It is at this point in the poem that the last bison, with its final breath, transforms the metalepsis of history to a prolepsis of the future, and makes a "prophesy" about the end of Western culture. As the "centuries in dim procession fly," the bison "see[s] our spoilers build their cities great," and then sees "grassy mounds, where cities once had been":

> Once more my vision sweeps the prairies wide,
> But now no peopled cities greet the sight;
> All perished, now, their pomp and pride.

Mair envisions for the colonists what they have done to the Indigenous peoples in both history and poetry—that is, depicting them as disappearing.[24] At the end of the colonial period with the conquest of all Aboriginal nations and the transition to Confederation, the bison's song foresees a decolonized future and the complete restoration of Indigenous life. Indeed, he takes it a step further, envisioning a more distant future when the First Peoples return to the land: "And savage nations roam o'er native wilds again!"[25] The bison's song ends, and the speaker returns to the present moment to witness its last death throes. As the Indigenous life source was ravaged by reckless colonization, Mair wishes to put this in the past as well and envisions a time when civilization will again have a respect for the land and animals, just as the Indigenous ancestors did.[26]

Taking a step back, one can see that Mair falls into an apocalyptic tradition that reflects the destructive aspects of Western culture and foretells the end of history, having recourse to a Romantic Aboriginal past that has disappeared, but will someday return. However, despite this self-critical view of his own culture, Mair still does not escape the status quo and the contradictions in the ideologies of his age. Associating the death of the last bison with the loss of Indigenous cultures, the poem is a classic instance of how the English Canadian speaker gives voice to that which he or she represents as dying and voiceless. Mair's use of an apocalyptic vision further allows him to diminish the destruction of one period of history by incorporating it into a larger, inevitable cycle. However, his nationalism comes into conflict with his literary aspirations and historical concerns. This is because although he attempts to romanticize an Indigenous way of life as somehow more pure than Métis or Western cultures, Mair himself was part of the process of destroying it.[27] Thus, Mair confronts a complex colonial condition that he is implicated in and which he cannot resolve without envisioning the end of all history.

Riel also turned to apocalyptic visions as part of his path to redemption, but for very different reasons than Mair. Throughout his life, Riel experienced several visionary experiences, which in turn affected his poetry's religious consolation. By the time of the Northwest Resistance, Riel's religious views had increased in intensity as he further proclaimed that the Métis cause was part of a greater transition in Christian eschatology. Indeed, after his trial, Riel wrote: "[t]o the Readers of *The Star*: I have devoted my life to my country. If it is necessary for the happiness of my country that I should now cease to live, I leave it to the Providence of God."[28] However, although many critics question Riel's apocalyptic beliefs, these poems reveal that essentially his views were at least morally equivalent to those of his contemporaries, and indeed go beyond them in terms of reconciliation.

An example of Riel's expression of divine consolation can be found in "Palpite! ô mon esprit" (How My Body Trembles) (1885), which he wrote in jail awaiting execution. Identifying himself with the entire Métis cause, Riel contemplates his own death and expresses grief over the loss of the Resistance.[29] However, he finds consolation in the promise of a divine apotheosis: "La paix et ses fruits font reculer le tombeau!" (The blooms of peace will keep death at bay!):

L'heureuse paix du coeur dans les plus grandes luttes
Toute seule vaut mieux que tous les autres biens.
Les revers, avec Elle, ont l'air d'être des chutes
D'abord; pour devenir ensuite des moyens.[30]

(Peace in the heart amid the great battles
Is even more precious than earthly treasures.
Perhaps our failures appear like shackles
To help us overcome our wretched fears.)

In his final days, Riel returns to a pursuit of spiritual transcendence over worldly ambition. For Riel, the only real peace is one found in Christ and God: "Ouvrons bien les deux palmes / Des nos mains vers le ciel. Rennaissons de nouveau!" (Let us open both hands so that our palms / Embrace the sky. Thus we will be reborn!). The promise of a divine rebirth releases a transformative consolatory revelation: "Sainte Vierge, obtenez qu'un torrent de lumières / Vienne éclairer le genre humain." (Holy Mary, may rivulets of light pour and pour / To enlighten all mankind). Riel arrives at an awareness, sudden and complete, as it brings all the conflicting elements and contradictions into a greater unity. We return to the Christian assurance that turns tears to joy in the context of an apocalypse or revelation of the ultimate knowledge of life and death at the end of the individual life and at the end of the world.

At the same time, Riel's view of death becomes more strangely personal and yet more socially relatable. He came to see death as a fiancée, who loves and embraces him; he also saw death as a thief. The most significant aspect of Riel's relation to death, though, is that because of the set date of his execution, he knew when the exact time of his death would be. This awareness led to a complex consolation, which is both comforting and mortifying: "Death has gained a day on me since yesterday [...] Death keeps guard at the door of my cell."[31] However, Riel finds consolation in a line of poetry that redeems himself and his nation's cause:

> And when His evidence
> Decides my acquittal,
> Let the Multitude dance
> In a move immortal.[32]

He no longer recognizes human justice, for that is based on revenge and division. Rather, he turns to God's judgment—and when he is acquitted in death, the "Multitude," the Métis, will "dance in a move immortal." In other words, the Métis were never conquered as they continue after Riel with a heightened consciousness of the displacement of a way of life that they had established over generations on the land. It is here that Riel emerges as the most pivotal and complex figure of the era, for his final poems show that apocalyptic views can also reveal the need to transcend the cycle of revenge. Rather than fear an end, he proclaims a beginning.

Conclusion
The conflicts of the Red River and Northwest Resistances encompassed an apocalyptic space. Within it, there was a volatile displacement of Aboriginal traditions and communities. Consequently, a motif of revenge for past losses became central to a poetics of place, and the turn to apocalyptic imagery helped the poets frame the effect of western expansion on Aboriginal cultures, whether from the Métis perspective of Riel or the English Canadian views of Hayes, Crawford, and Mair. The English Canadian poets turned to apocalyptic imagery in an attempt to legitimate their role in the conflicts over land because it provided the context to romanticize the same Aboriginal losses that their society was causing. As this is clearly a contradictory position, the poets added to their poems a vision of the eventual end of their own cultures as a way to include themselves in the fate of the cultures

they were displacing, implying that the displacement of Aboriginal cultures was something already historically determined. As this fight over homeland increased, Johnson, herself both English and First Nations, worked from both perspectives, envisioning a unified idea of nationhood based on a shared sense of loss and a shared sense of place. Indeed, Johnson's critique of using apocalyptic imagery to rationalize the moral consequences of western expansion helps emphasize the need to heal the rifts between divided peoples. Riel came to understand this, and although he also uses apocalyptic imagery as a form of closure, what is most important is that he uses it in a way that affirms the need to reconcile the conflicts rather than justify them.

Notes

1 The Cree word for this historical time is ê-kî-mâyahkâmikahk, literally "when it went wrong."

2 See G. F. Stanley, ed., *The Collected Writings of Louis Riel*, 5 vols. (Edmonton: University of Alberta Press, 1985).

3 Louis Riel, *Selected Poetry of Louis Riel*, trans. Paul Savoie, ed. Glen Campbell (Toronto: Exile, 1993), 42–45.

4 During the Métis raid on Dr. Schultz's house, where Mair had been staying, the only manuscript for his long narrative poem, "Zardust and Selima," was destroyed. See Fred Cogswell, "Charles Mair," in *Canadian Writers and Their Works*, vol. 1, ed. Robert Lecker, Jack David, and Ellen Quigley (Toronto: ECW Press, 1988), 151.

5 Ibid., 151.

6 *Toronto Globe*, January 20, 1869; letter from Mair, quoted in Doug Owram, *Promise of Eden: The Canadian Expansionist Movement and the Idea of the West 1856–1900* (Toronto: University of Toronto Press, 1980), 72.

7 For instance, Mair wrote: "Many wealthy people are married to half-breed women, who, having no coat of arms but a 'totem' to look back to, make up for the deficiency by biting at the backs of their 'white' sisters." Letter from Charles Mair to Holmes Mair, printed in the *Toronto Globe*, January 4, 1869, quoted in Maggie Siggins, *Riel: A Life of Revolution* (Toronto: HarperCollins, 1994), 87.

8 The significance of controlling Fort Garry cannot be understated, as Siggins explains: "The huge stone quadrangle, surrounded by walls fifteen feet high and protected by ten bastions mounted with six-pounder cannon, was the strategic centre of the Red River Settlement. Since all roads radiated from this point, it was understood that whoever controlled Fort Garry controlled all of Rupert's Land." Siggins, *Riel*, 109.

9 Ibid., 124.

10 Mair was interested in the history of Indigenous cultures throughout much of his career—in addition to "The Last Bison," Mair wrote *Tecumseh, a Drama*, *The American Bison*, and *Through the Mackenzie Basin: A Narrative of the Athabasca and Peace River Treaty Expedition of 1899.*

11 Charles Mair, "The Last Bison," in *Tecumseh, a Drama and Canadian Poems* (Whitefish, MT: Kessinger, 2005), 237–42.

12 Ibid.

13 See Siggins, *Riel*, 87–89.

14 Riel, *Selected Poetry*, 16–23.

15 Conflict in the Red River dates further back to its earliest days. The settlement was the first farming settlement in the Northwest, and was founded on land purchased from the Hudson's Bay Company in 1811 by Lord Selkirk. The settlement was across the river from an important fur trade route established by the Nor'West Company and run by the Métis. As Alan Wilson explains in "The 1810s," in *Colonists and Canadiens: 1760–1867*, ed. J. Careless (Toronto: Macmillan, 1971), 141: "Nor'Westers used intimidation and the threat of the Métis, and for a time completely dispersed the colony. A Hudson's Bay counterforce helped re-establish it; but in 1816 Robert Semple and twenty colonists were killed at Seven Oaks in a disastrous skirmish with the Métis. In response Selkirk engaged veterans from the War of 1812 as mercenaries [...] to restore his colony."

16 The irony is that the conflicts ultimately served English Canadian interests, as Siggins explains: "if the Canadian government perceived that a united form of opposition had cemented in the Red River Settlement it might sideline its plans to take over the West. It was important, therefore, to ferment conflict and discontent whenever possible." Siggins, *Riel*, 118.

17 Kate Simpson Hayes, "Riel," in *Canadian Poetry: From the Beginnings Through the First World War*, ed. Carole Gerson and Gwendolyn Davies (Toronto: McClelland and Stewart, 1994), 312–13.

18 Isabella Valancy Crawford, "Songs for the Soldiers," in *The Collected Poems of Isabella Valancy Crawford*, ed. Ethelwyn Wetherald (Raleigh, NC: Hayes Barton Press, 2006), 50–53.

19 Ibid., 50.

20 E. Pauline Johnson, "A Request," in *Collected Poems and Selected Prose*, ed. Carole Gerson and Veronica Strong-Boag (Toronto: University of Toronto Press, 2002), 22–23.

21 Ibid., 14–15.

22 Emma LaRocque, *When the Other Is Me: Native Resistance Discourse 1850–1990* (Winnipeg: University of Manitoba Press, 2010), 81. LaRocque makes a further salient point: "[i]t is intriguing that Johnson, herself an eastern Metis, refers only to Whites and Indians about a situation that principally involved the Metis of Red River. The issue of Metis loss of land space in western Canada is as much an issue about Aboriginal land rights as it is for other Native groups."

23 Mair, "The Last Bison," 237–42.

24 Leslie Monkman, in *A Native Heritage: Images of the Indian in English-Canadian Literature* (Toronto: University of Toronto Press, 1981), 89, explains: "More common in Canadian literature than a vision of the destruction of the white man's world by the Indian is the recognition that this world is subject to the same laws of chance, change, and death that have contributed to the red man's destruction."

25 Mair, "The Last Bison," 242.
26 Cogswell explains: Mair came "to see virtue in the Métis and in the Indian way of life which had altogether escaped him during his early Fort Garry days. He came to realize that, although the old way of life on the prairie was doomed by settlement, there was much more that was good in it than he had once conceded." Moreover, "his paper on the threatened extinction of the bison given before the Royal Society of Canada two years later, led to the Canadian government's purchase from the United States of the only remaining bison herd on the prairie and establishing it in a national reserve at Wainwright, Alberta." Cogswell, "Charles Mair," 127, 149.
27 Ibid., 149. Indeed, "at the time when these lines were published in book form, Mair was earning his living as a government agent furthering the process he described."
28 Quoted in Siggins, *Riel*, xvi.
29 Riel said at his trial: "I stand in this dock, not as myself only, but as the chosen representative of a whole people." Quoted in Margaret Gail Osachoff, "Louis Riel in Canadian Literature: Myth and Reality," in *Canadian Story and History 1885–1985*, ed. Colin Nicholson and Peter Easingwood (Edinburgh: University Centre of Canadian Studies, 1985), 61.
30 Riel, *Selected Poetry*, 124–26.
31 Quoted in Siggins, *Riel*, 437.
32 Ibid., 410.

Bibliography

Brummett, Barry. *Contemporary Apocalyptic Rhetoric*. New York: Praeger, 1991.
Burns, Robert Alan. "Isabella Valancy Crawford." In *Canadian Writers and Their Works*, vol. 1, edited by Robert Lecker, Jack David, and Ellen Quigley, 21–74. Toronto: ECW Press, 1988.
Cogswell, Fred. "Charles Mair." In *Canadian Writers and Their Works*, vol. 1, edited by Robert Lecker, Jack David, and Ellen Quigley, 119–58. Toronto: ECW Press, 1988.
Crawford, Isabella Valancy. "Songs for the Soldiers." In *The Collected Poems of Isabella Valancy Crawford*, edited by Ethelwyn Wetherald, 50–53. Raleigh, NC: Hayes Barton Press, 2006.
Hayes, Kate Simpson. "Riel." In *Canadian Poetry: From the Beginnings through the First World War*, edited by Carole Gerson and Gwendolyn Davies, 312–13. Toronto: McClelland and Stewart, 1994.
Johnson, Emily Pauline. *Collected Poems and Selected Prose*, edited by Carole Gerson and Veronica Strong-Boag. Toronto: University of Toronto Press, 2002.
LaRocque, Emma. *When the Other Is Me: Native Resistance Discourse 1850–1990*. Winnipeg: University of Manitoba Press, 2010.
Mair, Charles. "The Last Bison." In *Tecumseh, a Drama and Canadian Poems*, 237–42. Whitefish, MT: Kessinger Publishing, 2005.

Monkman, Leslie. *A Native Heritage: Images of the Indian in English-Canadian Literature.* Toronto: University of Toronto Press, 1981.

Osachoff, Margaret Gail. "Louis Riel in Canadian Literature: Myth and Reality." In *Canadian Story and History 1885–1985*, edited by Colin Nicholson and Peter Easingwood, 62–69. Edinburgh: University Centre of Canadian Studies, 1985.

Owram, Doug. *Promise of Eden: The Canadian Expansionist Movement and the Idea of the West 1856–1900.* Toronto: University of Toronto Press, 1980.

Riel, Louis. *The Collected Writings of Louis Riel*, 5 vols., edited by G. F. Stanley. Edmonton: University of Alberta Press, 1985.

———. *Selected Poetry of Louis Riel*, edited by Glen Campbell, translated by Paul Savoie. Toronto: Exile, 1993.

Savoie, Paul. Endnote to "Les chat et les souris." In *Selected Poetry of Louis Riel*, edited by Glen Campbell, 132. Toronto: Exile, 1993.

Siggins, Maggie. *Riel: A Life of Revolution.* Toronto: HarperCollins, 1994.

Wilson, Alan. "The 1810s." In *Colonists and Canadiens: 1760–1867*, edited by J. Careless, 122–48. Toronto: Macmillan, 1971.

17

My Poem Is an Indian Woman

Rosanna Deerchild

I.

The brilliant Thomas King said in his 2003 Massey Lecture that "The truth about stories is that is all we are."[1]

There are two basic rules to good storytelling. The story must be kept and the story must be given away. My story is a poem. My poem is an Indian woman.

People have always used stories as a means of sharing histories, way of life, and world views. Regardless of geography, colour, culture, or nation, stories inform our societies. Stories shape our moral beliefs. How we see ourselves. They influence how we see others. They seduce.

For Indigenous peoples, stories are intrinsic to our lives. Many nations had no written word, were nomadic, and spent a lot of time together, so you had to be a good storyteller.

Canada sought to silence that story. The aggressive assimilation policy imposed on Indians spawned the Indian Act, which deemed cultural gatherings, songs, ceremonies, even dancing, illegal.

The Indian Act also opened the door to the Indian Residential School Era. At its peak, 150,000 Indian kids were torn from their families and communities to be "educated" in the white man school system. Its intention, as then deputy superintendent of the Department of Indian Affairs, Duncan Campbell Scott said, was: "to continue until there is not a single Indian in Canada who has not been absorbed into the body politic and there is no Indian question and no Indian Department, that is the whole object of this bill."[2]

The objective of Indian Residential Schools, paid for by the Canadian government, was to kill the Indian within the child. Languages other than English were forbidden. Hair was cut and families torn apart. We were literally silenced.

Suddenly, everything we ever knew as Peoples was forbidden. Punishments were harsh, abuse was rampant, illness and death rates were abnormally high.

Meanwhile, those left behind were left to cope with homes empty of children, empty of laughter, empty of even sound. That silence meant stories—our stories—were gone.

Canada's act of cultural genocide was, of course, an utter disaster. Instead of killing the Indian within the child, it killed the child within the Indian. The effects are still being felt today. Indigenous peoples top every list of poverty, incarceration, health ills, child welfare apprehensions—all products of Canadian-made law.

But stories are never really gone. They have a funny way of showing up at just the right time. They're wily like coyote, just hiding out, waiting to be told.

II.

I Lost My Talk

I lost my talk
The talk you took away.
When I was a little girl
At Shubenacadie school.[3]

Mi'kmaq poet Rita Joe wrote that. She was born in 1932, in Wycocomagh, Cape Breton Island, and attended Shubenacadie Indian Residential School until grade eight.

She wrote about her experience in the 1970s, long before the dark legacy of the schools was completely revealed to mainstream Canadians. On reserves and in families, it was the fat white elephant in the room. No one wanted to say "residential school," much less talk about what happened there.

But Rita Joe did what silenced people do. She found other ways to communicate her truth. She reached for a pen and has said, "I write stories in poetry form."[4]

In her 1978 book, *Poems by Rita Joe*, she wrote about being Indian in Canada, being Mi'maq, and wrote in her own language,[5] a language Canada tried to choke out of her and every Indigenous person with assimilation, a language that was once forbidden. Rita Joe used poetry to break the rules and broke her silence.

My Poem Is an Indian Woman

slight
takes
just enough

room

thin lines
struggle
to be untangled

she doesn't need
to say any more
or any less

she will tell you
everything

III.

As a child I was tall, skinny, and socially awkward. I wore standard Indian Affairs–issued glasses that were too big for my face so I was always pushing them up, a habit I still have. You can imagine the anguish this would cause. But being a geek was the least of my problems. I was the last of six children, so my mother didn't have much time to pay attention to my neglected ego.

Born on a summer night in 1972 I was named—depending on who you ask—after my mother's best friend, the nurse who delivered me or one of my father's favourite Hank Williams Sr. songs, "Eleven Roses."

My family is from an isolated Cree community in northern Manitoba. South Indian Lake was part of the Nelson House Band until finally gaining recognition under the Indian Act and is now officially called O-Pipon-Na-Piwin (Winter Camp Along the Shores of South Indian Lake) Cree Nation.

But back in the 1970s, Hydro was flooding the North. A lot of people were displaced when the waters literally swallowed our homes. The community itself had to be relocated.

My father didn't have any interest in marriage or monogamy. My mother was tired of loving and fighting a man she would never really have, so she married another man—a white man—and he moved us 130 kilometres south to Thompson, Manitoba.

It was the 1970s and Indian people, as determined by the Indian Act, had been legally allowed off reserve without an Indian agent pass for only about a decade or so. Thompson was a nickel-mining town and a lot of mining families were moved in from other mining towns, towns where they were not surrounded by reserves or Indians. My first book of poetry, *this is a small northern town*, is based on my experience growing up there.[6]

To say the cultural divide was wide would be an understatement. Often we were the only Indian kids on the block. It meant being called "Squaw" and "Welfare Indian" on a daily basis. It meant my brothers came home, bruised and dirty from fighting and sticking up for us—a lot. It meant me and my sister could run really fast.

It meant we were raised in a home where the colour of our skin wasn't celebrated, it was denigrated. It meant my mother, in a loveless marriage, coped as best she could; often she found escape in alcohol.

I escaped into books. Stories were my refuge. From comics to novels, to encyclopedias, to the backs of cereal boxes and my mother's expansive record collection, I read insatiably.

But something was missing.

IV.

For a long time, I didn't know what that was. Then I stumbled on this poem during one of my many forays in the public library aisles:

The Cattle Thief

Stand back, stand back, you white-skins, touch that dead man to your shame;
You have stolen my father's spirit, but his body I only claim!
You have killed him, but you shall not dare to touch him now he's dead.
You have cursed, and called him a Cattle Thief, though you robbed him first
    of bread.[7]

I hand-copied that entire poem right then and there and carried it around with me, reading it over and over.

It was written by someone I had never heard of: E. Pauline Johnson, a woman and, upon further investigation, Mohawk. I imagined Pauline, who was known as a great performer in the late nineteenth century, narrating this poem in a great theatre in New York or London.

Up until then, I didn't really like poetry. Sure, I had some favourites. I loved the sly e. e. cummings, the gruesome Poe, and the haunting song of Sylvia Plath. But for the most part, poetry was written by dead white guys. It was staid, static, full of rules and language I didn't understand. Or want to. And always, that something that was missing.

But this, this poem was different. First of all, it was the first time I'd read about Indians like that. Sure, I'd seen countless movies of us getting shot off horses by John Wayne. In school we learned we were a "dead breed" with a dead culture and on the playground, it was open season.

In "Cattle Thief"[8] I found a story about my people: the Cree and a girl standing up to an injustice. At thirteen and having never seen a positive image of my Indian self, much less a defiant one, this was world opening. I realized that what had been missing was me. I was missing from the stories I read. I was nowhere to be found in the lines and stanzas of cummings, Poe, or Plath or any of the books I read.

V.

But here I was in a nineteenth-century iambic/trimeter poem. Here I was alive, while everyone else was writing me dead. Pauline's contemporary, Duncan Campbell Scott, while trying to legislate us to death, wrote our obituary in his poetry:

The Onondaga Madonna

She stands full-throated and with careless pose,
This woman of a weird and waning race,
The tragic savage lurking in her face.[9]

He was killing us in words but Pauline was keeping us alive. She wrote about race and gender and challenged the ideas of Scott and his ilk that the "red man" was dying. In an 1890 letter to a friend she writes of her life goals: "one is to upset the Indian Extermination and non-education theory—in fact to stand by my blood and my race."[10]

she writes us alive

while others
write our eulogy
erase us from
the lines
keep us
in the margins
she breaks through
all the boundaries

writes our lives
in her wide skies

My eyes were suddenly open. I started to look for other poets, other Indian women telling their stories. I found Joy Harjo.

Remember

Remember you are this universe and this
universe is you
Remember all is motion, is growing, is you.
Remember language came from this.[11]

Storyteller and poet Leslie Marmom Silko:

Toe'osh: A Laguna Coyote Story

In the wintertime
At night
We tell coyote stories
And drink Spanada by the stove.[12]

And the strong and beautiful Lee Maracle:

Bent Box (My Song)

My song hails
from a bent box
drums of earth tears
enjoys the unbending
of woman spirit.[13]

And more: Maria Campbell, Jeannette Armstrong, Chrystos, Skydancer Louise B. Halfe, Marilyn Dumont, Joanne Arnott, Kateri Akiwenzie-Damm, Emma LaRoque—all these women, Indigenous women, telling stories. They wrote about our pain, our injustices, and, most importantly, our stubborn refusal to die.

These women. These poems. Stories influenced by their people. The experience of their lives. The struggle of being Indigenous in a white world. These women grabbed that thread from her sister before—that fragile thread—and wove it into their own stories.

All adding to a collective memory, all continuing a living story.

So I grabbed my own thread, my own lifeline, and it was like I was hearing a language that sounded vaguely familiar. I wanted to be part of this voice. I wanted to add to the story.

So I am.

I Am an Indian Poem

I am my mother's story
My grandmother's story
My great grand

All the way back

I am the returning voice
From the silence of my mother
Who had her tongue stolen
In residential school

A thousand women
Stand behind me
Whispering
Singing
Holding the story
Blood line

I breathe them all in
And poetry breathes me out.

Notes

1 Thomas King, *The Truth about Stories The Truth about Stories: A Native Narrative* (Toronto: House of Anansi Press, 2003), 2.

2 Duncan Campbell Scott, cited in John Leslie, *The Historical Development of the Indian Act* (2nd ed.) (Ottawa: Department of Indian Affairs and Northern Development, Treaties and Historical Research Branch, 1978), 114.

3 Rita Joe, "I Lost My Talk," in *Native Poetry in Canada: A Contemporary Anthology*, ed. Jeannette C. Armstrong and Lally Grauer (2001), 14.

4 Joe, *Poems by Rita Joe*, 13.

5 Ibid., 13.

6 Rosanna Deerchild, *this is a small northern town* (Winnipeg: J. Gordon Shillingford Publishing, 2008).

7 Pauline Johnson (Tekahionwake), "The Cattle Thief," in *Collected Poems and Selected Prose*, ed. Carole Gerson and Veronica Strong-Boag (Toronto: University of Toronto Press, 2000), 97.

8 Editor's note: manitowêw (known in English as "Almighty Voice") was a Cree man who was arrested for killing a cow without the permission of the Indian agent of his reserve. He was arrested, broke out of jail, and was tracked down throughout the territory of present-day Saskatchewan in 1897.

9 Duncan Campbell Scott, "The Onondaga Madonna," in *The Poems of Duncan Campbell Scott* (1898; repr. Toronto: McClelland and Stewart, 1926), 230.

10 E. Pauline Johnson (Tekahionwake), personal letter, in *Collected Poems and Selected Prose*, ed. Carole Gerson and Veronica Strong-Boag (Toronto: University of Toronto Press, 2000), xvi.

11 Joy Harjo, *How We Became Human* (New York: W. W. Norton & Co., 2003), 42.

12 Leslie Marmon Silko, "Toe'osh: A Laguna Coyote Story," in *Storyteller* (New York: Arcade, 1981), 236.

13 Lee Maracle, "Bent Box (My Song)," *Bent Box* (Penticton: Theytus Books, 2000), 82.

Bibliography

Deerchild, Rosanna. *this is a small northern town*. Winnipeg: J. Gordon Shillingford Publishing, 2008.

Harjo, Joy. *How We Became Human: New and Selected Poems*. New York: W. W. Norton & Co., 2003.

Joe, Rita. "I Lost My Talk." In *Native Poetry in Canada: A Contemporary Anthology*, edited by Jeannette C. Armstrong and Lally Grauer, 14. , 2001.

Johnson, E. Pauline (Tekahionwake). Personal letter. In *Collected Poems and Selected Prose*, edited by Carole Gerson and Veronica Strong-Boag, xvi. Toronto: University of Toronto Press, 2000.

———. E. Pauline Johnson (Tekahionwake). "The Cattle Thief." In *Collected Poems and Selected Prose*, edited by Carole Gerson and Veronica Strong-Boag, 97. Toronto: University of Toronto Press, 2000.

King, Thomas. *The Truth about Stories: A Native Narrative*. Toronto: House of Anansi Press, 2003.

Leslie, John. *The Historical development of the Indian Act.* 2nd ed. Ottawa: Department of Indian Affairs and Northern Development, Treaties and Historical Research Branch, 1978.

Maracle, Lee. "Bent Box (My Song)." In *Bent Box.* Penticton: Theytus Books, 2000.

Scott, Duncan Campbell. "The Onondaga Madonna." In *The Poems of Duncan Campbell Scott.* 1898. Repr. Toronto: McClelland and Stewart, 1926.

Silko, Leslie Marmon. "Toe'osh: A Laguna Coyote Story." *Storyteller.* New York: Arcade, 1981.

Poetics of Performance

18

Interview with Marvin Francis

Conducted by Rosanna Deerchild and Shayla Elizabeth

This conversation between Marvin Francis, Rosanna Deerchild, and Shayla Elizabeth occurred when members of the Aboriginal writers group were visiting to perform at the Crow Hop. The interview took place at Sâkêwêwak First Nations Artist Collective on October 2001, Regina, Saskatchewan.

ROSANNA DEERCHILD (RD): Alright, now we are on the other side of the table with Marvin Francis and we are interviewing him. This is very exciting. Aren't you excited, Shayla?

SHAYLA ELIZABETH (SE): Very excited—my chance to—

MARVIN FRANCIS (MF): I'm so excited I didn't even make it to the Kleenex.

RD: This is starting to sound like that porn again. [laughter] So, Marvin, what is your deal? You're the most eccentric member of our group, as I often say. You have your own category. What is going on in that head of yours?

MF: Well everything, man! But it's kinda like, I'm not really eccentric. I'm just viewed that way. I'm misunderstood, eh? You know what I'm saying? [laughter]

SE: That's the typical lament of all men. [laughter]

RD: I'm just misunderstood... [laughter]

MF: What's going on in my head? I don't know, like, exactly what you mean. Life experiences shape you differently. Everybody's different. I mean, we're all eccentric, right, in our way, whether you're a writer or a bricklayer. You know what I'm saying? You know? We're all different. Some of us just perhaps are more honest about it, I think.

RD: You think, you figure you're honest, or are you a big liar? What's your deal?

MF: Or not dumb enough to cover up, right? [laughter] I don't know, I don't really consider myself a liar. I don't pretend to be something I'm not.

SE: So what made you join the writers group?

MF: Through Duncan, I guess. That's how I originally—for a while there, me and Duncan, before this group started, we had a couple of meetings of people there, but it just never really panned out. We didn't have a place to meet and, you know, people didn't show up much, and then it sort of petered off, and then when Rosanna started up the group again, then I came in, close to the very beginning there, if I remember, if my memory's correct. And it's sort of been there ever since, I guess.

RD: So you're pretty wide-ranging when it comes to your writing. How about you tell me—tell the audience, who is no doubt listening in droves right now—about some of your writing? What's your genres, etc.?

MF: Okay, well, I write poetry, obviously, because I'm here for the Crow Hop. I write screenplays for film and television, and stage plays, and one of my favourite means is radio drama.

RD: Tell us about your book. I understand you're getting a book published, which is very exciting, I'm sure.

MF: Yeah, I did an M.A. at the University of Manitoba, and for my thesis, for my creative M.A., I wrote a book of poetry, and the book's getting published by Turnstone Press, to come out in the spring, so that's cool. It's called *City Treaty*. And basically I examine the treaty as literature from an urban perspective as well, right? Because I think there's more attention paid to the Native people that live in the city now. They're sort of left out of the loop in a lot of senses. Until recently, you couldn't vote if you lived off-reserve, and in some provinces, I don't know if you can. In each and every province, I think in Manitoba you can now. I don't know how many people actually responded to that. Once you leave the reserve, you're gone, man. You're not involved in the politics, obviously, or in the personal lives. Like where I come from, I originally come from a reserve in northern Alberta called Heart Lake and it's getting to the point where only the older people remember me. The younger people, I'm just somebody that shows up once a year, or every two years, you know?

RD: Yeah. Is a lot of your work very political? I mean, just your book seems very political.

MF: Ah, everything's political. If you're a Native person, going to the washroom's political. [laughter]

RD: Depends how you pee. [laughter]

MF: Yeah, depends who you pee on, right? [laughter]

RD: Depends who you pee on.

MF: We're just peons, man.

RD: Back to the porn. [laughter]

MF: Yeah, I've never written a short story I really, really liked yet. So I haven't—I don't think a novel is in mind for me. Yeah, someday I will, though, write a novel.

SE: So what's the difference between playwriting, screenwriting, and writing a short story for you?

RD: Oh, damn good question!

MF: I guess the big difference is, it's just, you know, different mediums, right? I think [in] playwriting, you have to take into account the limitations of the stage, right? That's why I like, well, I'll get into radio drama too. One of the reasons why I really like radio drama, writing for the radio, is because you have this freedom of you can be here, and two seconds later be on Mars if, you know, if you want to do that, right? It doesn't cost you a thing. If you're making a movie, it costs a million dollars to do that. If you did it on the stage, you have to find complicated ways of staging that, right? But radio drama has that freedom of doing that, and radio drama has this sort of interactiveness with the listener because they don't know what your characters look like. So from the audio clues that you give them, they imagine them, you know?

SE: So it's pure imagination, and that's the purest form of writing for you?

MF: Well, in terms of playwriting, whether it's for screen, whether it's for stage or for television, I think, you know, poetry is probably, I don't know, the closest to the writer, I think. It's sort of more you, in a sense, than other forms of writing.

RD: That's what I was saying. You're like, echoing me, you know? It's sympatico.

MF: Are we in an echo chamber? [laughter]

RD: The same wave, which kind of scares me, being on the same wavelength as Marvin.... [laughter]

MF: Actually, we're here in Regina, in a booth, at Sâkêwêwak Gallery, and we're glad to be here.

RD: We are, awesomely, awesomely glad to be here. Does that make sense? Anyway, my last question for you, before we get kicked out of the booth...Marvin, earlier you were saying that life shapes you. Do you think that you became a writer, or a writer became you?

SE: Ooh, I like that one.

MF: When I was a kid, ever since I was little and I learned how to read at an early age, I wanted to be a writer. I just never really seriously pursued it until later in life. I used to draw comics and sell them to my brothers, okay? That was my first writing.

RD: And a businessman, too. [laughter] You'll buy the comic book! [laughter]

MF: That's just what you call a brother relationship.

RD: That's right.

MF: Pecking order in some cases. Buy this comic or I'll peck your eyes out, right? [laughter] I think most people have in them that desire to be creative whether it's writing, painting, sculpture, whatever, you know? It's just some people are more willing to pursue it. And like, say, poetry, you don't do it for the money, right? And if you do, you sure are a hungry cowboy, right?

RD: [laughter] Indian! Indian! Excuse me... [laughter] What's the matter with you?

MF: It's sort of like you do it because you like the creative act, you have things to say, etc., etc., right?

RD: It's like orgasming. [laughter] It is.

MF: I think there's a writer in everybody. I think some people just are more willing to take that chance of being rejected by publishers, being made indifferent by audiences when you read the poetry, by people saying, "No, I really liked your poem" without looking you in the eye when they say it, right? I mean, you have to be able to face rejection. But you also have to be willing to accept the good things, too.

RD: Which I hear is something you're good at—facing rejection. [laughter] So, did you answer my question? So you're a writer that became you? No, you're—you are you that became a writer.

MF: I think so—no—yeah, I think so. I don't know if the reverse is possible. You're a person first, right?

SE: But you're also a painter and that's a totally different medium than writing. Like, writing is more, like you said, invoking someone else's imagination. Like to me, painting is very concrete, very much in front of you, very dimensional. What's the difference?

MF: I think they're closer than you realize, or perhaps, or at least my art. I've learned, I think, just as much from looking at, say, a Van Gogh painting as I have from reading Shakespeare. Like it's just, you know, the words on the page are, in a sense, artistic. There's, like, there's different fonts, right? You know, there's different ways of laying the words out, and you get into what you call feel-poetry. You use the page in different ways, right? The visual world and the written world meet somewhere, right? Like, that image and text thing. It's something I'm very interested in, and I'm certainly not totally original on this, but somewhere they meet, right? And I'm in there somewhere. I'm somewhere in between painting and writing as me. I'm in there somewhere. I'm in there someplace.

SE: So what came first? Painting or writing?

RD: Chicken or the egg?

MF: Well, comic books. I drew and also wrote words. Yeah? Maybe it's not chicken and egg. Maybe it's just chicken and chicken.

RD: It's just chicken and taters. [laughter]

MF: Chicken and taters, man! [laughter] That's the story! Oh, that's gonna be our next poem.

RD: So you're an artistic force, basically.

MF: Well, that's nice of you to say.

RD: You are an artistic energy, baby. You're vibing all over the place.

MF: Well, so are a lot of people, right?

RD: Well, thank you very much for talking with us.

MF: Thanks for listening.

19

Blood Moves with Us—Story Poetry Lives Inside

Janet Rogers

We, as poets, respond to our history, social dynamics, culture (in whatever form it is saved and lost and lived now). We are the result of our environment resisting development and the battles our surroundings have lost to progress. And we, as poets, are here to witness, ruminate, and creatively express our stories in verse to all that has gone, all that is now, and visions for the future.

We are living culture. Our words are like the stars that helped navigate our ancestors. The words we choose to tell our story poems are themselves the stories and tell of our history of learning, the lost ingredients of culture, and our misunderstood truths. Our words are clues to our values, our experiences, and our words are literary territory on which we stand to represent ourselves (individually and as a collective). So to remove the right for Indigenous peoples to tell our own stories is like ripping the land from beneath us. We must tell our own stories to offer an honest definition of who we are. Our poetry is everywhere and is derived from everything above us, beside us, and below. The rest is politics. And the poet is inspired by that, too. However, the reality of who we are lives inside our art and our culture. Our art and our culture are informed by the physical land, so therein lies the bountiful inspiration, as well as the need to remain politically aware.

Why the Spoken Word?

The exact minute or literary experience that brought my words to be spoken/performed is not clear. However, I like to think of it as a meeting on middle ground, where the genre was there, waiting, and my words were travelling on a highway, then stopped to tour through the spoken-word territory and found a home. We are Indians, so we know "home" is as much rooted in a geographical place as it is within us. My words may, in time, travel away from this spoken-word place, graduate to new territory, or may separate like cells to occupy multiple territories at once. And to this possibility, I say "She:kon."

Like other writers, I believe in my words. And so it is perhaps for this reason, above all others, that became the catalyst for bringing my words into the spoken-word category. I wanted my words to be heard *and* experienced. I wanted *them* to have attention, not me. They wanted to live off of the page. At first, I was not an eager performer of them, but I trusted where they would take me. Too, it is important to define things by what they are not or, in this case, by what I didn't intend to do, and that was I didn't want to bore audiences with just another droning poetry reading. I, like many of us, have lived through that and I feel poetry presented in that style, or rather lack of style, is committing crimes against poetry and there should be punishment, at least as much punishment as the poet commits upon his or her audience.

So if the spoken word lives off of the page, where does it exist? It is delivered from the body, not the page. It lives in the memory of the poet, then as a remembered experience of the listener, and, if done well, passed on as an informal review. But I may be getting ahead of myself. Yes, the page is part parent of the spoken-word poem. It is birthed there. It is taught protocols and dressed up for public consumption from the page. So when we witness the spoken-word poet deliver, for the first time an oratory of verse, we witness the literary umbilical cord being severed. There, the poem lives as it was meant to live freely, taking on a slightly different personality with each presentation. Let's look at some of the characteristics of the spoken word poem:

energy: Spoken word is poetry on steroids. Energy matters. This, along with the message in the poem and the handsome order in which the words are strung together, are the offerings to the audience at a spoken-word event.

issues: Spoken word comes from street poetry. No good can come from poetry that is not rooted in individual truth and we all know truth ain't always pretty. The spoken-word poet can be described as a politically aware person, using his or her talents to relay passionate messages based on observations of social injustice, cultural prejudice, environmental exploitation, just to name a few. At times, spoken-word poets have been known to sing praises and raise their voices in celebration as well...there are no hard-and-fast rules here.

recitation: Spoken word is not for the absent-minded, but if it does happen during a poem, and it is inevitable that it will, just hang tough. Sometimes those words, like the names of important people, decide to take a vacation just when you need them most. However, the wonderful thing about being a spoken-word poet is that you are good to go at any given time, in any place and situation. We live with the poems in our memories, so like songs, we are able to offer them up as gifts.

performance: Embrace the theatrical. Allow your poems to have personality. Audiences listen with their eyes as well as their ears. Be interesting. Your body is telling your story as much as the message in the words, so move. Be aware that if you are introducing props to your spoken-word performance you are also cranking up the something-could-go-wrong factor tenfold. Keep it simple. Be aware of your personal dictionary of gestures and use the movements that are true to yourself. You'll know them once you try.

hooks: You need a hook to catch a fish. Repetition, pregnant pauses, asking questions, rhymes and rhythms—all these tactics are good hooks to catch the ear of the audience. A good spoken-word performer knows how to use them, and how not to overuse them.

originality: Stay true to yourself, stay true to yourself, stay true to yourself. Maybe you have seen some YouTube footage of a Def Poetry Jam presentation and are inspired to emulate the Def style of spoken word. Well, let me recommend you watch those video clips for an hour and you'll quickly tire of the sameness in delivery. To be clear, this is an honest observation, not a criticism of one presentation style. It is important, for the integrity of the genre alone, that we continue to discover, invent, and be open to new styles of spoken-word presentations. Again, there are no hard-and-fast rules in the world of spoken word. This baby is still growing and, to my pleasure, at this time defying limiting boundaries of definition.

Who's Doing It?

When I inquire throughout our communities as to who the spoken-word poets are, I get names of hip-hop artists and rappers. True, both hip hop and spoken word are two word-based performance art forms, but that is where their similarities end. True, some spoken word is recorded with music, but the delivery and the phrasing are quite different from hip hop. I am reminded, rap stands for "rhythm and poetry," so rap, hip hop, and spoken word likely have more in common with each other than I like to admit. Who's doing it? Joy Harjo. Zaccheus Jackson Nyce. Alex Jacobs. John Trudell. Cheryl L'hirondell. Surprise! When I googled "Native American spoken-word artists," my name and website came up first.

On more than one occasion, I have been approached after a spoken-word presentation by audience members who, in a confessional tone, expressed interest in turning their poems into spoken-word performances. One of those people was actually a very well-known, well-established writer who has inspired many, many Native writers after them to pick up the pen and embark on literary careers themselves. They were downright sheepish in their approach. I was honoured to be the recipient of their desire to expand creatively and flattered that my work had sparked something in them to take up the spoken-word torch.

Get It?

The best way to teach someone to build a house is to put the hammer in his or her hands. I invite you to recite a poem provided here. As you do so, be aware of your own tonality, natural inflections, where the poem lives in your body, where it moves out from your body. We all have a natural dictionary of gestures, and I recommend the next time you are in conversation with someone, get animated. Exaggerate your physical body language to teach yourself how you move and how you can use your movement to further enhance your poetry performance.

When I was developing the poem "Just Try," my intention was to recite it like my life depended on it. Considering the content, that wasn't too far from the truth. As well, "Just Try" was my response to being invited to compete in the first CBC Poetry Face-Off. The theme for the inaugural year was "belonging." I took a step back, and said to myself, "They are asking a Haudenosaunee poet, living on stolen colonized Indigenous territory, to address the theme of belonging? I got this." Subsequently I did not win the big prize, didn't even win the regionals with the poem, but was asked by the MC after my reading, "Is it really so innocuous to be Canadian?" Hmm, maybe they're not ready for this.

The History of Indigenous Oratory

Native American literatures scholars have widely recognized the importance and relevance of those literatures' oral storytelling roots as foundational to their literary development. With this understanding, the literary critical study of Native texts has often been interwoven with early orality studies by Native and non-Native ethnographers and folklorists. This notwithstanding, contemporary rhetoricians and literary critics have directed scant attention to those highly crafted Native American oral texts that were explicitly oriented toward the purposes of information and persuasion: namely, formal speeches.[1]

I continue to research Indigenous critical writings on Indigenous-delivered oratory. At this time, there are numerous examples of critical writings by non-Native individuals on Indigenous oration because, as we all know, once the colonizer "discovers" that which the original people have been practising since time immemorial, that practice is immediately validated in mainstream culture. But I digress.

Did I mention E. Pauline Johnson already? If not, I completely surprise myself. The Mohawk-English poet from Six Nations Reserve, I believe, was a writer who engaged in a type of spoken-word delivery well before the genre came into being. E. Pauline Johnson broke from the convention of her time to find notoriety as a writer solely in print. She took both her loves—her passion for writing and her limited experience and love of the stage—and sewed them seamlessly together in poetry recitals that commanded attention. She taught herself to be the star of her own written words, complete with costumes and theatrical recitation. And it is perhaps her pursuit of a literary career on the stage that kept her written work from print most of her life.

And what about all those beatnik poets? What were they doing? Paperless caffeine-and marajuana-induced verses with anti-war, anti-establishment sentiments...sounds like spoken word to me. Poetry at this time was almost the truest example of the writer discovering abstractism. Poetic laws were being broken left and right and left again. So perhaps the generation we now occupy has taken up the torch and recycled a word-based thing to make statements a straight poem can't convey. We can no longer simply say "The rain in Spain stays mainly on the plain." In spoken word, we want to personify the rain, give it a voice, and make it sing. We want to speak of the rights of that rain, and how the "plain" is playing the part of oppressor by making it stay there.

My spoken-word poems ask to be danced, and they have taught me how they need to be shared. Like any "good" writer, I want the work to speak for itself. I am not an eager performer of my words but the words demand it of me. The genre has brought me along so far to the point where I am now embarking on the vocalizing of my words—yes, singing. My one true love will remain the spoken word because it helped move me into categories of the literary arts I had no intention of entering, such as recording, video poetry, and cross-pollinations of poetry and dance and music. As a writer, the spoken word has been my greatest teacher. And yet the genre lives outside of classrooms, rejects dogmatic confines, and, like the northern lights, is constantly changing shape.

Note

1   Brill de Ramirez and Susan Berry, "Oratory in Native North America," *Studies in American Indian Literature* 16, no. 2 (2004): 88–92.

Bibliography

de Ramirez, Brill, and Susan Berry. "Oratory in Native North American." *Studies inAmerican Indian Literature* 16, no. 2 (2004): 88–92.

20

Revitalizing Indigenous Swagger: Poetics from a Plains Cree Perspective

Lindsay "Eekwol" Knight

Memory, thoughts, language, words, translations, recitation, and reaction. These are the stages observed with each piece released from whatever that place is in which the lyrics originate. I never know when the good ones will bubble and surface, exposing themselves into forms I process. Sometimes I feel captured, reluctant, and resistant to these persistent poetics, but then succumb to the grander notion of a bigger picture, a better future, a collective necessity for recognition of identity and self. It is for this process that I pay respect to the spirits and ask for strength, understanding, and guidance as I know that stories come to me with intention and purpose. Through my writing process, although I let feeling and heart sit paramount over practice and intellect, I still engage in academic and community research of the history of Indigenous music and then develop lyrical poetry with respect for our ancestral memory as I know that this discipline is the key to maintenance of Indigenous culture.

There is an obligation for recognition of Plains Cree music as part of complex and interrelated relationships and connections to land, spirits, and each other. For example, social and ceremonial events like the round dance and the sun dance are all focused on the use of song and instrument as a means of communication from the physical world to the spirit world. Beyond the old social and ceremonial songs and music, there is a continuum of recent Indigenous artists who create, practise, and perform all kinds of music, not in separate compartments or categories, but within an interconnected sameness that transcends time and place. Some examples are drum groups like the Young Scouts and rock musicians like Buffy

Sainte-Marie. The Young Scouts use a modernized style of drumming, quicker with stops, and some of their songs include a flute. Their songs are predominantly sung in the English language with parts in Cree. Well-known performer Buffy Sainte-Marie also uses the English language and includes Plains Cree–style chanting and drumming in her songs. References to her Plains Cree background and teachings are peppered throughout her music. Through their lyrics, both groups use poetics as a way of maintaining Plains Cree identity and are therefore responsible for presenting songs in a way that acknowledges our way of being. Contemporary Indigenous song stems from musical practices of the past, and although adapted and ever changing in language, sound, and style, it maintains the innate purpose of songs and music as an essential connector to all things spiritual, economic, political, and social within Indigenous peoples.

While not always intentionally reactionary, contemporary Indigenous artists in all areas of the arts are successfully capturing Indigenous cosmologies in the space of resistance movements. Plains Cree poets, through the use of words, using English and/or Cree, are re-establishing the definition of resistance within Indigenous cultures by relaying truths that can be translated and interpreted by a wider audience. It is because of this growing community that it becomes necessary to continue to build supportive discourse within Indigenous arts because they speak to resistance and become a tool for decolonization within contemporary Indigenous communities. For myself, I have always written lyrics from the perspective of a Plains Cree woman. I observe what I experience in my homeland, both dreaming and awake, and reinterpret it into words. The underlying, undeniable part of the process is that the foundation of everything I write and then say comes from the place of resistance, always consciences of our unique Plains Cree past, present, and future. And while I am not a poet in the "traditional" sense of the word, I view poetics as anything that flows—words, music, paint, beadwork, a river—there is poetry in it all. To me, poetics in Indigenous world views becomes something different and should be embraced as such as that is how we resist the loss of comprehension of and connection to both the physical and spiritual world.

Both traditional Indigenous and Western-educated Indigenous scholars adhere to the concept of music as a foundational necessity to all aspects of livelihood. As a form of Indigenous poetics, our music adds to the ongoing flow of poetry ringing throughout our history. Métis scholar Jo-Ann Episkenew claims that stories, dance, and song were considered beautiful each in their own way, and that they had always served as spiritual functions within communities.[1] This theme is also apparent within international literature, as Indigenous writer Ruby Langford articulates:

Our Ancient tribal people sat down and sang the spirits into this land giving it its physical form. Whiteman called our dreamtime a myth. Our people know it as fact, it was before creation(no break!)time! They sang the trees, they sang the mountains, they sang the valleys, they sang the rivers and streams...they sang life in its vastness, into this brown land; and the spirit lives still, never has it been silenced, by whiteman or his restrictive ways, and the song had a beginning, and there will never be an ending until justice is returned to the singers of songs, our ancient tribal people.[2]

Through this passage one can consider the richness of poetics used to describe essential teachings and conceptualizations that exist within Indigenous music as it is part of Creation stories and continued relationships with physical and spiritual beings. We know as Indigenous poets that there is more to the words and sounds of voice and instruments than pleasant, entertaining performance. Songs come from a place that we cannot name, and when sung, they create movement and motion in the universe. They are given, shared, and passed down. They are essential for miyo-wîcihitowin, which translates as "having good relationships."[3] They are a tiny part of the balance, a hint of the familiar in the vast unknown, and a whisper of truth in the great mystery that is life.

I am a rapper, so my genre of music exists bound in the realm of definitions and categories. However, because of my background and experience as a Plains Cree woman from my traditional territory (what is now known as Saskatchewan, Canada), I do not fit into any of these. My greatest influences are artists like The Wu-Tang Clan, Nas, and The Fugees, along with a huge appreciation for underground hip-hop movement coming out of LA in the mid-1990s. In the beginning I tried to emulate these rappers until I realized that my purpose was not to meet the standards of the mainstream record industry, but, more importantly, to be a voice from within my own community. And while maintaining a respect for the history of hip-hop music, which stems from struggling youth in the Bronx, New York, in the mid-1970s, I used what I learned, fell out of step with what was "fresh" and acceptable in hip hop, and made it my own by incorporating Indigenous understanding into my sound.

In addition to this shift in music, I also began learning and incorporating Plains Cree language into my poetry as I had always heard that our language encapsulates our world view. I also thought that it sounded pretty cool and hoped that the young people who listened to it would feel the same sense of pride that I felt in speaking my own language. I strongly believe that in order to really capture the attention of the younger generations, you have to have the ability to "cool it out," meaning that by respectfully fitting our traditional knowledge and language into examples of pop culture, we create a marketable tool that engages and teaches identity and values.

Like a ceremony, music is mostly beyond my level of awareness, yet I do it devotedly. As a performer I also succumb to the ways in which the energy within each word or phrase embodies my actions and movements. It comes to me in dreams, without thinking, without warning. It thumps out of my heart in drumbeat precision and I write what I capture, with hopes of respectfully relaying the meaning in the rhythm. I feel humbled, honoured, and burdened all within the same instant because some of the stories are so tragic, so painfully sad, that I am sometimes left sobbing uncontrollably, begging for strength by putting down the pen and picking up a braid of sweetgrass. And while not all the lyrics come from that place, they all have purpose. I use them to speak for those who cannot. I use them as an answer to struggle, both of others and my own.

I know that I will never be successful in the Western music industry, which, to me, is the ultimate success. I have chosen to continue my process of learning music in the Indian way, to think about the future generations and contribute to the process of decolonization. Among many roles, I am a mother, a music maker, and an academic, so I will always work toward this better good, which is the most rewarding path. By learning about and listening to Indigenous music, I will build with the continuum of artists from past to present, recognizing an ancestral memory that drives our intentions. Indigenous poetics are not about showing and convincing the rest of the world that we are capable; rather, they are about maintaining a compassionate mind within our own nations, rebuilding our history and strengthening our future, one rhyme at a time.

Notes

1 Jo-Ann Episkenew, *Taking Back Our Spirits: Indigenous Literature, Public Policy, and Healing* (Winnipeg: University of Manitoba Press, 2009), 192.
2 Ruby Langford Ginibi, *Real Deadly* (Sydney: Angus and Robertson, 1992), 36.
3 Priscilla Settee, *The Strength of Women: Âhkamêyimowak* (Saskatoon: Coteau Book, 2011), iv.

Bibliography

Episkenew, Jo-Ann. *Taking Back Our Spirits: Indigenous Literature, Public Policy, andHealing.* Winnipeg: University of Manitoba Press, 2009.

Langford Ginibi, Ruby. *Real Deadly.* Sydney: Angus and Robertson, 1992.

Settee, Priscilla. *The Strength of Women: Âhkamêyimowak.* Saskatoon: Coteau Book, 2011.

21

A Conversation of Influence, Tradition, and Indigenous Poetics: An Interview with Kateri Akiwenzie-Damm

Conducted by Rhiannon Johnson

When I was first asked to do this interview with Kateri Akiwenzie-Damm, I was overwhelmed with anticipation and excitement that I would have such an opportunity. Having been a fan of her book of poetry, *my heart is a stray bullet*, I was thrilled to have the chance to ask her a few questions after reading her work. Once I got more into her academic pieces, I realized that she is not only a talented poet, but also an extremely articulate intellectual with the ability to weave together words like cloth. I began to feel intimidated at the approaching interview while preparing the following questions. When the day finally came, I travelled to her home and was greeted with a friendly, warm face. She explained that she had just put her sons down for a nap. When we sat down to talk, I realized that Kateri Akiwenzie-Damm is not only a talented artist and academic, but also a warm and humorous individual with a wealth of knowledge concerning the Indigenous literary world and where that fits into the larger context of Indigenous art and its significance.

RHIANNON JOHNSON (RJ): What got you started in writing poetry?
KATERI AKIWENZIE-DAMM (KAD): Poetry specifically I can't actually say, but I think it was just part of an interest in writing and reading. My maternal grandmother, my Anishnaabe grandmother, Irene Akiwenzie, was a writer and a voracious reader. I spent a lot of time at my grandparents' house. I spent summers, weekends, holidays—we all

did—at my grandparents' place. It was just filled with books—there were just shelves and shelves of books, and my grandmother always had one or two books on her bedside table that she was reading. So, I was really fortunate that I grew up around that. She also wrote for the local newspapers and had a specific time—Monday morning at eleven—when she would sit at her desk in the midst of all this chaos and write her column. Everyone respected it so much and I can remember the grandkids—you know, we'd either tiptoe around in the living room or we'd go outside so that she could write. I think in retrospect that was really important to see that people respected her work as a writer so much, and I'm sure that had an impact on me. I come by it honestly because my grandmother was like that. She was part of the Kegadonce family (which her grandfather and father were named). It means an orator or speaker. My grandmother was also a public speaker and she told stories, so I think that interest in words and language and story comes naturally through her. My grandfather was a little bit different. He was more a man of few words, but they carried so much weight so I learned a lot from his way of speaking. His first language was Anishnaabemowin and he also spoke a bit of French, so English was his second or maybe third language. Then I had a Polish grandmother, who wasn't very well educated. She had come to Canada with the wars, the loss of her family, and so on. She had only about a grade three education and spoke English as a second language and with a fairly heavy Polish accent. She actually spoke several languages, but Polish was her first language. She worked as a cook and so she was around all these different kinds of people and other staff for these wealthy people whose homes she lived in and for whom she worked. She was always telling little anecdotes and the weirdest jokes. Some of them were really funny and some of them were quite crude, but it was the kind of stuff that I guess the staff told in the kitchen. So it was really interesting because I learned a lot from each of their ways of speaking and using language and working with as much or as little as they knew about English.

RJ: Can you tell me about your influences as a poet?

KAD: As a poet...I would say a big part of it is that I really see my work as a poet, as a writer, as arising from traditions, specifically from the Anishnaabe people and of my community. I mean stories, songs, invocations, and all of those traditional forms that we use. A little bit more broadly, those same kinds of traditions, but for Indigenous peoples generally because that's who I've been in contact with the most in terms of my writing and arts and just personally because a lot of writers are friends of mine, so I think that those have been the greatest influences. In terms of specific people and books, I've really learned a lot from some people whom I know and have had the opportunity to speak with about writing, including friends of mine like Patricia Grace, who's a Maori fiction writer, and Gregory Scofield. I also really like the writing of Ben Okri and Pablo Neruda, so there are some other people whose work I appreciate a lot. How much it influences me, I'm not exactly sure. Leonard Cohen—I love his work and I think just music and song lyrics and that sort of thing are a big influence as well.

RJ: Has becoming a mother influenced your writing? Do you find yourself drawing from different inspiration points since becoming a mother?

KAD: That's a really good question. I probably don't write as much since becoming a mother. They're so little now that it's hard to find the time and space. I do think it has influenced me because I've noticed some definite shifts in my thinking and in my priorities, and just the way that I engage with the world. It's been interesting to see some of the things that have suddenly just fallen away that I used to think mattered and other things that didn't matter so much to me are much more important. I have crazy fears that have come up since I have children that I never worried about or had to worry about—like retiring. I never thought about writing a will, but suddenly, when you have children, all of these things become so important because their future is more important than your own in a certain respect. I can't say specifically. I can't point to any poem or story at this point and say, "Well, that's since my sons," so you can see the change or the shift. But I'm sure it will because it's shifted my thinking.

RJ: What do you mean by *my heart is a stray bullet*, and why did you choose this as the title for your book of poetry?

KAD: "My heart is a stray bullet ricocheting in an empty room ..." I wrote that poem when I was quite young—in my twenties. It's really about that sense of loneliness and not knowing who to love or trust—that sort of thing. There's also another element, just in terms of not necessarily romantic love, but just being out in the world as an Anishnaabe person, an Indigenous person. The Oka Crisis was going on, there were all these things happening, and sometimes it kind of felt intermixed with this great love of my people and everything else, and there was kind of a sense of violence, of fear, and a kind of not really knowing what was going to happen, and to what lengths we might have to go to defend ourselves. I wanted to convey that element of chaos and the potential of danger and violence that sometimes accompanies those strong, passionate feelings.

RJ: How did you select the pieces to go into your book *my heart is a stray bullet*? Can you tell me about the editing process of the book?

KAD: I don't really remember how I selected the poems. I suppose it was a couple of things. One, I was in a writers group at the time here in Ottawa. It was a Native writers group...we called ourselves WINO. It was an acronym, but I think the acronym was made to end up with the word WINO. It was the Writers Independent Native Organization and there were people like Allen Deleary, otherwise known as Thom E. Hawke. He used to be in the band Seventh Fire and did a lot of writing and performance art. Joseph Dandurand, Ann Acco...I can't think of who else at the moment was part of that core group of people. We workshopped our stuff and did various things, so probably it was some things I had been working on—just the things that were important to me at the time. I probably just figured these were the best of what I had available at the time.

RJ: Who are you writing for when you write?

KAD: I think somewhere in my mind I'm always thinking about communicating with my own community. I mean that both in the sense of the Chippewas of Nawash community and also sort of my broader community: the networks I belong to, the friends, other Native writers, and Indigenous writers and so on, so basically the people whom I know. But there are also without doubt poems and stories that I know a non-Native audience is going to probably see because they're starting to get picked up by university courses. It was a shock to me before, the non-Native readers, because I was never really writing for them. Now I'd be lying if I said I didn't know that they're reading my work, so that's in the back of my mind as well. Sometimes things are more aimed toward my own people, some are more aimed outwardly. It varies from piece to piece and really, in a way, I never really write to please an audience. I just write what I want to write, and the way that I feel or think about things.

RJ: How would you define Indigenous poetics?

KAD: I'm sort of hung up on that whole concept of poetics and what does it mean in an Indigenous context. I suppose in a way it's kind of our sense of the aesthetics of language and story. That's how I see it anyway from an Indigenous point of view and within an Indigenous perspective, if that makes any sense. That's about as clear as I've been able to get to it myself, and part of the reason why I want to talk to some other people who have probably spent more time thinking about it. I want to speak with Gerald Vizenor and some other people whom I know who I could probably ask and they'd give me some amazing and articulate response. For myself, that's the best way I've been able to wrap my head around it.

RJ: You're also known for your performance works. While writing a piece, do you think about its potential as a performance piece or does this occur after?

KAD: Both. Sometimes I'm very aware. Really most of my poetry, when I'm working on it, I'm reading it aloud and really look at the way that it sounds and flows and how to perform it. I do this even though I don't know when I first started thinking about poetry as performance. When I belonged to that writers group, we did used to do performances that combined poetry with music and slide shows, all sorts of things. But we really never thought of ourselves as spoken-word poets—we were just writers. Some of us were musicians as well, and some of us were photographers, so we just put all this stuff together because it was fun. So, a little bit of both: sometimes I write specifically to perform and other times I have the poem and the more I read it aloud and perform it, the more I realize that it's better suited to perform than some of the others.

RJ: Are all of your pieces written to be performed? Or do you believe that some are better left to be read by themselves by an individual reader?

KAD: I think that there's power in performance, there's power in live performance, there's power in doing CDs that people can listen to on the radio or stereos. There's also tremendous power in the written word these days, whether it's paper or electronic, because it's portable and it's a different experience of the story or poem than if somebody reads it or performs it. So I think that for myself, I enjoy the imaginative solitude of reading something off the page. On the other hand, I really like being read to. There's something of a kid in me that just loves that sometimes. For example, Maria Campbell's *Stories of the Road Allowance People* really come alive when you hear her read them in her own voice. It adds a whole other dimension. Now every time I read those stories, I hear Maria's voice and through her the voices of the people whose stories they are.

RJ: Do you communicate an Indigenous consciousness through your work, specifically that from an Anishnaabe perspective?

KAD: I believe so because I'm always trying to learn more about who we are and our history and traditions. I'm proud of that part of who I am. It's probably the greatest part of how I identify myself, so I think in most things that I do, especially now that I'm older, that's been so integrated into my personality, my way of thinking, and my way of being in the world that I would have to make a conscious effort, I think, to try to remove it. So, yes, I think it's there. We're all individuals, so it's different for everybody. So the way I might think about something as an Anishaabe-kwe might be different than the way somebody from a different community, different experiences, and different age might think about it. I think that neither would be less Anishnaabe than the other.

RJ: Do you think it is important to have Indigenous publishing houses?

KAD: Absolutely yes, without doubt. I think that we're all at risk—all of the Indigenous publishing houses in Canada. We operate sort of on the edge of a cliff most of the time because we can't get stable funding. It's really difficult and the Canadian publishing industry has gone through some really difficult times over the last decade, so it takes its toll and filters down. I'm very proud that we've helped to launch careers of various writers and that we've supported and encouraged so many people. Even established writers are coming to us to be published, like Basil Johnston. I'm really proud of that. I'm proud that we can give them a home and do what we can to help get their work out there and work with them in a way that I hope is more comfortable for them because we do our best to always remember who we are, and to work in ways that uphold our own values as Indigenous peoples. We try to always be respectful and try to just maintain that integrity as Indigenous peoples and to be *Indigenous* publishers, not just publishers who happen to be Indigenous. We try to work in a way that makes that real.

RJ: How do you think that your work as an editor and publisher empowers emerging Indigenous poets and writers?

KAD: I hope that when I work with them that I do it in a way that respects who they are and the stories that they're trying to tell. I may not always understand them, especially if they're from a different First Nation or Indigenous background, but that's my starting point—just trying to offer people respect and sometimes that means that if I respect them that I give them a little kick in the pants and say, "You can do better." In doing that, I always try to be respectful. I've had writers whom I've worked with—one person in particular—and he's come to me with new work and the editing process broke down. To me, that's not a huge problem. It's a huge waste of time, but it's not a problem insofar as we're still really respectful to each other, we still like each other, and we still keep in touch. I don't know if he managed to find another publisher who had more of a similar vision as he did for what he wanted with his work, but I still think it was a very valuable experience for both of us. We remained friends and to me that's proof that we were able to work in a good way together. The process, to me, is just as important as the product in many respects.

RJ: What advice would you give to a young Indigenous poet?

KAD: Get a day job. [laughter] I have a Maori friend, her name is Briar Grace-Smith, and she said that being a writer is great food for the soul, but it doesn't necessarily help put groceries on the table, which I thought was really funny and witty and just too true. I think it's just really important to be true to who you are. Be open at the same time. It's your job as a writer when you're working with editors to protect the integrity of your work, but at the same time to be open to a process that can help you grow as a writer. It's difficult, I think, for emerging writers to find that balance sometimes where they're not overly protective and their work isn't too precious, but they don't get mortally wounded every time there's a red mark on the page or, on the other hand, where they give up control to the editor, which also is not a helpful thing to do. It's not necessarily good for your development as a writer to give that control over to somebody else. It's really about trying to find that balance of staying open and knowing where the line in the sand is. I believe you should write because you're a writer and that's who you are. Let everything else fall into place. Although I have to say Witi Ihimaera was on faculty at Banff a couple years ago when I was teaching out there, and one of the things he said to writers was "As soon as you finish a manuscript, start on the next one. Don't get caught up in the promotion too much. Of course you have to do that, but don't focus too much on 'Okay, now I've finished my book and it's celebration time.'" He said keep working, get on to the next one, and get it started. I thought that was really smart because I haven't done that. There's these big gaps. My poetry book was written ages ago, and I've done a bunch of other projects such as the CDs, but I think, "Oh my gosh, why can't I get my manuscripts finished?" He was giving that advice as a career writer and it was really good for me to hear. Even though I'm a career writer and I've been writing for a long time and getting published for a long time, I hadn't really thought of it that way, so I think that's really smart. Young emerging writers who do that will be way further ahead when they're my age than I am now because there will be that continuity instead of the big gaps and losing focus and things that can happen if you can't just keep writing. As writers, that's what we're supposed to do, right? Now there are so many demands on us to do performances, and do interviews, and be all these things that maybe writers in the past didn't have to. They didn't have to have a thousand Twitter followers and five thousand people on Facebook and all these other things that we're expected to do now. It's easy to get caught up in all of that and forget that the writing is what it's really all about.

RJ: So just stay focused on the writing?

KAD: Stay focused on the writing, stay true to yourself, stay open, and have fun. If it's not fun, stop doing it.

22

The "Nerve of Cree," the Pulse of Africa: Sound Identities in Cree, Cree-Métis, and Dub Poetries in Canada

Susan Gingell

Why Bring Together Indigenous and Dub Poetries from Canada?

Literary critics have generally shied away from bringing the writing of Indigenous and African diasporic peoples into conversation with one another, perhaps made wary by critiques of post-colonial theory that have rightly censured the tendency to make colonially centric and homogenous those peoples' radically different histories and experiences of colonialism and neo-colonialism.[1] However, Sophie McCall's "Diaspora and Nation in Métis Writing" and Renate Eigenbrod's "Diasporic Longings: (Re)Figurations of Home and Homelessness in Richard Wagamese's Work" follow Neal McLeod's "Coming Home Through Stories"[2] in framing Indigenous dislocations as productive of diaspora, thus preparing one kind of theoretical ground for bringing together Indigenous literature and writing more commonly recognized as diasporic. While analogous experiences of racism come quickly to mind as another basis for effecting the convergence, literary critics rarely consider issues related to audible difference. However, attending to the creative and regenerative responses that Cree, Cree-Métis, and Canadian practitioners of the reggae-born, politically charged, foundationally oral poetry known as dub have made to the systematic suppression of the ways their people sound reveals the significance of these issues. Indeed, orature and orality richly resource these poetries.

Any comparison of Indigenous and dub poetries in Canada needs to remain aware that the particular histories of (neo)colonialism suffered by Indigenous peoples in Canada and those endured by enslaved African Jamaican and related diasporic peoples are distinct except where intermarriage has taken place. "In These Canadian Bones," Lillian Allen thanks Native peoples for sharing the country she now calls home, and acknowledges that as a settler group, Jamaican Canadians have a different relationship to the land than Indigenous peoples do. Because the dub community in Canada is urban, Canadian dub characteristically thematizes city-based experience and rarely seems connected to the land beneath the asphalt and concrete. Urban Indigenous peoples, by contrast, may articulate a strong connection even when the land is paved over. Marvin Francis's *City Treaty*, for instance, asserts that *"native landscapes contain asphalt,"*[3] and that the "word drummers" (Indigenous writers) have rendered new Indigenous realities so that "the landscape now has city."[4]

Moreover, the two groups have been negatively impacted by quite different Canadian government policies, though often with depressingly similar, impoverishing results. Enforced residential schooling and the 1960s scoops that tore children away from their parents for adoption were uniquely Indigenous experiences, so Canadian dub poetry offers nothing quite like the wrenching accounts of families torn apart such as we encounter in Maria Campbell's translation of the Road Allowance people's story "Jacob," Louise Halfe's "The Residential School Bus," and Emma LaRocque's "My Hometown Northern Canada South Africa." Slavers did, however, permanently sever Africans' ties with homeland and family there; when plantation masters sold slaves, including children, to distant plantations, families were again violently ruptured; and, more recently, mothers and children were separated because of Canada's Caribbean Domestic Scheme's requirement that workers have no dependants.[5] Many Caribbean single mothers, pushed abroad by the collapse of their countries' economies in the post–Second World War period, had, as Allen's dub poem "I Fight Back" records, to leave their children with family members back in the Caribbean so they could care for others' children abroad.

Despite the two groups' different histories, orality is central to the social lives and verbal arts of each. They share both a belief in the dynamism and potency of the sounded word, and experiences of the silencing of their languages by (neo)colonizers. Moreover, Indigenous and dub poets frequently describe their work as extending ancestral oral traditions even as they thematize the muting of their mother tongues. The poetry of the Cree and Cree-Métis, and of Canadian dubbers reveals a pronounced degree of overlap in the groups' experience of the crucial place of language politics in colonization, so poets from these groups take up language as a primary vector of decolonization. In response to having English forced down their peoples' throats, they challenge the conventions of standard English, Indigenizing or dubbing it, but their respective strategies for "reinventing the enemy's language"[6] are conditioned by their peoples' quite different linguistic histories. nêhiyawêwin/Cree language is a living one in the Turtle Island context, so Cree and Cree-Métis poets can draw on it in a far more comprehensive way than dub poets can draw on African ancestral languages. These were stolen from Caribbean forebears centuries ago, though traces of African lexis, syntax, and phonology remain in Caribbean Englishes. The language that dub poets most often use is the "mix-up of west-afrikan languages/english/some spanish/some french, birthed from the trans-atlantic slave trade"[7] that Kamau Brathwaite in *History of the Voice* called "nation language"[8] and others call Creole. While recurrently pointing to the (neo)colonial subversion of their peoples' respective sound identities, then, both Indigenous and dub poets work through their language practices to recover and reconstitute culturally specific ones.

Theorizing Sound Identity
I adapt the term "sound identities" from music-education theorist Glenn M. Hudak who in "The 'Sound' Identity: Music-Making and Schooling" argues that music plays a key role in the formation of identity and the constitution of a sense of social context and place among school-aged youth. My usage recognizes the central role that music plays in the development, sustainment, and evolution of identity among people of Cree and Caribbean ancestry, but I expand Hudak's conception to include *language's* phonological aspect, and further draw on the polysemy of the word "sound" as verb (to gauge depths, here of self and community) and adjective (healthy, strong, valid, here as restoration of psychic and spiritual health after colonial depreciation and silencing, restoration evidenced by the proud sounding out of cultural difference).

Musical Sound Identities in Indigenous and Dub Poetries
No poet better illustrates the importance of music for Indigenous sound identity than Gregory Scofield. To him, poetry is song, as his book titles *Love Medicine and One Song/Sâkihtowin-Maskihkiy êkwa Pêyak-Nikamowin*, *Native Canadiana: Songs from the Urban Rez*, and *Singing Home the Bones* suggest. The Cree part of his sound identity, nurtured in him principally by his Cree-speaking Auntie Georgina, sings out from his earliest poems, as is attested by "Kookum's Lullaby" with its four Cree stanzas, and "Pêyak-Nikamowin," the "One Song" of the bilingual title of his third book. Moreover, his tribute to his two mothers, Dorothy Scofield and Georgina Houle Young, in *I Knew Two Metis Women*, plays to the soundtrack of the country

and western songs the women loved so much. In "I've Been Told, a poem near the end of the book," Scofield reveals that stories of Halfbreed heaven report it serving as a "rest-over" for country music luminaries,"[9] and to be full of the music and dancing of the people "in squeaky-wheeled carts / loaded with accordions, guitars / and fiddles."[10] Moreover, in Scofield's later work, Métis music and the strains of Cree songs are interwoven with the Hebrew prayer-songs of his father's Jewish heritage[11] so that Scofield's poems collectively play out a particularly complex sound identity whose multiple strains the poet holds in careful balance.

"Prayer Song for the Returning of Names and Sons" rebalances Cree and English by redressing the covering over of Cree names with English Christian ones. The poem is in part a sound memorializing, a ceremonial singing home of the remains of those sons of Hudson's Bay Company factors and Cree women who were sent to England for education and training by the Company and never returned to Canada. However, the poem also sings home the female ancestors whose sacred Cree names have been obscured by the patriarchal Hudson Bay Company's records so that only the alien English sound identity, encoded in the Christian names Charlotte, Sarah, Mary, and Christiana, was passed down. To make explicit the intent of his singing, Scofield directly addresses his "châpanak," his ancestral grandmothers, telling them he wants to restore "the spirit of your iskwew [Cree woman's] / names."[12] In his act of renaming, however, Scofield channels his ancestors' Cree names through English while preserving the form of traditional appellations, just as he channels the sounded through the written in the poem. He urges his "châpanak" and his reader-listeners "natohta,"[13] listen, so his foremothers can be called and sung with names like Tatooed from the Lip to the Chin Woman, She Paints Her Face with Red Ochre, and Charm Woman Who Is Good to Make a Nation.

Cree poets' references to music similarly suggest the hybridity of contemporary Cree sound identity. The round dance music to which the speaker moves in Halfe's *Blue Marrow* is constituted by strains of "Roy Orbison Hank Williams k.d. lang Otis Redding / Mosquito Drums Buffy Sainte-Marie Kashtin Murray Porter / Zamfir Enya B. B. King Glen Gould Riccardo Muti."[14] In "Holes in Sound," Neal McLeod relates a funeral trip back to the James Smith Cree reserve, which he locates "on the edge of English and Cree,"[15] and reports that even though Johnny Burns was a speaker of "high Cree," his cultural landscape and sound identity are textured by a multiplicity of traditions:

> they played old Cree songs
> and Buck Owens' "Act Naturally"

at his funeral
followed by Cree Anglican hymns
with the beat of the drum[16]

No one among the funeral attendees "seemed to notice / the buffet of sound,"[17] McLeod adds.

Dub poetry, for its part, is built upon musical and speech rhythms/ riddims. Oku Onuora, a pioneer of the genre, once said that the dub poem "has a *built-in reggae rhythm*,"[18] but he would later maintain that reggae was not the only music informing dub because "you can dub een a South African riddim,...a kumina riddim,...a nyabinghi riddim,...a jazz riddim,...a funk riddim...."[19] There is scarcely a dub poet who has not at some point poetically celebrated Bob Marley for providing Jamaicans with a proud sound identity, and in mandiela's tribute to slain Rastafarian-influenced dub poet Michael (Mikey) Smith, "Mih Feel It (Wailin for Mikey)," Marley's "Redemption Song" informs the representation of reggae's and dub's riddims as bringing a particular form of redemption: "Riddemshan for every dred / mus cum."[20]

Reggae's recording of Afro-Jamaican suffering is recognized in "I dub poet d'bi.young" when young speaks of "a slow rub-a-dub pounding the pressures / of a people transferred,"[21] while specifically Jamaican Canadian connections with Africa and struggles in a violent Toronto environment play through Cooper's "Africa Wailin" and a number of Lillian Allen poems, including "Riddim an Hardtimes," "Rub a Dub Style inna Regent Park," and "Dark Winds." Dub poetry makes clear, then, that Jamaican Canadian sound identity begins in reggae, yet is not limited to it. The Stereo-Prophet of "Africa Wailin," who "trow down / at Bathurst and Bloor"[22] and at the *Tequila* nightclub, creates a situation in which the black community blossoms in recognition of a shared sound identity as "300 sing as one / sing along wid the dj / sing along wid the singers" and "Black people dance / communally."[23] But the Africa that wails through this reggae cries out (neo)-colonized's people's pains of dignity-destroying unemployment ("no jobs here in Babylon / is jus pure batterayashan"), criminalization ("our men led like sheep to prison"), and deracination ("our sons lost in whiteness").[24]

If the violent music of the "Bu-bu-bu / Bullit [that] ah spit" and the "Ratta-tatta-tatta / [of the] Big gun dem [that] ah chatta"[25] are parts of the soundscape of the ghettos (whether in Kingston, Jamaica, or in North America), then Allen's "Rub a Dub Style inna Regent Park" suggests that an alternative, more peaceful soundtrack is Jamaican Canadian youths chanting out their frustration in a dancehall style: "could have been a gun / but's a mike in his hand."[26]

The poem's representation of frustrated youth being channelled away from self-defeating violence by dancehall performance creatively displaces with the "vessel" of reggae the slave ship that carried Africans to Jamaica. That ship enables a steady course by externalizing the particular heartaches of Jamaican Canadians stuck in a racist system in Canada and cut off in most ways from Africa and the fullness of sound identities Africa offers:

> riddim line vessel im ache
> from im heart outside
> culture carry im past
> an steady im mind[27]

Part of what dub poetry reflects back to Euro-Canada is that the sounds of violence are part of *its* sound identity. In "Dark Winds," for instance, the people who "just a uggle fi get a little space"[28] feel pressing down on them the weight of what many dub poets call the shitstem, which "just a progress pon them back / pon the[m] back."[29] Allen shows her people amid the music and the ganja of the reggae dancehall "seeped in a voyage of discovery / a mystic deep black journey"[30] and eased by the beat of the music so that "the tiredness and emptyness regress."[31] Then the sounds of repression break in upon this scene—"BAM!"—as the "p'lice them," objecting to "the noise" of the Jamaican dancehall, "kick down the door / put everyone pon the floor / face down flat."[32]

Yet even as Allen arraigns the police for the racist brutality of this assault, she conveys her community's resilience as the dub riddims keep driving the lines, and the rhymes and other repetitions just keep on coming:

> It was a brutal attack
> pon the spirit of survival
> pon the culture and the spirit of revival
> pon de youth of Jane & Finch
> cause them black, cause them black[33]

In this way Allen models a spirited sound identity that refuses to crumble under the weight of oppression and stands up to the violence in a way she urges is necessary for young people, who "just haffi find a way / fi stand them ground / and fight back."[34]

In Indigenous poetry, a similarly spirited and emphatic resistance is exemplified by Scofield's young Aunty Georgina in "A Jig for Sister" fighting back and ultimately dancing free of the (neo)colonial school's disciplinary power as she moves to an Indigenous music that only she can hear. When, after witnessing the chronic, violent, and often hysterical abuse of other girls by Sister Dennis, the teenaged Georgina is "once too often" slapped, "yanked around by her hair"[35] and otherwise physically and verbally assaulted; she sees red, chokes the nun, and pushes her to the floor. With her fist poised to strike, the girl becomes the embodiment of pent-up rebellion against abuse as she is urged on by her peers screaming, "Pukamow, Georgina! Pukamow!" (Hit her, Georgina! Hit her!)."[36] She declines, but her cultural victory is consolidated by her response to the Mother Superior's telling her that "such evil acts // wouldn't be tolerated."[37] Much as Allen's persona in "I Fight Back" rejects colonizing namings of her as "Immigrant, law-breaker, illegal, minimum-wager / refugee," in favour of "mother, ... worker, ... fighter,"[38] Georgina turns her back on Mother Superior's naming of the girl's behaviour as "evil,"[39] instead showing herself at this moment to be firmly and joyously self-determining. At sixteen, finally old enough to leave the residential school, she "[turns] on her moccasined heels," and performs a Métis cross-jig on her way out the door.[40]

Silencing Linguistic Sound Identities

Tuning in to the *speech* dimensions of sound identity enables recognition that both Indigenous and dub poets address the colonizer's muting power. On Indigenous territory, that power subverts and often all but destroys Indigenous sound identities whether manifested in speech in a mother tongue other than English or as Indigenous English. Reporting on the disruption of Indigenous soundscapes,[41] Francis remarks that the tearing away of language, its being rendered "sudden / illegal" in residential schools "equals ill eagle,"[42] i.e., results in unhealthy or unsound Indigenous peoples, here symbolized by the bird that embodies strength and acute vision. In the face of "word cannibals," he suggests, Indigenous youth "need some language insurance / dialect alarm system, too"[43] to protect them from linguistic losses, and his punning, counter-discursive use of "business talk,"[44] and his assertion that "language comes / from the / land" simultaneously model a "sound / escape" from the colonial sonic environment.

In Marilyn Dumont's "that tongued belonging," the persona and people like her face the painfully ironic situation of having lost most of their Cree sound identity because of the language having been "once forbidden"[45] and so not passed on by their parents, and then finding themselves depreciated by those who still speak Cree/nêhiyawêwin. The ones bereft of Cree are anguished to have a sound identity constituted linguistically only by alien English and occasional echoes of their ancestral Indigenous language. Nonetheless, in the opening stanzas, Cree is a living presence, however residual, because it makes itself felt in moments of intimate connection. The language vivifies the "borrowed sounds of English,"[46] when, for example, the affection carried by the word *niskwêsis* (meaning "my girl")—a single unit in a stream of Cree sound[47]—shoots life, warmth, and belonging through the English two-word phrase:

> Cree survives in the words
> my niece offers her tearful daughter, "It's O.K., my girl."
> "my girl," that tender way of affirming kinship
> "my girl," that recognition of being called into
> and belonging to Cree
>
> all of this, in a few borrowed sounds of English[48]

As Dumont explains, "the nerve of Cree remains / in mouths that have tasted a foreign alphabet too long."[49] This idea of the nerve of nêhiyawêwin still there in the mouths of Cree or Cree-Métis people who have been (neo) colonially habituated to speaking other languages communicates a felt connection to the all-but-lost ancestral language, a body memory of the movements and shapes of the mouth necessary for speaking Cree. That memory is just waiting to be reactivated even in those people who have never learned the language but whose ancestry is at least partly Cree. Sound identity by this understanding has a biological component whether as genetic inheritance and/or as neurological pathway laid down in response to the socio-cultural phenomenon of having repeatedly heard the language as a child.

Dumont's comment that "frequently we sound too little of ourselves"[50] suggests an infrequent and/or shallow sounding down into self and community and hence a compromised sound identity. Had deeper sounding been possible, the speaker believes, people like her would have been "spared...grief (not to mention, alienation)."[51] What the poem intimates, then, is that without the language fully alive in the mouth of such speakers and there to shape every connection to and perception of the world, bonds of relation attenuate, so that those who had the language taken from them are sometimes viewed by Cree-speakers as "illegitimate children"[52] held responsible for what they lack because in the post-residential school era, the "same sounds / once forbidden / are now pronounced."[53] The pain of loss is thus intensified. Moreover, by referring to the lost language as a "phantom limb" whose "ache"[54] is a constant reminder of amputation, Dumont conveys the sense of weakened sound identity impairing the whole being.

In two poems, Dumont makes clear that a Cree-inflected English is also subject to depreciation. In "The Devil's Language," she reports that a colonizing reconstitution of Indigenous identity is the outcome of breaking standard Canadian English's "syntactic laws"[55] by letting Cree erupt through the surface of the English: "use the wrong order or / register and you're a dumb Indian / dumb, drunk or violent." The force of the silencing "Great White way.../ [that] had its hand over [the speaker's] mouth since [her] first day of school"[56] is shown in "Memoirs of a Really Good Brown Girl" to specifically suppress sound identity. Dumont's persona testifies to this day being a muting experience, not because she didn't speak English, but because her English sounded different from that of her schoolmates: "I am a foreigner, I stay in my seat, frozen, afraid to move, afraid to make a mistake, afraid to speak, they talk differently than I do, I don't sound the way they do, but I don't know how to sound any different, so I don't talk.... "[57]

If Indigenous poets write about heritage languages depreciated and lost, as well as Aboriginal Englishes scorned, the major linguistic issue for Jamaican nation language poets, whose African ancestral languages were stolen centuries ago, is the devaluation of their creolized English. Jamaican speech, in its differences from British English, was judged bad and corrupted.[58] Satirizing this depreciation of her people's language was a recurrent concern of the Jamaican nation language poet Louise Bennett/Miss Lou, who, along with Marley, is one of the two artists without whom, Allen asserts, "there would be no dub poetry."[59] In the monologue "Jamaica Language," Bennett proudly asserts her sound identity and that of the majority of Jamaicans, offering a spirited defence of their way of talking by having her persona Aunty Roachy argue that it is no more a "corruption of the English language" than English is a "corruption of Norman French an Latin an all dem tarra language what dem seh dat English is derived from."[60] Auntie Roachy indignantly proclaims, "English is a derivation, but Jamaica Dialec is corruption! What a unfairity! We derive too!" before explaining that among the many roots of Jamaican speech is the Ghanaian language Twi. She reports, for example, that the Jamaican word *dutty* is often thought to be a corruption of the English word *dirty*, but is in fact a survival in Jamaican of the Twi word for ground or earth.[61] Contemporary dub poets' connection with African ancestral languages is, then, in some ways like that of the persona in Dumont's "that tongued belonging" with Cree, but, instead of the nerve of Cree making itself felt, the more distant pulse of Africa throbs in and through the dub poets' mouths.

Attempts to still that pulse are attacks on Jamaicans' sound identity as Allen makes clear. She reports that when she was growing up, "It was assumed that if you wanted to make something of yourself and get ahead, you had to leave your culture and 'bad talk' behind."[62] However, she says, "Very early I knew that this was not an attack on 'bad' culture or 'bad' language"; rather, she understood the assault as "an orchestrated strategy to 'keep these people in their place' and to stigmatize something so fundamental to a people's identity and sense of self"[63] as language. The assault, while "a deliberate attempt to degrade and destroy the very essence of who we are,"[64] is carried out by attacking the most broadly representative sound identity of Jamaicans, namely, that based on Jamaican Creole/ nation language.

Two poems by d'bi.young indicate that Jamaican schools, like Canadian ones, play a key role in subverting non-hegemonic sound identities. In her prose poem "letter to tchaiko," she speaks of spending the first half of her time at Campion College, "twisting my tongue into the queen's english"[65] and the second half "showing off my nation language because I was *authentic ghetto*." In "brown skin lady," young exemplifies the two modes of talk. First, she illustrates the "thick-ghetto-jamaican-accent"[66] that she "spoke…at home" with the assertion to her more economically privileged schoolmates: "'nuh becuz mi poor mean mi nuh belong 'ere / mi belong 'ere jus as much as you do.'"[67] Then she replays the same thought, this time phrased "the campion way / the british jamaican way / the best of the best way," claiming, "when I spoke like this at school / I fit / almost."[68] She glosses that *almost* by adding, "my ghetto-thick-jamaican-accent / refus[ed] to lie / still," and by breaking the predicate after the word *lie*, suggests that she felt prompted to mask her real sound identity, but it broke through the attempted muffling.

Re-Sounding Identities Through Code-Switching and Creolizing

In the racist contexts in which (neo)colonial depreciation and silencing occur along with similarly disempowering economic dislocations, both Indigenous and dub poets re-sound identities for themselves and their people. They do so, not by straining after some unrealizable pre-colonial sound identity, but by code-switching and creolizing language. A Jamaican girl like young, subjected to what St. Lucian poet Derek Walcott would call "a sound colonial education,"[69] at least still had nation language, or Jamaican Creole, as her mother tongue and could move between it and the "Mother country" tongue when doing so would be to her advantage. However, amuna baraka-clarke suggests that Canadian-born dub poets like her may well find themselves as bereft of nation language as Dumont reports some people of her generation were of Cree.

In "mih mudda tongue," baraka-clarke thematizes her desire to sound out the Jamaicanness in her identity above the white noise of her Canadian environment.[70] This desire entails being able to speak in the language of her mother, thus killing the colonizer ("gwan mek dih colonizer die / in me")[71] that she has internalized through Canadian English: "mih waan back mih tongue / (*but i was born in canada*)." The poem's code-switching between standard Canadian English—the pervasive source of the "noise... [that] jus a batta all around"[72]—and nation language is as deliberate as young's movement between nation language and Campion College English. baraka-clarke claims an Afro-Jamaican sound identity partly by aligning herself with the Rastafarian distrust of the colonizer's language when she remarks, "always wanted to liberate my tongue / from / my canadian downbringing,"[73] thus refashioning English in accord with the Rastafarian observations about the "Babylonian" tongue (read standard English). Rastafarians, having perceived that English is so deceitful that its word for pushing down, *oppression*, sounds like up-pression, began to record the maltreatment of African Jamaicans by coining the word *downpression*.[74] baraka-clarke further claims a Jamaican sound identity by making a deliberate decision to use nation language—"& now mih mek a choice / hear jamaican in mih voice"[75]— but the power of the language then seizes control, so she can "feel dih nation language / jus a tek hold ah mih."

Scofield's "The Poet Takes It upon Himself to Speak" acknowledges that after a period of trouble with English, his "lazy tongue / flopped involuntarily,"[76] his own version of a Canadian "downbringing." With the "pîkiskwewina" (Cree words) "locked in the attic" through the interventions of church and state, the liberation of Cree words is effected in this poem by asserting the language's connection to land and priority in Turtle Island sound identity: "*hâw-nikiskisin* [now I remember]/ first the language / was old earth." In retelling the Cree Creation story of the Earth Divers, Scofield re-sounds nêhiyawêwin, and as he imprints it on the white face of the page, he also stakes Cree's claim on the imaginative territory of the book. However, lest readers forget the importance of the sounded word, Scofield concludes the poem with a section in which Cree encloses and, for the first time in the poem, equitably counterbalances English lines: here "the language was spoken, / always spoken" is prefaced by "*hâw-nikiskisin*" and followed by "*êkwa êkosi kîtohta!*"[77] The final injunction to the reader here is to listen, to let Cree sound on the ear. In this way, Scofield confirms nêhiyawêwin as a key part of his sound identity and, by extension, that of other Cree-Métis and Cree people.

In "kipocihkân [a mute]," Scofield characterizes his own learning of nêhiyawêwin, the language of his second mother, Georgie, as giving him something to "cl[i]ng to life on"[78] in his difficult youth. In the nine-page poem, the sustained speaking about the many sources of the silencing in his life and his ancestors' lives is, in both form and theme, a refusal of silences born of shame about being Métis or Cree and, in his case, gay. It names those who pushed him into silence, and it honours those who helped him come to voice. The poem is also evidence that his discovery of his Jewish heritage led him to claim his Jewishness in part by integrating Hebrew and Yiddish into a sound identity principally linguistically constituted by Cree and English. He gives thanks in and for his ancestral languages, foregrounding Yiddish in phrases like "mein papa Ron, my father / whose tongue was a schmatteh [a rag]" and Hebrew in the blessing "Ba-ruch A-tah Ado-nai / E-lo-he-nu Me-lech Ha-olam" (Blessed are you, Lord our God / King of the Universe); toasts like "L'Chaim!" (To life); and prayers like "Alev ha-sholem" (May he rest in peace).[79] Rapid code-switches among four of his ancestral languages suggest the complexity of what he must integrate.

McLeod's poetic code-switching is simpler because to date at least he has found no place in his poetically recorded sound identity for the Swedish language of his mother, though he speaks the language.[80] His print textualizing of Cree orature and orality proceeds from his conviction, stated in "*mistasiniy*," that "stories and names are food / [that help] keep the life force / *waskawîwin* flowing."[81] Thus, his awareness of oral stories disappearing from the community's conversations—a loss thematized in "Holes in Sound"—motivated him to bring translated Cree oral stories to the page in both the scholarly study *Cree Narrative Memory* and his poems. Tutored by Elder Edwin Tootoosis, who said of colonized Cree land, "'*môy ê-kistawêt*' [It does not echo],"[82] McLeod asserts the sound identity of nêhiyaw-askiy, Cree land, discursively claiming it for the nêhiyawak, Cree people, by retelling traditional oral stories, and by frequently weaving Cree into poems set in Cree territory and often about specific places there.

His poetic and scholarly recountings of mistasiniy,[83] the great Grandfather Buffalo Rock in the Qu'Appelle Valley, exemplifies this practice. Because Cree people continue to tell the story of paskwâw-mostos awâsis, buffalo child, the great stone lives on, and Cree bodies are "tattooed / with land's memories / with land speak, *askîwêwin*."[84] But even more importantly, McLeod maintains that Cree traditional narratives give form to sound (healthy and whole) Cree identity while channelling the process of making Cree sound: "old stories give our bodies shape / and guide the path of sound / like trees guiding the wind."[85]

Similarly, traditional and other stories give discursive shape to the bodies of Jamaican people, guiding the path of Creole sounds to help form the sound identities of the dub nation. anitafrika explains of the people who surrounded her in her youth that "their bodies, faces, voices spoke the rhythms and rawness of their lives and expressed their feelings, thoughts, and disappointments in powerful and distinct ways…storytelling resided in their spirits."[86] She makes clear the centrality of sound to her people's identity when articulating what she calls the seven "orplusi" principles of storytelling. The first four—orality, rhythm, political content, and language[87]—are "fundamental pillars of dubpoetry" (Seven), and of these, three—orality, rhythm, and language—relate directly to sound. She identifies dub rhythm as the heartbeat of Africa in the bodies of black diasporic subjects when she explains that "afrikan peoples who were transplanted from their homelands on the continent and dispersed throughout the world, were not allowed to bring anything along with them, other than their bodies and the memories coursing in their veins. rhythm is the heartbeat, the memory that is stored in the blood, in the body."[88] Rhythm, then, is the pulse of Africa in the blood of transported Africans, and that pulse is transmitted when the lifeblood of Africa is transfused into the dub poem. It beats underneath the skin of English, transforming it into nation language, and helps bring to life Jamaican sound identities.

Dub from the outset spoke nation language, and its practitioners recognize Louise Bennett's language politics as foundational. Allen's "Tribute to Miss Lou" is an exemplary articulation of dub sound identity. The first section, "Heartbeat," opens by according Bennett space within the poetic tradition when for a long time literary editors refused to recognize her as a real poet. A. L. Hendriks and Cedric Lindo's *Independence Anthology of Jamaica Literature*, for example, placed her work outside of the poetry section, consigning her Creole verses to a miscellaneous section at the back of the anthology. Such treatment was the result not only of her reputation as an oral performer but also because in writing her poetry down, she did precisely what young says a dub poet does: "speaks to and for the people by breaking with british hierarchical linguistic rule."[89] Allen thus acknowledges Bennett's representing Jamaicans' experience through her poems' grammar, syntax, and style, praising her in the language she used: "Lawd, yu mek wi heart pound soh / yu mek wi just love up wiself / an talk wi talk soh."[90]

Bennett's legitimation of nation language, continued here by Allen, is analogous to Cree and Cree-Metis poets' indigenization of English. Halfe legitimates Creenglish in poems like "Valentine Dialogue," "Sugar Beat," and some of the *âcimowinisa* of *Blue Marrow*.[91] Campbell valorizes the village English of her father's generation in *Stories of the Road Allowance People*, as Scofield does the Michif-inflected English of "Conversation My Châpan Mary Might Have Had with Mrs. Sarah F. Wakefield" and the Creenglish of his "Oh, Dat Agnes." All these texts refuse the shame associated with speaking a socially stigmatized version of a language, doing so by rejecting standard orthography in favour of spellings guided by the pronunciation of Creenglish.

Sharing Strategies for (Re)Constituting Sound Identities

The kind of reaching out across the gulf of cultural and sound identity differences between Indigenous and Caribbean diasporic peoples in Canada that various dub poets have enacted in their writing may signal possible grounds for "communitist" (communal+activist)[92] strategic alliances in recognition of the two peoples' common experiences of socio-economic marginalization by neo/colonizing forces and of the neo/colonizers' culturally crippling, when not outright genocidal, activities. Allen long ago invited to a revolutionary tea party "You who know what the past has been / you who work in the present tense / you who see through to the future."[93] Those who take up Allen's invitation to "siddon and look at the system"[94] will also discover that hers is a joyous opening of doors to enable the sharing of experience and planning for ameliorative action: "let's talk, let's make art, let's love, dance / revel in the streets if that's the beat / protest demonstrate chant."[95] The opening is, however, made with full knowledge of the difficult struggle ahead and framed in a language that signals in its grammar and deliberately non-standard spellings a position taken up outside the pale of the colonizer's English:

> come sit here with we
> mek wi drink tea
> mek wi talk
> mek wi analyse
> mek wi strategize
> mek wi work together[96]

For some there is no choice but to work together, as George Elliott Clarke, an African-diasporic member of the Eastern Woodlands Métis Nation of Nova Scotia, argues because people like him can "no more separate [the two peoples'] [twin] struggles[s] for freedom than [they] could remove the Indian DNA from their bodies."[97] He, too, then, considers how alliances between the two groups might be built, maintaining that "any effective African-Canadian and First Nations reconciliation must begin...with an acknowledgement of each other's historical repression, genealogical bonds (as Métis) [when they do exist], and...mutual efforts, sometimes in coalitions...to insist on our rights and respect...."[98]

If Indigenous and Caribbean peoples in Canada *do* share enough to make them allies in the struggle for justice, poets from the two communities may be among the most advantageously placed to make clear the common ground and to build a productive conversation. Poets, especially those with roots in vibrant oral traditions such as Indigenous and Caribbean Canadian poets have, are both skilled listeners and speakers. They can thus communicate the shared experience of both language theft, which has so powerfully undermined a healthy sense of self, and other (neo)colonial stealing, which has impoverished both groups without being able to take away altogether the non-material treasures of their resilient cultures. Thus it is that their poets artfully employ the devalued tongues of their respective peoples to help restore health and wholeness, which is to say sound identities.

Notes

Acknowledgements: Thanks to Neal McLeod and Natasha Beeds for inviting me to participate in the Indigenous Poetics workshop at Trent University, to the Social Sciences and Humanities Research Council for the Standard Research grant that helped fund my participation, and to Neal McLeod and Margery Fee for skilled editing.

1 The imbrication of neocolonialism with colonialism will hereafter be lexically signalled by telescoping the pair into *(neo)colonialism* or its cognates.
2 The references to diaspora disappear in the version of "Coming Home Through Stories," in Neal McLeod, *Cree Narrative Memory: From Treaties to Contemporary Times* (Saskatoon: Purich Publishing, 2007), ch. 7.
3 Marvin Francis, *City Treaty* (Winnipeg: Turnstone Press, 2002), 66.
4 Ibid., 69.
5 See Agnes Calliste, "Canada's Immigration Policy and Domestics from the Caribbean: The Second Domestic Scheme," in *Race, Class, Gender: Bonds and Barriers* (2nd ed.), ed. Jesse Vorst et al. (Toronto: Garamond Press, 1991), 145.
6 Joy Harjo et al., eds., *Reinventing the Enemy's Language: Contemporary Native Women's Writings of North America* (New York: W. W. Norton, 1997).
7 d'bi young, *art on black* (Toronto: Women's Press, 2006), 4.
8 Edward Kamau Brathwaite, *History of the Voice: The Development of Nation Language in Anglophone Caribbean Poetry* (London: New Beacon Books, 1984), 13. Brathwaite's coinage names an English that throbs with the pulse of Africa and the agonizing pain of slave history, as well as the howling of the Caribbean hurricane and the crashing of waves on the shore.
9 Ibid., 132.
10 Gregory Scofield, *I Knew Two Metis Women: The Lives of Dorothy Scofield and Georgina Houle Young* (Victoria: Polestar Book Publishers, 1999), 131.
11 See, for example, "The Unorthodox Funeral of Ron Miller" and "kipocihkân."
12 Gregory Scofield, *Singing Home the Bones* (Vancouver: Raincoast Books, 2005), 29.
13 Ibid., 30.
14 Louise Halfe, *Blue Marrow* (2nd ed.), (Regina: Coteau Books, 2004), 65.
15 Neal McLeod, *Songs to Kill a Wîhtikow* (Regina: Hagios Press, 2005), 59.
16 Ibid.
17 Ibid., 60.

18 Quoted in Mervyn Morris, "People Speech," *Reggae Bloodlines: In Search of the Music and Culture of Jamaica*, ed. Stephen Davis and Peter Simon (London: Heinemann, 1977), 189.

19 Quoted in Christian Habekost, *Verbal Riddim: The Politics and Aesthetics of African-Caribbean Dub Poetry*. Cross/Cultures 10 (Amsterdam: Rodopi, 1993), 4.

20 Ahdri Zhina Mandiela, *Speshal Rikwes* (Toronto: Sister Vision Press, 1985), 47.

21 young, *art on black*, 6.

22 Afua Cooper, *Copper Woman and Other Poems* (Toronto: Natural Heritage Books, 2006), 67.

23 Ibid.

24 Ibid., 69.

25 "Getto Lingoz," in Klyde Broox, *My Best Friend Is White* (Toronto: McGilligan Books, 2005), 24.

26 Lillian Allen, *Women Do This Every Day: Selected Poems* (Toronto: Women's Press, 1993), 83. As many of the videos on nativehiphop.net suggest, hip hop arguably acts to articulate the rage of Indigenous youth in a way analogous to that in which it, dub, or rap music serves black youth.

27 Ibid., 82.

28 Ibid., 75.

29 Ibid., 77.

30 Ibid., 75.

31 Ibid., 76.

32 Ibid.

33 Ibid.

34 Ibid., 77.

35 Scofield, *I Knew*, 24.

36 Ibid.

37 Ibid., 27.

38 Allen, *Women Do This*, 140.

39 Scofield, *I Knew*, 27.

40 Ibid.

41 The coinage is R. Murray Schafer's. See *The Tuning of the* World (New York: Knopf, 1977).

42 Francis, *City Treaty*, 54.

43 Ibid., 60.

44 Ibid., 54.

45 Marilyn Dumont, *That Tongued Belonging* (Cape Croker Reserve: Kegedonce Press, 2007), 1.

46 Ibid.

47 This conception of sounded, as opposed to written, language stands behind McLeod's translation of *nêhiyawêwin* as "the process of making Cree sound." Sound is encoded in the very word nêhiyawêwi,n according to McLeod: literally "*nêhiyawêwin* means Cree language ... but if one examines the root of the word it really means 'Cree sound'—the '-*wê*' stem denoting sound." McLeod, *Cree Narrative Memory*, 6, 94.

48 Dumont, *That Tongued Belonging*, 1.
49 Ibid.
50 Ibid.
51 Ibid., 2.
52 Ibid., 1.
53 Ibid.
54 Ibid.
55 Marilyn Dumont, *A Really Good Brown Girl* (London: Brick Books, 1996), 54.
56 Ibid.
57 Ibid., 13.
58 See, for example, the comments on Jamaican language in the YouTube videos "Miss Louise Bennett," February 28, 2012, http://www.youtube.com/watch?v=W58MtDzanqA&feature=related; and "Miss Lou: Fi Wi Language (Jamaican Patwah)," February 28, 2012, http://www.youtube.com/watch?v=W58MtDzanqA&feature=related.
59 Allen, *Women Do This*, 12.
60 Louise Bennett, "Jamaica Language," in *Aunty Roachy Seh*, ed. Mervyn Morris (Kingston, Jamaica: Sangster's Bookshop, 1993), 1.
61 Bennett, "Miss Lou," http://www.youtube.com/watch?v=W58MtDzanqA&feature=related.
62 Allen, *Women Do This*, 11.
63 Ibid.
64 Ibid.
65 young, *art on black*, 80.
66 Ibid., 85.
67 Ibid., 86.
68 Ibid.
69 Derek Walcott, *Collected Poems, 1948–1984* (New York: Farrar, Straus and Giroux, 1986), 346.
70 Marilyn Dumont uses the term "white noise" counter-discursively to name a section of *A Really Good Brown Girl*, and in the poem "It Crosses My Mind."
71 amuna baraka-clarke, "mih mudda tongue," in *Utterances and Incantations: Women, Poetry, and Dub*, ed. Afua Cooper (Toronto: Sister Vision Press, 1999), 38.
72 Ibid.
73 Ibid., 37. The Rastafarians are (originally) African Jamaican believers in the divinity of the Ethiopian Emperor Haile Selassie, also known as Ras Tafari. They thus identify Ethiopia as the specific part of Africa to which they long to return from the generations-long "Babylonian" exile to which their ancestors were transported by slavers.
74 For a discussion of the language of the Rastafarians, see Velma Pollard, *Dread Talk: The Language of Rastafari* (Montreal: McGill-Queen's University Press, 2000).
75 baraka-clarke, "mih mudda tongue," 38.
76 Gregory Scofield, *Native Canadiana: Songs from the Urban Rez* (Vancouver: Polestar Book Publishers, 1996), 13.

77 Ibid., 15.

78 Gregory Scofield, *"Kipocihkân,"* in *Kipocihkân: Poems New and Selected* (Gibsons: Nightwood Editions, 2009), 16.

79 Ibid., 14.

80 In an interview with Renate Eigenbrod, McLeod reported, "Well, I am half Swedish too.... [But] I feel a sense of something that touches my heart with Cree speaking people—a connection I don't feel with Swedish speaking people." Renate Eigenbrod, Georgina Kalegamic, and Josias Fiddler, *Aboriginal Literatures in Canada: A Teacher's Resource Guide.* Toronto: Curriculum Services Canada, 2003), 32.

81 Neal McLeod, *Gabriel's Beach* (Regina: Hagios Press, 2008), 37.

82 McLeod, *Cree Narrative Memory,* 6.

83 "mistasiniy" and "Meditations on *pakskwâw-mostos awâsis"* in McLeod, *Gabriel's Beach,* 36–37, 39; McLeod, *Cree Narrative Memory,* 19–24.

84 McLeod, *Gabriel's Beach,* 39.

85 Ibid.

86 d'bi.young.anitafrika, "dub poetics and personal politics," in *Notes from Canada's Young Activists: A Generation Stands Up for Change,* ed. Severn Cullis-Suzuki et al. (Vancouver: Greystone, 2007), 140.

87 The other three are urgency, sacredness, and integrity. d'bi.young, "Seven Orplusi Principles of Storytelling: d'bi.young's Biomyth Monodrama Creative Process (pt 1)," October 25, 2010, http://www.summerworks.ca/2010/works4.php.

88 Ibid.

89 "di dub," in young, *art on black,* 4.

90 "Tribute to Miss Lou," in Allen, *Women Do This,* 43.

91 See, for example, the little stories of the Grandmother, identified only as *nôtokwêsiw*/old woman and of Born in a Tent Grandmother. Halfe, *Blue Marrow,* 38, 63.

92 Jace Weaver, *That the People Might Live: Native American Literatures and Native American Community* (New York: Oxford University Press, 1997), xiii.

93 "Revolutionary Tea Party," in Allen, *Women Do This,* 133.

94 Ibid.

95 Ibid., 134.

96 Ibid.

97 George Elliott Clarke, "Indigenous Blacks: An Irreconcilable Identity?", in *Cultivating Canada: Reconciliation through the Lens of Cultural Diversity,* ed. Ashok Mathur, Jonathan Dewar, and Mike DeGagné (Ottawa: Aboriginal Healing Foundation, 2011), 403.

98 Ibid., 404.

Bibliography

Allen, Lillian. "In These Canadian Bones." *Psychic Unrest,* 1–3. Toronto: Insomniac Press, 1999.

———. *Women Do This Every Day: Selected Poems.* Toronto: Women's Press, 1993.

anitafrika. d'bi.young (see also young, d'bi). "dub poetics and personal politics." *Notes from Canada's Young Activists: A Generation Stands Up for Change*, compiled and edited by Severn Cullis-Suzuki et al., 137–48. Vancouver: Douglas and McIntyre Publishing, 2007.

baraka-clarke, amuna. "mih mudda tongue." In *Utterances and Incantations: Women, Poetry and Dub*, edited by Afua Cooper, 37–39. Toronto: Sister Vision Press, 1999.

Bennett, Louise. "Jamaica Language." In *Aunty Roachy Seh*, edited by Mervyn Morris, 1–3. Kingston, Jamaica: Sangster's Bookshop, 1993.

———. "Miss Lou: Fi Wi Language (Jamaican Patwah)," February 28, 2012. http://www.youtube.com/watch?v=W58MtDzanqA&feature=related.

———. "Miss Louise Bennett," February 29, 2012. http://www.youtube.com/watch?v=C181G_s7h-s.

Brathwaite, Edward Kamau. *History of the Voice: The Development of Nation Language in Anglophone Caribbean Poetry*. London: New Beacon Books, 1984.

Broox, Klyde. *My Best Friend Is White*. Toronto: McGilligan Books, 2005.

Calliste, Agnes. "Canada's Immigration Policy and Domestics from the Caribbean: The Second Domestic Scheme." In *Race, Class, Gender: Bonds and Barriers* (2nd ed.), edited by Jesse Vorst et al., 136–68. Toronto: Garamond Press, 1991.

Campbell, Maria, trans. "Jacob." In *Stories of the Road Allowance People*, 86–104. Penticton: Theytus Books, 1995.

Clarke, George Elliott. "Indigenous Blacks: An Irreconcilable Identity?" In *Cultivating Canada: Reconciliation Through the Lens of Cultural Diversity*, edited by Ashok Mathur, Jonathan Dewar, and Mike DeGagné, 399–405. Ottawa: Aboriginal Healing Foundation, 2011.

Cooper, Afua. *Copper Woman and Other Poems*. Toronto: Natural Heritage Books, 2006.

Dumont, Marilyn. *A Really Good Brown Girl*. London: Brick Books, 1996.

———. *That Tongued Belonging*. Cape Croker Reserve: Kegedonce Press, 2007.

Eigenbrod, Renate. "Diasporic Longings: (Re)Figurations of Home and Homelessness in Richard Wagamese's Work." In *Cultural Grammars of Nation, Diaspora, and Indigeneity in Canada*, edited by Christine Kim, Sophie McCall, and Melina Baum-Singer, 135–51. Waterloo: Wilfrid Laurier University Press, 2011.

Eigenbrod, Renate, Georgina Kakegamic, and Josias Fiddler. *Aboriginal Literatures in Canada: A Teacher's Resource Guide*. Toronto: Curriculum Services Canada, 2003. http://curriculum.org/storage/30/1278480166aboriginal.pdf.

Francis, Marvin. *City Treaty*. Winnipeg: Turnstone Press, 2002.

Habekost, Christian. *Verbal Riddim: The Politics and Aesthetics of African-Caribbean Dub Poetry*. Cross/Cultures 10. Amsterdam: Rodopi, 1993.

Halfe, Louise. *Bear Bones and Feathers*. Regina: Coteau Books, 1994.

———. *Blue Marrow*. 1998. Rev. ed., Regina: Coteau Books, 2004.

Harjo, Joy, et al., eds. *Reinventing the Enemy's Language: Contemporary Native Women's Writings of North America*. New York: W. W. Norton, 1997.

Hendriks, A. L., and Cedric Lindo, eds. *The Independence Anthology of Jamaica Literature*. Kingston, Jamaica: Arts Celebration Committee of the Ministry of Development and Welfare, 1962.

Hudak, Glenn M. "The 'Sound' Identity: Music-Making and Schooling." In *Sound Identities: Popular Music and the Cultural Politics of Education*, edited by Cameron McCarthy et al., 446–74. New York: Peter Lang Publishing, 1999.

Kim, Christine, Sophie McCall, and Melina Baum-Singer, eds. *Cultural Grammars of Nation, Diaspora, and Indigeneity in Canada*. Waterloo: Wilfrid Laurier University Press, 2011.

LaRocque, Emma. "My Hometown Northern Canada South Africa." In *Native Poetry in Canada*, edited by Jeannette C. Armstrong and Lally Grauer, 154–58. Peterborough: Broadview Press, 2001.

mandiela, ahdri zhina. *dark diaspora . . . in dub*. Toronto: Sister Vision Press, 1991.

———. *Speshal Rikwes*. Toronto: Sister Vision Press, 1985.

Marley, Bob. "Redemption Song." http://www.metrolyrics.com/redemption-song-lyrics-bob-marley.html.

McCall, Sophie. "Diaspora and Nation in Métis Writing." In *Cultural Grammars of Nation, Diaspora, and Indigeneity in Canada*, edited by Christine Kim, Sophie McCall, and Melina Baum-Singer, 21–41. Waterloo: Wilfrid Laurier University Press, 2011.

McLeod, Neal. "Coming Home Through Stories." In *(Ad)dressing the Words of Our People: Aboriginal Perspectives on Aboriginal Literatures*, edited by Armand Garnet Ruffo, 17–36. Penticton: Theytus Books, 2001.

———. *Cree Narrative Memory: From Treaties to Contemporary Times*. Saskatoon: Purich Publishing, 2007.

———. *Gabriel's Beach*. Regina: Hagios Press, 2008.

———. *Songs to Kill a Wîhtikow*. Regina: Hagios Press, 2005.

Morris, Mervyn. "People Speech." In *Reggae Bloodlines: In Search of the Music and Culture of Jamaica*, edited by Stephen Davis and Peter Simon, 189–91. London: Heinemann, 1977.

Pollard, Velma. *Dread Talk: The Language of Rastafari*. Montreal: McGill-Queen's University Press, 2000.

Schafer, R. Murray. *The Tuning of the World*. New York: Knopf, 1977.

Scofield, Gregory. *The Gathering: Stones for the Medicine Wheel*." Vancouver: Polestar Book Publishers, 1993.

———. *I Knew Two Metis Women: The Lives of Dorothy Scofield and Georgina Houle Young*. Victoria: Polestar Book Publishers, 1999.

———. *Kipocihkân: Poems New and Selected*. Gibsons: Nightwood Editions, 2009.

———. *Love Medicine and One Song/Sâkihtowin-Maskihkiy êkwa Pêyak-Nika-mowin*. Victoria: Polestar Book Publishers, 1997.

———. *Native Canadiana: Songs from the Urban Rez*. Vancouver: Polestar Book Publishers, 1996.

———. *Singing Home the Bones*. Vancouver: Raincoast Books, 2005.

Stigter, Shelley. "The Dialectics and Dialogics of Code-Switching in the Poetry of Gregory Scofield and Louise Halfe." *American Indian Quarterly* 30, nos. 1 and 2 (2006): 49–60.

Walcott, Derek. *Collected Poems 1948–1984*. New York: Farrar, Straus and Giroux, 1986.

Weaver, Jace. *That the People Might Live: Native American Literatures and Native American Community*. New York: Oxford University Press, 1997.

young, d'bi. *art on black*. Toronto: Women's Press, 2006.

———. "Seven Orplusi Principles of Storytelling: d'bi.young's Biomyth Monodrama Creative Process (pt 1)." http://www.summerworks.ca/2010/works4.php.

23

Poetics of Renewal: Indigenous Poetics—Message or Medium?

Lillian Allen

De riddim and de heave an the sway of the beat
The rumblings an the tumblings down
To the dream to the beat
To the impulse to be free
To the life that spring up in the heat
To the pounding dance to be free[1]

Much of Indigenous poetics, like dub poetry, is about freedom—freeing up sounds, words, and ideas that need to be alive in the world. I believe that in our communities the search for beauty is the search for justice. Poetry, by its very nature, is the literary means of representing ideas, values, the world, voice, and our relationship to language. The great poet June Jordon said that there are two ways to "worry" words. One is hoping for the greatest possible beauty. The other is to tell the truth.

Writing is a kind of reaching out, of connecting, of reaching inside and touching. It's a reaching for words, for space, for breath, for a pause. It's the breath of our humanity. The poetic line glides, skips, is stubborn sometimes, it shouts, dances, whispers. And asserts itself as beings do in the world. We know that words are not just words as our voice is not just lines on paper. And text is mostly about the subtext.

Poet and Canadian literary cartologist Northrop Frye understood this power of poetic expression, this power of language, when he wrote; "Any word or phrase can become the storm center of meanings, sounds, and associations, radiating out and indefinitely like ripples in a pool."[2] This potential of language as power is especially important to us as we do not own or control the means of mass communication and its messaging in our society. Deciding to become a poet—most especially a spoken-word, dub, or performance poet—is seizing the moment to create our own media. Indigenous poets like dub poets have seized poetry as a necessary means to not just counter the meta-narratives and the absences of Indigenous and black communities, and communities seeking empowerment from the official version, but also as a way to vindicate our experiences, enrich our cultural voice, and to be fully in our humanity of art, ritual, and communication that the act of writing, reading, performing poetry is.

Poetry is certainly one way to reflect on and control the message, values, and visionary ideals on a tiny scale that we keep alive in our communities and in the world. There is a light that dances in poetry as poetry dances light into the world and we point to "the crack in things" so that the light can get through. It was Leonard Cohen who penned and sang:

> Ring the bells that still can ring
> Forget your perfect offering
> There is a crack, a crack in everything
> That's how the light gets in. (Chorus from "Anthem")

In this passage Cohen affirms that there is no one broad perfect sweep in confronting the massiveness of an unequal reality. He extols ringing the bell (our voices) that still can sing as a way of pushing through, breaking up, or affecting this dense monolith so that there can be illumination.

We're not lacking ideas in our communities. These are just not packaged on the scale or form of commerce. If we look at the ways ideas are expressed in our sense of justice, in our relationship with culture, through stewardship to the land, through rituals, and through weaving in and out of time, we can discern our own meta-patterns that correspond to our marks on paper, our words in pattern, and our recurring stories and images. These signify for us our vision, not only our pain and concerns. Indigenous and dub poetics call on embodiment as a signifier, the feel—"huggable" feel, like the feel in jazz, a sense of the whole self as holistic, and as holistic individual in community. The desire to mark, celebrate, probe, and give voice is at once the same desires. It is not just a belief but also an affirmation in the multi-dimensionality of life, including those unseen and unknown and unexplainable aspects. Possibly those we know from past life connections, the spirit of memory, whisperings from our ancestors, and those things we know and feel instinctively.

The poetry for dub poets and I believe the poetry of Indigenous artists have played forward the more iterative to being mostly concerned with being generative, less about copying, being like, imitating, shadowing, and getting approval from media-constructed mainstream society, and are as much a poetics of resistance, revival, renewal, and transformation. The

central question, I believe, is a spiritual one, not so much a political one, if
we must make those distinctions at all. For beyond the politics is the question: What is life about? And what is my/your life about? Who are we? How
do we fulfill what is worthy of us? The exploration through language and
the poetics are then about those values and actions that contribute to and
help to keep an expanding vision of this life alive in the world. In building
this vision, there are things to do and imagine, but unfortunately there
are also things to undo and overcome. Indeed, with a history of inequal-
ity and oppression against Indigenous peoples, black (African) peoples,
and peoples of colour and their cultures, there is much to be undone. As
we seek to chart our own expressions, it should come as no surprise, then,
that much of the poetry and poetic mission, as many dub and Indigenous
poets see it, will either directly or inadvertently confront those things that
have unfairly defined us and our communities. To do this we must liberate
words and forms to more closely reflect our rhythms and tempo. Out of
this journey we constantly negotiate between chaos, hard and harsh realities, and renewal. Lee Maracle wrote in her 1988 groundbreaking book *I
Am Woman*:

> ...*and the rain of our green meadows
> mingled with tears of pain
> pain healed by earth's soft damp.*[3]

Lee Maracle in this excerpt clearly moved way beyond the unrealized promised of "Justice for all" from what she called the "imprisoned word locked
into colonial bias" to a healing beyond man's or man-made institutions.
Maracle also shows us that poetry is important to comfort suffering, for in
its depths suffering is a silent thing, even if you scream it out loud. Poetry,
like the earth, can be the "wounded healer." Maracle's mingling of the rain
and the pain, the earth and the damp, the green and the soft, the meadow
and the tears, makes us lose ourselves in her images. In her words we see,
feel, touch, smell, hear, and remember. Maracle, as June Jordan would have
described, "worries words," and astoundingly achieves not just beauty and
truth, but transcendence.

In the best dub and Indigenous poetry, tone is very important and a clue
to understanding the poet's vision if you examine who the poem or persona is addressing and how the poet treats the audience, the subject matter,
and the community in the work. Tone in literature is about techniques
and modes of presentation the writer uses to reveal or create attitude and
feelings. We can ask the questions: What does the language and diction
(word use, style, and level of language) call upon the reader for? What
does the work promote? In dub and Indigenous poetry, the poet insists on

reminding us of historic and current injustices and inequalities, and a calling to account. At the same time, the poetics are always trying to create a new elevated space to nurture the craving in our aesthetic souls, and create understanding, new possibilities, and possible new beginnings.

Because by necessity this journey to healing and transformation must include a conscious or subconscious strategy of deprogramming in a market-driven society, the often identified political (us and them) nature of our work is glommed upon to the detriment of the integrative and generative nature of the vision, a vision whose very gesture is generosity. And it is because of this vision that dub poets have stepped up the discursive exchange with wider discourses on race, gender, equality rights, environmental justice, politics, and so forth, speaking within the community of origins radicalized in the West as black, and communities of colour, and communities of affinity, and communities of shared decolonizing values, shared vision, and communities of possibilities. For us this is spiritual work also.

Revolutionary beat poet Diane DiPrima, in her poem "Rant," asserts that without imagination there is no memory, but in her opening stanza she reminds us that:

> You cannot write a single line w/out a cosmology
> a cosmology
> laid out before all eyes

Further in the poem she states that everyone has a poetics:

> no matter what you do: plumber, baker, teacher
> You do it in the consciousness of making
> Or not making yr world

> You have poetics: You step into the world
> like a suit of readymade clothes.

> or you etch in light
> your firmament spills into the shape of your room, of yr body, of yr
> loves[4]

The poetics of dub poetry is a movement, a message, and a medium. I believe this might be similar in Aboriginal poetics in several ways. For one, dub poetry is a poetry of possibilities, forging new perspectives, new information, staking new ground of imagery and meaning, and applying a potent dose of creativity to specificity and the rigours of everyday existence. One of dub poetry's main concerns is community engagement, challenging notions of literature, reflecting back to the community their experiences and aspirations rooted in the fluidity of language. Dub poetry strives to bring creativity and voice into individual and collective process as a living being. Dub poetry brings literature to life, making it an engaged and interactive and democratizing process, an act of communion and community ritual. It is a web and a network of interconnections and cross-sectionality, messing up and meshing Western notions of history, language, literature, culture, community, and their traditional academic tropes that intersect categories of race, gender, class, mental health, sexuality, community, and spirituality.

Dub poetry emerged in Canada in the mid- to late 1970s simultaneously as it was establishing itself in Jamaica and other metropoles where Jamaicans found themselves. The first-generation dub poets were political activists who saw the poetry as part and parcel of the work of social and political transformation they were engaged in. In Toronto in the seventies we were poets who worked with words, sound, (em)power to celebrate voice, creativity, community, and to chart and chant our history, experience, and aspirations. We were fighting back against oppression. Our black community in Toronto was well accustomed to the call of reggae with its worldwide influence to feed the spirit of the tired, wake the sleeping, and champion the dispossessed. Reggae was sensual, beautiful, and fierce and carried our cultural rhythms and sense of beauty. The call of the black (African) American poets of black power and resistance and their processors of the Harlem Renaissance resonated with dub poets in Canada as we tried to negotiate our way and identities in an environment that did not reflect our existence, and one that we perceived as sometimes downright hostile. We also had great Caribbean poetic figures to look up to such as Kamau Braithwaite, Louise Bennett, and Claude McKay. So in Toronto in the 1970s and 1980s as we wrote our poems and participated in community events and marches and protests, the community validated our contribution with their support and appreciation. As Caribbean émigrés we were aware that we were helping to chart a new identity in a new place.

It is precisely because of this live and dynamic nature and dialectic that dub poetry has been a form that has developed a multi-media, interactive, democratizing stance in the writing and dispersal of ideas. One young man, who is now a successful media artist, recently spoke at a panel we shared in 2011. He said that when he was growing up and in high school, he heard my dub poetry (his parents are Caribbean). He said he didn't fully understand some of the "dialect" then or even some of the ideas, but he just knew that that voice and whatever I was saying and how I said it was on his side; here was someone in the media and on the air for the first time that he felt was rooting for who he was at his core. Comments like these in responding to the work of the dub poets are not unusual. But dub is also concerned that its process and reach continuously evolve, for if in such a small movement of dub poetry we can come to know so much, what more is there to know? And what are the other unknowns, especially to empower and move our creativity and communities forward?

In the fall of 2011, Native poet Janet Marie Rogers was a visiting lecturer/poet in one of my creative writing classes at OCAD University in Toronto. I first met Janet at the Banff Centre at the Spoken Word program, which I initiated in 2009 to multiply the power of the new and emerging poetics of dub and the spoken word. During the program Janet was an artist on fire and took on every creative challenge as if her life depended on it. Since Banff, she has become a publisher, video artist, sound poet, intensified her performance poetry, and broke into radio arts, in addition to her "page work" as a poet. Janet Marie Rogers talked to students about how to let the words/language, sounds, and utterance live in different mediums/media and how to work with these medium/media to transform the words and create voice and new meanings. What was most valuable for the students was not the "poetry" per se but the fact that they came away understanding that there are different ways of knowing—different epistemologies, if you wish—and possibilities in their own art for distinct voice and original thought.

> We Learned the language
> embraced paper and legislation
> to get our way by any means
> we maintain
> we reclaim
> the seas
> complex combinations
> of desert marsh
> and blizzard-ravaged northlands
>
> This land they call
> British
> We know
> we own
>
> The original names
> never forgotten
>
> they call it what they want
> we know it by another[5]

What of the often raised question of Indigenous, Native, Aboriginal, or First Nations poetics? Or poetics of Native poets?

One of the things my creative writing students do when a poet visits is to note those elements of the poet's work, particularly those literary and creative elements of the poet's writing/reading/performance/presentation that are successful in establishing the poet's "brand," so to speak. Students note how elements are played up or weighted; how elements are privileged and brought into focused; which elements are repeated. They discern recurring patterns of meaning and message to understand and distinguish a particular poet's unique voice and style. They explore what messages are important to the poet and what the poet values. We have learned that the poet can choose to bring elements into focus to reflect specific cultural values and priorities. Or they can choose to hit the default button.

While my creative writing students, who are art and design thinkers already at home in a multi-media environment, note these elements with an eye to improving and enriching their own writing and areas of practice, in the interactive learning environment of the classroom, the visiting poet must face probing. Students also collectively present the visiting poet with their list of her "poetics." A diagram on a blackboard might represent what students were able to come up with in deconstructing and engaging with a poet's work.

They noted her use of textures, sounds, silences, layering of voices, alliterations, assonance, subtle dramatics tension, bursts of words, phrases, embracing spirituality, erotic language, sensuality, exploration of emotion as sound, sound as emotion, sound as ideas, intimate, public, gestures as language, multiple images, multiple senses. Her use of language was contemporary, sassy, taxed the senses. Layers of meaning, use of patterns and recurring structures, use of explosive language, image that overwhelms, subtle language, use of quiet, multiple tone, sparse use of rhyme, quiet delivery, musicality, alphabet of gesture for delivery, playing with beats, multiple voicing techniques, direct language, different persona, juxtaposition, irony, use of symbols, allusions, referencing, looping, interesting information bits, history, vernacular, contrasts, idiomatic, insightful details, incisive details, mining personal experience and knowledge, confronts taboos, cultural coding, rhythmic, short stanzas, staccato, percussive, reflective, assertive, playful, no-nonsense, truth teller, metaphors, orality as talking-back, epiphany, insight, evocative, use of multi-media, intra-media, experimental.

Whenever this exercise is done, with the same or different students, it became clear that poets such as Janet Rogers, who sees a direct connection with her poetry and an audience and or community, has an engaged poetics. What was even more revelatory to students is that in addition to regular "poetics" of traditional English literature poetry such as meter, rhythm, image, metaphor, evocative language, and rhyme, the Indigenous and dub poets whose work they read and/or listened to, or watched in media, bring a host of additional poetics to the literary table, successfully expanding the poetic palate for the twenty-first century. For students, this opens up a range of possibilities for "reading" and appreciating all poetry, and engaging with poetics of the written and spoken words.

Our students today are at home with an expanding palate, a multimedia existence they are comfortable with in all aspects of their lives. It's no wonder, then, that young people are flocking to poetry as a contemporary, dynamic, and vital twenty-first-century form to carry their voices as they "worry words" and join spoken-word poets, dub poets, and Indigenous poets in the revolutionary creative movement of "word worriers."

MESSAGE : dub, spirituality, poet
Or : Native, Words,

MEDIUM : poetry, politics, kin, human, nature, bantu, self, community, culture, pimâcihowin aki

Marshall McLuhan's famous quote, "The medium is the message," is not solely about the technology or the "medium" or even the effects of the medium or the message, but about impact. About how the effect of message and medium/media change who we are as a society and as a planet. From this context, the impact of the work of Indigenous poets, not just their writing, is the real message, to be adequately charted, assessed, and understood. One way to begin this is to imagine where we would be as a culture without Indigenous poets: the fullness of their presence and who they are; their aesthetics, their work, their wisdom, their words, their questionings, their innovations, their very breath in this landscape.

The concluding lines of my opening poem trumpets

Revolution from de drums
Revolution from de beat
Revolution with heart
Revolution with da feet.[6]

Notes

1 Lillian Allen, "Revolution from de Beat," *Psychic Unrest* (London: Insomniac Press, 1999), 93.
2 Northrop Frye, *Fearful Symmetry: A Study of William Blake* (Princeton: Princeton University Press, 1969), 114.
3 Lee Maracle, *I Am Woman* (Vancouver: Press Gang Publishers, 1988), 95.

4 Diane Di Prima, *Pieces of Song* (San Francisco: City Lights Book, 1990), 158.
5 Janet Rogers, *Unearthed* (Lantzville: Leaf Press, 2011), 44.
6 Allen, "Revolution from de Beat," 93.

Bibliography
Allen, Lillian. *Psychic Unrest*. London: Insomniac Press, 1999.
Frye, Northrop. *Fearful Symmetry: A Study of William Blake*. Princeton: Princeton
   University Press, 1969.
Maracle, Lee. *I Am Woman*. Vancouver: Press Gang Publishers, 1988.
Prima, Diane Di. *Pieces of Song*. San Francisco: City Lights Book, 1990.
Rogers, Janet. *Unearthed*. Lantzville: Leaf Press, 2011.

Poetics of Medicine

24

Indigenous Poetry and the Oral

Lee Maracle

Despite the fact that assimilation and integration have witnessed a movement away from old social structures and old cultural forms of governance and leadership toward hierarchy, patriarchy, and coercion in recent history, the artistic expression in both the written and oral arts retains its non-hierarchical and non-coercive character. This chapter examines traditional poetry from inside the culture of the examiner from this perspective.

When we died we sang, we sang xway xway, we sang the poetic voice of rebuilding, of coming together, of reaching out, of touching one another, of really barrelling down and moving against the tide. That's what we call it—moving against the tide. And you can do that only in poetry. You can do that only in the poetic voice.

When we sing, the bones of our ancestors hear our songs and they work their way to the surface of the land, singing themselves up. The oldest songs come from the oldest bones. Our youth every now and then hear these old songs and they sing it and we are reminded of the thousands of years of history that the bones of our ancestors hold for us. All we need to do is create children who can hear them sing.

Oral poems formed an integral part of voluntary self-governance, community spirit, and influenced conduct when people had fallen from the path. They are remembered both for their beauty and because the community came to cherish the reframing of law, philosophy, or social governance contained in the poetry. Through the process of consensus between themselves and between the living and the dead, these poems became songs that preceded ceremony. Even love songs were committed to memory because the nation accepted the posited attitude of the singer as accurately reflecting the attitude of the community toward love and the women or men to be loved. Random love between two individuals could not be conceived of outside the love of community, so in our love stories, the path to community, the foundational means of building community, are remembered.

The dilemma of any oral culture (naturally, there is no word for "oral culture" any more than there is a word in French meaning "french fries") is who we are and what we do. The only reason we refer to it as oral culture is because we now have a written cultural experience; under scholarly examination, only the consensus languaged art is remembered. The value of written expression is that the artistic expression of artists who are opposed to the status quo is also remembered because it has been published despite the general rejection by segments of society. Examination is limited to what is remembered. (There is no word for memory; there is a word for word power [ha'weles stwoxwiyam], direction marker [ha'weles shxwi woxwt], thoughts and feelings [ha'weles sqwa:lewel:], and to remember [ha'weles]). So we can remember the words that govern us (the first one); we can remember the words that directed or guided us (the second); we can remember our thoughts and feelings about something that happened (the third one); and we can remember, but we cannot make an object of memory (the fourth one) and treasured or agreed upon, rather than as a survey of art, which expresses dissenting points of view. The value of oral remembered word art (sti'lem) is that each song, each poem, builds upon the original song, the original poem, and serves to deepen and strengthen the values of the people until it becomes sxwoxwiyam—a forever story or transformer story.

Because Native societies do not have institutions that are alienated from the family and social life of the community, oral language art became a powerful way to maintain governance of social and personal conduct without the use of force. Oral language art was foundational to the education process in Native societies.

Children were given stories rather than instructions to guide their conduct. I came to realize that one of the things in our sensibility of language in the poetic voice, the business of strengthening the voice, is that we are endangering ourselves by not promoting the poetic in our children.

Further, because force was never used to maintain internal discipline, choice, co-operation, and individual obligations became sacred. This condition led to the development of poetry and stories whose language refused to direct the listener to answers, but rather stimulated thought in the listener on a given condition, perception, or direction. Personal response to language art was connected to concepts of choice and tempered by the social value of co-operation. The listener then becomes central to the story or poem and is engaged in the process of imagining, building, constructing, and responding to the speaker's art.

The presence of the speaker is and was as much a part of the poem as the words used. Voice, choice of words, sound, tone, diction, style, and rhythm characterize both the poem and the speaker. A huge array of physical metaphors developed out of the experience of the collective in their relationship to their environment. The concepts of governance, the metaphor, must be understood by the listener and interpreted instantly in order to understand the poem. Because our art is community-based, the use of physical metaphor is understood in the context of the wellness of the whole, and the personal interpretation becomes the way in which the individual can use the poem as a guide to his or her contribution to the wellness of the whole. Over time, interaction of the individual from within the culture deepens both the individual's understanding and the community's understanding.

Figuring out the meaning through personal thinking (without community) of the listener, while not foreign, was only the first part of the process of coming to understand poetry and story. Once the story or poem was heard, it was discussed by other members of the community, evaluated and committed or not committed to. Two speakers may present the same story from opposing points of view and both are considered valid, just as the listener's interpretation of the poem is valid even though it may be different from both speakers and all other listeners. At the same time, the individual was expected to find a collaborative point of understanding with the whole. This led to a tremendous diversity of understanding of a single poem or story.

And one of the words in my language that I really love is Lummi; it means "face yourself." I grew up with that maxim. People would ask, "Are you listening to yourself?" if you were saying something a bit dense, or saying something negative about yourself or about somebody else. Facing yourself is one of the greatest gifts that human beings have. A whale is always a whale. They always behave as whales do. They have so much language and so much history, and so much knowledge, but they can't just get out of the water and go be a lawyer or drive a truck. They're always going to be a whale. Not so with humans. We were gifted with the capacity to fall off track and fail to carry out our original instructions. We were given the gift of choice. And in exercising those choices, when we fail to do so in a responsive, healthy way, we must face this and when we face ourselves through the poetic voice, we can overcome anything. We can move past anything.

Inherent in the oral poetry is a non-instructional subtext. The teaching power of the poem is provided by its aesthetic beauty and the philosophical socio-spiritual logic of the poet and his or her ability to achieve oneness with the listeners. Spiritual concatenation between poet and listener is quintessential to the articulation of oral poetry, and the governing poem rests on the achievement of this concatenation on the level of spirit.

The spirituality of the poetry of First Nations peoples is extremely misunderstood. Mistranslations of poetry, spoken to white scholars prior to our mastery of the English language, arises when well-intended European intellectuals attempt to fuse their extrinsic sense of the spiritual and/or poetics with the poetry of Indigenous peoples. Or, when dealing with someone whose English was deficient, white scholars might not bother to look deeper into the story or poem, so concepts of sun gods, war gods, etc., intervene and pose huge obstacles to understanding the nature of poetry and individual poems more frequently than not. Because the sense of the spiritual is expressed simply, the complexity of Native concepts of spirituality are often misunderstood and/or reduced to simplistic interpretation by scholars.

"All things possess spirit, Creation is sacred, transformation is being alive, oneness with all Creation is human" become tenets simplistically interpreted and applied to any and all circumstance, rather than explored for their range and complexity and place in the body politic and culture of the people. If all Creation is sacred, then words as created entities for facilitating oneness are sacred. If oneness with all Creation is valued, then words are intended to achieve oneness. The speaker then seeks oneness on a spiritual level with his or her audience. Through his artistic presentation of the sacred and thought, emotions, law, philosophy, and spirit, the speaker orchestrates the community process of spiritual concatenation. Voice, diction, tone, style, rhythm, and physical metaphor are intended to present the spirit of the poet, elicit the spirit of the listener, and conjoin all spirits into a single powerful sense of oneness with Creation. Thus the choice of words, the sound of language, the essence of meaning, and the attitude of the poet must all be carefully and prayerfully considered and transformed before the poetry of the poet can or will achieve spiritual concatenation.

We are trying to be ever stronger, ever greater, ever more interesting, collect more stories, create more stories, and see more and more of Shadowland so that when we enter the spirit world, we enter that world with a storehouse of imagery, poetry, and stories to share. That's the only reason I'm here, and that was impressed upon me when I was three or four years old. So that creates a different sort of visioning of what the spirit is all about, and what words are for. Words are to express that spirit of ever growing, ever strengthening, and ever walking toward the light, which is the spirit world, because we're in Shadowland. And so the language of expression among ourselves is tremendously metaphorical, tremendously poetic, even in our everyday speaking lives.

ok, Lm

The power of the speaker, the influence of the speaker, is dependent upon his or her personal capacity for eliciting oneness on the spirit level with the listener, the commitment of the speaker to the sense of community, and the speaker's exceptional sense of the desire for the good life that lies within each member. The remembered poems then remain treasured moments of spiritual concatenation. Spiritual concatenation between poet and audience has no equivalent among Europeans.

The objective of European poetry is not spiritual concatenation between the self and listener but rather self-expression. Spirit and spiritual concatenation cannot be understood mechanically or in terms of formulae, standard practices, basic characteristics; it cannot even be understood from the above perspective as it is a single view of a single wedge in a circle of understandings.

In order to understand original poetry, First Nations speakers must gather (and in fact they did so historically), engage the poem, engage the oratory around the poem, the circumstances that birthed the poem, and engage each other in discovering meaning (new, contemporary, and old) from the poem. They must do so in a manner that facilitates spiritual concatenation with one another. In this way the process of discovery, consensus of the speakers (male and female), and the spiritual concatenation births understanding between speaker and listeners and the results are taken to the larger audience. Poetics is the absence of separation between poetry, story, and song; our songs are poems and they are stories; our stories are poems and they are songs and include all the oratorical art of Native peoples. (The old poems are poems and stories.)

The poet elicits the imagination of the community, the heart of the nation, and the spirit of the present, past, and future. Poems must move people from where they are to where they need to go to ensure community concatenation. They must activate the community-based thought process of the listener without prescribing a response. Modern Native poetry needs to be understood in relation to the sense of community, spiritual concatenation, the positioning of the community in relation to the good life journey that being human is all about, and the direction the community must travel to return to the path to the good life. It is why a number of writers insist that they write for their communities.

We believe that words are sacred and have power and impact. Much of the words needed in the 1960s and through the 1990s were those words that would turn us from the trail of destruction that we were on and lead us back to our original path. Once on the path to the good life, our community needs the old stories, the old poems, and the old songs—our poetics— which have charted this journey to the good life for thousands of years. The revival of these songs, poems, and stories are critical to understanding that we are and always will be.

These poems have been told many times and change with each generation as word artists reform them to serve the moment. Even as we return to the good lifeways, we will continue to use study and discuss the word art that has always guided us. Our poems and stories will show us how to create oneness between ourselves and the world.

Poems as Healing Bundles

Gregory Scofield

kipocihkân

niya. I am the boy	*me*
whose tongue at birth,	*an obstruction*
hungered its blood root	
kept sacred by frogs,	

the keepers of stories,	
âcimowina.	*stories*

niya, I am the one whose mouth,	
kipocihkâna	*mute, someone unable to speak*
at night, alone,	
is a lodge of words, a frog-song	
croaking with the sound	
I sing from time to time.	

êkwa nitwew,	*and I say*
it is a good tongue	
housed in a good lodge	
that is mostly clean of pity,	
of anger.	

hâw, êkwa nistam	*but first*
a count of the names	
whose tongues	
I now call to prayer;	

â-haw kisê-manitow	*Oh, Great Spirit*
mâmaw-ôhtawîmaw	*Our Father*

kinanâskomitin	*I give thanks*

nicâpan Mary, my great-great grandmother
whose tongue was made homeless,
shame-shame
the day Riel slipped through the gallows.

Pîmâtisiwin pêtamawinân. Amen   *Bring us life*

â-haw kisê-manitow   *Oh, Great Spirit*
mama-ôhtawîmaw   *Our Father*

kinanâskomitin   *I give thanks*

nicâpanak Johnny êkwa Ida,
my great-grandparents
whose tongues, shame-shame
diluted the gene pool. Whose tongues,
chased up north
set others to wagging.

pîmatisiwin pêtamawinân. Amen.   *Bring us life*

â-haw kisê-manitow   *Oh, Great Spirit*
mama-ôhtawîmaw   *Our Father*

kinanâskomitin   *I give thanks*

nimosôm George, my grandfather
whose tongue, at fifty-nine
burst, shame-shame,
an illiterate blood clot. Whose tongue,
down south, he swallowed
for my grandmother.

pîmâtisiwin petamawinân. Amen.   *Bring us life*

God, Our Heavenly Father

I give thanks

My grandmother Avis, at ninety –three,
whose tongue, a chorus of etiquette
kept the secret
she hid in the barn
made by her brother. Shame-shame.

Bring us life. Amen.

â-haw kisê-manitow   *Oh, Great Spirit*
mama-ôhtawîmaw   *Our Father*

kinanâskomitin   *I give thanks*

nimâma Dorothy, my mother
whose tongue
swept the halls of psych wards,
her whore days made dead
by pills and wine. Whose tongue,
at forty-eight
she gave back to God. Fuck you!

pîmâtisiwin pêtamawinân. Amen.   *Bring us life*

Ba-ruch A-tah Ado-nai   *Blessed are you, Lord our God,*
E-lo-he-nu Me-lech Ha-olam   *King of the universe*
Toda, Toda.   *I give thanks*

mein papa Ron, my father
whose tongue was a schmatteh   *a rug*
to moth-eaten
to keep all his children.

Alev-ha-sholem – from hunger.   *May he rest in peace.*
Alev ha-sholem – from harm.
Alev ha-sholem – from pity.
Alev ha-sholem – from shame.
Alev ha-sholem – from our own poisoned tongues.
L'Chaim! Amen.   *To life.*

â-haw kisê-manitow   *Oh, Great Spirit*
mâmaw-ôhtawîmaw   *Our Father*
Ba-ruch A-tah Ado-nai   *Blessed are you, Lord our God*
E-lo-he-nu Me-lech Ha-olam   *King of the universe*

Kinanâskomitin   *I give thanks*
Toda, Toda.   *I give thanks*

Tapiyaw nîtsânak,   *my half siblings*
Mein shvester, mein bruder   *my sister, my brother*
the one before me
whose tongues and names
I pray be sacred in the world,
without shame. Shame.

pimâtisiwin petamawinân.   *Bring us life.*
L'Chaim! Amen.   *To life*

God, Our Father

I give thanks

Ann, my stepmother whose tongue,
half charitable, half grudging

held all these years my father's pardon,
my own half tongue
growing back in fragments.
To hell with shame.

Bring us life. Amen.

God, Our Father

I give thanks

Gary, the kimotisk who threw us away,   *thief*
whose tongue, shame-shame
made her heart a morgue, and me,
the one – hope in life – to bury it.
Bring us life. Amen.

God, Our Father

I give thanks

Gerry, the Terrible One whose tongue,
whose fists
left her a pile of broken bones,
shame-shame, and me,
the one—micihicy—to fix her.   *hand*

Bring us life. Amen.

God, Our Father

I give thanks

Sean, the môniyâw-nâpesis whose tongue   *white-boy*
chased me home from school,
his footsteps, shame-shame
reeking of come and awkward hope.

Bring us life. Amen.

God, Our Father

I give thanks

Robert, the Wîhtikow whose tongue   *Legendary eater of humans*
shame-shame
made marks in my case file,
whose tongue in the dark
made me his boy,
his wild kipocihkân boy.

Bring us life. Amen.
pîmâtisiwin pêtamawinân. Amen.   *Bring us life*

â-haw kisê-manitow   *Oh, Great Spirit*
mama-ôhtawîmaw   *Our Father*

kinanâskomitin   *I give thanks*

nimâmasis Georgie, my little mother
whose tongue, nehiyawaywin   *the Cree language*
no shame, no shame
I clung to life on.
Nehiyawaywin, I clung onto life,

her tongue
my kipocihkân hope, my tongue
tasting frog-songs
she brewed in a teapot,
maskihkîwâpoy   *liquid medicine, tea*
she made medicine, her stories
no shame, no shame.

pîmâtisiwin pêtamawinân. Amen.   *Bring us life*

â-haw kisê-manitow   *Oh, Great Spirit*
mama-ôhtawîmaw   *Our Father*

kinanâskomitin   *I give thanks*

niwicewâkan, the one I go around with
whose tongue, âya, kotak mina niwî-âtotî   *the one I love*
kâ-kay sakihyak ana ê-wî-acîmak,   *I am going to tell a story about*
him
is the rope
I climb back to myself, my lips
the lodge door
he calls me into ceremony, the one
I go around with whose tongue, in the dark,
is a rattle, a frog-song
chasing out kipocihkân

pîmâtisiwin pêtamawinân. Amen.   *Bring us life*

â-haw kisê-manitow   *Oh, Great Spirit*
mama-ôhtawîmaw   *Our Father*

kinanâskomitin   *I give thanks*

the ones I've left behind, the ones
whose tongues I've made kipocihkân.

pîmatisiwin petamawinân. Amen.   *Bring us life*

â-haw kisê-manitow   *Oh, Great Spirit*
mama-ôhtawîmaw   *Our Father*

kinanâskomitin   *I give thanks*

the ones who are my relatives
whose tongues
I've neglected to mention.

pîmâtisiwin pêtamawinân. Amen.   *Bring us life*

piyisk êkwa, I pray   *and last*
the return of frogs,

the keepers of stories,	
âcimowina.	*Stories*
â-haw, kisê-manitow	*Oh, Great Spirit*
mâmaw-ôhtawîmaw	*Our Father*
kinanâskomitin	*I give thanks*
the ghost	
who is my tongue, niyakâtôtamân.	*I am responsible, a plea of guilty*
kinanâskomitin	*I give thanks*
the bitch	
who is my tongue, niyakâtôtamân.	*I am responsible, a plea of guilty*
kinanâskomitin	*I give thanks*
the beggar	
who is my tongue, niyakâtôtamân.	*I am responsible, a plea of guilty*
kinanâskomitin	*I give thanks*
the glutton	
who is my tongue, niyakâtôtamân.	*I am responsible, a plea of guilty*
kinanâskomitin	*I give thanks*
the mute	
who is my tongue, niyakâtôtamân.	*I am responsible, a plea of guilty*
kinanâskomitin	*I give thanks*
the singer	
who is my tongue, niyakâtôtamân.	*I am responsible, a plea of guilty*
pîmâtisiwin nipêtamawîna. hâw!	*Bring me life. Amen*

(2009)

I normally don't introduce that poem and talk about it. It's a poem that I normally don't read a lot in public. Maybe because it's a long poem, maybe because when I originally worked on it, it was for this particular book. In order to talk about my presentation today, I need to talk first about the piece I just read to you.

I don't necessarily consider this a poem. I really don't know what I consider it. It came from a place of birthing; Joanne Arnott talked about birth and how it was from a place of death that had reached a new light. That particular piece is the introductory poem for my book called *Kipocihkân*. The word "kipocihkân," in Cree, is a slang word. It means "to be muted" or "to be silenced." And I suppose that this is the reason why I was drawn to poetry, into the world of storytelling. My sense of kipocihkân—that sense of being muted, and the need and desire to be heard, I guess you could say to make sound—was my inspiration for this particular poem. Perhaps my greatest difficulty in life has been the silence and being silenced. I've never been afraid of the silence because there are a lot of things within that silence, but I've struggled very much with being silenced, I think, as a lot of people have, probably a fair number of my colleagues. That's probably the reason why we write.

This presentation is entitled "Poems as Healing Bundles." I want to talk to you about my approach to writing. My seventeen-year career of writing was something that I had been drawn to as a means of survival. I talked about silence, I talked about being silenced and trying to find sound. Neal McLeod mentioned in his paper the names that are filled with sound. Joanne also mentioned this. She said the lines of a poem are sung into being. I believe that sound is life and singing is living.

With this in mind, I think about how we are all given bundles, and that there are some bundles that I believe are meant to be untied and opened. There are others that are meant to remain closed. We all carry, within ourselves, sacred bundles. I'm fond of the idea of being a collector, a reporter, a witness, a tattletale—anything other than being an observer of my own life. I realized that the silence that I have been talking about, and the silence that punctuates the piece that I just read, caused me to be the observer of what was happening to me. And I realize that within that, I was trapped within the silence. I was allowing myself to be silenced.

The polar opposite of that, of course, is being drawn to sound. I often tell emerging writers and young poets that "poetry is in your body. You have to use it like a rattle. You need to shake it. You need to move the silence around. You have to do something with it." When you think about the way medicine people work, they work with the body. My writing has been really an exploration of the medicine of myself, ourselves. It's been an exploration of the medicine of our communal and individual selves and our struggles. The medicine that we carry from our communities of origin—and, for some of us, the medicine of those communities that we're searching to find, searching to locate, relocate, associate, or disassociate with—is something that we are all blessed with. Having said this, we therefore become responsible for bringing it forward to share with one another. A lot of what we have been talking about the last couple of days is traditional storytelling. We have talked about the sacred stories, we have talked about personal stories, family stories. I talk about being a tattletale—for example, the piece that I read is filled with a great deal of vulnerability. In order to create a new space for ourselves and our rhythms, and for the rattle, we need to be tattletales. We need to speak and tell our stories.

People have often asked me how it is that I can talk about such personal things. Of course it is difficult. We are all self-conscious. But when you consider that we all carry our vulnerabilities, it makes it much easier to stand in front of people and speak our truth. When you think about it, we are able to open those bundles of ourselves, we are able to unwrap them in front of each other in ceremony. We don't need to be in a sacred lodge, and we don't need to have our traditional medicines laid out because this is already happening—for example, like the work that we are doing at this poetics symposium. Each day ceremonies have happened in this very room, ceremonies in which we have opened bundles in front of each other.

From this place, we have been able to look and see many things. We are therefore able to walk away and take with us the memory of these ceremonies. In the privacy of our own homes we are then able to start untying our own bundles. From there we are able to take out our little stones, that little claw, the roots, the feathers, the bones, all of the things that are part of our bundles. In doing so, we are able to listen to something other than our own voices. We create a new sound—a sound with names—the names of our ancestors, the names of ones who violated us, the names of ones who gave us strength and gave us hope, the ones that give us anger and move us to a place of eventual healing.

I thank you so much for giving me the time to speak. I'm so honoured, as I always am, to be in the company of my fellow wonderful poets, writers, and storytellers. Thank you so much. kinanâskomitinâwâw.

26

Small Birds / Songs Out of Silence

Joanne Arnott

Nestlings have so much faith, awaken into this world with the full expectation of being loved, cherished, cared for, and protected. Guided, succoured: How is it that we small birds go about our living? Learning the cultural patterns ("This is what is," "This is what we do') from our elders, we move through into a fledgling state, and then—fly from the nest when we are able. We then rebuild the world for the young and for all whose lives touch upon ours.

When I gave birth for the first time, at the age of twenty-five, I was pretty much blown out of the water by the experience. All of my systems were amazed and impressed! It was like dumping out fourteen buckets of anything, and then stirring them up altogether. Dreams, nightmares, weeping, thinking fast—I was trying to sort out my understanding of the world, and finding out how to be me in the new context.

I followed my baby's father to a tiny upstairs Taoist temple, or tan, on Pender Street in Vancouver. There were so many women who knew just exactly what to do, to ease and succour my baby! One Elder offered me healing help, but my level of paralysis meant that I never did get out the door to visit her to accept the help that she was moved to offer. (This is a pattern I have not fully overcome. I used to give myself a very hard time for it, and now, I just accept that it is hard for me to trust sometimes.)

I was, by definition and a lifetime of training, an outsider, but this was nonetheless a safe harbour and a teaching space for me, a cultural immersion among working-class Chinese Canadians with a spiritual focus. It was highly effective in undoing some of the hurts and contradictions of Catholicism/my particular life. I participated in a group translation project, learning much, and connecting with other people in a gentle way. The most important lesson that I carried away with me were the words of an Immortal, speaking through the comfortable working class priest writing in a box of sand in classical Chinese: "Given birth, but not nour-ishment, we die" (Lui Jo).[1] That was and is the basic life orientation that I received, the premise out of which I have since built and adapted my basic job description in relation to my children, self, Elders, audience as a writer, and the people around me. (To be clear, I am not an initiate, and no longer attend the tan or any church. I do participate in ceremony when invited, but infrequently.)

My family of mixed-bloods was very peripheral. While growing up, I moved to a different province every five years, so I didn't really settle in and learn much of anything coherent from any specific community or side of the family. Vancouver held mostly my mother's extended family, who were French Catholic; rural Manitoba was my dad's family's realm; south-ern Ontario was just Mom and a handful of daughters. What I had, by age twenty-five, was an overwhelming overload of impressions, many very dangerous, many gentle and kind, and a lifetime job of trying to decode and organize it all.

To counter the chaos that I had grown up with, to heal the injuries and the reactions to injuries that formed and informed my family and my self, this is the path that I followed, beginning with this gentle cultural immer-sion experience. Probably the most important book that I read in those years, besides the Taoist classics (each one succinct and more coherent than the Roman Catholic Bible), was a gentle how-to book by Lin Yutang, popu-larizing Taoist tenets for modern readers, *The Importance of Living* (1937). I immersed myself in martial arts classes, books about Chinese scientific and medical thought, poetry and aesthetics, alongside Western dance classes and bodywork, co-operative involvements in the community, and unlearning racism workshops (thought and peer counselling strategies for building alliances and releasing the pain and confusion of the past).

I remained for decades a person more comfortable in my mind than in my body, as my body was the route by which harm came to me. Hyper-vigilant responses of withdrawal from engagement have been hard to over-come. By creating my own family, and slowly over time remaining engaged as they grow and change, my ability to extrapolate "safety" from the small inside group (my children and their dads and I) to the larger world and community, including the community of writers, has also grown and changed. Through the leadership of small children and through friend-ships in community, I came to accept that we will not be immediately (or even in the afterworld) punished for being human beings.

Whether the newly born, newly arrived can be said to have an "expecta-tion" or not is neither here nor there. The upsurge of energy of birth and springtime are everywhere evident, and do not need a string of authorities, or trees built of peer-reviewed scientific studies, to feel or notice or respond to. In classical Chinese aesthetics, creative expression is considered a natural response to living, and nowhere have I found a better description of why we do what we do: it's just natural. We're alive, aren't we?

Through my years as a writer, meeting and getting to know several very distinguished writers—whom I could at first hardly look at for the glow of divine light they threw off, standing as I was in the deep shadow of my overwhelming sense of insignificance—and later, seeing political leaders who were surprised and amazed to discover what a hotbed of cultural activity Indigenous writers are in Canada today, it has come clear to me that there are much wider applications for what I have learned and experienced. We are all a wealth and a resource to one another, each one carrying precisely what another most deeply needs: what is obvious to you may be the answer that resolves three generations of pain in my family, while what is obvious to me may arrive as a shock to your system, and soften your shoulders, perhaps, lighten your heart.

In this way, I have a sense that we are all small birds still. No matter how big and powerful we grow, we have questions, vulnerabilities, and tasks that we need help completing. This is the realm of poetry, for me, perhaps all of literature: the whole-bodied response to our worlds, making gifts of whatever makes sense to us, and the process of making sense through making art. Honouring ourselves by speaking our truths, and sharing our stories with others; receiving stories with dignity, thereby honouring others.

My body does not belong to me, my body is me. I'm not knocking self-possession, or self-regency, these are valid and important in some situations. I am acknowledging the continuity between myself and my circumstances. The people and vitalities around me all influence my being on levels that can sometimes be caught in words, in thoughts, and more often are simply experienced as organic reality, a continuity. I wake up in the morning and the birds are in song, and I wonder what it is they are telling one another this morning.

To write is to give voice to that reality, by focusing in on some part of "what is" and singing it into being. Words and images are the beads and threads, the meat and potatoes, and the guiding principle is sense and song. By shining my attention and focusing my receptivity, and by giving a little push, I can craft a new something that is expressive of the moments of truth that are stirring inside me. Sometimes these truths are clamoring for attention; sometimes these truths move very softly, shyly beckoning, almost preferring to be overlooked.

I am a poet. I have been a poet for so long that I can hardly describe the work: it is like going to sleep or getting up, or like giggling, or like responding to a conversation midstream: you just do it! The only real rules are these: stop stopping yourself. Value the work enough to linger over it and return, nudging the words on the page and the voice in the air until you have achieved satisfaction, and then set it free to the world. Be willing to follow the deeper direction, and if fear gets in the way, make a poem of it, too. Whatever rises to the top, whatever presses or creates a disturbance within, whatever contradiction needs to be pulled into some form of reconciliation, just carry on creating as life passes through.

Sharing the work is as important as honouring the first impulse: *to make* is followed by *to give* or *to share*. If you recognize the need of a voice to be heard, a poem to be shared, a gift to be received from one to another, then you will not pile up bones and branches at the door of your cave. You will be really out there, flying and singing, flocking and teaching, nesting and mating.

For myself, poetry comes out of struggle, and this can be pleasurable struggle—trying to capture a moment or a morning, trying to vision a future or settle the past from the surge of feelings let loose by falling in love—or it can be difficult, reluctant, a struggle, like trying to find my way past my own bigotry to see something from a more true or a broader perspective.

After doing a whole lot of abuse-focused work, I started to think of writing poetry as not just archaeology, but dumpster-diving. I shifted my focus to writing about my kids, or to happy grown-up things—I got the idea from Kateri Akiwenzie-Damm, *Celebrate everything*. After spilling out far too much love poetry, feeling about as solid as a cloud in the sky, I started to think of writing poetry as a way of escape from what is, in the here and now. And so, change again, I started to focus more on what is tangible and immediate, rather than what is possible—quite a different thing.

For me, the motivation to start a poem is either excess energy, or because I'm uncomfortable. I return to perfect the poem so that it makes sense to someone who is not me—I do that because I like to communicate, it is pleasurable for me. Every moment may not feel great, but the immersion in the work, and the satisfaction of sharing something coherent to others, is well worth it.

I did learn over time that what I put out there would come back to me. If I share stories of tragedy, tragic stories will come forth from the people around me. If I share particular kinds of troubles, I will hear more from those who share those elements of life experience. This is excellent to know. What it means is for any writer, what you need to hear about, you should just start talking about in poetry, essays, or performance. And if you are becoming overwhelmed with a particular kind of story, you should set the tone, provide leadership, and focus on a different theme. Redirect the conversation. The role of poet is, in this way, a leadership position.

I think about an important long poem from my early days as a mum, which I fussed with for over a year. Working on the poem helped me in working out who I will be, and the big question: how to make family on the perch of a great deal of unhappiness. The poem is called "Enchantment & Freedom." It could be called other things, given the ideas that I was grappling with—"Tradition & Innovation," say, except that the traditions I was looking at were the ways we abandon and protect ourselves from one another, and I was looking for a way to be different for my son and his father. "Enchantment" in the sense of these are the things we tell ourselves and show one another, over and over, and so they become engraved, negative teachings. My interest was a question, and working on the long poem was the process of reaching for answers, how to work free of those multi-generational bad habits, and find better things to be and to teach and to say.

The other key concept was "freedom." I was coming to motherhood after decades of feminist impact in the mainstream, which had profound effects on my mother, my family, and me, my family became "the truth" for a time, and they were the only people that I wanted to hear from. I received many blessings and good guidance, through feminist magazines, people, and books, despite my ongoing resentment for the catastrophic impact it had on my childhood family.

At the same time, I had both a profound love for and need for my family, and home, and a complete lack of confidence in (read terror of) the same. The feminist perspectives were useful, but not wholly useful, given how steeped in the either/or of Judeo-Christian philosophy the thinkers were. Susan Griffin's *Woman & Nature: The Roaring Inside Her* was an excellent way to see how the meta-philosophy of oppression operates in a Christian colonial context, but, it didn't tell me how to raise my son. While many writers of the time were radicalized by Audre Lourde's essay, "The Master's Tools Will Never Dismantle The Master's House," the essay of Lourde's that I found most empowering and useful—and went back to again and again—was "Uses of the Erotic: The Erotic as Power." Aligned as it is with considering people in groups, and energy dynamics, harmony and conflict, and acknowledging the base necessity as a feminist mother of sons to "be honest," this was the most useful of Audre Lourde's texts for me.

The majority voice of feminism in those days was all innovation and none affirmation of the basic, fundamental ways that humans organize ourselves: the families we rise out of and the mates we lay down with, the Elders we care for and the children we tend to. It was all about rights and little about responsibilities. For me, I just had to keep trying to reconcile the two—tradition and innovation, enchantment and freedom—and writing has been what I made while working it out. It's good not to be impatient because I am still trying to work this bit out, day by day and moment by moment. Terror suggests that being free from the world is the best thing, but that is not—in those long painful moments of longing— what a person really wants to believe in. Something positive to reach for, strive for, and hold on to, is the very best food there is.

Performing this long poem, with the music of church and the placement of church beside temple, love beside despair, actual family words beside the words of an Immortal Being and my own common sense, has had a synthesizing effect for me, as an individual. The fact that people have chosen to publish it tells me that in this one place, at least, I am speaking for more than just me. I am putting words to a common problem or complexity that many other people are sitting with, or struggling with, in their own lives and minds.

When I travelled to Australia in 1994, I was in for a big surprise. This poem that spoke well to the audiences I was used to—feminist or woman-positive urban people who were poor or poor-aware—arrived like a big bomb for some of those people who I most expected to "get it"—other Indigenous and miscegenated women in Australian audiences. Some got mad at me, some just sat in the front row, so I could watch them transform from happy and open, to sucker-punched.

I am very lucky, although of course it didn't feel like good fortune for a while, that some cared enough to come up to me after and let me know where the pain was coming from. My unrestrained volley of rage against my Elders was only possible because I was completely oblivious to my own and my family's historical context. That was a turning point, for me, in beginning to learn a lot more about these things—"community, "family," "history." When I came back to the West Coast after these experiences, I began looking for a different sort of teaching.

Becoming aware of the impacts of multi-generational living and community context was the next giant step, the next leg of my journey. Bonnie Fine Day did a very profound presentation that helped me to come to grips with all this, bringing home words and concepts to apply the inside story and life as a parent, teacher, person in the world. Many contributors to the Indigenous Poetics gathering have been my teachers, too.

It is my pleasure today, to show a little kindness, to show some respect, to look on the bright side, to try for balance along with the truth, and to have a heart. Suppressing the truth isn't going to teach us much. It's only a workable life strategy for times of danger, and then when we have sufficient safety, the suppressed truth wants its day. Whether it works its way up from the gut or is showcased on another person's face, the truth is truth and we have to accept it, accommodate it, and learn from it as gracefully as possible.

We have often been told that what makes us unique as human beings is that we have language, and conceptual thinking, and that we use tools. Most of our traditions do not make these distinctions, and common sense and my body tells me that none of this is so. I am no more and not less than the crow, and I can hear the languages of the world, even when I am not privy to the details of the words' meanings. This striving individualism, which imbues the English language and colours the thoughts we have been taught at church and school, and creates false hierarchies and inhuman versions of everything, the promulgation of fragmentation and "thingness"—dead entities—that we come to believe is the base reality of our worlds, is a creeping distortion. However pervasive the thought form, it simply isn't so.

Communal reality and the continuity of our being is the sensual reality, and it is the space and energy between so-called individuals that are luminous. Like the scientists discover, who look at atoms and sub-atoms and sub-sub-atoms, there is ultimately no thingness in our worlds, and the closer we look at any given individual, the more multi-porous and participatory and co-influential a being we find, smaller flocks among the larger flocks of being.

I believe that we need to be careful with our language/s, and the thoughts suggested by the construction of our language/s, and that we need to honour the truth of our experiences. Allow the truth of our experiences to be the base, and be willing to bend and shape language/s to reflect our deeper truths.

Allow the possibility that rocks, stars, winds, waters, plants, and bears all have language, all have teachings, congruity, dignity, and an equal or possibly a much greater place, and keep listening. Keep in touch. Relax completely into who you are and what is, and give voice.

We have a base language, the language of living. Beyond that we have common languages and uncommon languages, and sometimes we leap or fumble between the many languages. We exist between two cultural patterns, a textual and print-driven over-culture, and the whole wealth of orality, buoying up and articulating the real world. Many people over many generations have worked along the interface between languages, and between oral cultures and textually driven realms in hopes of making peace and truth. We are building upon that interface each and every day.

When I look back to discover who were the poets who inspired me, I have to say that they were the singers, both folk tradition songful southern Manitoba, settler and Métis without distinction, and the Roman Catholic

Church (oral and hymnal). During my formative early teen years, I spent a lot of hours in the grass and the bush playing with an old poetry book that my mother had left behind. I wrote the poems out by hand, and the ones I loved were the ones that spoke of something that I could actually understand—the language of Robert Frost's poem, turning a mouse's nest over with his plow, described things I was familiar with—the mouse, the fields, the dirt, the plow, fear, tragedy, loss of home, loss of mother—in heavily inflected English I could hardly understand, but loved the music of. Most importantly, it was a love poem, a poem of compassion.

Around the same time, my dad taught me three notes on the guitar, unleashing a cascade of three-note love songs, and through occasional insults, and even fewer commendations, he bumped me toward discovering (in a physical, self-expressive way) my voice. Most of the songs I knew I learned from my dad or mum or elder sisters, and besides the tattered tome of poetry, I inherited a wealth of handwritten songs, with three (or more) chords above the words. I taught myself some of the songs, but always in a way that felt right to me, never in a way that has rendered me a contender on the karaoke scene. I also had a close friend, also from a guitar-playing family, who was a big influence, if not precisely a tutor. She was a fantastic singer-guitarist, and a very fun friend, and she also made it possible for me to get my first work published (she was failing a class and asked for an assist, so I gave her some things I'd been playing with: whether or not her teacher actually published them, the fact that she asked permission of my friend, and my friend asked it of me, made me feel *great*).

I don't remember if I read it in junior high (Manitoba) or high school (Ontario), but one Canadian book that profoundly affected me as a writer was Takeo Ujo Nakano's *Within the Barbed Wire Fence*. His straightforward storytelling of the dislocation of a Japanese Canadian family during the war, and the deeply moving poetry interspersed with that telling, to share and to show another side of the same experiences, was the teaching that I needed on how to put all the layers of lived life together, and make it beautiful by sharing it with the world.

The drive toward literacy can be a drive away from a greater wealth, an embodied voice that holds a larger reality embedded and vocalized in a far richer way than the text on the page. So we must be conscious, to give our words voice and body, to hold onto our orality and embodied continuities and connections, our sensitivities to silence and to meaning beyond words, even as we develop the textual savvy and finesse that we need to make our way, collectively and in smaller groups, in this text-sexy world. Through the stages of our lives, we need to honour the wholeness of ourselves, of humanity, by remembering or allowing ourselves to teach and to be taught directly, human to human, and not leave it all to the transmissions of books and the web. There is much more to us than the words only, and participating directly, be that one to one, small group, large group, vast gatherings—all of these are necessary ways of connecting and nourishing. For balance, as much as is possible, we need them all.

Hearing Beth Brant read "Turtle Gal," or Maria Campbell reading "Joseph's Justice," are ways of connecting with ourselves and our histories more broadly than the solitary enjoyment of receiving each of these works from the printed page. Either way we are called to witness, and the fullness of being persons together—seeing, hearing, scenting, becoming utterly absorbed as a group—is an outstanding experience, and an antidote to solitude.

When I attended the Strong Words gathering in BC, bringing together singers and poets from across BC, I had a glimpse of the range of our voices from completely traditional to utterly texty, and it was a revelation: most powerful in effect were the traditional singers, whatever languages they were singing in. From talking heads, trained away from our bodies, to embodied humans sharing in full voice and full dimensionality, is not only the range of persons that I observed and experienced, a spectrum of poetics that I somewhere along the line fit into, but a human process that every one of us can undergo. We re-inhabit ourselves after a grave shock, or find our ways back to fullness after being for generations trained away, schooled to be much, much smaller and less powerful. The larger voice of indigenous culture sings directly, in many ancient and continuous forms, and we never grow so sophisticated, so assimilated, so empowered that we can do without that nourishing.

When I was a body in a body, inside my mother's womb, I heard the voices of my family, laughing and bickering, and I heard the sound of the guitar. I felt what it meant to my mother to be a mother, to be a wife, to be a participant in the Roman Catholic Church, the incantations, the singing. I felt her bodily responses to everything before I was born, and this continued after I was born, and it continues to this day.

As I grew I came to sense more and more of this world, and more and more people, and to focus my attention on ever-greater patches of reality. Like many of us gathered here today, there were great lacks, neglected realms where I had only absence, and there were areas of overwhelming intensity that sent me to what may have seemed to be an unworldly place.

These absences and these overwhelms are simply a part of the all of our all, and they are not everything. We give voice to these and to the more poignantly beautiful, and we seek balance within the ocean of vitality. Shifting this way and that—a time for listening, a time for contemplation and respite, a time for sharing our stories, and a time to work hard and capture nothing, simply dive in and participate.

My body does belong to me. Despite the continuities, the thoughts and emotions flowing from person to person and from realm to realm, the actions that impinge upon and those that express my self, there is a certain realm which is smaller than my realm of influence, and that is me. That is the level where my willingness to live in truth is most essential. If I feel I am locked in a small place, and I am not really locked in a small space, I may use more strength and ferocity than the current situation really requires; it is when I am feeling most powerless, but am not really powerless, that I do the most harm.

Whatever comes at me from the world, only I can choose how I receive these gifts, how I think about what I have received, and how I choose to conduct myself. We are sometimes given gifts that are so overwhelming that it takes a lifetime, or even many lifetimes, to learn how to be in relation to these experiences. The stories that we draw from them change from year to year, from age to age.

I have come to think of body tension as stories. The way to return to a relaxed and centred place at peace with myself is to share stories. Not just any story, but the right story, the story that is creating tension, the story that is pushing for consciousness and air. That may be a community story, it may be a simple human story, and that really doesn't matter: it is the necessary story, and I honour it by giving it birth. I honour our world by taking the time to share it, to stand and deliver.

Note
From an unpublished translation project; words of Lui Jo as channelled by a Taoist priest using Fu Ji 扶乩 (sandwriting) at Po Yuen Taoist Tan, Vancouver, 1986

Bibliography
Po Yuen Taoist Tan. Unpublished Fu Ji 扶乩 (sandwriting divination) translation project, Vancouver, 1986.

27

Stretching through Our Watery Sleep: Feminine Narrative Retrieval of cihcipistikwân in Louise Halfe's *The Crooked Good*

Lesley Belleau

The narrative of Louise Halfe's *The Crooked Good* is a long poem that holds a multi-layered voice, profuse with story and choices, and offers a feminine perspective within the story of cihcipistikwân[1] (Rolling Head). The reader steps into the language of the Rolling Head, whose feminine voice reveals a notably different interpretation from the version of the same story seen in *The Journal of American Folklore*, as written by Edward Ahenakew, a Cree theologian, writer, cleric, and vice-president of the League of Indians, and has quite different considerations. Louise Halfe actively retrieves the feminine voice from the poetic pathways of the narrative past, and allows the voices to come back to life within the contemporary frame of her text through ancient storylines.

Feminine narrative retrieval not only reclaims the voices and experiences of our grandmothers and ancestral feminine narrative lines, as seen through the historical narratives of all Indigenous women collectively, but interweaves the ancient stories into the contemporary narrative memory landscape. Kim Anderson asserts that "the recovery of our peoples is linked to digging up the medicines of the past," and through this, it is possible to understand that the retrieval process is also a process of restoration, as well as one which acts to re-align a colonial imbalance that has placed our women aside, silenced and distorted, a long way from home."[2]

There is a sacred journey that must be travelled in order to begin to understand how and why feminine Indigenous narratives must be retrieved

from the ancestral past. It is important to consider the reasons why Louise
Halfe acted to retrieve the female voice from the narrative of the Rolling
Head, which contrasts with Edward Ahenakew's masculine version of Rolling Head. Feminine narrative retrieval can be looked at simply as bringing
the submerged collectivity of voices and experience as envisioned by the
writer through their personal pathways, and through their own feminine
voices, as well as the voices entwined within them through collective memory within the ancestral pathways. This action allows the author's contemporary way of seeing the story emerge. Leanne Simpson in *Dancing on My
Turtle's Back* expresses that "those old stories hold the beginnings of the
new stories we are about to create.... As it is so often in my culture, the old
story this time begins with the women."[3] These stories are alive, their pulsa-
tions beating us forward and inward like a drumming heart, and by placing
the feminine voices within the scope of Indigenous literature, a narrative
empathy is created, along with a strengthening of female conceptualization.

By understanding this through Louise Halfe's retrieval of the story of
the Rolling Head, one could conceptualize this collectivity as the interconnected experiences and pathways of our female ancestors, and how they
would remember and conceive of the Rolling Head as both an Indigenous woman and as an Indigenous mother, bearing in mind the historical
representations and acts of colonial submersions that are, and have been,
present in our country, as well as the positionality of women through history and on a contemporary landscape. Through this feminine narrative
visioning, it is significant in understanding the powerful way in which
our ancestors are part of our narratives and stories as Indigenous women,
and how this changes the way in which we might individualize the act of
memory. Jennifer Andrews in *In the Belly of a Laughing God* quotes Diane
Glancy as stating that "history can...be seen as the writing of one's own
story into the fabric of the written text. Maybe even the *rewriting* of one's
own story into the *rewritten* text."[4] This reinforces the collectivity of our
individual experience as Indigenous peoples; that our stories are fused
within a great body of prevailing composition, a sea of voices and experiences, gathered together.

In Louise Halfe's *A Crooked Good*, as well as within her ancient story of
the Rolling Head, lies the very crux of memory. Once considering individual and then collective memory, one could also consider the idea of embodied memory within an Indigenous framework. Embodied memories are
the root in which Indigenous stories are grounded. Embodied memories
can be envisioned as what they are and have been; as well, the potentiality
for the future vision is through the particular memory, within the preservation of language. Halfe is very aware of this when she says: "The preser-

vation of language is important. Every artist, regardless of what media they use, calls upon the invisible, calls forth memories through sound, sight and emotion. Language is its voice."[5] Halfe suggests that through memory lie the voices that can be portrayed and expressed through language, and she is successful in doing this in *The Crooked Good* as well as through her version of the story of the Rolling Head. Halfe says:

> We seek...memory, again related to the wind. This inherent memory that asks us to reflect from the blessed heart, in other words, the sacred things we have eaten from our heart and have gathered through the wind. Knowledge is alive, aware is intelligent and responsive. One must embody it to have a truly intimate relationship.[6]

By gathering these things through the wind, Halfe suggests that "the breath of everything, all my relations and those that ever inhabit this earth is captured by infinity in the wind."[7] By connecting the memory of our ancestors and relations as being captured, the wind holds a position as gatherer of memories; as the embodiment of memory and the core of all Indigenous stories and relationships. The eternal wind, heard as a whisper and a breath behind all of Creation, holds the totality of memory within its being, and is a place to be retrieved and remembered through the act and journey of language, under the hand of its Creator.

Cree writer Louise Halfe, also known as Sky Dancer, is from the Saddle Lake Reserve, Alberta. She is the author of *Bear Bones and Feathers* and *Blue Marrow*, which was nominated for a Governor General's Award and was instrumental in bringing forward a strong voice and experience of the Indigenous female.

In her third book, *The Crooked Good*, Halfe fluidly creates a powerful narrative as the reader of her poetry is thrust within the life-voice of her female protagonist, ê-kwêskît, who describes herself as a dreamer who "dreams awake. Asleep. On paper."[8] The character ê-kwêskît, otherwise known as "Turn-Around Woman"[9] is listening to her mother, aspin, tell the story of Rolling Head as her "ears witnessed the story."[10] Aspin is described in *The Crooked Good* as the mother who is also known as Gone-for-Good and who is, as ê-kwêskît describes, "is anything but gone."[11] Aspin can be seen as one who unfurls stories with a "bitter-root mouth,"[12] and is the one who is the teller of the story of Rolling Head as seen in the poem "Listen: To the Story."[13] Within Halfe's poetic visioning, the reader is amidst a clamour of voices; some whisper a gentle exalt of beginnings, others wail of a building of lairs that house the tongues of these stories; constructions exude the power in the telling of a story that followed as ê-kwêskît's "memory sniffs the woven trail."[14] The image of the woven trail portrays a pathway with voices, experiences, and stories woven tightly together throughout the centuries, pulsing with the beat of all memory.

Louise Halfe's poetic narrative embodies a feminine voice in *The Crooked Good*, most profoundly within the sacred story of cihcipistikwân/Rolling Head. The story of Rolling Head is told in an earlier version published in 1929 by Edward Ahenakew and varies in some greatly distinct ways from Louise Halfe's portrayal, which should be examined as the variation between versions shifts the way in which the reader understands the story and understands those within the story. The two versions are two different dreamings coming from the same bed, one from the masculine and one from the feminine, the landscape of their vision a long-ago remembrance of âtayôhkêwin,[15] bearing the sacred dreaming of the "ancient story-keepers."[16] In "Cree Poetic Discourse," Neal McLeod writes: "Poetic thinking involves dreaming, relying on the visceral, like a painter.... A poetic way of thinking urges us to radically rethink the surface of things, like a dreamer."[17] By experiencing and responding to both versions/dreamings, the reader gains an inner sense of the emotive qualities that are present within each version, along with the delicate shifts of narrative flow and abundance found within the Indigenous imagination. McLeod further states: "Just like Nôhtokwêw Âtayôhkan (The Old Grandmother Spirit) keeps the stories, the mamâhtâwisiwak, the poetic dreamers, keep ancient poetic pathways."[18]

Dreaming is powerful communication, and involves a sacred passage of understanding and expression. In *The Crooked Good*, Louise Halfe's dreamer, ê-kwêskît, describes dreaming throughout the poetry as a potent part of reality and communicating, and articulates that "The Old White Man taught me to unfold night visits and The Old Woman taught me all of it was real."[19] Halfe writes about "dreamers"[20] and expresses the livings and dreamings within her language, creating a near indivisibility between the two. In "Poetics as Medicine," Louise Halfe expresses that:

> A dream is simply not a dream. Crees believe it is a spirit that fills one with stories. It is up to us to discern the teachings, whether or not they're meant for others or just for oneself. In its power place a guardian presides, is alive, resourceful and intelligent. The dreamer and dream embody themselves.... A dream in many respects is a quest that plants the seeds of wonder.... One must make concrete the secret language of one's dream.[21]

Halfe's poetry in *The Crooked Good* does this. Rolling Head is described as a dreamer when Halfe writes: "I give in to Rolling Head / though I don't yet know this. / I was in a dream that was all /...I went to the dreamer. Rolling Head."[22] By thinking of Rolling Head as dreamer, Rolling Head comes to embody a spirit of stories, and embodiment of the self as dream and dreamer. It is quite possible then to view the story of Rolling Head as a story of dream embodiment, where the element of possibility exists and the perspective of the dreamer prevails.

Halfe successfully retrieves the ancient narratives and brings them forward into the present through a poetic vision by using her feminine understanding to carry the voices both respectfully and with intent to walk the sacred stories into the contemporary landscape, creating a weaving of worlds, narratives, and collective experience. Jennifer Andrew's *In the Belly of a Laughing God* quotes Jeannette Armstrong's words during a 2007 keynote address: "this ability to bring things that are sacred forward into the human realm is absolutely essential."[23]

Contemporary Indigenous poetics approach and capture many elements from identification to politics, to relationships, and more. In *Native Poetry in Canada: A Contemporary Anthology*, the editors Jeannette Armstrong and Lalage Grauer express that contemporary poetics involve a way of getting "through to an audience and voice what matters to us as subject. Not unrequited love and romance, not longing for motherland, not taming the wilderness, nor pastoral beauty, nor driving railroad spikes, nor placing the immigrant self, but our own collective coengaged in speaking out."[24] Also, the contemporary poet who is Indigenous shares "experiences of racism and continuing colonial attitudes that...suggest histories of being Native in Canada."[25] In *The Crooked Good*, Halfe expresses colonial images throughout her work, such as "Governor Simpson disposed of his Indian bride"[26] and "the gentle Cree thawed the foreign tribes,"[27] acting as a contemporary action to express Indigenous history as well as speaking as part of a collective memory. There is an explicit sense of accord within the Indigenous narrative canon that creates an interbraiding of ideologies, experiences, and a common knowledge of shared history among other Indigenous writers, which draws a contemporary frame around the voicing of self through narrative expression.

Sacred stories differ from contemporary poetics, and it is interesting how Louise Halfe's use of both creates a powerful coherence of the two narratives, integrating the sacred Cree story into a contemporary narrative plain through the lens of her feminine perspective. The joining of the sacred with the contemporary is reflective of Halfe. However, on a deeper level, the use of Indigenous sacred stories is employing an ancient voice within the space of a narrative, one that holds the memories, experiences, and understanding of our ancestors on a level worthy of extreme honour and respect for the sacred spirit within. In *The Crooked Good*, Halfe's use of the sacred is evident as she is using a sacred story of cihcipistikwân, who is the mother of wîsahkêcâhk, who is a sacred figure in Indigenous culture. In the foreword of *Life Stages and Native Women*, Maria Campbell explains the sacred story. She asserts:

My Cheechum [cîhcam] also told the *ahtyokaywina* [âtayôhkêwina], which were told only in the spring when the frogs started to sing. *Ahtyokaywina* told how we came to be here as well as taught us the taboos and laws of our people.... The stories were multilayered with knowledge and teachings interwoven into each of them. The keeper of these stories was Notokwe Ahtyokan [nôtôkwêw âtayôhkan], the old woman spirit who was the first grandmother, and as keeper of the *ahtyokaywina*.... I am sure our first grandmother Notokwe Ahtyokan is walking with us on this journey as we do the work of communicating our family histories and community laws in new ways.[28]

Maria Campbell outlines the sacred nature of the story that Louise Halfe employs by carrying the Indigenous female voice forward to the contemporary present.

The Indigenous imagination can be contrasted with the colonial imagination; however, a narrative imaginative response has occurred from colonialism. The colonial imagination has placed Indigenous nations within the historical context of becoming people, places, and voices that were vastly far removed from reality. This historical and social repositioning shows a direct imperial intentionality that distorted and displaced Indigenous peoples in terms of positionality, political roles, social roles, and created a great period of silence, most specifically within the Indigenous female. Because of this shift, the Indigenous female writer had to actively learn and gather strength to rewrite the position of women in history. Linda Tuhiwai Smith asserts that "Indigenous people want to tell our own stories, write our own versions in our own ways, for our own purposes."[29]

This silence from the Indigenous female emerged from colonial subjugation of women. Distortion and silencing of women in any mode is a predecessor of social chaos within the balance of our nations. In "Trauma to Resilience: Notes on Decolonization," Cynthia C. Wesley-Equimaux states that "Contact with Europeans imposed alien social structures and disrupted gender relations. The roles women played in their homes and communities were increasingly altered by external influences and demands."[30] Historically, women were pushed out of their inherent positions and were consistently forced into a submissive stance by the colonial hand. Wesley-Equimaux continues:

Almost immediately after the influx of explorers, Native women came under the gaze of missionaries, men who could not see women as equals, because these men were coming from a place where women were inferior to men. Native women were removed from their traditional roles and responsibilities and pushed to the margins of their own societies.[31]

From the instigation of Christianity's steadfast repression of the historic women of Indigenous nations, the contemporary Indigenous female has continued to be submerged through governmental action such as the Indian Act, which stripped women of their right to be a legal Indian on their own; a woman had to have an Indigenous husband or father in order to have the privileges or rights that came with being an Indigenous person. Indigenous women were consistently and gradually submerged until they were marginalized and completely silenced. Julie Andrews emphasizes that from this silencing, the Indigenous "women writers give voice to stories of marginalization through a process of imaginative retelling."[32] Halfe's version of cihcipistikwân emerges from the silence and moves toward a new vision.

On the other side, the Indigenous imagination is a crucial factor in the realignment and retrieval of what Leanne Simpson describes as "a vision of life or a social reality that is different from the one the individual, clan or community is currently living within."[33] Another way of seeing this could be called visioning, which would open our imaginative minds to vision the world and social reality in which we truly belong in, which drastically contrasts with the images and standards set by the colonial imagination. Such use of the Indigenous imagination also creates a pathway for storytellers to recreate and revise our ancestral past, present, and future. Feminine narrative retrieval, in this sense, is a vision of a better world for the Indigenous female, one that strengthens, enhances, and propels her forward by retrieving a strong ancestral voice from our histories. Without the occurrence of colonialism, such visioning wouldn't be necessary; therefore, the contemporary Indigenous imagination is largely shaped by and from the colonial actions. However, with ancient stories, art, and literatures from a pre-colonial era still in existence, the Indigenous imagination is as ancient as the first breath of our grandmothers from the dawn of Creation.

A feminine retrieval of the story of cihcipistikwân creates a knowledge pathway on how to proceed to begin the process of narrative retrieval. In his work "Cree Poetic Discourse," Neal McLeod discusses this idea when he writes:

> In *The Crooked Good*, Halfe discusses the classic Cree narrative Rolling Head and reframes it by retrieving the feminine voice through the sound of the colonial imagination. In this work, Cree poetic memory is essential to the process of retrieving the hidden and submerged female perspective.[34]

McLeod's use of the words "hidden" and "submerged" express that the female perspective is alive and functioning, but in need of retrieval through the use of poetic memory by visiting the poetic pathways of our ancestors, and even through creating new paths and interpretations. Within Louise

Halfe's *The Crooked Good*, this submersion of cihcipistikwân is evident throughout, but specifically in the poem "Braids,"[35] when the Rolling Head's submersion is described as:

> cihcipistikwân stretches through her watery sleep.
> Phantom arms. Feels. Squeezes, shuffles phantom toes.
> Moves a foot. Through a membrane, a slight split in the
> Water, stretches her skin. Crawls through blubber.
> Parts the belly of her eye. Centuries of waiting.
> Where does the gathering of self begin?
> What form?[36]

The Rolling Head's own submersion (as namêw,[37] the sturgeon, in Ahenekew's version), and her difficulty in finding a way out of such a restrictive and complete containment, speaks to all stories, histories, and voices of Indigenous women. It is realistic to view the "slight split in the water"[38] as the opening for our own voices and stories and languages to fit through. As Indigenous women, the Rolling Head's questions of identity are our own, and as Indigenous women, the period of waiting is felt in the depths of our own sinew and in the wind against our faces, the same wind that holds memory, that blows over the narrative pathways toward our grandmother's voices. Through Halfe's description of cihcipistikwân, it is possible to view Rolling Head's emersion from submersion as symbolic of our own stories' potential for coming out their watery sleep through memory and language.

Gayatri Chakravorty Spivak, in "Can the Subaltern Speak," describes this hidden and submerged existence as the "margins...the silent, silenced center of the circuit marked out by epistemic violence."[39] Spivak continues by stating: "If in the context of colonial production, the subaltern has no history and cannot speak, the subaltern is female is even more deeply in shadow."[40] Within her discourse, Spivak recognizes the gendered function of the female within the colonial imagination and against the colonial ideal, ultimately causing a rift between voice and expression, based on femininity, which enhances McLeod's image of the submerged female. Also, Spivak's discourse asserts that the subaltern have no history within colonial production, so in this colonial historical erasing, it is even more vital to wade through the imperial murky currents to pull out and take home our women's voices. In "Between Subalternity and Indigeneity: Critical Categories for Postcolonial Studies," Jodi A. Byrd and Michael Rothberg write:

> Both subaltern and Indigenous name problems of translation and relationability; or, to put it slightly differently, subaltern/Indigenous dialogue is, among other things, a dialogue within and about, incommensurability....

Incommensurability in "Can the Subaltern Speak," in other words, refers to the gap between the "sender" and "receiver" of messages, inflected by power, a gap that has considerable implications for the subaltern and Indigenous histories....[41]

By looking at Spivak's subaltern argument in this way, the shift would move from the submerged female to the gap between submerged Indigenous female and those who cannot and will not hear her voice over the surface as she reaches out of the water of her submersion as either a complete failure to listen or a blurred distortion of speech. In this way, we see the submersion of Ahenekew's Rolling Head as a subaltern position, and her reaching out of the water as identification and a voicing of the self, through Halfe's retelling in *The Crooked Good*.

Subaltern can be a point of issue as there are many intellectual scholars and activists within the Indigenous communities that are getting a great deal of attention and respect. People are listening to many Indigenous women today. However, many Indigenous women are still not being heard. Michael Rothberg describes Robert Warrior as estimating that:

> There is more than enough subaltern experience in Native communities—including abject poverty and continued political disenfranchisement, but there are also already spaces within those communities where alternative formations persist which can't simply be termed subaltern.[42]

From Warrior's observation, it is possible then to be fully aware of the subaltern positionality within Indigenous voices. However, one must be conscious of the spaces that contain voices that cannot be viewed as the subaltern within Indigenous society. Looking at Spivak's, McLeod's, and Warrior's ideas of submersion and subalternity, the significance of bringing these Indigenous women out of hiding into a place of visibility and speech is all the more urgent. By narratively incorporating poetic memory to retrieve this voice, Indigenous writers are active in changing the narrative landscape through the act of treading the ancient trails of poetic memory to do so.

Relative to the idea of retrieval, it is possible then to consider the issue of necessity and interpretation within narrative retrieval. Kim Anderson considers that many storytellers and writers use the stories of the past in order to allow the story to fill a contemporary need. In *Life Stages and Native Women*, Anderson writes:

> Although some stories maintain consistency over time, some stories change with time. These stories vary according to the life stage of the participants telling them or according to what is important to them at the time of telling.

Because the subjectivity of the storyteller is understood, it is without question that stories of the past will reflect the needs of the present... there is a purpose in every telling, which is not seen as detracting from the "truth."[43]

By understanding what Anderson suggests in terms of Louise Halfe's retrieval of the feminine from within the story of Rolling Head, it can be perceived that Halfe had intended to feminize the story and that there is a present-day need for her choice. This need is evident as Indigenous women writers are voicing their dreamings and imaginative narratives from the boundaries of their own experiences, as well as from the embodied memories of their grandmothers or other female ancestors and influences from the past in ways that are both purposeful and truthful, according to the way the world is seen in their temporal or contemporary space. Halfe's purpose may be to create a newfound sense that reinforces the feminine narrative in the story, as well as a subjective choice to retrieve the story out of the masculine command to shift the reader toward a more relational perception of Rolling Head as a woman, as a lover, as a wronged wife, and mostly as a mother.

Rolling Head in Edward Ahenakew's account of "chichipischekwân/ Rolling Head" falls under a masculine narrative, in which Rolling Head is cast as a wicked, vengeful, and crafty woman with a restless spirit who ultimately comes to a deserved end of disembodiment, left literally as a rolling head bent on destroying and harming her children. There is no narrative empathy toward the female in the earlier version of the story, and this alone creates a narrative that privileges the male. Suzanne Keen describes "narrative empathy" as "the sharing of feeling and perspective-taking induced by reading, hearing, viewing, and imagining narratives of another's situation or condition."[44] Keen expresses the fact that both author and reader can have narrative empathy. She writes: "Author's empathy bears on fictional worldmaking and character creating. It may influence writer's choices about narrative techniques, evincing a desire to evoke an empathetic response in the narrative audience...."[45] Perhaps Louise Halfe's own feelings of empathy in seeing and hearing the story of the Rolling Head may be within her feminine retrieval process in her work.

Narrative empathy makes the reader empathic toward a subject within a fictional or poetic work, which produces an understanding on the part of the reader. This understanding creates an attachment formed of vision and connectivity between the readers of Louise Halfe's retrieval of the feminine voice in *The Crooked Good* and the character of the Rolling Head itself. Neal McLeod affirms that:

Central to an embodied poetic understanding of the world is what I would call a "poetics of empathy" which could be translated into Cree by the term wâhkôtowin (kinship/relationships). Through relations we are able to create the web of understanding of our embodied locations and stretch it outwards to a wider context of collective historicity and through a poetics grounded in dialogue and an open-ended flow of narrative understanding. A poetics of wâhkôtôwin and empathy are key to a thorough engaging with history. These concepts are at the heart of Louise Halfe's *The Crooked Good*.[46]

McLeod's insights centralize empathy's role within poetic understanding in Louise Halfe's narrative retrieval, and find the relational context and historical engagement within the voice of the Rolling Head. Such connections further fuse the collectivity of our voices and create a deepening of our sense of the Indigenous narrative spaces and the very intricate layering and weaving that lie beneath the stories.

Without narrative empathy, there is a distinct feeling of narrative male-privileging in Edward Ahenakew's version of the story of Rolling Head. Ahenakew's version was published in 1929, which leaves a vast span of just under eighty years between his publication and Louise Halfe's 2007 publication. The Canadian political spectrum has shifted considerably in a multitude of ways in that time period, so the retrieval of the lost feminine voice from within Ahenakew's version will have an enormous connotative difference on a contemporary narrative landscape. Jennifer Andrews and Renate Eigenbrod in "The Love of Words" write that Ahenakew was a "Cree activist who was also an Anglican cleric who lived at the time of the height of the government's assimilation policies."[47] This suggests a political atmosphere of governmental aggression, cultural and gender violence, and an intense Christianization of the people and land, which may have influenced the narration of the time, perhaps masculinizing the language and storyline in the story of Rolling Head. The voice of the female within the story is without empathy, without feelings other than lust and anger, and maintains a male positioning of voice and feeling and perspective that has consequences for the female within the story, who has no hope for reader redemption or connectivity.

In Ahenakew's Rolling Head story, the wife, whose name is wâpi-mîkwan (her classical name before she is transformed into the Rolling Head),[48] has a "restless preoccupation"[49] and takes walks into the forest to fondle snakes in a provocative manner, horrifying her husband. There is mutual trickery in which the man feigns illness and the woman uses magic in order to return home quickly to the safety of her family's dwelling place in the bush. This is not in Louise Halfe's version of the Rolling Head story. Upon the wife's departure from the dwelling of her snake over, the man kills the snakes and curses them to a lowly position on Earth. Both the magic and the curse have Christianized overtones of woman-as-witch and is the first reptilian curse in the Garden of Eden, creating a patriarchal narrative within the text. Once the husband disembodies his wife and she becomes Rolling Head, she says "I will go after his sons."[50] This statement denies her motherhood; the sons are *his* offspring now and not hers, so she can kill them without remorse for revenge, screaming "I am going to kill you!"[51] However, within the next page, it is written that "She gave chase to her children,"[52] which casts her as a mother-turned-demon, who becomes a murderous predator of her own children. Ultimately, Rolling Head is described as having a "naturally wicked nature"[53] with "evil ways,"[54] which again has a patriarchal overtone and is suggestive of the sinning female.[55]

Louise Halfe sets the familiar story within a contemporary and feminine narrative voice in *The Crooked Good* in a way that creates narrative empathy and embodied understanding toward Rolling Head. Halfe's version in "Keynote Address: The Rolling Head's Graveyard" has the boys grudgingly let the father know where their mother goes during the day. This does two things. It shows that the children have a stronger loyal to their father or that they are afraid to be caught lying. It also leads the husband to discover his wife with her "raven braids untied,"[56] her hair entwined with a large snake, and the babies by her feet. He becomes "engorged with jealousy"[57] and decapitates his own wife. The man's violence is unjustified, which further increases the reader's narrative empathy and understanding for the woman.

Halfe's version includes a physical description of the woman's beauty and female sensuality as she makes gentle, loving movements with the snake. This contrasts with Ahenakew's physical description of Rolling Head as unsightly and vicious. In Ahenakew's story, the woman "tapped"[58] against the wood to attract the snake, whereas Halfe writes that she "drummed."[59] Halfe's description of the woman's physicality and sexuality portrays the wife and mother as filled with desire and saddened by loneliness because her husband is often away, which contrasts with the evil-at-heart character in Ahenekew's version. Halfe's empathetic portrayal shows the woman's loneliness and the solace she found in the company of the snakes, making the motivation for her adultery understandable and beyond the dualism of right or wrong.

When the wife and mother becomes Rolling Head, Halfe describes that "the head wept, rolled and squeezed through the trails,"[60] a description that has an emotive quality and lends a deep sense of humanity to the now non-human Rolling Head and her loss of love, of choice, of motherhood. Her pain over the loss of her children is furthered by the description that "She struggled, ripped her face, gouged her eyes. She called. Called."[61] Halfe interprets the empathetic presence of animals also in her text. She writes that "a fox trotted by, heart filled by the Rolling Head's wail."[62] The fact that the animals of the forest feel sympathy for her shows that she is worthy of sympathy, and that her pain is so deep that it affects the life around her. Halfe's use of narrative empathy in *The Crooked Good* is in sharp contrast to the monstrous characterization of the woman in Ahenekew's version of the story. In Halfe's story, the reader can understand that Rolling Head is a victim of her husband's jealousy and rage, a woman left suddenly without her physicality, without her husband, lover, and, most of all, without her children.

The relationship between Rolling Head and her children is an issue that is highlighted with the feminine telling of the story of Rolling Head, which creates a deeper sense of narrative empathy in the work. In Louise Halfe's story, Rolling Head laments "âstamik pê-kîwêk. Come home. Come home. I love you my babies.... My babies, my sons."[63] The boys continue to run away from their mother, with "their father's wrath and words coiled inside their guts."[64] These lines show the torment of the mother who has been separated from her children. She is not focused on the pain of losing her lover or her own pain, but the pain of losing her children is evident. This is the most prominent feature of the feminine retrieval and the most poignant for several reasons. She is now bodiless and destroyed by the evil of her husband's jealousy and intent to slay her. She is a torn mother, and all mothers—regardless of culture, space, or time—can hear her cries or imagine the intensity of losing her babies. With the historical reality of the residential school experience, where Indigenous mothers felt the heartbreak of having their children forcefully removed from them, the pain of loss becomes far more palpable and truthful for the reader. This pain is more understandable and more conceivable when described from a contemporary and female perspective than Ahenakew's portrayal of a vengeful and heartless monster who wishes to kill her children.

The positionality of Rolling Head's children is also something that must be considered in the version narrated by Louise Halfe. In the Ahenakew version, the mother wants to kill her children, who are victims of a monster. They fear her and want to flee from her. In Louise Halfe's feminine retrieval, the boys reject their murdered mother, who is disembodied. They further disembody her motherhood through their rejection and choice to stay loyal to their father. They will not help their mother, and use their father's weapons against her in an attempt to destroy her a second time, acting as extensions of their father's rage.

In Louise Halfe's "The Rolling Head's Graveyard," she states that "In order for young boys to attain manhood, the umbilical cord must be cut."[65] The fact that the boys' attachment to their mother was severed at the same time that the mother was decapitated is significant. Before the attack against the mother, the family was happy: "in the pines they gathered blueberries and cranberries, and what the sparrows left of dried saskatoons, chokecherries, and rosehips."[66] This is an image of a peaceful family unit. When he discovered the snake lover, the father "took his sons aside, and gave them a sharp bone, a file, a flint, and a beaver's tooth. He filled their heads with plans should he not return."[67] In this version, the father's words are not narrated, but through the boys' actions later, when they reject their mother's calls and her love, their father's intentions are clear.

Louise Halfe continues: "The woman's love for her offspring, as indicated in this story, has the potential to be destructive to young men. Therefore it becomes helpful for the husband/father/man to help the young man not only grow up, but to sever the maternal bond or tie. However, to sever this tie too early in a child's life is detrimental."[68] The reader is aware that it is natural for young men to break ties when they choose to walk in their own direction, but this is not a natural development in the process of growing up. The boys' rejection of their mother has been ordered by their murderous and jealous father, bent on revenge and retribution. Halfe continues when she asserts: "The father, in this case, is unable to accept the circumstances of his wife's affection for the snakes and speeds up this severing by demonizing his wife."[69] The father instils fear in his sons, does not take any accountability for his actions, and severs family ties, leaving his wife childless and his children motherless, all for his own benefit. He forces his boys to accede to his will, not realizing that by murdering their mother, he is depriving them of her nurturing and abandoning his children. Ultimately, he makes his children orphans and commits a colonial act of violence against an Indigenous woman on the basis of sexual jealousy and personal feelings of betrayal.

An interesting character in this text is wîsahkêcâhk, who is the elder of the two brothers. Wîsahkêcâhk (also known as Elder Brother, Nanabush, Nanaboozho, and more) plays a significant role in Indigenous literatures, and is sometimes understood as the trickster. Linda Morra, in *Troubling Tricksters: Revisioning Critical Conversations*, writes: "tricksters need to be relocated within specific Indigenous socio-historical contexts."[70] The stories of both Ahenakew and Halfe each have wîsahkêcâhk in their narratives, and he is the older son in both stories. Seeing wîsahkêcâhk as the child of Rolling Head and the man who killed her and gave him an escape plan places wîsahkêcâhk within an interesting family unit and childhood. Deanna Reder, in "Sacred Stories in Comic Book Form," writes: "for the Cree, our strength is in our storytelling. It is clear that the form is not rigid or resistant to innovation.... The way [Wesakeck] looks is really up to the imagination of the storyteller."[71] Halfe continues to keep wîsahkêcâhk and the younger brother as they are, but shifts the parental action surrounding them, thus contrasting the actions of the two brothers in her feminine narrative with Ahenakew's masculinized story of Rolling Head.

By viewing wîsahkêcâhk as a child, in this way, it becomes clear why the father would give his son the tools to enable him to use the land as a barrier between him and his mother, rather than leave wîsahkêcâhk to his own transformative devices. Perhaps the child might choose to transform into a being to save his mother and to help her, so the father offers a tool to help his sons maintain a physical divide between themselves and their mother, setting them up for a motherless life, and giving them the skills to modify the environmental. The father chooses to vanquish the mother, and although wîsahkêcâhk is the one throwing the devices, it is his father who has ordered him to use such tools. The reader can view the child as an obedient and fearful child, rather than a single-minded, cunning child.

Rolling Head is featured in three tellings: Ahenakew's version, Halfe's version in *Rolling Head's Graveyard*, and Halfe's retelling through the character of aspin in *The Crooked Good*. Each is housed within the confines of the sacred story of cihcipistikwân, and doesn't deviate from the ancient storyline. Of course, there are revisions and feminine narrative retrievals, but the story still recounts the family unit, the infidelity, the decapitation, the chase of the children, and ultimately with the mother's restless rolling and plunge into the depths of the water, where the story ends. Within the larger framework of *The Crooked Good*, however, the Rolling Head is further retrieved in a very contemporary and meaningful way beyond the original storyline. Halfe gives cihipistikwân a stronger voice, as well as a more potent being in the contemporary physical world. In *The Crooked Good*, Louise Halfe describes cihipistikwân's life as:

> Over brooks, ponds, rivers, lakes and seas,
> Her winds caused great floods. She cleared
> Her throat, swelled, tore dirt, shot arrow-spiked rains.
> She sent flying flames, blistering fired.
> She'd glide over mountains, unbuckle her soul ...
> She slept so long. Rocks are her spine, rivers
> Bury her seeds. No one knows her age. In the spring
> Rolling Head awakens, becomes Rib Woman.
> The lodge, her hair.
> Willow people form her flesh, a basket woven
> Over weeping dreamers. The spring berry is her heart.[72]

Halfe gives Rolling Head a stronger essence and more humanity through this narrative as she describes her soul as well as her heart. Louise Halfe gives a sense of the passing of time, the feeling of a contemporary landscape, a sense of the place where Rolling Head went after she chased her children, and of the being that she became as she lived on. Also, through Halfe's use of the Rolling Head within a contemporary framing, cihcipistikwân is able to relate to and influence the other characters within *The Crooked Good*, giving the contemporary reader a poetic framing and understanding of how Rolling Head's existence plays into the greater world of contemporary Indigenous society and relationships.

The Rolling Head is also envisioned as one who visits dreamers when she says that "I'll enter your sleep...I will harvest your bed,"[73] as well as a place of refuge for the lost dreamer when ê-kwêskit "swam in her skull, gouged and borrowed her eye, her tongue...the only safe place."[74] Halfe voices the Rolling Head as one who speaks, offers suggestions about love and lovers, "guides"[75] and "coaches,"[76] and also inspires and touches people. She is portrayed as a great influence and one to whom people "give in to,"[77] and in this sense, she can be seen as one who has a power over humanity, a being with a familiar core, as much as our own consciousness. Halfe is building the memory of cihcipistikwân, attaching her ancient story to the breath of the contemporary Indigenous woman. At the very end of *The Crooked Good*, in the poem "Gave My Name"[78] the Rolling Head becomes entwined with ê-kwêskît as she lives, and it becomes clear to the reader that the two beings are braided together to form a conjoined entity. Jennifer Andrews states that "the speaking 'I' and the eyes of the Rolling Head seem to have transformed into two parts of the same figure, and this duality is rendered visible on the page through the presentation of the poem in two columns."[79] Also, at the end of the poem, the Rolling Head says:

> I'm earth
> Born each moon,
> Waxing and waning,
> Bleeding eggs.
> I'm painted red on rocks;
> I swim the caves in lakes
> Where my head sinks.
> And I drink to roll again.[80]

Halfe alludes to the cycle of femininity and reproduction, connecting it with Mother Earth, and ending in the images of rolling again, cycling the universe. Halfe has cihcipistikwân describe herself as the rock paintings swimming in lake caves, which creates a connection to the first stories and to the expression of Indigenous peoples. Finally, when the Rolling Head says she must ingest water in order to exist as a Rolling Head, this underlines cihcipistikwân's sacred connection to water in order for her to exist. Louise

Halfe creates a deep and meaningful retrieval of the feminine narration of the sacred being of the Rolling Head, and offers the reader a glimpse into the essence of humanity through this story.

Louise Halfe's retrieval of the feminine from the narrative past proves to be a powerful and strategic yet imaginative way of walking the woven trail of memory in a meaningful way. Halfe reaches within the ancient storyline and brings cihcipistikwân forward to a contemporary landscape, offering a present-day voice through which her femininity and motherhood are reconsidered and the truth is retrieved. Halfe visions a cihcipistikwân that the reader can empathize with. At the New Sun Conference on Aboriginal Arts 2012, Louise Halfe contends that "I think of myself as Rolling Head."[81] She further asserted, "We are all Rolling Head."[82] She includes all of humanity within the sacred story, and in this statement directly suggests that each of us may have aspects of Rolling Head, thus reinforcing Rolling Head's humanity itself within Indigenous women's entireties. Halfe understands the significance of honouring the strengths in Indigenous femininity and the power in refusing to be blocked in the poetic pathways toward our true voices and honoured histories. By creating a feminine narrative retrieval in the story of cihcipistikwân as portrayed in *The Crooked Good*, Louise Halfe has, with a sacred step, walked through the grassy trails of narrative memory to find the sounds of these voices and bravely cradled them in her arms to take them home, where we wait to nourish them and follow the honour song of the narrative journey, all the way through.

Notes

1 cihcipistikwân is the Cree word for Rolling Head and is used throughout Louise Halfe's *The Crooked Good* interchangeably with the English version of Rolling Head throughout the poetry book. With Cree orthographic practice, Cree words are not capitalized.

2 Kim Anderson, *Life Stages and Native Women* (Winnipeg: University of Manitoba Press, 2011), 4.

3 Leanne Simpson, *Dancing on My Turtle's Back* (Winnipeg: Arbeiter Ring Press, 2011), 106.

4 Jennifer Andrews, *In the Belly of a Laughing God* (Toronto: University of Toronto Press, 2011), 131.

5 Louise Halfe, "Poetics as Medicine" panel, Sounding Out: Indigenous Poetics, Trent University, Peterborough, November 5, 2010, 211.

6 Ibid., 212.

7 Ibid.

8 Louise Halfe, *The Crooked Good* (Regina: Coteau Books, 2007), 4.

9 Ibid., 130. Also written as meaning "She turns around"; personal name given to a female: Turn-Around Woman.

10 Halfe, *The Crooked Good*, 22.

11 Ibid., 5.

12 Ibid., 37.

13 Ibid.

14 Ibid., 28.

15 âtayôhkêwin is a sacred story in Cree.

16 Halfe, *The Crooked Good*, 3.

17 Neal McLeod, "Cree Poetic Discourse," in *Across Cultures, Across Borders*, ed. Emma LaRoque et al. (Peterborough: Broadview Press, 2009), 112.

18 Ibid., 89.

19 Halfe, *The Crooked Good*, 4.

20 Ibid., 81.

21 Halfe, "Poetics as Medicine," 210–11.

22 Halfe, *The Crooked Good*, 45.

23 Andrews, *In the Belly of a Laughing God*, 156.

24 Jeannette Armstrong, *Native Poetry in Canada: A Contemporary Anthology* (Peterborough: Broadview Press, 2001), xvi.

25 Ibid., xxii.

26 Halfe, *The Crooked Good*, 60.

27 Ibid., 61.

28 Maria Campbell, *Life Stages and Native Women* (Winnipeg: University of Manitoba Press, 2011), xvii–xix.

29 Linda Tuiwai Smith, *Decolonizing Methodologies* (Winnipeg: Zed Books, 2012), 28.

30 Cynthia C. Wesley-Equimaux, "Trauma to Resilience: Notes on Decolonization," in *Restoring the Balance: First Nations Women, Community, and Culture*, ed. Gail Guthrie Valaskakis, Madeleine Dion Stout, and Eric Guimond (Winnipeg: University of Manitoba Press, 2009), 13.

31 Ibid., 16.

32 Andrews, *In the Belly of a Laughing God*, 140.

33 Leanne Simpson, *Dancing on Our Turtle's Back* (Winnipeg: Arbeiter Ring Press, 2011), 146.

34 McLeod, "Cree Poetic Discourse," 113.

35 Halfe, *The Crooked Good*, 19.

36 Ibid.

37 Edward Ahenekew, "Chichipischekwân (Rolling Head), in *The Journal of American Folklore* 42, no. 166 (1929): 313.

38 Halfe, *The Crooked Good*, 19.

39 Gayatri Chakrovorty Spivak, "Can the Subaltern Speak?," in *Marxism and the Interpretation of Culture*, ed. Cary Nelson and Lawrence Grossberg (Champaign: University of Illinois Press, 1988), 78.

40 Ibid., 83.

41 Jodi A. Byrd and Michael Rothberg, "Between Subalternity and Indigeneity: Critical Categories for Postcolonial Studies," in *Interventions* (Champaign: University of Illinois Press, 2011), 5.

42 Ibid., 11.

43 Kim Anderson, *Life Stages and Native Women* (Winnipeg: University of Manitoba Press, 2011), 22.

44 Suzanne Keen, "Narrative Empathy," in *The Living Handbook of Narratology* 14, no. 3 (Hamburg: University of Hamburg Press, 2012), 1.

45 Ibid., 28.

46 McLeod, "Cree Poetic Discourse," 90–91.

47 Jennifer Andrews and Renate Eigenbrod, "From Conference to Special Issues: Selected Articles on the Love of Words," in *Studies in Canadian Literature* (Fredericton: University of New Brunswick, 2008), i.

48 Neal McLeod noted that his great-grandfather, Peter Vandall, had confirmed orally that wâpi-mîkwan was the original name of the Rolling Head, Peterborough, Ontario, 2012.

49 Edward Ahenakew, "Chichipishekwân (Rolling Head)," *Journal of American Folklore* 42, no. 166 (1929): 312.

50 Ibid., 313.

51 Ibid.

52 Ibid., 312.

53 Ibid., 313.

54 Ibid.

55 Ibid.

56 Louise Halfe, "Keynote Address: The Rolling Head's Graveyard," *Journal of Canadian Studies* 31, no. 1 (2006): 1.

57 Ibid.

58 Ahenakew, "Chichipishekwân (Rolling Head)," 313.

59 Halfe, "Keynote Address," 1.

60 Halfe, *The Crooked Good*, 27.

61 Ibid.

62 Ibid.

63 Ibid.

64 Halfe, "Keynote Address," 1.

65 Ibid.

66 Ibid.

67 Ibid.

68 Ibid., 2.

69 Ibid.

70 Linda Morra, *Troubling Tricksters: Revisioning Critical Conversations*, ed. Deanna Reder and Linda M. Morra (Waterloo: Wilfrid Laurier University Press, 2010), xii.

71 Deanna Reder, "Sacred Stories in Comic Book Form: A Cree Reading of *Darkness Calls*," in *Troubling Tricksters*, ed. Deanna Reder and Linda M. Morra (Waterloo: Wilfrid Laurier University Press, 2010), 190.

72 Halfe, *The Crooked Good*, 20.

73 Ibid., 33.

74 Ibid., 45.

75 Ibid., 54.

76 Ibid., 101.

77 Ibid., 45.
78 Ibid., 126.
79 Andrews, *In the Belly of a Laughing God*, 75.
80 Halfe, *The Crooked Good*, 126.
81 Louise Halfe, New Sun Conference on Aboriginal Arts, Wanwkewin Heritage Park, Saskatchewan, March 29–30, 2012.
82 Ibid.

Bibliography

Ahenakew, Edward. "Cree Trickster Tales." *Journal of American Folklore* 42, no. 166 (1929): 309–53.

Anderson, Kim. *Life Stages and Native Women*. Winnipeg: University of Manitoba Press, 2011.

Andrews, Jennifer. *In the Belly of a Laughing God*. Toronto: University of Toronto Press, 2011.

Andrews, Jennifer, and Renate Eigenbrod. "From Conference to Special Issues: Selected Articles on the Love of Words." *Studies in Canadian Literature* 31, no. 1 (2008): 3–9.

Armstrong, Jeanette. *Native Poetry in Canada: A Contemporary Anthology*. Peterborough: Broadview Press, 2001.

Byrd, Jodi A., and Michael Rothberg. "Between Subalternity and Indigeneity: Critical Categories for Postcolonial Studies." *Interventions*, 1–12. Champaign: University of Illinois Press, 2011.

Halfe, Louise. *The Crooked Good*. Regina: Coteau Books, 2007.

———. "Keynote Address: The Rolling Head's Graveyard." *Journal of Canadian Studies* 31, no. 1 (2006): 65–74.

———. "Poetics as Medicine" panel. Sounding Out: Indigenous Poetics, Trent University, Peterborough, November 5, 2010.

Keen, Suzanne. "Narrative Empathy." In *The Living Handbook of Narratology*, 1–35. Hamburg: Hamburg University Press, 2012.

McLeod, Neal. "Cree Poetic Discourse." In *Across Cultures, Across Borders*, edited by Emma LaRoque et al. Peterborough: Broadview Press, 2009.

Morra, Linda. *Troubling* Tricksters, edited by Deanna Reder and Linda M. Morra. Waterloo: Wilfrid Laurier University Press, 2010.

Reder, Deanna. "Sacred Stories in Comic Book Form: A Cree Reading of *Darkness Calls*." In *Troubling Tricksters*, edited by Deanna Reder and Linda M. Morra, 177–94. Waterloo: Wilfrid Laurier University Press, 2010.

Simpson, Leanne. *Dancing on My Turtle's Back*. Winnipeg: Arbeiter Ring Press, 2011.

Smith, Linda Tuiwai. *Decolonizing Methodologies*. Winnipeg: Zed Books, 2012.

Spivak, Gayatri Chakravorty. "Can the Subaltern Speak?" In *Marxism and the Interpretation of Culture*, edited by Cary Nelson and Lawrence Grossberg, 271–313. Champaign: University of Illinois Press, 1988.

Wesley-Esquimaux, Cynthia C. "Trauma to Resilience: Notes on Decolonization." In *Restoring the Balance: First Nations Women, Community, and Culture*, edited by Gail Guthrie Valaskakis, Madeleine Dion Stout, and Eric Guimond, 13–34. Winnipeg: University of Manitoba Press, 2009.

28

"Learning to Listen to a Quiet Way of Telling": A Study of Cree Counselling Discourse Patterns in Maria Campbell's *Halfbreed*

Gail MacKay

Introduction

This is an exercise in Indigenous poetics. It contributes to theorizing Indigenous poetics to the extent that it describes how the rhetorical form of Indigenous Elders' discourse is a pathway to Indigenous knowledge and a tool for finding and structuring the meaning in a contemporary Indigenous written text. This study belongs to Indigenous poetics because it relies on a Cree and Saulteaux oral form and cultural knowledge to interpret the Indigenous poetic meaning of *Halfbreed*.

A clarification of terms prefaces the chapter. Defining my understanding of the terms "poetics," "rhetoric," and "Indigenous rhetoric" characterizes my academic study as interdisciplinary with links to Indigenous studies, literature, and education. I qualify my use of insider and outsider naming and explain why I use the terms "Cree," "Saulteaux," "Indigenous," "Halfbreed," and Métis, depending on the pre-eminent relationships particular to the situation being addressed.

I argue that *Halfbreed* adapts rhetorical patterns of Cree and Saulteaux Elder's oral discourse in an interplay between orality and literacy to affect a learning experience for the reader. I begin by describing the characteristics of Cree and Saulteaux Elder's counselling discourse and relate these to Cree and Saulteaux epistemology. I describe the listener's engaged role in oral discourse and parallel this with the reader's interaction with written records of Indigenous oral discourse. I examine the patterns of Elder's discourse as they appear in the story of *Halfbreed* in the following sequence: the introduction of the book, which establishes author's authenticity, authority, and humility; deliberate connection of the audience to time and place; the use of a second person narrator; and the use of metaphor to leave the learning to the reader.

Clarification of Terms

Indigenous poetics as the theme of this book prompts me to clarify what the term means to me and why I think my interpretation of Maria Campbell's *Halfbreed* belongs in the group here. Indigenous poetics for me is a study of the meanings and values that are infused in the recorded verbal forms in Indigenous literature. Indigenous poetics, being an interpretive study of verbal art forms, rests within the broader category of Indigenous rhetorics. And Indigenous rhetorics I understand to be the interpretive study of meaning in diverse Indigenous art forms, including forms that are alphabetic and non-alphabetic, literate, performative, aural, and visual. Relating our study of Indigenous cultural expressions to the fields of poetics and rhetorics is useful for purposes of cataloguing and accessing our work. It is also a useful reminder of an ideological stance on the very ways our study is similar to and yet significantly different from Western literary criticism.

Scholars in American Indian rhetorics mark this position clearly in their definitions of rhetoric.[1] Malea Powell delineates her opposition to a belief commonly held in rhetorical studies, specifically:

> the belief that there is *a* rhetorical tradition around which all other rhetorical traditions constellate...that *all* rhetorical scholarship must somehow, some way, show a genealogical or thematic relationship to that mythical Greco-Roman origin story in order to be counted as "really" (or "just") about rhetoric.[2]

She states that when she uses the word *rhetoric,* she refers to "systems of discourse through which meaning was, is, and continues to be made in a given culture.[3] Ernest Stromberg, editor of *American Indian Rhetorics of Survivance,* defines rhetoric to go beyond the study of persuasion and eloquence of expression. He writes:

> a definition of rhetoric as the use of language or other forms of symbolic action to produce texts (in the broadest possible sense) that effect changes in the attitude, beliefs, or actions of an audience. In this sense, rhetoric is both an art of persuasion and epistemic–epistemic inasmuch as Native Americans use language to alter our understanding of the world we inhabit.[4]

Thus implicit in the term "Indigenous rhetoric" is the sense that cultural knowledge is constructed within language structures, expression, and interpretation. Critical work by Gingell, Neuhaus, and Acoose demonstrate that study of Indigenous rhetoric may include works recorded in Indigenous languages or in translation, or in creative adaptation and syncretic blending of languages.[5] Beyond the underlying assumptions about the terms used to define the field are distinctions in ethical motivation and a commitment to interdisciplinary study.

Writers of Indigenous poetics operate from a de-colonial impulse. And though we may draw from Western literary theories to associate our critical work with the four literary theoretical orientations identified by Abrams as a focus on the author, the text, the world, or the literary work's effect on the audience, we must use all available methods, knowledge, and practices in order to achieve the purpose of Indigenous cultural vitalization.[6] Indigenous poetics reach beyond Western literary theoretical orientations to bring Indigeneity to the forefront of all factors being considered. Indigenous identity of authors and audiences, the contexts of Indigenous cultural survival in various eras and regions, the foundation of Indigenous philosophy in language structure and discourse patterns, tropes, symbols, metaphors, and methods: in sum these contribute to a reading in survivance.[7] Therefore our study of Indigenous poetics may necessarily draw from diverse fields to provide us with insight into Indigenous consciousness, and understanding how meaning is coded, transmitted, and decoded. Methods and analytical tools from Indigenous philosophy, Indigenous language, ethno-poetics, and sociolinguistics are some ways to access interpretation of meaning in Indigenous cultural expressions. But in effect all of these are academics' efforts to access Indigenous knowledge recorded in literate forms and apply them to our interpretation of the meaning and values in Indigenous literature.

For the idea of using an Indigenous framework for interpreting the embedded orality in *Halfbreed*, I am indebted to Womack's book *Red on Red: Native American Literary Separatism*.[8] However the cultural contexts of Cree, Saulteaux, and Métis challenge the unequivocal use of "tribally specific" concerns of literary separatism because the notion of "tribe" imposes artificial and mutually exclusive categories upon Nēhiyawak, Nahkowēwak, and Métis groups who have cohabited in bands, shared kinship, and had cultural exchange for centuries.[9] Innes argues that rather than tribe or race, kinship more accurately describes the social organization of groups of Indigenous peoples in the northern plains region.[10] He references Macdougall's work, which challenges the essentialized cultural standard of Métis, and McLeod's work, which describes genealogical ambiguities

in First Nations bands.[11] St-Onge characterizes Métis and Saulteaux eth-
nic identities as "fluid, relational and situational," which is most helpful
in understanding that there are similarities and cultural sharing between
communities of people.[12] These scholars have affirmed that the nuances of
relationships and situations make it appropriate and necessary to use different terms for the group being discussed. And so I use "Cree," "Métis,"
and "Indigenous" for the discussion here. I use the term "Cree" with some
confidence knowing that Maria Campbell and her family are Cree speakers.
In her story, Campbell describes the kin, cultural, and political relationships between the Cree and Halfbreeds, and refers to the political organization of Métis. I use the term "Halfbreed" to reference the title of the book,
and to insider self-naming of the community to which Maria Campbell's
family belonged in the parkland region of the northern plains in the late
nineteenth and first half of the twentieth century. I use the term "Métis"
as it is currently and commonly used by academics to refer to the diverse
historically rooted cultural manifestations of the relationships among Cree,
Saulteaux, English, and French in the northern plains region. I also use the
inclusive term "Indigenous," partly to acknowledge Campbell's cultural and
political self-identification as Halfbreed, but also to acknowledge the multicultural Cree and Saulteaux sources that are the basis of my interpretation
of the rhetorical form. I draw my understanding of Elders' oral discourse
from the recorded, translated, and interpreted counselling speeches of Cree
Elder Jim Kâ-Nîpitêhtêw from Onion Lake, Saskatchewan, Cree Elder Louis
Sunchild from Hobbema, Alberta, and Saulteaux Elder Alfred Manitopeyes
from Muskcowekwun, Saskatchewan.[13] From these and other cited sources,
I concluded that the cultural ethic of personal autonomy, characteristics of
Elder's discourse, and features of high and low rhetoric are shared among
the groups.[14] For this reason, I interpret the authority of Saulteaux teachings and philosophy to also apply to Cree and Métis in this region. If I am
overgeneralizing, I trust future writers will offer clarification.

Characteristics of Cree and Saulteaux Elders' Counselling Discourse
Readers of Cheechum's counsel in *Halfbreed*, who attend to the text as if listening to an Elder's quiet way of telling, open themselves to understanding
the wisdom conveyed by an Elder's counselling discourse.[15] My phrase "listening to a quiet way of telling" is inspired by Elder Jim Kâ-Nîpitêhtêw, who
in a counselling speech, referenced a certain old man who had counselled
him on the topic of counselling the young. The Cree word okakêshkihkê-
mowina with the verb root kakêskim meaning "counsel him" is transitive
and animate.[16] Linguistically and ontologically this indicates relationship
between animate beings. He said:

Our children and grandchildren do not understand us in anything, even when we tell them about something quietly, they do not understand us. They have to be made to understand in particular how young people used to be counseled in the old days, young women and men; how they have always accepted the good things which their parents have been telling them, or their grandfathers and grandmothers.[17]

Elder Kâ-Nîpitêhtêw uses the phrase "telling them about something quietly" to refer to the counselling that is given to the younger generation. It is a subtle but powerful reference to the philosophy of teaching and learning.

Elder Alfred Manitopeyes tape-recorded a talk about Native education and Linda Akan translated and interpreted it for publication. Elder Manitopeyes refers to Elders' counsel using the word "keekimiquotoh-kainuk" modified by the word "soohngun," meaning "She received a powerful teaching."[18] But he prefaces this with "My grandchild also listened to them—I will say first—she listened to her grandfather, and also to her grandmother —when they raised her as a young girl."[19] From Elder Manitopeyes we understand the pedagogical importance of being in relationship with, and listening to, the Elder. Elder Manitopeyes names her by kinship term and acknowledges that she received her counselling/teaching from her grandparents, her grandmother in particular.

Education has a spiritual foundation, and an Elder's role is to engage the learner in a process of making him or herself wholly human.[20] In his interpretation of Elder Louis Sunchild's discourse, Lightning echoes this understanding of the spiritual foundation of education:

Learning is not a product of transferring information between a teacher and a student. It is a product of creation and re-creation, in a mutual relationship of personal interaction, of information. It is not just a cognitive (mental) act, but an emotional—thus physical act. Learning is felt. It is a sensation. It is something that involves emotions. And as the elder here points out, learning is a spiritual thing, because the compassionate mind is one that is spiritually centered.[21]

The Elder's counselling discourse has a formal intonation, is spoken quietly and gently like a prayer, and helps the learner to connect to time, place, and self in the cosmos. Akan interprets Manitipeyes's words about Native education for us by writing: "Learning involves thinking hard about who you are; ultimately learning is a process that 'resolves,' involves,' and 'revolves.' Learning is good thinking."[22]

Akan tells us that an Elder's counselling discourse is "a process of give and take that is implicit in the discourse" and that "if we can imagine a visual representation of this process, we would see two acts occurring simultaneously from different perspectives."[23] She explains that the listener's role is active because

> Saulteaux discourse leaves things out —leaves them unsaid—when the point is thought to be pertinent to the learning of the student. Thus a "good talk"...will invite students to do their own work, to find their own answers. The Elder simply makes the connection to our Ancestors.[24]

The ethic of individual autonomy guides the philosophy of education wherein the learner is responsible for his or her own learning. Lightning informs us that the Elder, in a relationship of engagement and attention with the learner, uses systems of implications to guide the learner in making meaning. That is, the Elder "state[s] things in such a way that there is a continuing unfolding of the meaning, as the learner follows the implications of a statement...."[25] The Elder does not state things categorically or specifically, and uses metaphors so that the learner must "look for relationships and metaphors that he is going to specify. Remembering the metaphors and relationships, we will gain understanding as we develop."[26] We will see how this aspect of Indigenous education is a keen part of the development of the narrator guided by Cheechum. An Elder's teaching is an act of love. The learners, being respectful of the Elder's compassion, experience, and wisdom, engage as active participants hearing what the Elder tells them in a quiet prayerful way.

"Learning to listen to a quiet way of telling" is key to understanding Cree epistemology and pedagogy. Willie Ermine explains that a legitimate way to construct knowledge in Cree world view is through subjective inward exploration. He names it "mamatowisowin" and explains that "is the capacity to tap the creative force of the inner space by the use of all the faculties that constitute our being—it is to exercise inwardness" (104). It "refers not just to the self but to the being in connection with happenings."[27]

This concept of inward exploration is the process described by Elder Alfred Manitopeyes whereby the Elder, through his or her counselling speech or "good talk," facilitates the young person's inward exploration and use of all faculties of his or her being to increase self-knowledge as a spiritual, physical, intellectual, and emotional being.[28] Thus the cultural context of listening to a quiet way of telling is one in which the listener constructs knowledge using all faculties of his or her being. Listening to an Elder's counselling speech is meditative, collaborative, and active. Learning is the listener's responsibility. The Elder respects the learner's autonomy and does not impose understanding upon the learner. This last feature is the basis of the interactional reading by which a reader sensitive to Indigenous Elder's counsel would recognize the teaching Cheechum shared with Maria[29] and, by extension, the reader.

Patterns of Elder's Counselling Discourse in Halfbreed

A close reading of *Halfbreed* lends an Indigenous perspective of the author's expression of cultural, sacred, and historical knowledge. The Cree counselling discourse patterns that work rhetorically to effect learning in the reader are found in the introduction of the book, the connection of the audience to time and place, the use of second-person narration, and the use of metaphor.

"Learning to listen to a quiet way of telling" is a phrase that identifies the process of learning from her Cheechum that Maria, the primary narrator of *Halfbreed*, experiences and reveals for the reader. The narrator, in recounting her remembrances of her great-grandmother, reflects on the teachings she received in childhood and her understanding that developed in adulthood. The phrase also instructs contemporary audiences how to read written records of Indigenous oral discourse. Encouragement and guidance may be intuited from the words of Elder Kâ-Nîpitêhtêw when he gave permission for his speeches to be recorded and used for future educational use. He said, "[t]hat is why it is better that we should leave behind good things for them to use, for example, that they might listen on this kind [points to the audio-recorder] and that the young might thereby remind one another."[30] *Halfbreed* is a powerful "good thing" for us to use because the author deftly incorporates through Cheechum the teaching philosophy of Cree counselling discourse within the telling of her own story. Some may argue that *Halfbreed* belongs to the genre of Western auto-biography.[31] But Campbell herself says that she thinks of it as her story, not an autobiography or "full life story" because she was a young woman, barely thirty years old when she wrote it.[32]

Interpreting meaning in this story about her life, which the young Métis woman prepared for a largely non-Native Canadian audience, requires a conscientious understanding of the work's features, which draw upon the tradition of a Cree counselling tradition. First, the purpose of an Elder's counselling speech is to assist young people to find peace of mind through proper conduct. "Finding peace of mind" with the guidance of an Elder is an anchor in the story that provides coherence throughout. Indeed, the text is a record of her writings that Campbell engaged in to find peace of mind.[33] In the introduction, the narrator explains, "[l]ike me the land had changed, my people were gone, and if I was to know peace I would have to search within myself. That is when I decided to write about my life,"[34] The search within herself is the inward exploration described by

Ermine. Second, Maria's great-grandmother Cheechum functions as a secondary narrator of the text because more than half of the book involves
Maria's recollection of her memory of and interaction with Cheechum,
who personifies the cultural traits of a Cree Elder and teacher. Cheechum
left the learning to the individual, a clear expression of the value of the
autonomy of the learner identified by Akan and Lightning. Examples of
this are how the great-grandmother did not interfere in the narrator's decision to marry and move to Vancouver, and of her non-judgment when the
narrator returns home as a young woman and confides her experiences.
"When I had finished, she said, 'It's over now. Don't let it hurt you. Since
you were a baby you've had to learn the hard way. You're like me.'"[35] The
subsequent section, which discusses second-person narration, will argue
that Cheechum as an Elder functions as an integral link in the transmission of knowledge accessible through the book.

A brief review of some salient features of counselling texts as they are
explicated by Lightning, Akan, and Wolfart are useful to qualify the argument that *Halfbreed* draws from the tradition of Indigenous Elder's oral
discourse. The Elder's discourse conforms with its expressions of humility,
gratitude, and phrases to connect listeners to the four domains[36] and link
listener and speaker.[37] Wolfart, in his notes and commentary about Elders'
oral discourse, draws attention to the *apologia* at the beginning wherein
the speaker declares that he or she has been bidden to speak by those in the
audience and by the Elders. Akan and Wolfart note the trope of beginning
with the Elder making reference to the present place and the people in the
audience. The Elder identifies himself by name and place. Wolfart notes
that Elder Kâ-Nîpitêhtêw's counselling speech begins and ends with specific events, and affirms the authority of the speaker invoked by relating his
father's visionary experiences, thereby linking the audience and speaker to
the ethos, connecting the physical and spiritual domains.[38] Though *Halfbreed* is a written text, and as such it precludes the union of the audience
to the spiritual and physical domain in the face-to-face happening of the
discourse, it features forms and structures reminiscent of the Cree rhetoric
employed by the example studied by Wolfart. A close reading of the introduction and the first three chapters reveals that these structures survive the
translation and literation.

In the introduction of *Halfbreed*, the narrator expresses humility and
places herself in relation to the land, her ancestors, and the audience. The
image of "gophers scurry[ing] back and forth over the sunken graves"[39]
reveals the attitude toward life that Akan calls "accept[ing] life at face
value."[40] To a Euro-Canadian sensibility, the image may seem an opposi-

tional pairing of the profane and the sacred, the lowly and the revered, yet from an Indigenous perspective, it is an image of the everlasting life energy that animates the gopher and that also once animated the human beings whose remains have returned to the earth. The absence of her people and the buildings that housed the work they did, juxtaposed with the thriving roses, tiger lilies, thistle, and poplar trees, emphasize the place of human beings in the physical and spiritual domains. The book was originally published for a Canadian audience and this demographic is appealed to in the introduction. The narrator addresses them directly by telling them, "I write this for all of you, to tell you what it is like to be a Halfbreed woman in our country. I want to tell you about the joys and sorrows, the oppressing poverty, the frustrations and the dreams."[41] The Canadian audience would recognize the pine trees and beavers, icons of Canadian national identity, that appear in the first paragraph of the introduction. So too would the audience recognize their familiar stereotypes of "[t]he Halfbreed families who squatted on the road allowances [and who] have moved to nearby towns where welfare hand-outs and booze are handier, or else deeper into the bush as an escape from reality."[42] The emotions of the audience are stirred by the image of a ghost town and of the old generation, "the crippled, bent old grandfathers and grandmothers on town and city skid rows...in the bush waiting to die or baby-sitting grandchildren while the parents are drunk," and of the young generation like the narrator, who "continue[s] to struggle for equality and justice for their people."[43] The historical references to her ancestors in chapters 1 and 2 establish the temporal and spatial orientation of the narrator, the Canadian audience, and the subject of the story. However, this historical orientation also affirms the authority of the narrator in the tradition of Cree storytelling.

Wolfart explains that it is customary for the speaker at the beginning of any Cree discourse—historical, factual, counselling, or prophetic—to legitimate his or her authority to speak and to affirm the veracity of the story.[44] In *Halfbreed*, the narrator recalls historical dates, events, and geographical locales that are familiar to the audience's conception of reality. In Cree tradition the function of such an introduction goes beyond simply establishing the setting of the story. It establishes the authority, veracity, and deference of the speaker. It connects the audience to the subject matter and qualifies the trust they grant the narrator in her account. The narrator starts by calling forth her ancestors and recounting their lives lived from the 1840s to the 1930s. This appeal to aid of the ancestors, those gone to the spirit world, effectively swears to the truth of the story presented to the limits of the storyteller's capacity. In a discourse that unites speaker and listener in physical and metaphysical domains, and affirms the authority of the narrator to tell her story as she understood it at the age she was, the importance of the appeal to ancestors cannot be overstated.

The introduction reveals other characteristics of counselling discourse. For one, it conforms to the convention in Cree storytelling to avoid personal names where kin terms will serve instead.[45] Nowhere in *Halfbreed* does the great-grandmother's given name appear. The convention comes into greater focus in the reading of Chapter 2. This very key figure in the text is initially identified not by name but as a woman in reference to her husband: "Great Grandpa married a Halfbreed woman, a niece of Gabriel Dumont" and "both brothers had wanted the same woman."[46] Her identity and suffering is affirmed by the stories told by the old people about her husband. "They say he was very cruel and would beat his son, his wife, and his livestock with the same whip and with equal vengeance...."[47] Her character emerges standing in active opposition to the oppression of a husband's misogyny and the Canadian government's colonization. "She in turn passed on all the information she heard at these meetings to the rebels and also stole ammunition and supplies for them from his store."[48] Her competence and certainty are revealed in the narrator's telling us:

> She built a cabin beside Maria Lake and raised her son. Years later when the area was designated for the Park, the government asked her to leave. She refused, and when all peaceful methods failed the RCMP were sent. She locked her door, loaded her rifle, and when they arrived she fired shots over their heads, threatening to hit them if they came any closer.[49]

A full paragraph follows, detailing her physical appearance before the author offers: "Great Grandma Campbell, whom I always called 'Cheechum,' was the niece of Gabriel Dumont and her whole family fought beside Riel and Dumont during the Rebellion."[50] Cheechum thus is a link to the land, the ancestors, and the self-reliant spirit of Métis people.[51]

The line following this identification of Cheechum is the first direct quote of her speech. This brings into focus a very important characteristic of Cree counselling text that is foundational to the power of the teaching potential of *Halfbreed*: the idea that Cheechum is one of two narrators. The use of two narrators is a convention found in recorded Cree historical, factual, prophetic, and counselling texts. Wolfart notes that "Cree texts seem to have a high proportion of directly quoted speech."[52] Further repetition of quotatives accentuate the fact that the story is another person's first-person narrative. The secondary storyteller adds commentary in the form of parenthetical asides, the use of the third person, and the use of direct speech, which authenticates the orally transmitted dialogue.[53] Maria, the first narrator in *Halfbreed*, uses all these devices to subtly incorporate Cheechum's voice. The book began as a search for peace of mind and it is culturally appropriate to recall Elder's discourse and weave it into the narrative to achieve this effect.

Cheechum's first quoted speech articulates the theme that is fundamental to the story. Maria narrates:

> She often told me stories of the Rebellion and of the Halfbreed people. She said our people never wanted to fight because that was not our way. We never wanted anything except to be left alone to live as we pleased. Cheechum never accepted defeat at Batoche, and she would always say, "Because they killed Riel they think they have killed us too, but some day my girl it will be different."[54]

The narrator characterizes Cheechum as a Cree Halfbreed woman certain of her identity and philosophy of life. The narrator interprets Cheechum for us in asides and third-person paraphrase:

> Cheechum hated to see the setters come, and as they settled on what she believed was our land, she ignored them and refused to acknowledge them even when passing on the road. She would not become a Christian, saying firmly that she had married a Christian and if there was such a thing as hell then she had lived there; nothing after death could be worse! Offers of relief from welfare were scorned and so was the old age pension. While she lived alone she hunted and trapped, planted a garden, and was completely self-sufficient.[55]

But we must not forget that the story traces the route of a young woman's gradual comprehension of the Elder's teaching, and arrival at self-knowledge. The narrator deftly traces this route through the stages of her own development. The reader similarly progresses through stages of understanding. This rendering of the story conforms to the Cree cultural counselling discourse.

Akan explains that among the features of an Elder's teaching discourse or "good talk" is that the story is deliberately told in simple language so that it is accessible to all ages of maturity and understanding.[56] *Halfbreed* is like this. Cheechum's words are very simple and seemingly straightforward in meaning, but they are complex in that they convey meaning at multiple levels. At the beginning, the story seems historical and sociological, but by the end of the book, and certainly with subsequent readings at stages of growing maturity, the story has teaching about human psychology and spirituality. The inward exploration that it invites is as complex as the reader permits. The narrator within the book realizes her own development. An example of this can be discerned by examining the metaphor of the blanket. In adulthood, the narrator recalls Cheechum's use of the metaphor of the blanket:

> My Cheechum used to tell me that when the government gives you some-thing they take all that you have in return—your pride, your dignity, all the things that make you a living soul. When they are sure they have everything, they give you a blanket to cover your shame. She said that the churches, with their talk about God, the Devil, heaven and hell, and schools that taught children to be ashamed, were all a part of that government.[57]

As a child, the narrator reasoned with her great-grandmother that the gov-ernment was made by the people, to which the old lady said, "It only looks like that from the outside my girl."[58] As an adult the narrator witnessed Indian parents who cowered in the face of racist brutality, and she under-stood the meaning of her great-grandmother's words and related it to her own self-understanding:

> I understood about the blanket now—I wore one too. I didn't know when I started to wear it, but it was there and I didn't know how to throw it away. So I understood about those boys' parents—it was easier for them to stay in the car. If they came out from under their blankets, they'd have to face reality, ugly as it was.[59]

When the narrator as an adult speaks to her great-grandmother of her com-munity activism and her understanding that people need their dignity and self-reliance to survive, her Cheechum responds by employing the metaphor of the blanket again:

> I'm glad you believe that, and I hope you will never forget it. Each of us has to find himself in his own way and no one can do it for us. If we try to do more we only take away the very thing that makes us a living soul. The blanket only destroys, it doesn't give warmth. But you will understand that better as you get older.[60]

The Elder uses the mnemonic device of the blanket metaphor to help the narrator comprehend her own development, maturity, and identity. She alludes to the narrator's future reference to the mnemonic device that will identify for her continued maturation and growth of understanding.

In 1988, Elder Kâ-Nîpitêhtêw explained how youth and Elders relate to each other in a counselling talk:

> A young woman listened most carefully to the things her grandmother, especially, warned her about. Of course the "old woman," as she was called, had come to be experienced in always treating everything with respect. That is what she used to pass on to her grandchildren, how the children and grandchildren have peace of mind, how they would be given peace of mind.[61]

Cheechum's counsel in *Halfbreed* affords the readers a valuable lesson about learning to listen to a quiet way of telling a serious story. *Halfbreed* is an example of a story that relies on two narrators, Cheechum and Maria, as two links in the cultural transmission of counselling the young generation. Campbell has recorded the words of her great-grandmother that are good things left behind so that we may use them and thereby remind one another of how to seek peace of mind through proper conduct. What Cheechum gave to her great-grandaughter, Maria Campbell has shared with us: the experience of interacting with Elder's counselling discourse to pay attention to the relationships of implied meaning and metaphors to check our own development. In the field of Indigenous rhetorics, *Halbreed* provides an example of a contemporary work of literature that draws upon its heritage of a cultural discourse to convey meaning and motivate readers to reflect and act on the values that guide peace of mind.

Notes

I wrote the first iteration of this paper for a graduate course "Imagining an American Indian Intellectual Tradition" taught by Malea Powell at Michigan State University. For stimulating my thinking about Indigenous rhetorics as material and textual productions, I extend my thanks to Dr. Powell and my classmates Qwo-Li Driskill, Angela Haas, Rain Gomez, Julie O'Connor-Colvin and Andréa Davis. I am grateful to Neal McLeod, who offered suggestions and questions that helped me improve the paper. I am especially indebted to Maria Campbell and Danny Musqua, who have generously shared good talks with me.

1 Malea Powell, "This Is a Story about Belief," for "Octalog III: The Politics of Historiography in 2010," *Rhetoric Review* 30, no. 2 (2011): 120–23; Ernest Stromberg, *American Indian Rhetorics of Survivance: Word Medicine, Word Magic* (Pittsburg: University of Pittsburg Press, 2006).
2 Powell, This Is a Story about Belief," 121.
3 Ibid., 123.
4 Stromberg, *American Indian Rhetorics of Survivance*, 4–5.
5 See Susan Gingell's critical work on linguistic blending of Cree and English in the writing of Cree and Métis authors. Susan Gingell, "Lips' Inking: Cree and Cree-Metis Authors' Writings of the Oral and What They Might tell Educators," *Canadian Journal of Native Education* 32 (Supplement) (2011): 35–61. Also, Marieke Neuhaus examines the linguistic transference of the holophrase (one-word sentence) form to identify a textualized orality of an Indigenous author's works. Marieke Neuhaus, *"That's Raven Talk": Holophrastic Readings of Contemporary Indigenous Literatures* (Regina: Canadian Plains Research Center, 2011). Janice Acoose explores how Nehiyawiwis-Métis storytellers fuse written and oral forms of knowledge through mastery of Indigenous languages and English. Janice Acoose, "Honouring *Ni'Wahkomakanak*," in *Reasoning Together: The Native Critics Collective*, ed. Craig Womack, Daniel

Heath Justice, and Christopher B. Teuton (Norman: University of Oklahoma Press, 2008), 216–33.

6 M. H. Abrams, *A Glossary of Literary Terms* (7th ed.) (Fort Worth: Harcourt Brace College Publishers, 1999), 51–52.

7 Vizenor coined the term. "Survivance is an active sense of presence, the continuance of native stories, not a mere reaction, or a survivable name. Native survivance stories are renunciations of dominance, tragedy, and victimry." Gerald Vizenor, *Manifest Manners: Narratives on Postindian Survivance* (Lincoln: University of Nebraska Press, 1994), vii.

8 Craig Womack, *Red on Red: Native American Literary Separatism* (Minneapolis: University of Minnesota Press, 1999).

9 Naming of groups immediately delineates the conventions of a historical period, status of insider/outsider, the privilege and power of self-naming and outsider naming, the primacy of selected relationships, and the lines distinguishing a separate sense of belonging. For the purpose of this chapter, I use the terms "Cree" to refer to the people self-named as Nêhiyawak who speak or whose ancestors spoke Nêhiyawêwin; "Saulteaux" to refer to the people outsider-named as Plains Ojibwa and self-named as Nahkawêwak who speak or whose ancestors spoke Nahkawêwin, the plains dialect of Anishinaabemowin; "Métis" to refer to the peoples self-named as Métis and Halfbreeds who speak or whose ancestors spoke a number of languages, including Michif, Cree, Saulteaux, French, and English. Even so I add the acknowledgement that multilingual ability and cross-cultural sharing constituted a norm up to the early twentieth century. Indeed, the name Nahkawê is reputed to be a name given to the Plains Ojibwe by the Cree and is understood to refer to their close alliance with the Cree. See Diane Knight, *The Seven Fires: Teachings of The Bear Clan as Told by Dr. Danny Musqua* (Muskoday First Nation, SK: Many Worlds, 2001), 30. Depending on the pronunciation and spelling of the regional dialect, the term is interpreted to mean either "middle of the road" or "brothers who speak in a start and stop pattern." Danny Musqua, personal communication, May 23, 2012.

10 Robert Alexander Innes, "Multicultural Bands on the Northern Plains and the Notion of 'Tribal Histories,'" in *Finding a Way to the Heart*, ed. Robin Jarvis Brownlie and Valerie J. Korinek (Winnipeg: University of Manitoba, 2012).

11 Brenda Macdougall, "*Wahkootowin*: Family and Cultural Identity in Northwestern Saskatchewan Métis Communities," *Canadian Historical Review* 87, no. 3 (2006): 431–62; Neal McLeod, "Plains Cree Identity: Borderlands, Ambiguous Genealogies and Narrative Irony," *Canadian Journal of Native Studies* 20, no. 2 (2000): 437–54.

12 Nicole St-Onge, "Uncertain Margins: Métis and Saulteaux in St. Paul des Saulteaux, Red River, 1821–1870," *Manitoba History* 53 (2006): 2–10.

13 Jim Kâ-Nîpitêhtêw, Freda Ahenakew, H. Christoph Wolfart, and Algonquian Text Society, *ana kâ-pimwêwêhahk okakêsihkêmowina: The Counselling Speeches of Jim Kâ-Nîpitêhtêw, Publications of the Algonquian Text Society*

(Winnipeg: University of Manitoba Press, 1998); Linda Akan, *"Pimosatamowin Sikaw Kakeequaywin*: Walking and Talking; A Saulteaux Elder's View of Education," *Canadian Journal of Native Education* 23, no. 1 (1999): 16–39; Walter Lightning, "Compassionate Mind: Implications of a Text Written by Elder Louis Sunchild," *Canadian Journal of Native Education* 19, no. 2 (1992): 217–53.

14 See Joseph Couture, "What Is Fundamental to Native Education? Some Thoughts on the Relationship Between Thinking, Feeling, and Learning," in *Contemporary Educational Issues: The Canadian Mosaic*, ed. Leonard L. Stewin and Stewart J. H. McCann (Toronto: Clark Pitman, 1987), 178–91; Willie Ermine, "Aboriginal Epistemology," in *First Nations Education in Canada: The Circle Unfolds*, ed. Marie Battiste and Jean Barman (Vancouver: UBC Press, 1995); Basil Johnston, *Ojibway Heritage: The Ceremonies, Rituals, Songs, Dances, Prayers, and Legends of the Ojibway* (Toronto: McClelland and Stewart, 1998); Knight, *The Seven Fires*; Alexander Wolfe, *Earth Elder Stories: The Pinayzitt Path* (Saskatoon: Fifth House, 1998).

15 *Cheechum* is the spelling as it appears in *Halfbreed*. The Plains Cree spelling of the word is cīhcâm. Neal McLeod, personal communication, April 30, 2012.

16 Jean Okimasis, *Cree Language of the Plains, Nehiyawēwin Paskwawi-pīkiskwēwin* (Regina: Canadian Plains Research Center, 2004), 189.

17 Kâ-Nîpitêhtêw et al., *ana kâ-pimwêwêhahk okakêskihkêmowina*, 47.

18 The spelling of the Saulteaux words in quotation is written as it appears in Linda Akan's article. A reference for standard Saulteaux or Nahkawēwin orthography has not yet been published. The Saskatchewan Indian Culture Centre's (SICC) website attests to the regional variance in the language, indicating that the language is influenced by Cree, and that the ten Saskatchewan First Nations communities have their own unique dialects of the language. See SICC, "Nahkawē," http://www.sicc.sk.ca/nahkawe.html. Arok Wolvengrey has published a paper outlining the commonalities between Cree and Saulteaux language features and spelling systems. Arok Wolvengrey, "On the Spelling and Pronunciation of First Nations Languages and Place Names," in *Prairie Forum* 23, no. 1 (1998): 113–25.

19 Akan, *"Pimosatamowin Sikaw Kakeequaywin,"* 19–20.

20 Ibid., 19.

21 Lightning, "Compassionate Mind," 232.

22 Akan, *"Pimosatamowin Sikaw Kakeequaywin,"* 17.

23 Ibid., 18.

24 Ibid., 30.

25 Lightning, "Compassionate Mind," 232.

26 Ibid., 233.

27 Ermine, "Aboriginal Epistemology," 104.

28 Akan, *Pimosatamowin Sikaw Kakeequaywin*, 19.

29 Following the conventions in literary criticism, I use "Maria" when referring to the narrator in the story, and "Campbell" when referring to the author.

30 Kâ-Nîpitêhtêw et al., *ana ka-pimwewehahk okakeskihkemowina*, vii.

31 Armando Jannetta examines *Halfbreed* as autobiography using postmodern deconstruction (citing Foucault and Barthes). He resolves it with collaborative and collective aspects of Native preliterate narratives (citing Bakhtin, Bierhorst, Brumble, and Krupat) and concludes that it represents a new genre of autobiography as resistance literature (citing Allen and Derrida). See Armando E. Jannetta, "Métis Autobiography: The Emergence of a Genre Amid Alienation, Resistance, and Healing in the Context of Maria Campbell's *Halfbreed* (1973)," *International Journal of Canadian Studies* 12 (Fall) (1995): 169–81; Michael Bakhtin, *The Dialogic Imagination: Four Essays by Mikhail Bakhtin*, ed. Michael Holquist (Austin: University of Texas Press, 1981); Roland Barthes, "The Death of the Author," in *Issues in Contemporary Critical Theory*, ed. Peter Barry (London: Macmillan, 1982); John Bierhorst, "Introduction," in *In the Trail of the Wind: American Indian Poems and Ritual Orations*, ed. John Bierhorst (New York: Farrar, Straus and Giroux, 1971); David H. Brumble, III. *American Indian Autobiography* (Berkeley: University of California Press, 1988); Jacques Derrida, *Of Grammatology*, trans. Gayatri Chakravorty Spivak (Baltimore: Johns Hopkins University Press, 1976); Michel Foucault, "What Is an Author?," in *Language, Counter-memory, Practice: Selected Essays and Interviews*, ed. Donald F. Bouchard (Ithaca: Cornell University Press, 1977); Arnold Krupat, *For Those Who Come After: A Study of Native American Autobiography* (Berkeley: University of California Press, 1985); Paula Gunn Allen, *Spider Woman's Granddaughters: Traditional Tales and Contemporary Writing by Native American Women* (London: Women's Press, 1990).

32 Maria Campbell, personal communication, April 29, 2012.

33 In an interview with Hartmut Lutz, Maria Campbell explained that *Halfbreed* began as letters she wrote to herself seeking peace of mind. See Hartmut Lutz, "Interview with Maria Campbell," in *Contemporary Challenges: Conversations with Canadian Native Authors* (Saskatoon: Fifth House Publishers, 1991).

34 Maria Campbell, *Halfbreed* (Toronto: McClelland and Stewart, 1973), 7–8.

35 Ibid., 149.

36 Lightning names these as "mental, physical, spiritual, along with behavioural, emotional, and sensory." Lightning, "Compassionate Mind," 233.

37 Ibid., 229–30; Akan, "*Pimosatamowin Sikaw Kakeequaywin*," 17–19.

38 H. C. Wolfart, "Commentary and Notes," in Jim Kâ-Nipitêhtêw, Freda Ahenakew, H. Christoph Wolfart, and Algonquian Text Society, *Ana Kâ-pim-wêwêhahk Okakêskihkêmowina: The Counselling Speeches of Jim Kâ-Nîpitêhtêw*, *Publications of the Algonquian Text Society* (Winnipeg: University of Manitoba Press, 1998), 141–42.

39 Campbell, *Halfbreed*, 7.

40 Akan, "*Pimosatamowin Sikaw Kakeequaywin*," 18.

41 Campbell, *Halfbreed*, 8.

42 Ibid., 7.

43 Ibid., 13.

44 Wolfart, "Commentary and Notes," 141; Alice Ahenakew, Freda Ahenakew, H. Christoph Wolfart, and Algonquian Text Society, *âh-âyîtaw isi ê-kî-kiskêy-ihtahkik maskihkiy: They Knew Both Sides of Medicine: Cree Tales of Curing and Cursing, Publications of the Algonquian Text Society* (Winnipeg: University of Manitoba Press, 2000), 145.

45 Ahenakew et al., *âh-âyîtaw isi ê-kî-kiskêyihtahkik maskihkiy*, 168.

46 Campbell, *Halfbreed*, 14.

47 Ibid., 14.

48 Ibid.

49 Ibid., 15.

50 Ibid.

51 Cheechum was also the niece of Atâhk-akohp. This and other details of the genealogy came to Campbell's attention in the years following the publication. Maria Campbell, personal communication, April 29, 2012; Neal McLeod, personal email, April 30, 2012.

52 Ahenakew et al., *ah-âyîtaw isi ê-kî-kiskêyihtahkik maskihkiy*, 145.

53 Ibid., 145–46.

54 Campbell, *Halfbreed*, 15.

55 Ibid.

56 Akan, "*Pimosatamowin Sikaw Kakeequaywin*," 33.

57 Campbell, *Halfbreed*, 137.

58 Ibid.

59 Ibid.

60 Ibid., 149–50.

61 Kâ-Nîpitêhtêw et al., *ana kâ-pimwêwêhahk okakêskihkêmowina*, 47.

Bibliography

Abrams, M. H. *A Glossary of Literary Terms* (7th ed.). Fort Worth: Harcourt Brace College Publishers, 1999.

Acoose, Janice. "Honouring *Ni'Wahkomakanak*." In *Reasoning Together: The Native Critics Collective*, edited by Craig Womack, Daniel Heath Justice, and Christopher B. Teuton, 216–33. Norman: University of Oklahoma Press, 2008.

Akan, Linda. "*Pimosatamowin Sikaw Kakeequaywin*: Walking and Talking; A Saulteaux Elder's View of Education." *Canadian Journal of Native Education* 23, no. 1 (1999): 16–39.

Allen, Paula Gunn. *Spider Woman's Granddaughters: Traditional Tales and Contemporary Writing by Native American Women*. London: Women's Press, 1990.

Bakhtin, Michael. *The Dialogic Imagination: Four Essays by Mikhail Bakhtin*, edited by Michael Holquist. Austin: University of Texas Press, 1981.

Barthes, Roland. "The Death of the Author." In *Issues in Contemporary Critical Theory*, edited by Peter Barry, 114–37. London: Macmillan, 1982.

Bierhorst, John. "Introduction." In *In the Trail of the Wind: American Indian Poems and Ritual Orations*, edited by John Bierhorst. New York: Farrar, Straus and Giroux, 1971.

Brumble III, David H. *American Indian Autobiography.* Berkeley: University of California Press, 1988.

Campbell, Maria. *Halfbreed.* Toronto: McClelland and Stewart, 1973.

Couture, Joseph. "What Is Fundamental to Native Education? Some Thoughts on the Relationship Between Thinking, Feeling, and Learning." In *Contemporary Educational Issues: The Canadian Mosaic*, edited by Leonard L. Stewin and Stewart J. H. McCann, 178–91. Toronto: Clark Pitman, 1987.

Derrida, Jacques. *Of Grammatology*, translated by Gayatri Chakravorty Spivak. Baltimore: Johns Hopkins University Press, 1976.

Ermine, Willie. "Aboriginal Epistemology." In *First Nations Education in Canada: The Circle Unfolds*, edited by Marie Battiste and Jean Barman, 101–12. Vancouver: UBC Press, 1995.

Foucault, Michel. "What Is an Author?" In *Language, Counter-memory, Practice: Selected Essays and Interviews*, edited by Donald F. Bouchard, 114–37. Ithaca: Cornell University Press, 1977.

Gingell, Susan. "'Lips' Inking: Cree and Cree-Metis Authors' Writings of the Oral and What They Might tell Educators." *Canadian Journal of Native Education* 32 (Supplement) (2011): 35–61.

Innes, Robert Alexander. "Multicultural Bands on the Northern Plains and the Notion of 'Tribal Histories.'" In *Finding a Way to the Heart*, edited by Robin Jarvis Brownlie and Valerie J. Korinek, 122–45. Winnipeg: University of Manitoba, 2012.

Jannetta, Armando E. "Métis Autobiography: The Emergence of a Genre Amid Alienation, Resistance, and Healing in the Context of Maria Campbell's *Halfbreed* (1973)." *International Journal of Canadian Studies* 12 (Fall) (1995): 169–81.

Johnston, Basil. *Ojibway Heritage: The Ceremonies, Rituals, Songs, Dances, Prayers, and Legends of the Ojibway.* Toronto: McClelland and Stewart, 1998.

Kâ-Nîpitêhtêw, Jim, Freda Ahenakew, H. Christoph Wolfart, and Algonquian Text Society. *ana kâ-pimwêwêhahk okakêskihkêmowina: The Counselling Speeches of Jim Kâ-Nîpitêhtêw, Publications of the Algonquian Text Society.* Winnipeg: University of Manitoba Press, 1998.

Knight, Diane. *The Seven Fires: Teachings of The Bear Clan as Told by Dr. Danny Musqua.* Muskoday First Nation, SK: Many Worlds, 2001.

Krupat, Arnold. *For Those Who Come After: A Study of Native American Autobiography.* Berkeley: University of California Press, 1985.

Lightning, Walter. "Compassionate Mind: Implications of a Text Written by Elder Louis Sunchild." *Canadian Journal of Native Education* 19, no. 2 (1992): 217–53.

Lutz, Hartmut. "Interview with Maria Campbell." In *Contemporary Challenges: Conversations with Canadian Native Authors*, edited by Hartmut Lutz, 41–65. Saskatoon: Fifth House Publishers, 1991.

Macdougall, Brenda. "*Wahkootowin*: Family and Cultural Identity in Northwestern Saskatchewan Métis Communities." *Canadian Historical Review* 87, no. 3 (2006): 431–62.

McLeod, Neal. "Plains Cree Identity: Borderlands, Ambiguous Genealogies, and Narrative Irony." *Canadian Journal of Native Studies* 20, no. 2 (2000): 437–54.

Neuhaus, Marieke. *"That's Raven Talk": Holophrastic Readings of Contemporary Indigenous Literatures*. Regina: Canadian Plains Research Center, 2011.

Okimasis, Jean. *Cree Language of the Plains, Nehiyawēwin Paskwawi-pīkiskwēwin*. Regina: Canadian Plains Research Center, 2004.

Powell, Malea. "This Is a Story About Belief" in "Octalog III: The Politics of Historiography in 2010." *Rhetoric Review* 30, no. 2 (2011): 120–23.

St-Onge, Nicole. "Uncertain Margins: Métis and Saulteaux in St. Paul des Saulteaux, Red River, 1821–1870." *Manitoba History* 53 (2006): 2–10.

Stromberg, Ernest. *American Indian Rhetorics of Survivance: Word Medicine, Word Magic*. Pittsburg: University of Pittsburg Press, 2006.

Vizenor, Gerald. *Manifest Manners: Narratives on Postindian Survivance*. Lincoln: University of Nebraska Press, 1994.

Wolfart, H. C. "Commentary and Notes." In *ana kâ-pimwêwêhahk okakêskih-kêmowina: The Counselling Speeches of Jim Kâ-Nîpitêhtêw, Publications of the Algonquian Text Society*, edited, translated, and with glossary by Freda Ahenakew, H. Christoph Wolfart, and Algonquian Text Society, 139–230. Winnipeg: University of Manitoba Press, 1998.

Wolfe, Alexander. *Earth Elder Stories: The Pinayzitt Path*. Saskatoon: Fifth House, 1998.

Wolvengrey, Arok. "On the Spelling and Pronunciation of First Nations Languages and Place Names," in *Prairie Forum* 23, no. 1 (1998): 113–25.

Womack, Craig. *Red on Red: Native American Literary Separatism*. Minneapolis: University of Minnesota Press, 1999.

About the Contributors

Kateri Akiwenzie-Damm

Kateri is a proud member of the Chippewas of Nawash First Nation and lives and works in her community at Neyaashiiningmiing, Ontario. She is an internationally known writer, spoken-word performer, editor, and publisher. She has developed and taught university-accredited English and Creative Writing courses at the University of Manitoba and at the En'owkin Centre, led creative writing workshops, taught creative writing at the Emerging Indigenous Writers Program at the Banff Centre, and is the Managing Editor and Acquisitions Editor of Kegedonce Press. She has published fiction, creative non-fiction, poetry, and non-fiction internationally, recorded two acclaimed CDs of poetry and music, worked as a librettist with a classical composer, written for radio and television, and performed her work internationally. Kateri was profiled on the TV series *Heart of a Poet*, was featured in the documentary film *Words from the Edge*, and has appeared on nationally televised programs such as *Contact*, *Buffalo Tracks*, *First Arts & Music Take 3*, and *Writing on the Wall* and radio programs including *The Next Chapter, Sounds Like Canada, Ontario Morning, Between the Covers*, and *Morningside*.

Lillian Allen

Lillian Allen hails from Spanish Town, Jamaica, where she attended Barracks School (now Spanish Town Primary) and St. Jago High School. Lillian lives in Toronto and is a cultural strategist and professor of creative writing at the Ontario College of Art & Design University (OCAD). An internationally renowned dub poet, writer, and multi-dimensional artist, Lillian is a two-time Juno award-winner for her recordings of her dub poetry and music, *Revolutionary Tea Party* and *Conditions Critical*. Allen's work seamlessly combines art, social critique, community engagement, and transformation. In 2011 Lillian received a Cultural Champions award from the City of Toronto. Lillian publishes widely in performance and in a variety of media. She has published several books of poetry, including *Psychic Unrest*, *Women Do This Every Day*, and work for young people, including *Why Me?* and *Nothing But a Hero*.

Jesse Rae Archibald-Barber

Dr. Jesse Archibald-Barber is originally from Regina. He began his post-secondary studies at the Saskatchewan Indian Federated College before completing his B.A. in English at the University of Victoria and his graduate degrees at the University of Toronto, where he wrote his thesis on forms of elegy and consolation in Aboriginal literatures. Presently he teaches First Nations and Métis poetry, fiction, and drama at the First Nations University of Canada. His recent interests also involve representations of games of chance in First Nations and Western literatures, film, and popular culture.

Joanne Arnott

Joanne Arnott is a Métis/mixed-blood writer from Manitoba, and has lived on the West Coast since 1982. Her first book, *Wiles of Girlhood*, won the Gerald Lampert Award (LCP, best first book of poetry, 1992). She has published five other books: *Breasting the Waves: On Writing & Healing* (creative non-fiction), *Ma MacDonald* (illustrated children's book), and three more books of poetry—*My Grass Cradle, Steepy Mountain Love Poetry* (Kegedonce, 2004), and *Mother Time: Poems New & Selected* (Ronsdale, 2007), with two more on the way. Mother of six young people, all born at home, Joanne is a founding member of the Aboriginal Writers Collective West Coast, for whom she edited the self-published collection, *Salish Seas: An Anthology of Text and Image* (2011). Joanne is on the Author's Committee, The Writers Trust of Canada, hosts two occasional blogs (*Vera Manuel Tribute* + *Joanne Arnott*), and has published two chapbooks, *Longing: Four Poems on Diverse Matters* (with Aaron Paquette, Rubicon Press, 2008) and *the Family of Crow* (with various artists, Leaf Press, 2012), as well as a new collection, *A Night for the Lady Ronsdale*.

Tasha Beeds

Tasha Beeds is of nêhiyaw, Scottish, and Caribbean ancestry. She grew up in the territories of her mother's family in Saskatchewan: mistawâsis, atâhk-akohp, and nêwo-nâkiwin (Mont Nebo). Tasha taught English and Indigenous studies at First Nations University of Canada for eight years, and credits her many Indigenous students for inspiring her own return to university. She has also taught at the University of Saskatchewan and at Trent University. She has published articles in *Saskatchewan Indian*, *Eagle*

Feather News, Saskatchewan First Nations, and the *Native Studies Review*. She co-wrote a piece with Janice Acoose for the anthology *Me Funny* and has poetry published in *Mixed Race Women Speak Out* and *From Turtle Island to Abya Yala*. Tasha was also honoured to be production assistant for the National Film Board documentary *Finding Dawn*. She is currently a CGS SSHRC award holder and is in her second year of the Indigenous studies Ph.D. program at Trent University.

Lesley Belleau

Lesley Belleau is an Anishnaabekwe and Swedish writer from the Ojibwe nation of Garden River, located outside of Sault Ste. Marie, Ontario. She is a Ph.D. student in the Indigenous Studies Department at Trent University and is focusing on studying Indigenous literature. Lesley enjoys writing fiction and poetry and is the author of *The Colour of Dried Bones*, a collection of short fiction published by Kegedonce Press, as well as other publications both nationally and internationally. Lesley is currently awaiting the release of her second novel, *Sweat*, a full-length fiction novel, published by Your Scrivener Press. She is finishing a poetry manuscript, as well as some book reviews and academic essays. Currently, Lesley resides in Peterborough, Ontario, with her husband and four young children, ages ten, seven, three, and two.

Warren Cariou

Warren Cariou was born in Meadow Lake, Saskatchewan, into a family of mixed Métis and European heritage. He has published numerous articles on Canadian Aboriginal literature and has published two books: a collection of novellas, *The Exalted Company of Roadside Martyrs*, and a memoir/cultural history entitled *Lake of the Prairies*. He has also co-directed and co-produced two films about Aboriginal peoples in western Canada's oil-sands region: *Overburden* and *Land of Oil and Water*. He is General Editor of the First Voices, First Texts series at the University of Manitoba Press and editor of *W'daub Awae: Speaking True* and co-editor of *Manitwapow: Aboriginal Voices from the Land of Water*. He is a Canada Research chair and director of the Centre for Creative Writing and Oral Culture at the University of Manitoba.

Rosanna Deerchild

Rosanna Deerchild is Cree from South Indian Lake in northern Manitoba. Her first book, *this is a small northern town*, won and was nominated for several awards. These poems are about what it means to be from the North, a town divided along colour lines, and a family dealing with its history of secrets. She is also a broadcaster and performer who lives in Winnipeg.

Marilyn Dumont

Marilyn has worked in the Edmonton Indigenous community since moving to Edmonton in 1985. Her family is from Kikino Settlement, Fishing Lake Settlement, Lac Ste. Anne, St. Albert Metis community, St. Paul des Metis, and Onion Lake First Nations. She taught a non-credit course in Aboriginal Women's Literature for the University of Alberta's Faculty of Extension in the late 1980s and co-anthologized *Painting the Town Red*, a collection of Indigenous student writing, with Anna Marie Sewell and Peter Cole. Her poetry collections have won provincial and national poetry awards. In 2015, two titles will be published: *A Really Good Brown Girl*, in its fifteenth printing, will be issued as a special edition, and a new collection , *The Pemmican Eaters*, is forthcoming from ECW Press.

Shayla Elizabeth

Shayla Elizabeth is a Cree/Iniwe writer/storyteller, poet, emerging playwright, and spoken-word performer living in Winnipeg. She has been a member of the Aboriginal Writers Collective since 1999, with poetry in the group's *Urban Kool, Bone Memory*, and a spoken-word CD, *Red City*. Also, her poetry has appeared in *Contemporary Verse 2, Urban NDN*, and on the CBC and the Aqua Books Speaking Crow reading series, with the most recent being in *Manitowapow: Aboriginal Writings from the Land of Water*. She also has participated in "Stone Soup Storytelling Cafe" at McNally-Robinson bookstore, Winnipeg.

Marvin Francis

Marvin Francis, a Cree from Heart Lake First Nation in Alberta, was born in 1955 and after leaving school in 1971 he travelled throughout much of western Canada before settling in Winnipeg in the late 1980s. There he quickly established himself as an innovative figure in Winnipeg's burgeoning Aboriginal arts scene. He was a founding member of the Manitoba Aboriginal Writers' Collective and was active with the Urban Shaman Gallery. His art took many forms, including poetry, oral performance, visual art, and radio drama, all of it marked by playful irony, formal experimentation, and streetwise philosophy. During his M.A. studies at the University of Manitoba, he wrote his first book of poetry, *City Treaty* (2002), which won wide acclaim for its mingling of postmodern play, tricksterism, and serious examinations of urban Aboriginal identity. His second book, *Bush Camp*, was completed just before he succumbed to cancer in January 2005 at the age of 49. Published in 2008, *Bush Camp* solidifies Marvin Francis's legacy as one of Canada's most innovative poets.

Susan Gingell

Susan Gingell teaches decolonizing and diasporic literatures at the University of Saskatchewan. Her current research on Canadian poets' writing of oral traditions and ethnically specific Englishes pays significant attention to the work of Indigenous poets. She is the author of numerous essays, principally on the literatures of Canada and the Afro/Afraspora, and has edited two volumes in the *Collected Works of Canadian E. J. Pratt* and *The Bridge City Anthology: Stories from Saskatoon*. Recent publications include two co-edited books, *Listening Up, Writing Down, and Looking Beyond: Interfaces of the Oral, Written, and Visual* (WLU Press) and *Gendered Intersections: An Introduction to Women's and Gender Studies*, 2nd ed.

Alyce Johnson

Alyce Johnson is a member of the Kaajèt–Crow clan, and the Tsäyda Tà–Jimmie Johnson and Á Tsʉa–Emma Johnson family, as well as the Copper Chief families from Alaska. She is from the Yukon Territory and followed trails that have led her to both the University of British Columbia and Trent University. She has two degrees in education from the University of British Columbia, and a Ph.D. from Trent University. Alyce grew up on the trails of the Kluane Lake region with her parents' teachings that narratives are mnemonic maps and trails that guide us into who we are as Indigenous to knowledge. She has seven grandchildren who also walk the trails on the landscape. As an assistant professor, Alyce Johnson teaches at the University of Northern British Columbia.

Rhiannon Johnson

Rhiannon Johnson grew up on Hiawatha First Nation reserve just south of Peterborough, Ontario. She began writing at a young age and exploring different poets through Indigenous writing courses at Trent University while pursuing a degree in politics and Indigenous studies. She is currently living in the Ottawa area, working and creating more poetry of her own.

Lindsay "Eekwol" Knight

In Lindsay Knight—a.k.a Eekwol's—world, mothering, music, and academics are chaotically coordinated into a delicate balance. As a dedicated hip-hop emcee, Eekwol astounds her listeners with honest, direct, and revolutionary words that come from places original, unknown, and always groundbreaking. As a member of Muskoday First Nation, she has a lifelong background of Plains Cree Indigenous music and culture, and invites the audience into a space of experimental hip hop unique to her land and place while respecting the origins of hip hop. She is currently completing her master's degree at the University of Saskatchewan. Not surprisingly, her area of research is Indigenous music.

Michèle Lacombe

Michèle Lacombe is an Acadian/Québécoise/Maliseet/Métis literary scholar and associate professor of Canadian and Indigenous studies at Trent University. Born on the east bank of the St. John River on the Maine/Quebec/New Brunswick borderlands, she was raised on the north shore of the Gulf of St. Lawrence. Her research interests in comparative literature extend to Indigenous literatures from Atlantic Canada and Quebec, Indigenous literary history and literary criticism from Canada and the United States, and cross-cultural perspectives on women's writing. Her recent publications include "Indigenous Criticism and Indigenous Literature in the 1990s: Critical Intimacy," in *Unruly Penelopes and the Ghosts: Narratives of English Canada*, ed. Eva Darias-Beautell (Wilfrid Laurier University Press, 2012); "'Come on, Dave': Indigenous Identities and Language Play in Yves Sioui Durand's *Hamlet-le-Malécite*," in *Indigeneity in Dialogue: Indigenous Literary Expression across the Linguistic Divides*, a special section of *Studies in Canadian Literature* 35, no. 2 (Winter 2011), which she co-edited with Heather MacFarlane; and "Colonialism, Métissage, and the Logic of (Imperial) Relations: la Sagouine 'parmi les sauvages,'" in *Open Letter: A Canadian Journal of Writing and Theory*, a theme issue "Remembering Barbara Godard" 14, no. 6 (Summer 2011). In her spare time, she dabbles at creative writing and studies earth medicines.

Gail MacKay

Gail MacKay, Anishinaabe-Métis from Sault Ste. Marie, is a Ph.D. candidate at the University of Saskatchewan. Her doctoral research focuses on Indigenous students' discourse in their transition to higher education.

Lee Maracle

Ms. Maracle is the author of a number of critically acclaimed winning literary works, including: *Sojourner's and Sundogs, Ravensong, Bobbi Lee, Daughters Are Forever, Will's Garden, Bent Box, I Am Woman,* and *First Wives' Club: Salish Style,* and is co-editor of a number of anthologies, including the award-winning *My Home as I Remember, Telling It: Women and Language Across Culture.* Ms. Maracle is a member of the Sto:lo nation. Maracle has served as the Distinguished Visiting Professor at both University of Toronto and Western Washington University. In 2009, she received an Honorary Doctor of Letters from St. Thomas University and the Jane Stewart award for her body of work. Her upcoming work: *Memory Serves: and Other Words* and *Celia's Song*. Maracle currently teaches at the University of Toronto (Aboriginal Studies) and at the Indigenous Theatre School.

Sam McKegney

Sam McKegney is a settler scholar of Indigenous literatures. He grew up in Anishinaabe territory on the Saugeen Peninsula along the shores of Lake Huron and currently resides with his partner and their two daughters in traditional lands of the Haudenosaunee and Anishinaabe peoples, where he is an Associate Professor at Queen's University. He has published a collection of interviews entitled *Masculindians: Conversations about Indigenous Manhood* (University of Manitoba Press, 2014), a monograph called *Magic Weapons: Aboriginal Writers Remaking Community after Residential School* (University of Manitoba Press, 2007), and articles on such topics as environmental kinship, masculinity theory, prison writing, Indigenous governance, and Canadian hockey mythologies.

Neal McLeod

Neal McLeod is Cree (from the James Smith reserve in Saskatchewan) and Swedish, having had the fortunate opportunity to study abroad at the Swedish Art Academy at Umeå. He was one of the founders of the legendary Crow Hop Café in Regina, Saskatchewan, which was a venue for Indigenous comedy, music, and poetry. Building from this in 2002, Neal directed *A Man Called Horst*, a comedy film that was screened in Berlin and across Canada. Neal has exhibited his artwork throughout Canada, including the 2005 exhibition *au fil de mes jours* (in my lifetime) at Le Musée national des beaux-arts du Québec, which was remounted at the Museum of Civilization in 2007. Neal has published two books of poetry, *Songs to Kill a Wîhtikow* and *Gabriel's Beach*. In 2007 he published *Cree Narrative Memory*, which was nominated for book of the year at the Anskohk McNally Aboriginal Literature Awards. Neal has two other books in press, *A Cree Word a Day* and *cîhcêwêsin: New Writing from Indigenous Saskatchewan*. He is also working on a book of poetry called *Dreams of My Father's Horses*, a novel called *Neechie Hustle*, a retranslation of *Plains Cree Texts*, and an anthology of Indigenous science fiction and speculative storytelling for Theytus Press.

Duncan Mercredi

Duncan Mercredi—Cree/Métis poet/writer/storyteller—is originally from Misipawistik (Grand Rapids, Manitoba), has published four books of poetry, and has also had his work featured in three anthologies of Native writings and in other periodicals such as *Prairie Fire* and *CV2*. He attended the Banff Centre screenwriting workshop after receiving the Ross Charles Award where his work, *oomsikakispanik*, was chosen for further develop- ment. Duncan has participated in the Winnipeg International Writers Fes- tival, the Winnipeg Storytellers Festival, the University of Manitoba's For the Love of Words conference, Brandon University's Aboriginal Writers and Storytellers Festival, the Prince George Storytellers and Writers Festival, the Singing Waters Storytellers Gathering, and has conducted workshops for the Young Authors Conference in Winnipeg. He has held readings in and around Winnipeg, Calgary, and Regina. He is currently working on a manuscript, which has been a ten-year project to date. Most of this work consists of writ- ing he has done as a member of Manitoba's Aboriginal Writers Collective.

Daniel David Moses

Poet, playwright, essayist, and teacher, Daniel David Moses is a Delaware who hails from the Six Nations lands in southern Ontario, Canada. He holds an Honours B.A. in general fine arts from York University and an M.F.A. in cre- ative writing from the University of British Columbia. His poetry collections are the books *Delicate Bodies*, *The White Line*, and *Sixteen Jesuses*, and the CD *River Range Poems*, which includes music by David Deleary. He is the co-editor of Oxford University Press's *An Anthology of Canadian Native Literature in English* (4th and 20th Anniversary ed., 2012), the editor of *The Exile Book of Native Canadian Fiction and Drama*, an anthology (2010), and *A Small Essay on the Largeness of Light and Other Poems* (2012). His honours include a James Buller Memorial Award (for the play *The Indian Medicine Shows*), the Har- bourfront Festival Prize, and a Chalmers Fellowship. He teaches playwriting in the Department of Drama at Queen's University as an associate professor.

David Newhouse

David Newhouse is Onondaga from the Six Nations of the Grand River near Brantford, Ontario. He is chair of the Department of Indigenous Studies at Trent and an associate professor in the Business Administration Program. His research interests focus on the emergence of modern Aboriginal society. He lives in Peterborough, Ontario, in Ashburnham Village (now East City) on land mysteriously acquired from the British Crown by the Burnham family in the mid-1850s.

Janet Rogers

Janet is a Mohawk/Tuscarora writer, spoken-word poet, video poet, record- ing artist, performance poet, and radio host. She lives on the traditional territories of the Coast Salish people and is proud to call herself a West Coast Mohawk. Janet is Victoria's current poet laureate until 2015. Her latest book is *Unearthed* (Leaf Press, 2011), with a new collection, *Peace in Duress*, forthcoming in 2014 from Talonbooks. She is an E. Pauline Johnson enthusiast and has been studying the life and work of the Mohawk poetess for over fifteen years. Janet has contributed text to the Vancouver City Opera's program notes for the production *Pauline*, to open in Vancouver in May 2014. She also writes reviews and is a regular contributor for *BC Musician* magazine, Indian Country Today Media Network, *First Nations Drum*, and *The Two Row Times*.

Armand Garnet Ruffo

Armand Garnet Ruffo was born in Chapleau, northern Ontario, with roots to the Sagamok (Ojibway) First Nation and the Chapleau Fox Lake (Cree) First Nation. His work includes *Grey Owl: The Mystery of Archie Belaney* (Coteau Books, 1996) and *At Geronimo's Grave* (Coteau Books, 2001), which was the winner of the Archibald Lampman Award for Poetry. In 2010, his feature film *A Windigo Tale* won Best Picture at the 35th American Indian Film Festival in San Francisco. In 2013 he co-edited *An Anthology of Canadian Native Literature in English* (Oxford University Press). *Man Changing into Thunderbird: The Life and Art of Norval Morrisseau* (Douglas & McIntyre) and *The Thunderbird Poems* (Insomniac Press) will appear in 2014. He is currently co-editing a collection of seminal critical essays on Indigenous literature for Broadview Press. He lives in Kingston and teaches in the Department of English at Queen's University.

Gregory Scofield

He is known for his unique and dynamic reading style, which blends oral storytelling, song, spoken word, and the Cree language. His maternal ancestry can be traced back to the fur trade and to the Métis community of Kinosota, Manitoba, which was established in 1828 by the Hudson's Bay Company. His poetry and memoir, *Thunder Through My Veins* (Harper-Collins, 1999), is taught at numerous universities and colleges throughout Canada and the United States, and his work has appeared in many anthologies. He has served as writer-in-residence at the University of Manitoba and Memorial University of Newfoundland. His other publications include *Kipocihkan: Poems New & Selected, I Knew Two Metis Women, Love Medicine and One Song*, and *Louis: The Heretic Poems*. He currently lives in Maple Ridge, British Columbia.

Leanne Simpson

Leanne Simpson is a writer, storyteller, educator, and activist of Mississauga Anishinaabeg ancestry. She is the author of *Dancing on Our Turtle's Back* and

The Gift Is in the Making, the editor of *Lighting the 8th Fire* and *This Is an Honour Song.* Leanne and was also on the editorial collective that produced *The Winter We Danced: Voices from the Past, the Present & the Idle No More Movement.* In her debut collection of short stories, *Islands of Decolonial Love*, Leanne vividly explores the lives of contemporary Indigenous peoples and communities, especially those of her own Anishnaabeg nation. She teamed up with musicians to record some of her writing as spoken word/musical performances. You can stream or download these tracks for free at http://arpbooks.org/islands.

Niigaanwewidam James Sinclair

Niigaanwewidam James Sinclair is Anishinaabe, originally from St. Peter's (Little Peguis) Indian Settlement near Selkirk, Manitoba. He is a regular commentator on Indigenous issues for CTV, CBC, and APTN, and his work can be found in books such as *The Exile Edition of Native Canadian Fiction and Drama*, newspapers like *The Globe and Mail*, and online with *CBC Books: Canada Writes.* He is also a co-editor of the award-winning *Manitowapow: Aboriginal Writings from the Land of Water* (Highwater Press, 2011), *Centering Anishinaabeg Studies: Understanding the World Through Stories* (Michigan State University Press, 2013), and *The Winter We Danced: Voices of the Past, the Future, and the Idle No More Movement* (Arbeiter Ring Press, 2014). Currently at the University of Manitoba, Niigaan teaches courses in Indigenous literatures, cultures, histories, and politics.

Waaseyaa'sin Christine Sy

Waaseyaa'sin Christine Sy is Ojibway Anishinaabe of mixed ancestry from Obishkikaang (Lac Seul First Nation) and Bawating (Sault Ste. Marie, Ontario). She resides in Mississauga Anishinaabe territory in the Williams Treaty 1923 area as a visitor with her family. She is a mother, Anishinaabe land-based learner and educator, adult language learner, and photographer, and has been writing, performing, and publishing poetry since 2006. Significantly inspired by the poets, storytellers, and academics at the Sounding Out: Indigenous Poetics Conference in 2009 (on which this book is based), she has expanded her creative practice into spoken word (including sound recording) and storytelling, as well as short story writing. Her short story "How to Be Lonely" won the Briarpatch Creative Writing (fiction) Contest in 2013 and has been forwarded to the 2014 Journey Prize competition. She is presently completing her Ph.D. dissertation, "Following the Trees Home: Ikawewag Iskigamiziganing (Anishinaabe women at the Sugar Bush)."

Index

Books in the Aboriginal Studies Series
Published by Wilfrid Laurier University Press

Blockades and Resistance: Studies in Actions of Peace and the Temagami Blockades of 1988–89 / Bruce W. Hodgins, Ute Lischke, and David T. McNab, editors / 2003 / xi + 276 pp. / map, illustrations / ISBN 0-88920-381-4

Indian Country: Essays on Contemporary Native Culture / Gail Guthrie Valaskakis / 2005 / x + 293 pp. / photos / ISBN 0-88920-479-9

Walking a Tightrope: Aboriginal People and Their Representations / Ute Lischke and David T. McNab, editors / 2005 / xix + 377 pp. / photos / ISBN 978-0-88920-484-3

The Long Journey of a Forgotten People: Métis Identities and Family Histories / Ute Lischke and David T. McNab, editors / 2007 / viii + 386 pp. / maps, photos / ISBN 978-0-88920-523-9

Words of the Huron / John L. Steckley / 2007 / xvii + 259 pp. / ISBN 978-0-88920-516-1
Essential Song: Three Decades of Northern Cree Music / Lynn Whidden / 2007 / xvi + 176 pp. / photos, musical examples, audio CD / ISBN 978-0-88920-459-1

From the Iron House: Imprisonment in First Nations Writing / Deena Rymhs / 2008 / ix + 147 pp. / ISBN 978-1-55458-021-7

Lines Drawn upon the Water: First Nations and the Great Lakes Borders and Borderlands / Karl S. Hele, editor / 2008 / xxiii + 351 pp. / illustrations, maps / ISBN 978-1-55458-004-0

Troubling Tricksters: Revisioning Critical Conversations / Linda M. Morra and Deanna Reder, editors / 2009 / xii+ 336 pp. / illustrations / ISBN 978-1-55458-181-8

Aboriginal Peoples in Canadian Cities: Transformations and Continuities / Heather A. Howard and Craig Proulx, editors / 2011 / viii + 256 pp. / colour and b&w photos / ISBN 978-1-055458-260-0

Bridging Two Peoples: Chief Peter E. Jones, 1843–1909 / Allan Sherwin / 2012 / xxiv + 246 pp. / 15 b&w photos / ISBN 978-1-55458-633-2

The Nature of Empires and the Empires of Nature: Indigenous Peoples and the Great Lakes Environment / Karl S. Hele, editor / 2013 / xxii + 350 / 3 b&w photos / ISBN 978-1-55458-328-7

The Eighteenth-Century Wyandot: A Clan-Based Study / John L. Steckley / 2014 / x + 306 / ISBN 978-1-55458-956-2

Indigenous Poetics in Canada / Neal McLeod, editor / 2014 / xii + 404 pp. / ISBN 978-1-55458-982-1